The Intelligent Soccer Coach

CARL WILD

THE INTELLIGENT SOCCER COACH

PLAYER-CENTERED SESSIONS TO DEVELOP CONFIDENT, CREATIVE PLAYERS

Meyer & Meyer Sport

British Library of Cataloguing in Publication Data
A catalogue record for this book is available from the British Library

The Intelligent Soccer Coach
Maidenhead: Meyer & Meyer Sport (UK) Ltd., 2022
ISBN: 978-1-78255-225-3

Aachen, Auckland, Beirut, Dubai, Hägendorf, Hong Kong, Indianapolis, Cairo, Cape Town, Manila, Maidenhead, New Delhi, Singapore, Sydney, Tehran, Vienna
Member of the World Sport Publishers' Association (WSPA), www. w-s-p-a.org

Credits
Cover and interior design: Anja Elsen
Layout: DiTech Publishing Services, www.ditechpubs.com
Cover illustration: © AdobeStock
Interior figures: Carl Wild
Managing editor: Elizabeth Evans
Copyeditor: Stephanie Kramer

Printed by: Print Consult GmbH, Munich, Germany
Printed in Slovakia

ISBN: 978-1-78255-225-3
E-Mail: info@m-m-sports.com
www.thesportspublisher.com

Contents

INTRODUCTION

For many of us, our coaching journey begins because we have volunteered to help out with a team. It may be that our son or daughter plays for the team or we know someone who is already involved and we just want to help give this group of players an opportunity to play soccer. Therefore, the reason that we have entered coaching is a completely unselfish act; we have done it to allow young children the chance to play a game that they love to play, most likely with their friends. There is also a good chance that we have had some attachment to soccer already, whether this is playing the game ourselves, watching it as a spectator or even taking on the role of an official. And through this involvement, the game has provided us with an endless amount of enjoyment that we now want these young players to experience. This involvement would also have allowed us to gain and increase our knowledge of the sport, which we are keen to pass on to the players to help them develop and improve and become better players. In short, we enter coaching with all of the right intentions and these usually stay with us throughout our journey as a coach. However, what we might not fully understand is the correct approach that we need to apply, to be able to achieve these intentions. And this is merely because we only know what we know and therefore we will rely on our previous experiences and what we perceive to be the right thing to do.

These former experiences and beliefs will often lead us to the full version of soccer, as well as the professional game. For instance, when we watch the professional game, we will look to identify what the successful teams do well or the new trends that characterise the modern game. So we see tactics such as the high press and we will look to introduce this to the young players that we are working with, or we are influenced by the statistics that show the total distance that a professional player will run during a game and we will look to get the players 'fitter' so that they can run more when they are playing in a match. And though these observations are correct, in that they are key characteristics of the modern game and it is how we would want or like the players to be able to play the game, what we do not necessarily recognise or fully understand is that the players we are observing are adults and professional athletes and that they are in a completely different place in their journey as a soccer player compared to that of the players that we are coaching. We therefore need to recognise what is right for adult players and professional players is completely unsuitable for the young players that we are working with.

The chapters of this book will, first of all, provide a clear outline of what the game of soccer actually involves and consists of, specifically the format of the game that young children play. It will then go on to provide you with a more in-depth understanding of what your role is as a coach and the qualities that are needed to achieve this, many of which you probably already have, but you either did not realise were needed or you were just unaware that you actually had them. The remaining chapters will then concentrate on what the players need at this specific stage of their journey as soccer players. This includes the types of practices that they need to participate in; how we support them whilst they are involved in these practices; the different areas of performance that need developing; and how we can do this, not only throughout training but also on match days as well. This new information can be used, alongside the existing knowledge that you already have, to provide the players the best possible experience whilst playing the game that they love. To support your understanding of each of these areas, a range of different practices will be used, not only to show how it can be easily achieved, but to provide you with ideas as well that will hopefully inspire your own creativity and encourage you to produce stimulating and fun practices for the players to play and learn from.

Even though we have more than likely volunteered or requested to become the coach of the team with which we are working, we should not forget or take for granted that we are in a privileged position. We have an opportunity to work with a group of young children that have chosen to come to training and play matches because of their love for the game and their desire just to play. They will look up to us as role models, whilst also looking to us for guidance, support and help. They will be willing to listen and learn and will have a real yearning to become better players and reach their full potential. So not only are we privileged to be able to have such a positive impact on these young lives, but we also have a great responsibility to do our very best for these players. The experience that we give them will undoubtedly stay with them for the rest of their lives, whether it is a good experience or one that they would rather forget. We must therefore, make it a positive one and one that they will always remember and will use in other aspects of their lives as they get older. We need to make sure that when they think back on the times that they came and played soccer with their friends and teammates, that they look back on them with fondness and joy; they need to be priceless memories which they would not change for anything. So what we must not and cannot do as a coach is let them down.

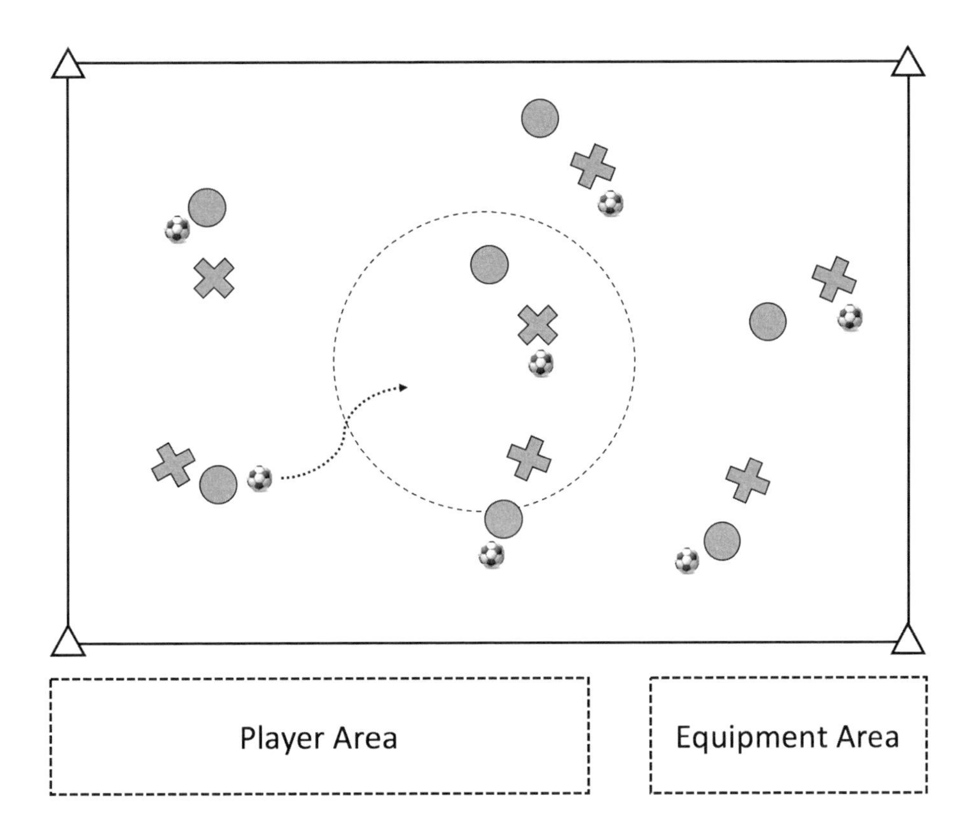
Player Area
Equipment Area

CHAPTER 1

UNDERSTANDING THE GAME

As coaches, if we are going to help the players that we are working with reach their full potential, then we need to make sure that we actually fully grasp the game itself and what actually makes it 'soccer'. Without this understanding, the practices that we use and the support that we provide may not be relevant or actually helpful in helping the players develop. And when we are talking about understanding the game, this is not just limited to the different tactics that can be used or the individual requirements needed for each different position. It is more about the different elements that, first of all, make it a game and then also the unique characteristics that are found firstly within invasion games and then soccer itself. If we can gain this awareness, then it will enable us to be able to put the players into an environment that is both relevant and realistic to the game, whilst also providing them with the support that will allow them to develop a much deeper game understanding that is essential to their development.

The main attraction of playing soccer, for most players, is the fact that it is a 'game' and children enjoy playing games. There is a concept within youth soccer that there should not be any form of competition and that young players are not bothered about winning. This is not necessarily true. Children usually enjoy winning, and whether this is a game of soccer, a board game or a school playground game, they will play the game and they will try to win it. However, what we do not always understand or recognise is that if they do not win, then it is quickly forgotten and that it is not that important to them. Children will try to win a game of soccer, as the format of the game makes it competitive, but they are not overly concerned if they are not successful, it is usually the adults who are the ones that find it harder to accept. Children will very quickly forget about what happened in the game that they just played in, including the result, and they will move onto and focus on whatever happens next in their day-to-day lives. If a child decides to stop playing soccer, it is very unlikely that they came to that decision because they are not winning games. The reason a child will no longer want to play soccer is because they are no longer enjoying it or because something else comes along that they want to do instead.

This desire to want to play the 'game' is reinforced within the training environment. The most common question a coach will be asked by the players is usually, 'When are we playing a game?' Children will not start playing soccer because they want to take part in a passing practice or learn how to improve their defending; they start playing because they want to play the game. It is not that they do not enjoy training or learning, it is just that the biggest attraction is to actually play the game of soccer. It is therefore important that as a coach we utilise and capitalise on this desire to want to play games and whilst we cannot just constantly allow them to play in a game, as this will not support their development as a player, what we can do is design our practices so that they contain the characteristics of any game, whilst also resembling as many aspects of the game of soccer as possible.

As a coach you would never deliberately design or deliver a practice that is unrelated to the game. The perception will always be that the activity is relevant for the group of players that you are working with and that it is something that they need to practice and improve. What we do not always remember to do is to include essential components that when joined together make the practice both realistic and applicable to an aspect of the game of soccer. To start to include these essential components within our practices, we must first of all identify and understand the characteristics that are needed to make any activity a 'game'. After this, we must break this down further into the distinguishing factors of the game of soccer.

What Is a Game?

When we consider the games that we used to play as children growing up, whether this was on the playground during school or after school on the street or in the park, and the games that children play today – board games or even computer games – it is possible to ascertain key characteristics that they all have in common. Games are basically a form of 'play', and playing an organised game just provides structure to this play. To achieve this structure, there need to be a number of specific features which then differentiate a game from random play.

Every game has a set of rules, which all players need to understand for the game to be played correctly. These rules, however, can be changed or adapted provided everyone understands and agrees to them. When we play a game of rock, paper, scissors, among the first questions we will ask before the game starts are, 'When do we show which option we have chosen?' and 'Is it on "scissors" or is it on "shoot"'? We are basically clarifying the rules of the game to ensure that both players understand how the game is to be played. Similarly, if we buy a new board game, we will usually read the rules that come with the game before we start to play it, because if we don't, we are unable to either play the game at all or we will play it incorrectly. If we do decide to play without reading the rules, we usually end up referring to them at some stage because something has come up in the game and we are unsure what it means or what happens next. Therefore, if we are going to play some form of game within our sessions we need to ensure that there are clear rules to the game and that everyone understands them. The easiest way to achieve this is by making sure that there are as few rules as possible and that these rules are simple to follow. If need be, further rules can be added as the game is played to make the game more challenging, and by adding them later on, this allows the players to grasp the game quickly which in turn allows it to get started more quickly.

In addition to rules, every game needs some form of scoring system so that there is not only the element of play but also some form of competition. Scoring systems can come in a wide range of formats. Whether it is a board game that requires the accumulation of monetary value or the number of bibs that you can grab in a game of 'tails', a game needs a scoring system that allows for the identification of a winner. This scoring format could be where the opponent/opponents are in 'direct' opposition, i.e., the actions of the other team or individual, directly affect you, and as a result of this, the score in the game. An example of these types of games are racket sports (tennis, squash, badminton, etc.). Or it could be a scoring format where you are competing against other individuals or a team, but their actions and the 'points' they obtain do not directly affect you, such as in a game of golf. Scoring systems can also be adapted to challenge players or to influence a particular outcome. For example, if you are doing a session that has a narrow focus on passing, when you a play a game within the session, whether this is a normal game of soccer or some other form of game, the passing that takes place within the game influences the number of points scored. It could be that to score a point a player has to pass the ball to a teammate in an 'end zone' and that the number of passes made by the team before the final pass into the 'end zone' is the number of points awarded.

When we look at scoring systems, it is a good opportunity to start to consider how we implement a new form of game that is now commonplace for this current generation of player, i.e., the computer game. There is a clear argument that the evolution of the computer game has had a major impact on the amount of time young children participate in physical activity, which will subsequently have an impact on their physical literacy and motor skill development. But it also needs to be recognised that this form of play is not just a fad that will eventually disappear; instead it will continue to develop and will remain popular with young children. Therefore, though we should persist in encouraging children to spend less time playing these games, we should also identify that we can take concepts from these games and use them for our coaching that will then make the environment for the players more recognisable and also more fun. One of these concepts involves the scoring systems found within computer games. Quite often progression through computer games involves the player 'leveling up' and they often also have an opportunity to complete a 'bonus round'. Therefore, where possible, when planning our practices we should look to incorporate opportunities for players to 'level up' or obtain 'bonus points' within the scoring systems.

When we refer to games we also need to consider where they are played, i.e., the boundaries in which the game takes place and the equipment needed to play the game. Even in the games we played in our childhood in the local streets, there were restrictions in the form of the boundaries in which the game was played, whether this was the road kerb, a lamppost at the end of the street or a specific tree. Therefore, a game needs to have boundaries and we need to consider what happens if the game goes beyond these boundaries, whether it is a player in a game of tag or the actual ball in some form of ball game. We also need to consider the size and shape of the area that is formed by these boundaries, as this will have a major impact on how the game is played and the outcome of the game. How we manipulate an area and the effects this has on a practice will be discussed further in chapter 3.

The equipment needed for the game to be played and the purpose of this equipment also needs to be considered. The main consideration is: Do we have the required equipment to play the game? And if not, can we be resourceful and creative with what we do have available, so that the game can still be played? We also need to ensure that the equipment is both safe and appropriate for the age, ability and experience of the players. It could be that the game being played is some form of catching game, where the players have to catch and throw a ball. The ball that is used for the game needs to be appropriate so that it allows for achievement and success, whilst also supporting the safety of the game. Therefore, instead of using a ball that the players usually use, a smaller ball could be used such as a size 1 training ball or a tennis ball. The important thing to remember is that without the relevant equipment the game cannot be played, or it will need to be adapted so that it can be played with the equipment that is available. It is quite often the equipment, alongside the rules that make the game; badminton without a shuttlecock is no longer badminton.

We also need to consider players. How many players are needed and how they are divided has to be decided. The number of players playing a game is significant in terms of whether the game can actually be played and how much we enjoy playing the game. Every game will have a minimum number of players necessary for it to be played. More often than not this will be two, but quite often the game will become enjoyable if there are more than two players, but at the same time it can be less fun if there are too many players. If we look at a game of 'tag', it can be played with just two players but becomes much more enjoyable if we add further players. Part of the fun within tag is being chased. But enjoyment also comes from the unpredictability and anticipation of when you will be chased; therefore, if there are just two players then this element of the enjoyment you get from the game is lost. These parts of the game that provide enjoyment can also be reduced if there are too many players, increasing the number of players will mean that the likelihood of being chased is less likely and we spend more time being inactive.

How we divide players within the game can also be significant in how it is played and the experience the players gain from playing it. If we return to the game of tag, how we divide the players between those who are trying to avoid being tagged and those who are attempting to tag other players will affect the involvement the players have within the game, the difficulty of the game and therefore the enjoyment of the game. We may also need to consider whether the players are playing the game individually or whether they are in teams, and if they are in teams how do we organise the teams in terms of numbers? Are they equal or is there a deliberate overload towards one team, and is this because they have different tasks within the game? Again, all of this can be seen within the game of tag; the players attempting to tag the other players can be working alone or they could be working in a team; or the players could be split into two teams with both teams attempting to tag each other in some format; or it could be that there are three teams and each team takes turns being the one that is tagging; or all three teams are trying to tag each other at the same time. The important part is that the players are organised to maximise their involvement and enjoyment of the game.

The final and most important element is obviously the fun factor. If a game is a structured form of play, then we need to remember that the main purpose of play is to provide enjoyment. This is usually taken for granted. Because it is a game, we automatically assume that the participants will enjoy it. However, to ensure that it is fun, a number of specific components of the game need to be carefully planned. The game needs to be simple to understand and simple to play. Progressions can be added to the game step-by-step to make it more difficult, while allowing it to continue to be easy to understand. The game itself needs to be challenging, but also achievable for the participants to remain interested and motivated; if it is too easy or too difficult then the game will quickly lose its appeal. The enjoyment of the game can be increased further if within the game the

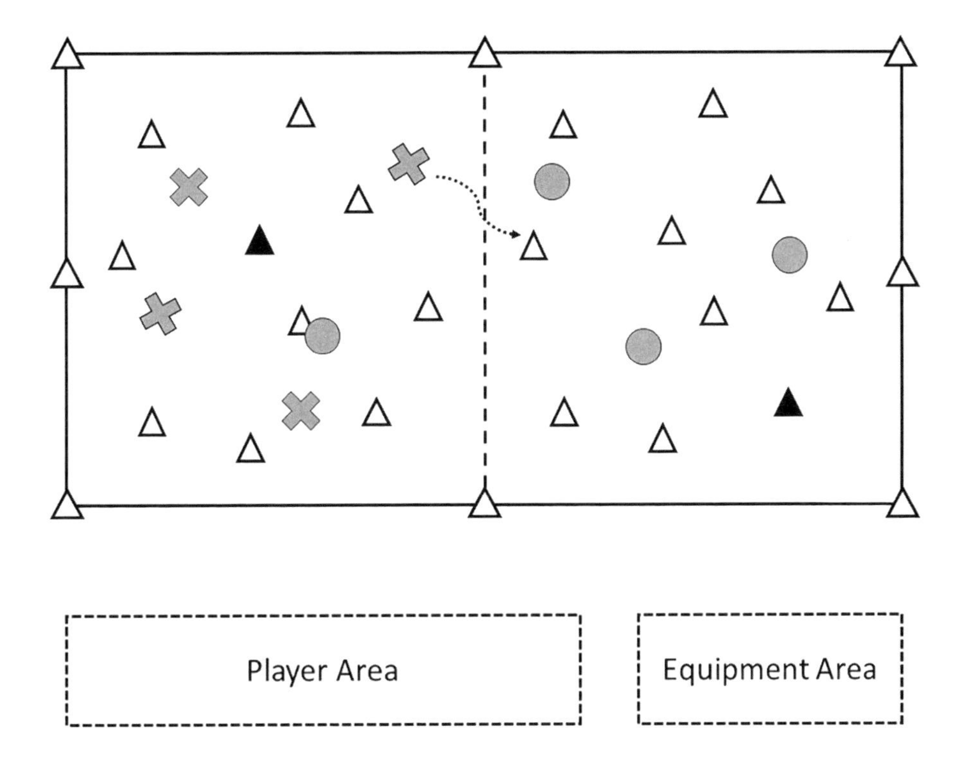

Practice One

Players are split into two teams, with each team defending the cones in their half of the pitch whilst also trying to steal the cones from the other team's half of the pitch. Players can stay or leave their half of the pitch when and as they please. If a player is 'tagged' in the opponent's half whilst in possession of a cone, they must drop it where they were tagged and return to their own half and touch the far end line before returning to the game. Each cone is worth one point apart from a number of 'bonus' cones (these are a different colour to the rest of the cones), which are worth extra points (the exact number can be decided by the players). After a set amount of time, the game ends, and the team with the most points in their half wins.

participants have different options for scoring points, with the level of difficulty linked to the value of the points awarded.

All of these elements can be found within our first practice: *Practice One*. The game has clear and simple rules and boundaries that are easy for the players to understand. The players are divided into two equal teams and there is a clear purpose for the equipment that is being used. There is a scoring system that will ensure some form of 'result' in that there will be either a winner and a loser or a draw. It also allows for different levels of challenge, which helps with the fun element for the players. And as will become clear later in the book, this particular game has clear and significant links to soccer and through playing it, the players will be developing key skills that they can transfer over when they are playing the actual game of soccer.

Invasion Games

Soccer is classified as an invasion game, alongside other sports, such as netball, rugby, hockey and basketball. The key characteristics of invasion games are that they are team games with an equal number of players where the overall aim is to attack the opponent's territory to score some a goal or point. Alongside these main characteristics, there are other fundamental factors that make a sport an invasion game. These include the game being played on some form of field or court that has clear boundaries as well as specific areas within it. In addition to this, some form of object is used to score a goal or point, these can be in a range of forms including a ball, puck and disc. As well as these key characteristics and factors, there are also three main concepts that are common to all invasion games: in possession, out of possession, and transition (this can be from possession to out of possession, or from out of possession to in possession).

Though soccer has its own unique characteristics (these will be discussed in greater detail later on in the chapter), because it is an invasion game, we can take key concepts of all invasion games or an exclusive concept from a specific sport and adopt these within our training to help the players in their development and learning process. For instance, in the majority of invasion games, a key skill that players have to learn is when to release the ball (or puck or disc) and when to retain it (i.e., dribble, run with it, or shield it). Therefore, we can either introduce these actual sports or similar rules from these sports into our training. Within netball, players cannot travel with the ball and must pass the ball. Therefore, we may use the concept of netball when we are delivering a session with an outcome that is focused on passing or receiving or something similar.

So if we look at *Practice Two*, the practice begins with the players having to transfer the ball between their hands and not being able to move when in possession of the ball. This is very similar to the invasion game of netball, where passing and moving to receive the ball are key aspects of the game. This practice could then be adapted to make it similar to the games of basketball or rugby. It could be that you allow the players to dribble with the ball when they are in possession of the ball (basketball) or you could just allow them to run with it (rugby). The important part is that a rule is introduced where possession of the ball can be turned over if a player is caught in possession of the ball. This might be in the form of a tag, e.g., if a player in possession of the ball is tagged by an opposition player, then possession is transferred over to the other team.

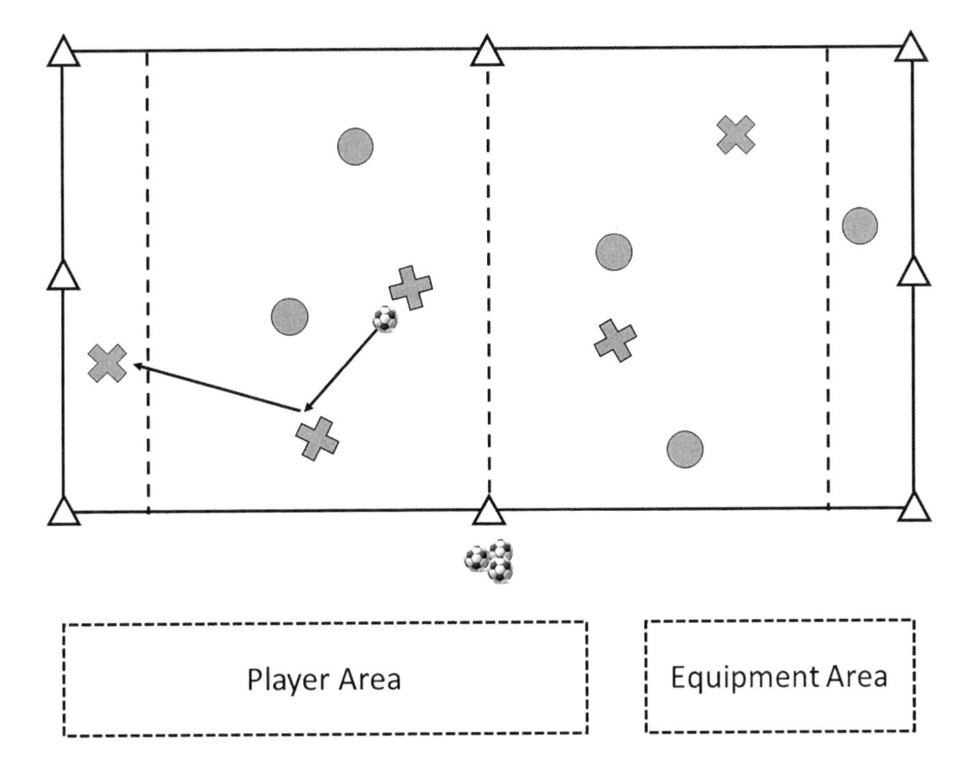

Practice Two

Players are split into two teams. Each team has a target player in an end zone. Teams win a point by playing the ball to the target player. Players use their hands only to receive and pass the ball (similar to netball, when in possession of the ball, they cannot move). If a target player receives the ball, it is a point, and they pass the ball to the opposition.

A key characteristic of all invasion games and a factor that we often remove from our practices, especially when we look at retaining possession is direction. *Practice Three* is an example of a common rondo practice that is used regularly by most, if not all, coaches.

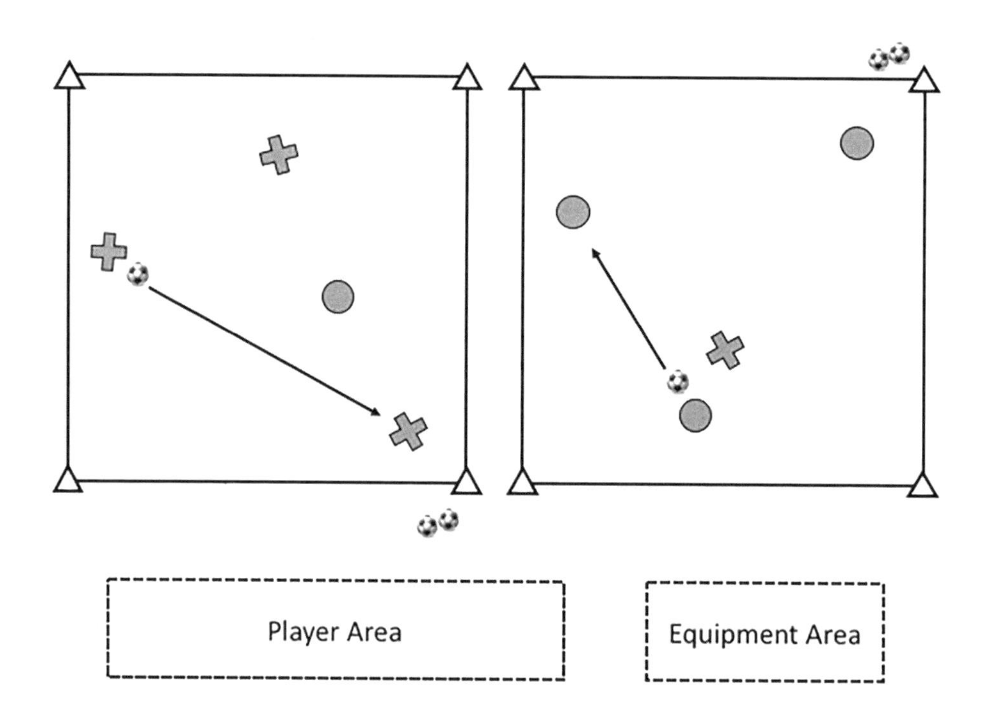

Practice Three

Three-versus-one practice, where the three attacking players look to retain possession of the ball. The player looking to intercept the ball remains as a defender for a set period of time or until they gain possession of the ball. During the practice, consider rotating the participants between the different grids so that they play with and against a range of players. Or you may want to organise the players so that they are playing with and against players that will challenge them.

Though there is absolutely a time and a place for these type of practices, as you will achieve a number of returns from them – such as touches on the ball, high intensity and development of the players' first touch – you will also lose key concepts, such as penetration and defensive principles. As mentioned earlier within the chapter, the main aim of an invasion game is to attack the opponent's territory with the aim of scoring a goal or point. Whilst doing so, the opposition are attempting to regain possession of the ball (or whatever object is used) and at the same time protecting the area in which the goal or point can be scored. Therefore, if we look at the defensive elements of a rondo, the clear difference between the practice design and the game of soccer is that the defenders have nothing specific to protect. At the same time, the players in possession of the ball are attempting to retain possession for no specific reason or as a means to an end. This will usually result in the defending players chasing the ball around the area, whilst the attacking players make a number of passes until, finally, an error is made and possession is lost. As a coach, you would not want to see the team play in this manner, either in or out of possession, during a game. When the team has the ball, you would not want them to just keep possession for the sake of keeping possession; you would prefer them to make progress into the opposition's territory and attempt to create a goal-scoring opportunity. It could be argued that a team may look to just retain possession towards the end of the game if they are winning. But it would be hoped – due to the age and level of players that we are likely to be working with – that these types of tactics or thought processes would never be considered. Similarly, when the team is out of possession, we would not want the players to run around the pitch chasing the ball. Instead, we would want the players to retain the correct shape so that they are in the best possible position to protect the goal and win the ball back. However, the current practice design for the rondo does not allow for these key principles of the game to occur. The design of *Practice Three (b)* has the main components of a rondo, but by including direction as well, it allows the practice to incorporate more key principles of an invasion game and therefore makes it more like a game of soccer.

Another key characteristic of all invasion games, which was touched upon earlier in the chapter, is that they are played with an equal number of players on both teams. This is a fragment of the game that again we quite often move away from during training, apart from when we play a game or deliver some form of one-versus-one practice. The fact that we often use overloads or underloads within practices can, however, quite often be realistic and relevant to the game, provided that we have considered carefully the desired outcome of the session and how these situations look in the actual game. Though a game of soccer usually takes place with an equal number of players on each team, the actual areas on the pitch where the action takes place, i.e., where the ball is situated at that specific moment in time, are more often than not competed for between an uneven number of players, i.e., three-versus-two or two-versus-four. This may be seen when a ball is played forward to a striker and they find themselves up against two defenders; or when the ball is being competed for in the midfield area between an odd number of players; or when a wide player, who is in possession of the ball and is up against the opposition full-back, is overlapped by

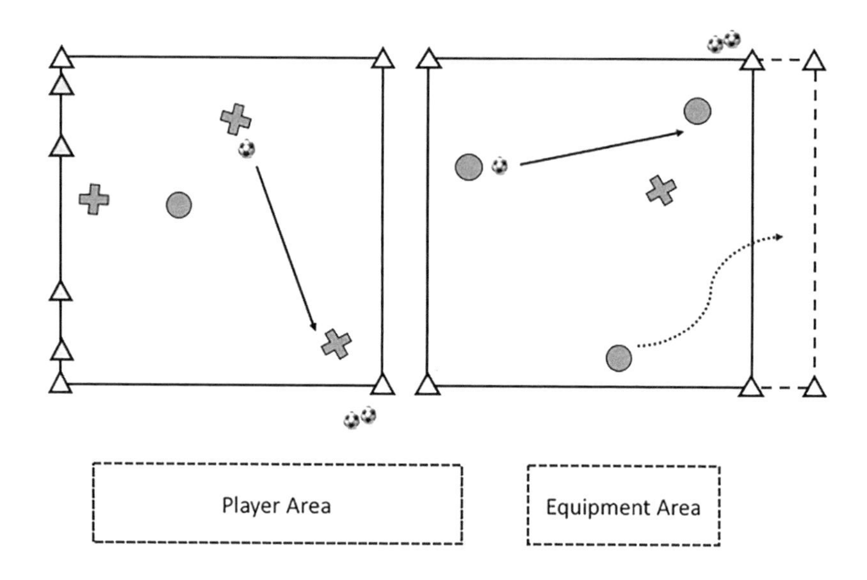

Practice Three (b)

Three-versus-one practice, where the three attacking players look to retain possession of the ball, whilst attempting to achieve a set number of passes. On completion of the set number of passes, the attacking players then look to complete a given task. In the first practice, a player has to dribble through one of the two gates, whilst in the second practice a player needs to receive a pass within the 'target zone'. Similarly, if the defending player wins the ball they have to dribble through a gate or into the target area.

one of their teammates. Overloads and underloads occur constantly throughout the game and therefore players should be exposed to them regularly within training.

Overloads within a practice are usually achieved when we find ourselves with an odd number of players during training. To deal with this 'extra player' we will often designate a player as a 'floater' or the 'magic player'. There are most definitely arguments for and against the use of these types of players within practices. One reason not to use 'floaters' is that it is unrealistic and not applicable to the game; you would never play a game of soccer in which there is a player who plays for both teams, depending on who has possession of the ball. The argument against this is that unless you play the 'actual game' then there will be elements of the practice that are not realistic. However, it could be argued that the practice becomes very unrealistic for the player who adopts the role of the 'floater' as they will not experience being out of possession, nor will they have to react to transitions in the game. Therefore, instead of using a 'floater' it may well be more beneficial to play with uneven teams, in terms of the number of players. How the make-up of the teams is decided, i.e., which team has the extra player, can be dealt with in a number of ways. It may well be that the players that are perceived as the 'stronger' players are put on the team with fewer players to challenge them. Or it could be that halfway through the practice a player is 'transferred' between the two teams so that both teams experience having one extra player versus being short one player. It could possibly be that the teams are just selected randomly or the players themselves decide which team has the extra player, giving you the opportunity to see how they react and deal with the different situations in which they find themselves due to the uneven numbers.

There is, of course, another side to the argument in that there are a number of returns you will get from using a 'floater'. There may be a particular reason why you select a certain player to be the 'floater', as it is beneficial to their development; why and how this can be done will be discussed further in chapter 5. Or it could be that you use a 'floater' or 'floaters' as they are needed to help the players find success within the practice, or to allow more players to be more active during the practice. An example of this can be seen within *Practice Two*, where two 'floaters' are now being used on the outside of the practice area, which makes it easier to retain possession of the ball. Instead of using 'floaters', two players from each team could have been used instead, with them supporting their teammates when they have possession of the ball. However, this would mean that the support players would only be active when their team was in possession of the ball.

Therefore, the decision about whether or not to use a 'floater' is the same as most decisions that are made with regards to the planning and delivery of your coaching sessions: the outcome should always be the same in that the option you choose is the one that is the most beneficial to the players.

All invasion games will take place within a designated area whether this is in the form of a court or pitch with clear boundaries as well as specific areas within it. The shape of the areas in which these games are played is usually in the form of a rectangle, which supports the main aspect of the game – to invade the opposition's territory – as it inherently provides direction to the game. The first point that we need to take from this is that the games are played within boundaries and that the dimensions of these boundaries are pertinent to the players within the game, the number of players and the age of the players, as well as the rules and distinctive elements of the actual game. Players therefore need to be used to playing within restricted spaces, to have the experience of coming up against boundary lines, and then working out what to do when they do. As coaches we can support players with this part of their development by ensuring that the practices in which they participate are within specified areas. It is not unusual for a coach to set up a practice that does not have a boundary, whether this is because it is a line drill, such as dribbling around a set of cones, or because we do not believe there is a need to have an actual area, in which case the players are allowed to go where they please. The importance of providing the players with

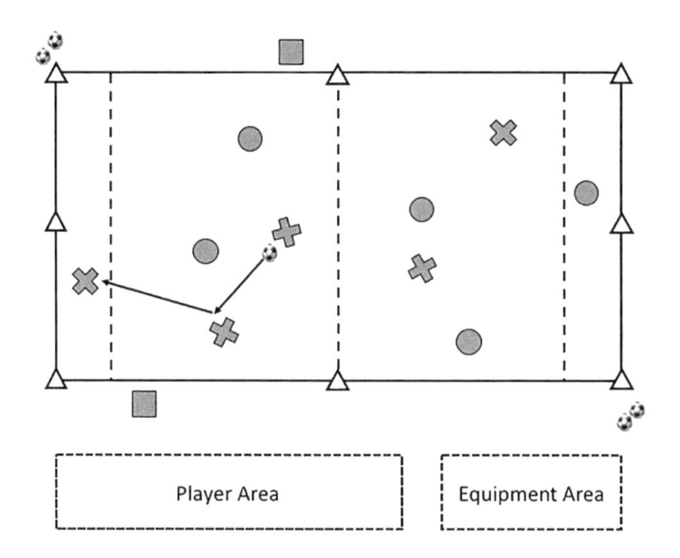

Practice Two

Players are split into two teams, with each team having a target player in an end zone, with an additional two neutral players on either side of the area. The neutral players support the team in possession of the ball and are limited to two touches. Teams win a point by playing the ball into the target player.

'freedom' will be stressed throughout the book, and therefore not providing the players with boundaries is considered far more preferable to restricting and forcing them to travel in exact patterns from one cone to another cone. As the game is played within boundaries, however, they need to be used to being restricted by these limitations. This is particularly important when they are playing some form of game. Boundaries need to be in place alongside rules that specify the outcome should a player go outside of the boundaries. For instance, if we look back at *Practice One*, if a player collects a cone from the oppositions half but then goes out of the area whilst avoiding being tagged, there needs to be a rule in place that outlines what happens if this situation occurs. It is also important that these rules are then enforced by the coach, so that the players get used to playing in this type of environment.

Invasion Games – The Three Phases of Play

The three key principles of being in possession, out of possession, and transition have been touched upon throughout the chapter within the other key characteristics, which provides an indication of their importance to invasion games. When we are considering the outcomes of the session and the designs of the practice we must first consider which of the three principles we are working on. It may be that you decide which of the three principles you want to work on and then from that select a narrower focus. For example, you may want to work on when your team is in possession of the ball and then you narrow the focus down further and you concentrate on passing or penetration. Alternatively, your planning may take you directly to your narrow focus. For instance, you may decide that the players need support in defending the ball in one-on-one situations and therefore this is your narrow focus; however, you must still take into consideration that this happens 'out of possession'.

Though there might be some small differences in the actual components of the three key principles across the various invasion games, they will on the whole be the same. In addition to this, the prominence of the three principles within each specific game does not differ, nor does the importance of understanding them. For example, one of the

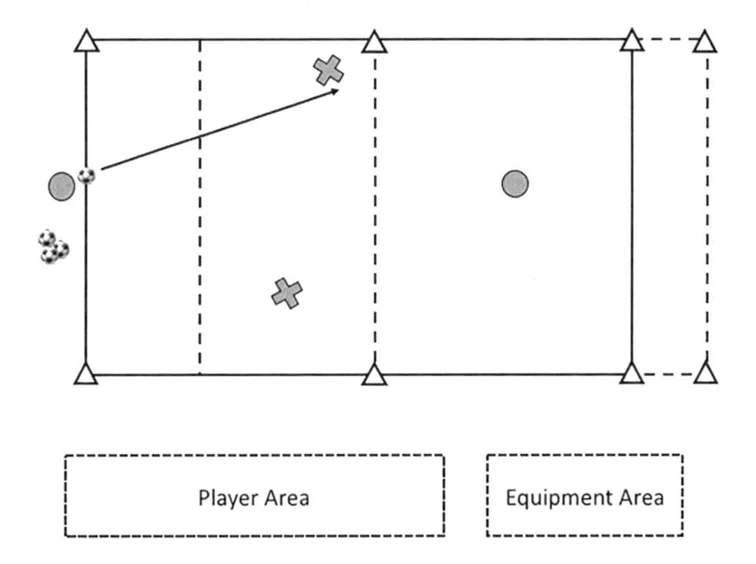

Practice Four

Two-versus-two practice, with the area split into thirds (the thirds are not equal in terms of size and need to be set up to meet the needs of your players). The server plays the ball into the attacking players who enter the final third and look to score a point when one of them receives a pass in the 'target zone'. Once the attacking players have entered the final third, the server then becomes a second defender and makes a recovery run to support their team-mate who has been attempting to delay and prevent the attacking players from scoring a point. Should the defending players win the ball, they look to get the ball back to the first third by having either one of the players dribbling the ball into it or receiving a pass within it.

components in soccer when your team is out of possession of the ball is to 'delay'. As an individual player, and as a team, when you are out of possession you should look to delay or slow down the attack, as this will then allow the team to get organised, allow teammates to recover and get goal-side, and ensure that you are not outnumbered. This component of being out of possession will be found in most, if not all, invasion games – it may just look different. For instance, in soccer you would look to delay your opponent by forcing them backwards or out wide or by reducing the amount of time and space they have. Though this component of delaying will be evident in all invasion games, in some games it will look the same, such as hockey, while in other games, like rugby union, it will look different. So within *Practice Four* we are asking the first defender to try to delay the two attacking players long enough to give the other defender enough time to recover and support their teammate.

At this stage of your coaching journey it is helpful to have an understanding of the different components that make up the three principles of the game. Having a basic understanding of the three principles will provide you with the necessary knowledge when it comes to the designing and delivery of your sessions.

In Possession

Width: By having your players stretched across the full width of the pitch when your team is in possession of the ball, it is more likely that you will also stretch the opposition, making them less compact. This in turn will create larger gaps between their players which will make it easier to penetrate through their defensive 'lines'. In addition to this, you are more likely to isolate their players into one-versus-one situations or possibly even create overloads, i.e., two-versus-one. Finally, using the full width of the pitch will make the pitch bigger, which will make it easier to create gaps; it will allow players more time and space on the ball and it will make it harder for the opposition team to regain possession of the ball.

Depth: Similar to width, it allows the team in possession to make the pitch bigger and therefore it will produce similar outcomes of allowing players more time and space on the ball as well as making it more difficult for the other team to get the ball back. In addition to this, stretching the opposition team the length of the pitch will increase the distances between the defending team's units, i.e., defensive unit, midfield unit and attacking unit. Doing so will allow the players on the team in possession of the ball to find space in between these units.

Progression: If a team is to invade another team's territory, then it has to be able to make progression up the pitch. Whether they start with the ball from a goal kick, in the centre of the pitch from a throw-in, or by winning the ball off the opposition in their own half, a team has to progress up the pitch to get into a position where they can have an attempt at goal. Progression can be achieved in a number of ways and is quite often the area of the game that generates the biggest discussion, with some coaches preferring the more direct and quickest option, whilst more recently the more popular option is for teams to get closer to the opposition's goal through short, quick, accurate passing. Whatever way a team chooses to move the ball up the pitch, the essential element is that they move the ball farther away from their own goal and closer to the opposition's.

Penetration: One of the main reasons to maximise the width and depth of the team when in possession of the ball is to create gaps in the opposition team, with a view to 'penetrating' the different units or lines, with the ultimate aim of penetrating the final unit/line of the opposition, i.e., the defensive line. Penetrating this final line can lead to turning the opposition players to face their own goal, crosses or cut backs and, of course, attempts at goal. Therefore, penetrating or playing through opposition lines is a crucial element of an invasion game, in terms of progressing into the opposition's territory and ultimately creating scoring opportunities.

Support: Providing support to the player on the ball is clearly important in retaining possession within the game. When providing support to a player, you may ask the players to concentrate on three guidelines that will help them be in a position that will support their teammate: distance, angle and sight. When considering distance, a player does not want to be too close to their teammate; if they are, it makes it easier for the defending player in terms of their positioning and decision making. Ideally, a supporting player will also position themselves so that they create an angle between themselves and the player on the ball. This should make it easier for the receiving player to see more of the pitch and to play forward because of their body position. In addition to this, an angled pass is not as risky or dangerous as a flat pass which is easier to block or intercept. Finally, the player looking to receive the pass needs to ensure they are in a position where they can see the ball, i.e., there is nothing blocking their view and there is a clear pathway for the ball to travel between the player passing the ball and the player receiving it.

Creativity: To be able to get through a defence and create goal-scoring opportunities, teams and players inevitably will need to be creative or imaginative in their play. They need to be able to find solutions and make decisive decisions within the situations in which they find themselves, whilst also reacting and adapting to the ever-changing environment that is a game of soccer. This is just one of the reasons why a key theme running throughout this book is the need for a coach to provide players with an environment that allows them freedom on the ball and encourages creativity. At the same time, it should also put them in positions that replicate what happens in the game so that they gain experience of being in these situations, which in turn will develop their decision-making skills.

Retention: Though the main purpose of having possession of the ball is to make progression up the pitch and to create goal-scoring opportunities, it is not always possible to do this. In these situations, where it is not possible to make progression or to create an opportunity, there is a need to just retain the ball, whether this is as an individual or as a team. Sometimes it is helpful to play backwards or sideways, as it will help shift or stretch the opposition, which in turn will then allow the team to play forward or to produce an opportunity. It should also be remembered that if you do not have the ball, you cannot score, but the opposition can; the importance of having the ball cannot be overstated. Therefore, when we are happy for a player to put the ball out of play or just to clear it up field, we are actually just encouraging the players to hand over possession to the other team.

Out of Possession

Compact: Staying compact within units, and as a team as a whole, will restrict the amount of space that the opposition can exploit. The smaller the amount of space that there is between the defending players, the more difficult it is for the team in possession to be able to penetrate lines and to make progress into the opposition's territory.

Denying: When the opposition has the ball, it is important that they are denied time on the ball as well as space. Denying a player time on the ball will give them less time to make the right decision and reduce the options available to them. Similarly, by denying the opposition space on the pitch it will be more difficult for them to be creative and for them to make a vital pass, or for them to beat an opposition player that will create goal-scoring opportunities, especially in the final third of the pitch. Or if it is done higher up the pitch it will reduce the space that they have to play out of their defensive third. Overall, it will significantly increase the difficulty to make progression and to generate opportunities to make an attempt at goal.

Delay: If you delay the opposition making progress up the pitch towards your goal, it will give you more time to get players back behind the ball, i.e., between the ball and the goal that you are protecting. It will also give the team time to get 'organised' in terms of the team shape and the positioning of players. If a defending team can get organised, it is much easier to achieve the other principles for when you are not in possession of the ball, i.e., being compact, denying space and time, etc.

Protect: The ultimate aim of soccer is to score in the opposition's goal. Therefore, when you are not in possession of the ball, the main aim is to win the ball back so that you can look to score; however, in the process of doing this, your own goal must be protected. When we relate this to an individual one-versus-one situation, the priority for the defender is to get themselves between the ball and their goal while attempting to win the ball back and, if not, forcing the attacking player away from the goal, i.e., backwards or wide. It is the same principle for the defending team as a whole: the pathway to the goal needs to be blocked and the main danger area, in and around the penalty box, needs to be guarded.

Cover and Support: It is essential that when defending, players do not get isolated; if they do and then get beaten by an attacking player, it will open up the pitch for the team in possession of the ball. If the pitch is opened up, the attacking players will have more time and space on the ball. To prevent this, defending players need to have support with them when they engage the player on the ball. Therefore, if the first defender does get beaten the second defender can engage the attacker. By supporting the first defender, the second defender can also cover the space in which the attacking player wants to go whilst also making it more difficult to pass the ball forward.

Transition

Decisive: Having just won or lost the ball, players need to make decisions quickly and stick to them once they've been made. If a player is indecisive, it will slow everything down which can cause result in missed opportunities or danger. If the team has just won possession of the ball, there are a number of decisions to be made, such as whether to pass or dribble – or if you are going to pass, to whom and where. These decisions need to be made and they need to be carried out straight away. If the player on the ball has a change of mind or if they are unsure it is the right decision, then the opening could disappear as the defending team have had time to get organised, compact and to close down space. Similarly, if players are indecisive after they have just lost the ball, the opposition team will have more time and space on the ball, making it more likely that they will produce a goal-scoring attempt. Especially when the team has just lost the ball, it is important that eventually these decisive decisions become instinctive decisions.

Speed: Similar to being decisive in their decision-making, the players also need to be quick in their actual play. If the team has just won possession of the ball, it needs to be moved quickly. This could mean moving it quickly up the pitch or quickly to the other side of the pitch where there is more space. Or it could be that it has been won close to the opposition goal and then it needs to be moved quickly to a player who is in a position to have an attempt at goal. As well as moving the ball quickly, players need to be fast in supporting their teammates, having just won the ball means that players would currently be in a position to protect their goal and will therefore need to move with speed to get in a position to support their teammate. It is the same having just lost the ball: the team would have been set up to create width and depth and there will be a need to recover quickly to get goal-side and to be compact.

Reaction: Before a player can be physically quick in changing their position during transition, they need to be mentally quick. They need to identify that possession has changed hands and that there is either immediate danger or a limited opportunity to create. More often than not, players have the opportunity to react before the transition occurs. By reading the play or by gambling players can give themselves an advantage in terms of gaining time and distance in altering their position to suit the changing picture within the game. Should they gamble and the anticipated change in possession does not take place, then it is important that they react again and return quickly to their original position.

Balance: As previously discussed, when transition happens within a game, it is important that players react to this change in the game and alter their positions accordingly. However, what we do not want to happen is for all of the players to react in the same way, in that they all do not go from defending to attacking or vice versa; it is vital that balance remains in the set-up of the team. As a loose guideline, you would want a minimum of one extra player left defending the number of players that the opposition leave upfront, i.e., if the other team leaves two players up the pitch as front players, there need to be at least three players holding their position to defend against these players. Doing so allows some of the key principles of defending to be implemented should the opposition win the ball and play the ball up quickly to the two front players: cover, support, protect, etc. Balance is just as important when your team has just lost the ball; though we want players to recover and get back behind the ball, we still need at least one player to remain up the pitch, ahead of the ball, occupying some of the opposition defenders. Doing so provides the team with an 'outlet' for when they win the ball back and it immediately achieves one of the key principles of when you are in possession of the ball: depth.

Characteristics of Soccer

Soccer has a number of individual traits that are exclusive to it and not seen within any other game, as well as a couple of traits that are specific to some of the different formats of the game. The most obvious and probably most important trait of soccer is, of course,

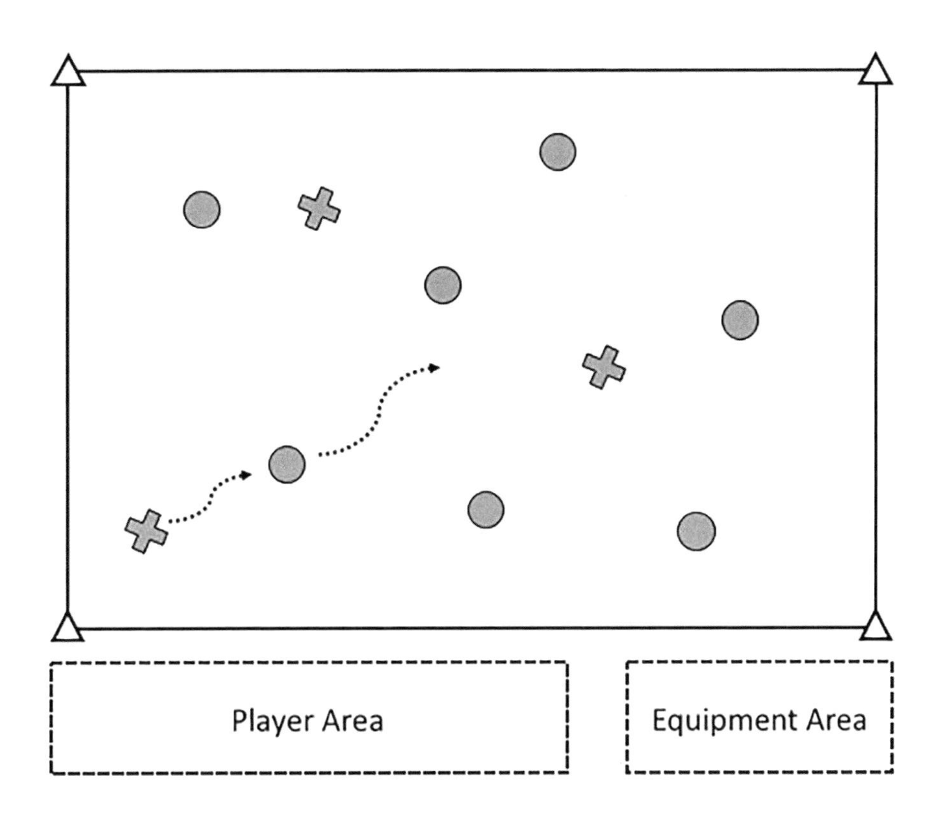

Practice Five

A small number of taggers attempt to tag the rest of the players. If a player is tagged, they are 'frozen' and must remain still until they are released by one of their team-mates. (This could be with a 'high five' or by running under the frozen players outstretched arms.) Taggers aim is to try and tag all of the players so that they are all frozen. Also consider giving the players a challenge to complete whilst they are frozen to increase the physical returns you get from the practice. For instance, you might challenge them to balance on one foot.

the ball and how it is used within the game. Though it may sound strange, there are times that as a coach we forget this most important concept of the game and exclude it from our training. There are times, of course, when we deliberately exclude it due to the outcomes we are looking to achieve. As we just discussed, this could be because we are using another invasion game, and transferrable skills within it, to help the players' cognitive development. Or it could be that the outcome of the practice is focusing on the physical corner of the player's development (see chapter 4) and therefore something like a game of tag might be used. However, even then there is still the opportunity to include the main element of soccer, i.e., the ball and replicating some of the ways in which it is used in the actual game.

Practice Five shows a normal game of tag in which a number of taggers are attempting to tag the other players. Using this form of practice at the start of the session will get the players active really quickly and there will be a high level of returns in regards to the players' fundamental physical development. These physical returns include agility, acceleration and deceleration, all of which are not only essential requirements for soccer, but all invasion games and most other sports.

Now consider introducing a ball or balls to this game of tag and how this will increase the returns you will get from the practice. This can be done in a number of ways. It could be that you give every player within the practice a ball and the game continues as normal, but just with the ball as well. It could be that you give the players who excel (see chapter 5) at this type of game – i.e., the quick and agile players – a ball to make it more difficult for them. Another option would be to reduce the area size which will make it much more difficult for those players who are trying to avoid being tagged and then to counterbalance this, you give the players who are tagging a ball to make it more difficult for them. Alternatively, if you are focusing on passing within your session, you may introduce one or two balls to the game of tag and these can be passed around by the players who are avoiding being tagged, with the rule that if they are in possession of the ball they are safe. The options and possibilities are endless; it just takes the coach to be creative in their thinking whilst ensuring the concept remains consistent in terms of the outcomes for the session and that it is relevant to the game.

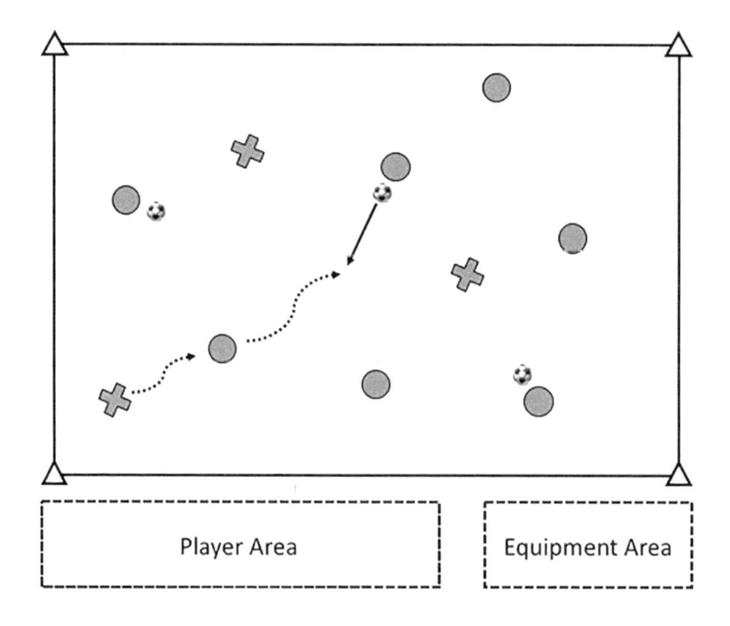

Practice Five (b)

The same set-up as Practice Five but with the addition of a small amount of balls. The balls are used by the players avoiding being tagged; if a player is in possession of the ball they cannot be tagged. The players are encouraged to pass the ball to teammates who are in need of the ball, i.e., they are in danger of being tagged. In this practice the tagger's aim is to try to tag enough of the players so that the number of players left equals the number of balls being used within the practice.

Quite often as a coach we become consumed with the need to improve the player's levels of 'fitness'. There is a clear and justified need to develop the physical attributes of all players and this will be discussed further within chapter 4; however, this should not come at a cost to their technical development and game understanding. Quite often we will refer back to what we experienced ourselves as a player, or what we see other coaches do, whether this is what we may see on television or on the pitch next to us on a training night. This then usually results in players doing a lot of constant running without the ball or a number of 'physical exercises', neither of which replicate what players do during a game. If you look at running in particular, players do not constantly run during a game, their movement patterns are very stop-and-go at various levels of speed and intensity. Running constantly for a set period of time or distance has no relationship to the physical requirements for soccer. If we refer back to *Practice Three,* within this practice the players are getting plenty of opportunities to imitate the physical demands they will face during a game, whilst being able to practice with a ball at the same time. There are other simple ways in which we can get physical returns from practices without compromising the technical and tactical returns. Simply increasing the pitch size will put more physical demands on the players; or reducing the number of players within the practices of the games will ensure the players are constantly involved and active. For instance, instead of playing a game of six versus six, play two games of three versus three.

Another key characteristic of the game of soccer are the goals in which the teams either look to score or protect, with scoring usually being the main aspect of the game that the players enjoy the most. Again this does not mean that every practice should include goals, or that when we do include goals they have to be exact replicas of the goals that we use within the game, or even the same number of goals. They do not have to be actual goals; they can just be a set of cones – they just need to represent goals. But when we do design a practice, can we take time to consider whether by adding a goal or goals it would improve the practice further? And when we do add goals to a practice, they can represent a number of things; they do not have to just represent the goals within the game. Within a practice you could use small goals, which could be a target that the players need to play the ball into. The goals would then be representing specific areas of space within a game or a specific player, such as the striker. Or it could be that they are used in a one-versus-one practice that is focusing on being out of possession, and the goal provides the defending player with a specific target to protect.

If we look at *Practice Six,* it is a one-versus-one practice with a focus on the attacking player. Usually within these types of practices we will ask the attacking player to get past the defender and then stop the ball on the line. This is an excellent practice in that it is encouraging players to be positive on the ball and to go past a defending player. But what happens next is not realistic or something you would want a player to do: when in a game would we want a player to beat a defender and then just stop the ball?

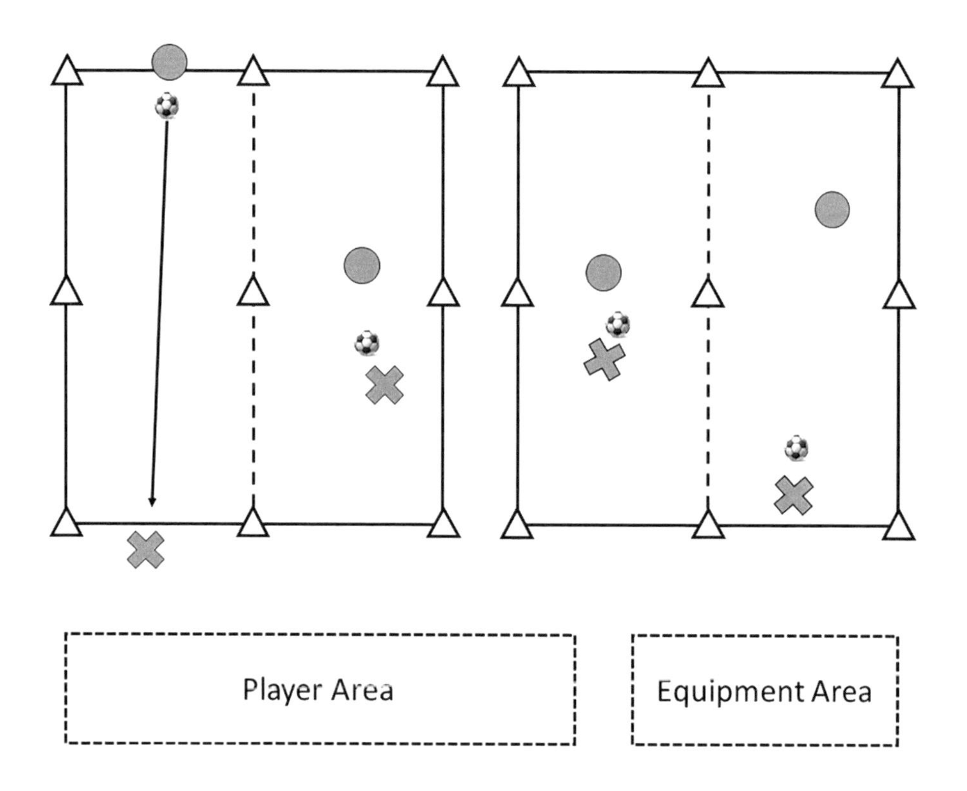

Practice Six

Defender plays the ball to the attacker who looks to dribble the ball over the defender's line. If the defender wins the ball, they look to dribble over the attacker's line. After each go, rotate the roles of the players.

Therefore, can we add something to the practice that the attacking player has to achieve after they have beaten the defender? Within *Practice Six (b)*, a small goal has been added for the attacking player to play the ball into after they have beaten the defender. The goal is positioned to help replicate a player beating a defender in a wide position and then crossing the ball.

Whilst *Practice Six (c)* has a focus on the defender, a small goal has been added to give the defender something to protect. In addition to this, two goals have been added for

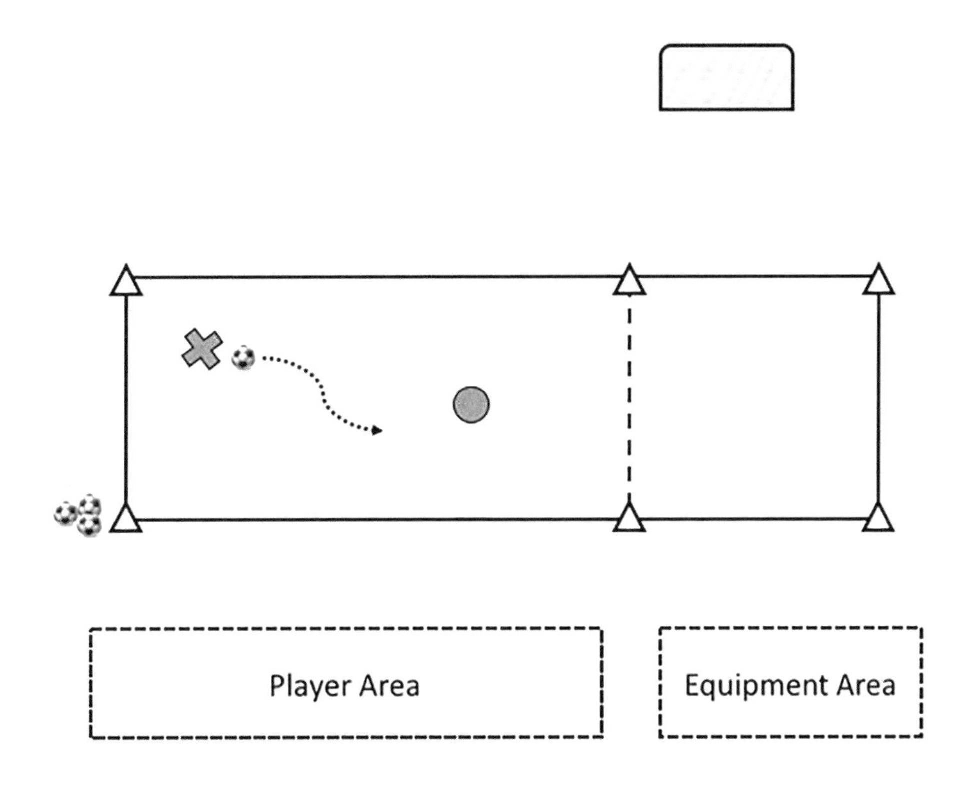

Practice Six (b)

The defender starts with the ball on the line that separates the two playing areas. They play the ball into the attacker who then looks to dribble the ball into the second area. Once they are in the second area, they attempt to pass the ball into the small goal that is situated to the side and slightly away from the area. Should the defender win the ball, they look to dribble the ball over the line where the attacker started the practice.

the defender to dribble through if they win the ball. The defender has been given two options to attack as it aims to replicate the different options a player would have, having just won the ball. This is another example where as a coach we can be creative in the planning and delivery of our practices. By distinguishing between the two goals, this could be done by using different coloured cones so that each goal could have a different meaning. One goal could be worth more points because of where it is positioned or because it is narrower. Or it could be that one goal you have to pass into (this then represents a teammate), and the other goal you have to dribble through (this goal would have to be created using cones and would represent the space the player has to drive into).

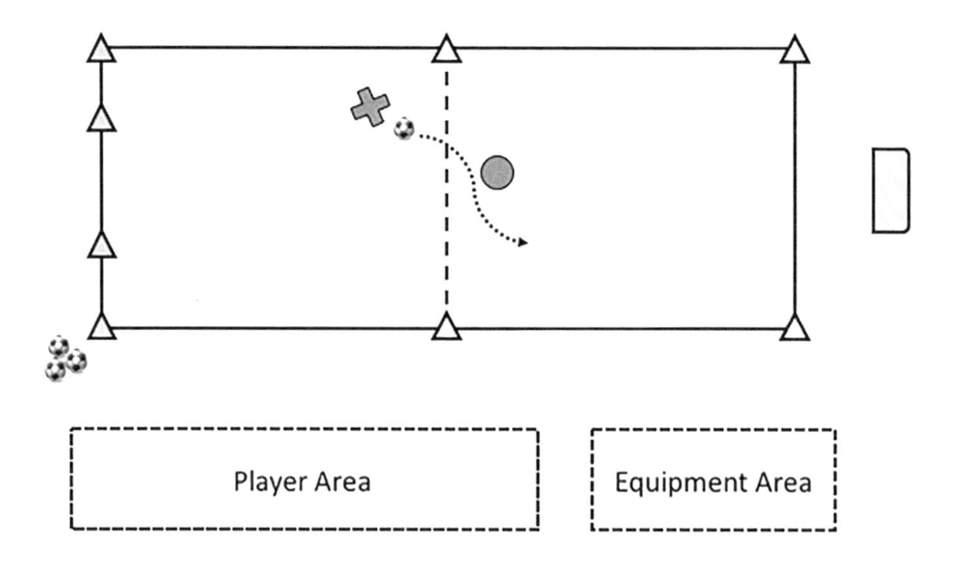

Practice Six (C)

The defender starts with the ball on the halfway line and they play the ball into the attacker who then looks to dribble the ball over the halfway line. Once they are over the halfway line, they attempt to pass the ball into the small goal that is situated slightly away from the area. Should the defender win the ball, they look to dribble the ball through one of the two gates that are situated on the line where the attacker started the practice.

The set-up and focus of *Practice Six (c)* also provides a good opportunity to revisit transition, specifically within soccer, and the need for it to be included more often within our practices. Earlier in the chapter we discussed how, though there might be some small differences in the actual components of the three key principles across the various invasion games, they are basically the same. The actual principle of transition within soccer is quite different to a number of other invasion games. For instance, in netball a change of possession does not usually provide opportunities to exploit the opposition due to the positions of the players being restricted. Similar to netball, basketball possession changes hands regularly, usually from either a successful or unsuccessful attempt to score a basket, which allows the team about to lose possession to get organised in preparation to defend their basket. If possession is lost beforehand, i.e., within the build-up, this usually results in the team losing the ball conceding points, as there is no time to recover and protect the basket. In rugby (both formats), a change in possession usually occurs from one team kicking or a foul being committed. Rarely does a pass get intercepted or the ball break free and get collected by the defending team; therefore, there are limited opportunities for taking advantage of a team that is short of numbers or is disorganised. However, during a game of soccer, transition regularly happens in a number of different ways and in a number of different places within the pitch, resulting in a range of outcomes, including the opposition being organised or disorganised and being close or far away from the opposition's goal. Therefore, there is a greater amount of emphasis on transition in soccer compared to other invasion games.

As coaches we do, of course, need to have a clear and narrow focus for our session, such as dribbling, passing or one-versus-one defending. That does not mean, though, that when these focuses are achieved or break down that the practice needs to stop and restart. *Practice Seven* is a possession-based practice that has a focus on passing and receiving the ball; there is an overload for the team that starts with the ball which is looking to complete a set number of passes. As would be expected, the team in possession of the ball will not always achieve their target number of passes required; if they were to do so, as coaches we would need to consider whether the practice is too easy, and if so, it would need to be adapted (see chapter 5). Once the required number of passes has been established to make the level challenging but also achievable, then we need to start to consider what happens when the defending team stops them and wins possession of the ball. In these instances, we will quite often ask the defending team to return possession back to the attacking team or to play it out of the area. Though this would allow the practice to return back to its main focus of passing and receiving, it would remove a key aspect of soccer (transition) from the practice. Furthermore, what motivation is there for the team that is defending to win the ball if they have to give it straight back? If they have no motivation to win the ball back, then they are unlikely to defend correctly which will result in the practice becoming unrealistic and it will be difficult to achieve the planned outcome of the session.

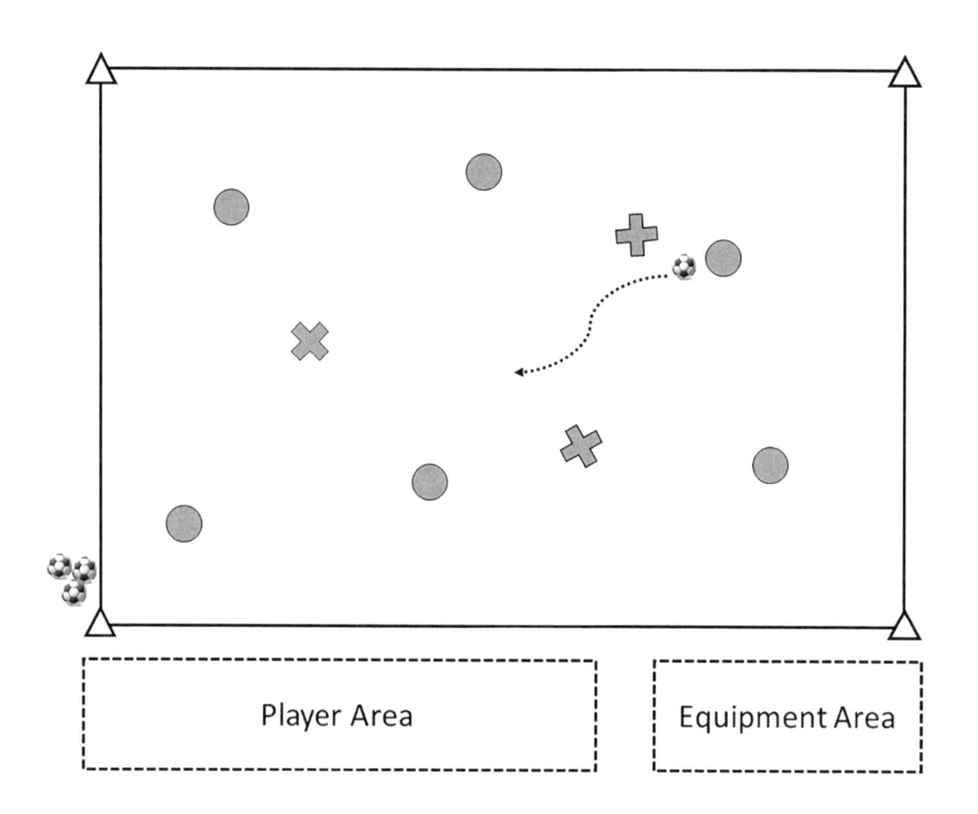

Practice Seven

The attacking team looks to complete a set number of passes to achieve a point. In doing so, they will gain a point and the practice will continue. Should the opposition win the ball or if the ball goes out of play, the pass counter is reset, and the practice continues. If the defenders win the ball, they win a point if they successfully break out of the area. Rotate the role of the defenders regularly throughout the practice.

Providing the defending team with a challenge or a target if they win the ball introduces transition to the practice. It also makes it more realistic and motivating for the defending players. This challenge again could come in a range of forms, such as dribbling out of the area (this helps players to get the ball out of tight, congested areas and into space) or passing the ball to a goal or target area away from the grid (representing a teammate).

Different Formats of the Game

There are a number of different formats of the game, and with these different formats come slight amendments in terms of the rules and how the game is played. It is important that we remember these unique characteristics and use them within our practices. Usually this means that the practices the players take part in mirror the format of the game that they play. However, sometimes we can use elements of one format of the game within practices for players that play in a different format, as it helps achieve the desired outcome of the session. If we consider the retreat line that is used within mini soccer, this can be used within practices for players that use it and do not use it within the matches that they play. Within *Practice Two,* the retreat line rule could be applied, with teams having to retreat to their own half each time they achieve a point by getting the ball to their target player. For young players playing in the mini soccer format, this will replicate what they need to do in a normal game. For older players, the rule could be used to allow them to practice against teams that defend deep.

An obvious difference between most formats of the game is the number of players. The younger the players the smaller the number of players there are on each team. There are two reasons for this: firstly, to allow the players to have more touches during the game and, secondly, because of the size of the pitch that the games are played on. However, a further advantage of having fewer players for younger children is that the larger the number of players on the pitch, the more possible solutions there are to the decisions that a player has to make. In an eleven-a-side game, the player on the ball will have a number of options available to them. Specifically, there are a large number of different options in terms of who they can pass to. In addition, there are the alternative possibilities to passing, i.e., running with the ball (if the player chooses this, they need to decide where exactly to drive into), turning,with the ball (in which case they need to decide how they will turn and in which direction), etc. By reducing the number of players on the pitch, the player on the ball will probably only have one or two options in terms of who they can pass to, whilst the possible decisions about where on the pitch to move into with the ball will also be reduced, due to the smaller amount of opposition players. It is the same for all decisions that a player will have to make during the game, whether they are in possession of the ball or not. If a player is defending, it is much easier to decide whether to close down the player on the ball or make a different decision, such as provide support and cover for a teammate or track the run of a different opposition player. Because there are fewer players on the pitch, the number of solutions available to the decision that has to be made is significantly reduced.

The reason for this reduction in numbers – the difference in rules and equipment within the mini soccer format compared to a full-size game – is simply to make it easier to understand and participate in and, of course, more enjoyable to play. This thinking therefore needs to be taken into our coaching. Most interactions a player that plays mini soccer will have, whilst in possession of the ball during a game, will be with a small amount of other players, from both their own and the opposition's team. More often than not, it will be with just one other player, i.e., it will be one versus one, which could then develop into one-versus-two, two-versus-one or two-versus-two situations. As coaches we therefore need to ensure that we frequently replicate these conditions within training. Instead of having a possession practice that is six versus four, could we have two separate practices of three versus two instead? If we overload practices with too many players, it will go against what we are trying to achieve within the mini format of the game. Though it could be argued that a six-versus-four practice has the same number of players that will play in a game of five versus five, the smaller dimensions of the area compared to the size of the pitch will result in players having more solutions to the questions they are faced with, which is unrealistic compared to what they will experience in a game.

Another aspect of the game that changes are the dimensions of the pitch. As the players get older, the pitch size increases to accommodate the extra number of players that are involved within the game as well as the development of the players in terms of their physical attributes. It is therefore expected that similar practices for different age groups would be completed in dissimilar area sizes because of the difference in terms of numbers within the practice, remembering that the younger age groups need smaller numbers in their practices, as well as the physical characteristics of the players and the type of passes that they make. However, it is not uncommon for practices to be delivered in comparable areas, with no consideration of the game format. Other factors may well be considered instead: quite often a small area will be used, as the coach wants a high tempo to the session. However, this only replicates a small section of the game, more often players will be looking to retain possession of the ball across larger areas of the pitch. Even in small-sided formats of the game, the pitch dimensions are quite substantial and the passing and receiving of the ball will be completed over considerable distances.

Therefore, when designing a practice or laying out the practice area, not only do the age and the ability of the players need to be taken into consideration but also the game that they play at the weekend. When you are deciding upon whatever you want the players to practice, you need to consider what does it look like when they are doing it during a game on Saturday or Sunday? What is the number of players that are involved from both teams? What is the area size in which the action is taking place? What are the specific rules that can affect this part of the game? We need to ensure that whatever we are asking the players to practice during training replicates as closely as possible what it looks like when they are doing the same thing during an actual game. We will look at this in greater detail in chapter 3.

Competition

At the very start of the chapter, the importance of embracing the fact that soccer is competitive by its very nature was highlighted, as are the people who play it, whether they are small children or fully grown adults. Therefore, if we are to fully understand the game, we need to remember that competition is at the very heart of it, which means it needs to be an integral part of everything that we do. It is just a matter of remembering that when we are working with young players competition is important, but the result has no importance whatsoever and therefore this competitive element of the game should be used to create an environment that is not only fun, but where learning will take place as well.

Players will generally enjoy a practice more if it involves an element of competition within it. Adding competition to a practice provides the participants with the motivation to complete the task as well as they possibly can, and it also provides a purpose to it – there is now a reason for doing whatever they are being asked to do, and there is a target or goal to achieve, which they will need to do as an individual or part of a team. Adding this competitive element to a practice also brings it closer to the actual game of soccer; it makes it more realistic and relevant. The easiest way in which we can add competition into a practice is by adding a scoring system, which was outlined earlier within the chapter. So, for example, if we refer back to *Practice Six*, which is a one-versus one-practice, having a scoring system provides a purpose for both the attacking player and the player who is defending. The attacking player knows that each time they are able to dribble over the line that the defender is protecting, they will earn a point and will therefore try to earn as many points as they can. Whilst the defender is trying to stop them, in their mind they are not trying to prevent them from crossing over the line, but from winning a point – and they get the added bonus of winning a point themselves if they can steal the ball from the attacker and dribble over their line.

Another advantage of introducing competition to a practice is that it is likely to increase the tempo in which the practice is being played. By increasing the intensity of a practice, we will be placing the players in an environment which will be close to the one they will find themselves in on a match day, in terms of how the players will approach and play the game, the speed in which the game will be played and the determination of the players to either win the ball or to retain it. There is the argument that if we remove the competitive element from the practice, it will allow the players just to concentrate solely on what they are trying to learn, such as dribbling, short passing, etc., without the added pressure of competing against other players. And there are definitely some advantages to this, as players will find completing the task easier and therefore are able to work on enhancing it in their own time. But it must be remembered that they will not be able to do this within the actual game; therefore, we can increase the level of intensity by adding competition, but this does not have to be directly opposed competition, it can, for instance, just be which pair of players can complete the most amount of passes, or which player can dribble through the most number of gates. By inserting a competitive element, we will increase the level of intensity within the practice. And remember: competition does not have to be against other players; we can also compete against ourselves. When you have another go, can you beat the number of passes you and your partner made? Can you dribble through more gates than you did last time?

Finally, as previously mentioned, children generally enjoy competition and it is one of the main reasons that they will play the game of soccer. They enjoy playing all types of games, whether it is video games, board games, card games or even games that they have made up themselves. And when they play these games they enjoy trying to win them, and they have fun playing against their friends and trying to do better than they do. And, generally, if they do not win they just want to play and try again. If they do win, they usually enjoy the fact that they won, but as with the child that just lost, they will just want to play again. The common theme throughout these different game formats is that the children playing enjoy the competitive element to them, but the actual final result is not overly important and will not affect their decision as to whether they will play again or not. Therefore, we need to provide the players with this element of fun within the practices; we need to let them feel the achievement of winning a point or scoring a goal, that could then contribute to them winning the game. Then, whatever the outcome of the game, we need to give them the opportunity to play the same game again or a different game, as they will just want to play again.

By introducing competition within our practices we are not only giving the players what they want, but we are also producing a training environment which is much closer to the game of soccer, when compared to one that does not have any. It makes the session more enjoyable and realistic, which helps the players to prepare more effectively for a game by practicing in a similar environment to that in which they will find themselves on match day. Competition is a key element of the game of soccer and should not be confused with a 'need to win' or 'results ahead of development'. Recognising the importance of competition – not only to the game itself, but to a child in terms of their enjoyment of an activity – it should be used whenever it is feasible to support the development of the players.

Having a full understanding of what a game is, and specifically appreciating the key characteristics of the game of soccer, is essential if we are going to provide the best possible support for the players. By fully understanding the game, we can ensure that within the training session, the players are practicing something that they will actually do in a match. We can put them in situations that are similar to what they will find themselves in during the actual game. Therefore, they are practicing something that they will actually do in a match, which is vital if they are going to be able to reach their full potential. Part of this is understanding the specific format of the game that they are currently playing and ensuring that the unique aspects of these formats are included wherever possible within the practices, as well as the key characteristics that occur in every format: possession, out of possession and transition. By producing these forms of practices, not only can we optimise the players' learning, but we can also create an environment which the players will find simulating as well as enjoyable, as they will basically be playing one of the many mini games that continuously occur throughout their normal game of soccer.

CHAPTER 2
UNDERSTANDING YOURSELF AND THE QUALITIES NEEDED TO COACH

Now that we have a better understanding of the make-up and the purpose of the game of soccer, it is important to understand the role of the coach within the development process. And when we refer to the coach, it is imperative that we see beyond the person that provides the players support in terms of their development as a soccer player, the role of the coach goes much further beyond this. As part of the player-coach relationship, the coach will need to offer support across many aspects of the players' lives and therefore it is not just knowledge around the game of soccer that is needed. A coach also needs to understand children and people and, just as importantly, they need to understand themselves and the skills and characteristics that they have developed in all aspects of their lives and how they can transfer and use them whilst supporting the players with whatever help they need.

The best coaches are not necessarily the coaches who have the greatest level of technical or tactical knowledge or the most experience or even the highest qualification. The most effective coaches are usually those that have and demonstrate effective people skills. This is particularly evident when working within grassroots soccer where it is extremely unlikely that any of the players you come in contact with will make it as professional players in the future, therefore it could be argued that the role of the coach is not to just improve them as players but more importantly improve them as people, whilst fuelling their love of the game. Fast forward ten, fifteen years' in time and you come across one of the players you worked with when they were first starting their soccer journey. How would you want that meeting to go? Think about how you would feel if they took the time to cross the road to speak to you, greeted you with a handshake and then told you how they were still playing the game and were finding success and fulfilment in other aspects of their life, whether this is in their careers, education or family life. Outside of a player's main social influence group, which usually consists of their close family, friends and teachers, it is highly likely that as a coach you will have the greatest impact on their lives, and in some instances your influence on their behaviour and life journey could actually be greater than some of or all of the members of their social influence group. Consider the child whose current experiences within school are not positive, or the child who is socially awkward and finds it difficult to make friends, as well as the child whose home life is not a happy one. The time that they spend in the environment that you create could be their weekly release where they can just concentrate on having fun and being a child, whilst the social interaction they have with you and everyone else involved with the team – players, other parents, etc. – is positive and supportive.

Throughout this chapter, the key qualities needed to be an effective and successful coach will be discussed and examples of how they can be incorporated within both training and match days will be provided. Through adopting and developing these qualities it is expected that it won't be just your players' experience that improves and becomes more positive, but your own as well, which is an essential element when volunteering and working with young children. Volunteering as a soccer coach is time-consuming and can often be quite stressful, which will only lead to one of two outcomes: either the coach will stop volunteering, or they will unconsciously pass their stress or negative feelings onto the players they are working with. As with all aspects of life, it is important that you enjoy what you do; by doing so you will be motivated to carry on doing it, and to do it as well as you can and subsequently your positivity and enjoyment will be passed on to, and absorbed by, the players.

Connecting With Players

When discussing a coach's connection or relationship with the players with whom they work, the conversation usually focuses on trust and the need to have the players' 'buy in' or their willingness to run through the proverbial 'brick wall'. And whilst these commonly used sayings are not relevant when working with young players, or in fact unsuitable, the importance of trust and mutual respect between the players and the coach cannot be overstated. Without this trust or respect, it is not possible for the players to flourish or to maximise their development and enjoyment of taking part. It is therefore essential that the right environment is created where players are comfortable enough with both you and the other players to express their full personality, to experiment and be creative in their play, whilst not being fearful of making mistakes.

Whilst there are a number of factors that can contribute to the connection between the coach and the players they are working with, the most important attributes a coach must display are being both understanding and attentive. When trying to understand the players, the most important thing you need to remember is that they are children and not small adults. Because of this, they will differ to you in so many ways, including: their understanding and interpretation of words, their ability to concentrate and absorb information, their social development and overall life experience. Therefore, it is essential that we adopt a patient approach and adapt some of our usual behaviours to ones that the players will more easily recognise and grasp. To achieve this kind of environment, a number of strategies and habits can be used to enhance and strengthen the relationship between the coach and the players. Introducing good habits or changing bad habits into appropriate habits for both you and the players will be a common theme throughout the book.

How you meet and greet your players can have an instant impact on how the coach connects with the players and can also provide a helpful insight into the players' mood and frame of mind ahead of the session or the game. On arrival the players' minds are understandably focused on getting a ball and playing, but before doing so, introduce the routine of the players coming to you and shaking your hand. It is not necessarily the handshake that is important, but rather the interaction that takes place during the action, as it presents an opportunity to find out how each player is feeling, what they have been up to that day and it also gives you a chance to let them know what the starter activity for the session is going to be. Introducing starter activities to your sessions will be discussed later on in the book, and how they can change a bad habit your players might have into a really good habit. This form of greeting could also be broadened to include the players greeting each other on arrival as well, which will then also help with their social development, which we recognise as an area they currently lack. It could also be extended further with the players shaking each other's hands before they leave, as well as yours, which will then allow you to provide praise and feedback to each individual player on their performance within the session. Of course it does not have to be a handshake; it may well be a fist bump or a high five. The way in which you greet the players is not important; what is, is the culture and environment you are creating and to which you are exposing the players.

Whilst having any interaction with the players, it is important to be mindful to keep it precise and concise, remembering that their concentration span is very short and therefore they will be eager to move onto the next thing, whatever that may be. So though you might be eager to pass on lots of information or ask a number of questions, it is important that you keep it short or the connectivity you are trying to achieve will get lost as the players begin to focus on something else. Another factor to consider is changing your body language or position and also your terminology, so that they are on a similar level to theirs. For instance, when talking to young children an adult can come across as an authoritarian or a dominant figure just through the language that they use or by towering over the child to whom they are speaking. Simply crouching or sitting down when speaking to players can make it a more relaxed and enjoyable experience for the child; it also allows for you to make eye contact which demonstrates that they are important to you and that you are listening and interested in what they have to say. Using language that they are used to and find easy to understand will help keep them engaged and attentive. This is particularly important when providing soccer-specific information or feedback. Commonly-used jargon that an adult may easily understand could be very difficult for a child to understand – 'find a pocket of space' or 'get in the hole' are examples of such phrases too often used. The language that you use needs to be clear and simple, so that the information you are passing on cannot be misinterpreted.

Finally, as coaches and as people we need to be approachable. The players that you are working with need to feel comfortable in approaching you to either ask you a question or tell you something that is important; this could be a minor matter, but is seen by them as being of high importance, or it could well be something that is vital to their well-being. Regardless of the reason they want to speak to you, they should not hesitate or consider whether or not to approach you. To achieve this type of relationship with the players, you need to constantly consider and review your behaviour and how you respond or react to the players. It helps in the first instance if you stay true to yourself and do not try to be something or someone that you are not. The players will respect you for this and they will also have a clearer picture of you as a person. If you try to be someone you are not, then it is more likely that your personality and behaviours will frequently change and as a result the players will find it difficult to read you as a person and understand you. As a result, they will find it difficult to approach you, as they will be unsure whether it is a good time to do so.

The other way in which we can build trust with the players is simply to get to know them and to understand them as people and not just as soccer players. Going beyond the player and getting to know them as a person will obviously help build a stronger relationship between you and the players; it will show them that you are interested and that you care about them. Subsequently, the players are more likely to trust you and be able to approach you, if you have built up a relationship with them. Simply finding out more about them outside of soccer, whether this is how they are getting on at school or finding out what other interests they have along with soccer, will help you to learn more about your players and, in addition to this, it will also allow the players to get to know you better as well. Strengthening the relationship between you and your players not only will enable you to become more approachable, it will also provide you with a far greater understanding of who they are, which is a key factor in coaching that will be discussed in different sections of the book.

Communication

As coaches we often get frustrated when the players do not understand the instructions we give them and the practice does not materialise as we had visualised it would when we were planning it. But should we really be blaming the players that they do not understand what we are asking them to do, or should we look closer to home and consider that we have not explained it clearly enough? As humans we usually have one of three preferences in how we learn. We either like to listen to the information being given (auditory), or we like to see it (visually) or, finally, we like to try to work it out ourselves by just having a go at it (kinaesthetically). Therefore, within the group of players you are working with, you will more than likely have players with all three different preferences, and more often than not as an individual we have more than one preference. So when we are explaining what we would like the players to do, it should be expected that all of them would benefit from receiving the information in a different way.

Providing information visually can be a powerful tool and is usually the easiest way for people to absorb instructions quickly. It can be done using a number of different methods. The easiest way to understand the practices within this book is to look at the diagrams and read the brief instructions that accompany them. If you were unable to see the diagrams and someone else read the instructions out loud to you, then you would probably get a general idea of how the practice is set up and what the players are required to do. But it is probable that you would not fully understand the information that is being relayed to you. It is the same situation for the players at the start of a practice: they will probably get an idea of what they need to do from the information given by the coach, but they would definitely benefit from some visual aids as well. One of the most effective ways to achieve this is by using a tactics board, where a simple diagram of the practice alongside short and precise instructions can be shown to the players whilst verbal information is being provided at the same time. Using a tactics board not only allows the players to visually picture the practice, it also allows them to revisit it as many times as they need to before they fully understand what they need to do.

Another effective visual aid is a demonstration or a walk-through of the practice. Going through a step-by-step process provides the players a clear picture of not only how the practice works, it also gives them an idea of the area and environment they will be working within. If we are to use this strategy, then we do not need to give them information beforehand, as we will only repeat it again as we complete the walk-through and therefore we do not want to waste time repeating the same information when that time could be added to the players' playing time. Another way in which a demonstration could be used is that if an individual player is still struggling to comprehend what they need to do, they can step out of the practice and watch the other players whilst being supported by the coach. Though this may eat into their own particular playing time, it does not affect the rest of the players and if they need this extra minute or two to help with their understanding of the practice, then this is time well spent.

Once we have provided the information to the players both verbally and visually, we must now allow them the opportunity to explore and work out how to complete the task they have been set themselves (kinaesthetic learning). At this stage, our communication needs to be quite minimal and needs to shift from providing information to providing praise and encouragement, because if we just give them the information, then there is the risk that we prevent the players from working it out themselves.

The other key ingredient in effective communication is the ability to actually say nothing at all and listen to what is being said by the players and then show the players that you were listening and that you were interested in what they were saying. Simple actions, such as maintaining eye contact with the player and not interrupting or jumping in before they have finished, are effective ways to show a person that you are listening. This can be enhanced further by responding afterwards, whether this is a question to clarify a point or to get further information from them, answering a question that you may have been asked or providing an opinion on the information that you received from the person who was speaking. Being an effective listener allows the person speaking to feel valued and that they have a voice and can have an input whenever they want to contribute. This will also have an impact on the person's self-esteem and will provide them with the confidence to speak to other people as well.

Organisation

Being organised will have two major impacts on your coaching: first of all, it will help you maximise the contact time that you will have with the players. One of the greatest frustrations of a grassroots coach is the limited amount of time they get with their players, especially as the allotted time you get with the players is quite often affected by the teams using the pitch before and after your session. Being organised will allow the players to spend more time actually playing and practicing, rather than waiting for the next practice to be set up or trying to figure out the configuration of the area in which they are working. As well as maximising the time you have with the players, being organised is also an effective tool in managing the behaviour of the players, as it will ensure the players are always active and therefore have fewer opportunities to become bored or distracted; it also allows the coach to have greater control over who the players work with and when and how the equipment is used.

One of the easiest ways to manage the behaviour of the players is through organising the equipment and the players into two separate areas. By simply identifying two separate areas using cones (to make the two areas easily distinguishable, use a different colour for each area), you can control when the equipment is used and who collects it, and you can also have a more controlled environment when you want to speak to the players. These can be seen in the diagrams used throughout the book and are there as a visual reminder of the importance that they play in enabling a session to run both smoothly and effectively. Earlier in the chapter we spoke about changing and managing the habits of the players, and using these two areas will provide a further opportunity to transform and develop their behaviours.

Later on in the book, the importance of allowing the players to 'play' will be stressed, as well as allowing practices to be 'messy' where creativity and problem solving can take place within a safe, fun and challenging environment. A similar environment to this can be found within schools, a place with which your players will be more than familiar. When it comes to painting within the classroom, students are encouraged and allowed to paint whatever they want and they are inspired to be creative with their ideas, shapes and colours. However, what they are not allowed to do is to go and grab the equipment or the materials whenever they want, as the teacher recognises and understands the need primarily for a safe and controlled environment. There is no difference between this setting within the classroom and the one on the pitch. As the players arrive for training or match day, and after they have shaken your hand, they can drop off their drinks and any extra clothing they have brought into the 'players area' where they will also find the instructions for the starter activity (chapter 3), which might include collecting equipment from the equipment area (e.g., 'collect a ball from the equipment area'). Both areas can then be used throughout the session or the game, for instance, the first part of the session may require one ball per player and the second part only one ball between two; the balls no longer needed can be returned to the equipment area. The 'players area' can also be utilised throughout; for instance, if you need to make changes to the area for the next practice, the players can wait in the 'players area', during which time they can have a drink and also be completing a task – 'in the last practice you completed, can you make a list of everything that you had to do well, to be successful?' Or if you want to pass on some important information about the practice and you need to ensure the players are listening and concentrating, you could return to the 'players area' where there are fewer distractions and the environment is much more controlled.

Positioning of these two areas is also important and can depend upon what it is you want to achieve in terms of the players' development. You may be looking for some or all of your players to become more independent and less reliant of their parents or guardians. In this situation, you would place both areas away from where the parents and guardians usually stand so that during the session or the game the interaction between them and the players is limited, allowing the players to be more independent. Or, alternatively, you may want the parents or guardians to have a better understanding of what it is you do and what you are encouraging the players to do. For example, if the theme of your session is dribbling, you might tell your players in front of the parents or guardians that you want them to do lots of dribbling in the next game and that they will get lots of praise if they try to dribble past an opposition player. This then could help avoid the players' getting mixed messages during games, instead of possibly encouraging the players to pass the ball during the game, parents and guardians will now, hopefully, remember to encourage and praise players dribbling. If you have some form of group contact, whether this is via text or email or some other format, you could also send out a message the night before, or on the morning of the game, as a further reminder of the area of focus for praise and encouragement.

Changing the area set-up to move into another practice during the session quite often causes stress and frustration, and perhaps more importantly, it disrupts the session. Therefore, a carefully organised practice set-up can allow a session to flow whilst also helping to utilise the small amount of time you have with your players. It will also act as a deterrent to disruptive behaviour as players will have fewer opportunities to become bored or distracted. A simple strategy of adding or removing cones to existing areas is the easiest and most effective way of achieving this. If we look back at *Practice Six* from the previous chapter, the set-up allows the players to experience one-versus-one situations where the coach can concentrate on the player with the ball, before the session progresses into a two-versus-two situation, by simply removing a small number of cones. This progression then provides the player on the ball a completely new situation with different problems to solve, such as whether to retain the ball or pass it to their teammate. The coach can now work with the player on the ball as well as the player supporting them, where they can provide assistance about the types of runs that they make or the angle and distance of their support. Though the content and the exact focus within the area would be expected to be different, in that it would be adapted or altered to meet the needs of the players, the set-up allows for a smooth transition into the next practice that continues with the theme of the session.

Another strategy that can be used is to use the same area throughout the entire session, which will therefore require no changes to be made and should therefore limit any disruptions. The key element in these types of practices is that the coach is organised and prepared in terms of the progressions and challenges they introduce, so that the players remain motivated and do not become disengaged. The area layout used for *Practice Two* will not change throughout the entire session. Along with making it easier to set up and minimising any disruptions, it also makes it much simpler for the players to understand and process what they are being asked to do, as they remain in the same area with the same constraints throughout the session.

Patience

As coaches, we can find it difficult to watch and not intervene when the practice we have devised and set up is not going the way we had imagined it would – whether it is because the players do not fully understand the conditions and constraints, or because they are finding it too challenging and are struggling to find success. It is important to realise and understand that just because the players are not doing what you intended them to do, doesn't mean that learning is not taking place. In fact, there is actually more skill development happening than if they were doing everything exactly how you wanted it done. This is not to say that if a practice is not working due to one of the four main reasons which will be discussed in chapter 3, that you should not intervene and make necessary changes, it just requires the coach to demonstrate a level of patience, during which time the players are given an opportunity to work out the solutions themselves first. For instance, some of the players may need some help with the different spaces and dimensions within the practice area or the constraints and rules that have been put in place. They will attempt to solve the problems they are facing through trial and error, observing others, or by asking questions, and it will take each player a different amount of time to fully understand the concept and rules. At this stage, it is important that you are flexible and lenient with the rules and constraints, allowing the session to flow and just providing reminders to the players about what they can and cannot do within the practice. Some players may benefit from stepping out of the practice and watching what the other players are doing whilst being guided by the coach; this will support the player in their understanding, whilst allowing the rest of the players to continue playing.

Earlier in the chapter the importance of allowing practices to be 'messy' was introduced, and if some practices are to be 'messy' the coach needs to be patient as well as trusting in the process. It can be difficult to stand back and watch when a practice is not going exactly how you envisaged, especially when you have the added pressure of your colleagues and the players' parents observing your session. The easy option here would be to step in and support the players to help them complete the task in the way you want them to, so that the practice becomes more 'easy' on the eye. However, a key element of the players' development is trial and error; therefore, if we intervene too early because we want the practice to look better, or the players to be better at what they have been asked to do, then we are in fact restricting their learning and development. As coaches we need to be patient whilst the players figure out what needs to be done and how it is done. This can be achieved by allowing the players an opportunity to explore and find the solutions to the challenges they are facing themselves. Further ways in which you can help players with the understanding of what they need to do within your sessions can be found within chapter 3, which discusses the design of the practices.

Similarly, we need to be patient with the long-term development of the players, remembering their age and how long they have to learn and understand the game. Using the example of education again, you would not expect your child's primary school teacher to be teaching maths equations that they need to understand for their final exams. Too often, coaches working with young children expect the players to produce skills or carry out tactics that they have seen in the elite game. A prime illustration of this is when new trends evolve within the game, such as the 'number 10' role and then we ask a seven-year-old to find the space between the midfield and the striker, or when the 'press' became popular an under-nine team is asked to work together in units to close down space and win the ball high up the pitch. If we go back to the teacher in the primary school teaching maths, they will help children learn and develop the fundamental maths skills such as multiplication and subtraction. They will then use these skills throughout their mathematical journey, including the final exams, where despite facing considerably more difficult and challenging problems, they will still use and need the fundamental maths skills that they learnt and refined in their early years. In the same way, it is essential that we provide young players an environment where they can learn and refine the fundamental skills that they will always need whenever they play soccer.

The content of *Practice Eight* allows the players to develop a range of fundamental skills that contribute towards the foundations of playing soccer. Specifically, they will develop key physical attributes such as agility, balance, acceleration, deceleration and strength, as well as essential technical characteristics including close control, turning, running with the ball and one-versus-one defending. In addition to this, the practice allows the players to unconsciously improve a number of the psychological requirements of the game, such as awareness, confidence and problem solving.

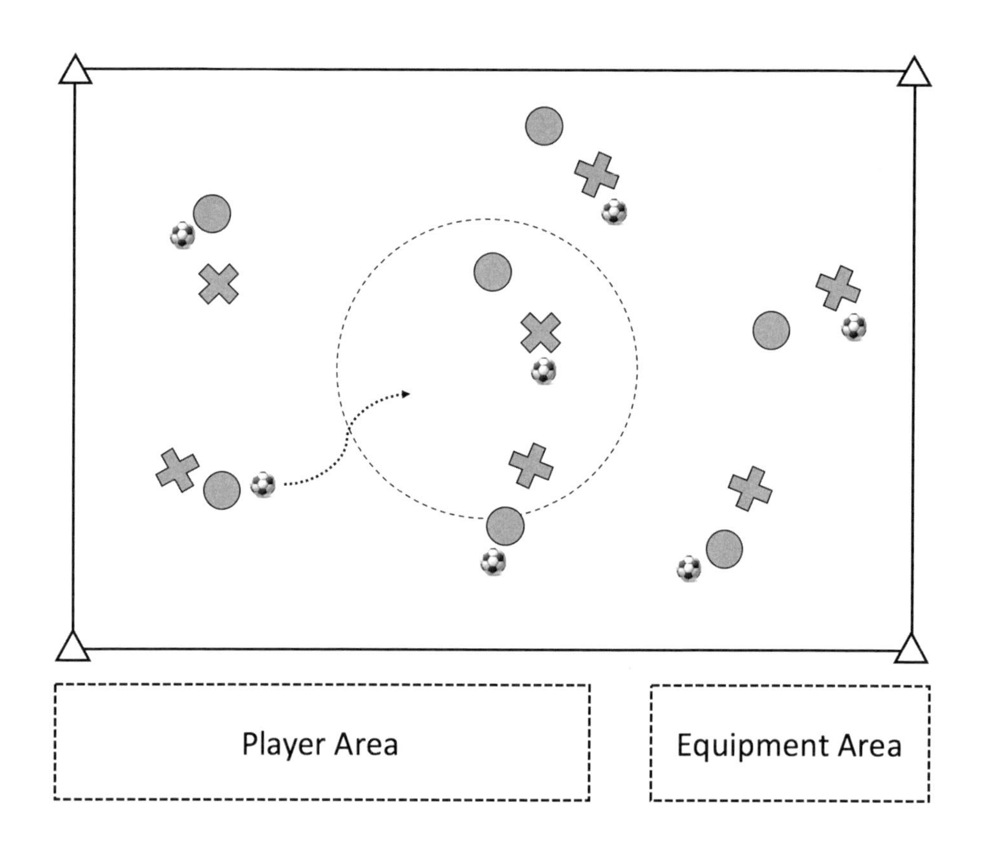

Practice Eight

Players are split into pairs, with a ball between each pair. The players look to keep the ball away from their partner for as long as possible. If the partner wins the ball, they then look to retain the ball. An additional area can be introduced to the practice and can be used in a number of different ways. For instance, players are challenged to dribble through the area to achieve a point.

Finally, the most important part of working with young children is remembering that they are children and therefore will behave as children. If you can accept and understand this, then it is much easier to be more tolerant and remain patient, which will go a long way in creating an environment in which the players will flourish and that they enjoy. Children want to actively socialize with each other and instinctively want to play and explore; therefore, we should not be surprised or disappointed if they become distracted or go off task. Instead, we should expect it and subsequently prepare for it. It is expected that a young child will have an average attention span of just fifteen minutes before they lose interest and this will significantly be reduced if they are not enjoying the activity. If players do start to stray away from the task at hand, the first question we need to ask ourselves is: does it matter? Is the safety of the player or any other players at risk? Are they affecting the learning or the enjoyment of other players? If the answer to these questions is 'no', then we may not need to intervene straight away. This possibly could be the child's way of exploring and they should be allowed time to finish what they are doing and find their own way back to the task at hand. They may need some guidance and support with this, through gentle reminders that are in the form of questions or by intervening and progressing the practice to help re-engage the child.

Alternatively, we could look at ourselves for the reason that the child has become disengaged; quite often their concentration span can be reduced if the activity they are participating in is not challenging or is too difficult. As an adult we can perceive things differently to children. What we may see as essential in terms of what they need to know and need to practice does not come across as being important or fun to a child. Similarly, when we are giving information to the players, the manner in which we do it and the amount of time it takes can often seem to us as being relevant and delivered in an appropriate and timely manner, whilst the young players are quickly losing interest and focus. It cannot be expected that young children will understand and retain large amounts of information or be motivated and absorbed by the same type of activity. We therefore need to remain patient with the players and also ourselves while we work out what it is that they enjoy and will apply themselves to, whether this is the type of practice, the duration of the practices, the difficulty of the practices, how information is given to the players or the time that it takes. Though certain guidelines can be followed to aid the process, all of which will be discussed throughout the book, the main ingredients for success in this area of coaching are both time and experience, and experimentation is needed to find out what does and does not work. During this period of experimenting, there will be times when what you are trying is not successful and at these points in time it is more important than ever to persevere with the process and stay patient, especially if the players show signs of frustration. It will inevitably take time to find the formulas that work and these will then need to be constantly reviewed as the players develop and mature.

Creativity

As coaches we are very much like magpies in our behaviour; if we see a practice that we like, or if we see it being used by a coach that we perceive as being more skilled or experienced than ourselves, then understandably we will 'take' the practice and use it with the players we are working with. However, unlike a hat or a watch, when it comes to practice design 'one size does not necessarily fit all'. It can take just one of a number of factors to prevent a practice for one group of players being suitable for another group. These include the more obvious factors such as chronological age, technical ability and playing experience, as well as the less apparent ones, like the format of the game in which they play and their understanding of the game.

This does not mean that we should not use the ideas of other coaches. In truth, if the concept of the practice design is effective in that it allows the desired outcomes of the session to be achieved, or that it promotes one or more of the key aspects of player development, such as decision-making or improving technical performance, then it could be argued and rightly so, that it should be used by other coaches. However, before we use it we need to ask ourselves a number of questions: are the anticipated outcomes of the practice relevant to the players that you are working with? Is the focus of the practice suitable for the players? Is the purpose of the practice appropriate for the players' current stage of development? If we were to ask these questions, then it is more than likely that the answer would be 'no' to at least one of the questions and if this is the case, then the practice should not be used. Instead, the possibility of adapting or changing the practice so that the answer to all of the questions is converted to a 'yes' could be explored. Ideally, the principles and foundations of the practice should only be used to help produce a practice that is relevant and effective for the players you are working with.

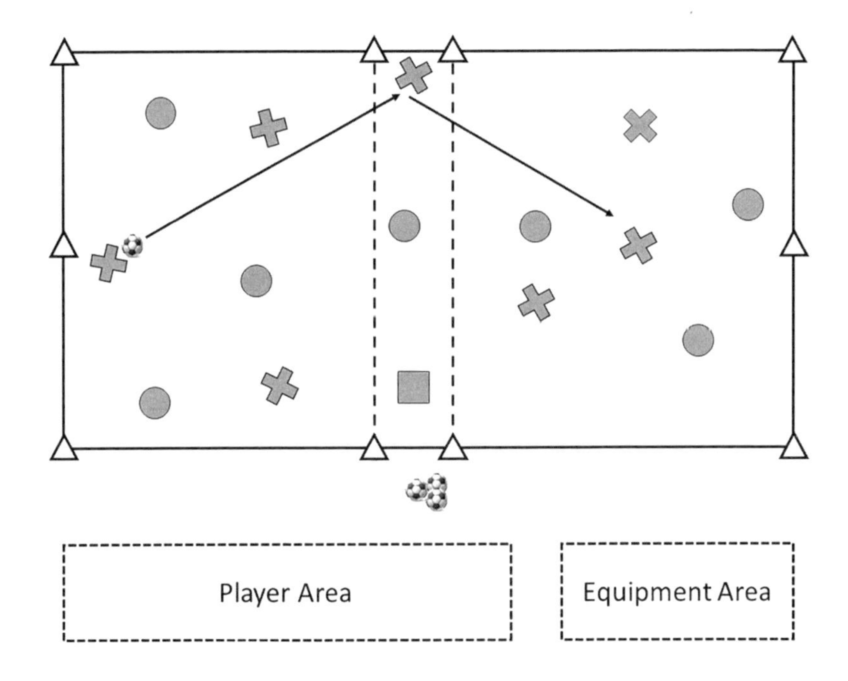

Practice Nine

Players are split into two teams with three versus three in each of the two zones. In between the two zones there is a central zone where there is a player from each team, with an additional neutral player. The neutral player always stays in their wide position, whilst the other two players rotate their position depending on which team has possession of the ball. If your team has possession of the ball, you go into the wide position; when your team loses the ball, you move into the central position. Teams have to complete a set number of passes before they look to transfer the ball from one zone to the other via the central zone using either their own player or the neutral player.

The set-up for *Practice Nine* is quite complicated and challenging and is therefore aimed at players with a good level of technical and tactical ability as well as a good understanding of the game. However, it can be adapted for players who might not have the same level of ability or experience or who might just be younger.

Even though a number of changes have been made to the practice, the principle of players transferring the ball from one end zone to the other end zone via a central zone, i.e., playing the ball forward through the thirds, remains the same. Other changes could also be made and a process that you could use to make these changes is discussed further within chapter 3, but what is important is that the practice is adapted to meet the needs of the players. Whatever changes are made, they need to be made so that the players find the practice challenging but achievable, easy to understand, and relevant to wherever they are on their developmental journey as a player.

When it comes to practice design, the ideal position to be in as a coach is that you do not need to use other coaches' practices, but instead you are able to design and produce your own practices. For that reason a whole chapter of this book is devoted to practice design and key aspects, such as direction and being like the actual game, although these key elements of practice design do not mean that you cannot be creative. Introducing additional features to the session that are fun and associated with the players' lives, apart from the time that they spend with you and their teammates, will help make the practices more enjoyable and engaging. It could be that your players enjoy playing video games and are therefore used to progressing through 'levels' or 'powering up', so incorporating these within a session can aid with learning and player development. For instance, if your session topic is to improve passing, then teams could 'power up' during a game by completing a set number of passes and then any goal they score is worth two or three. Or if your session focus is on dribbling, the players could progress through the 'levels' by

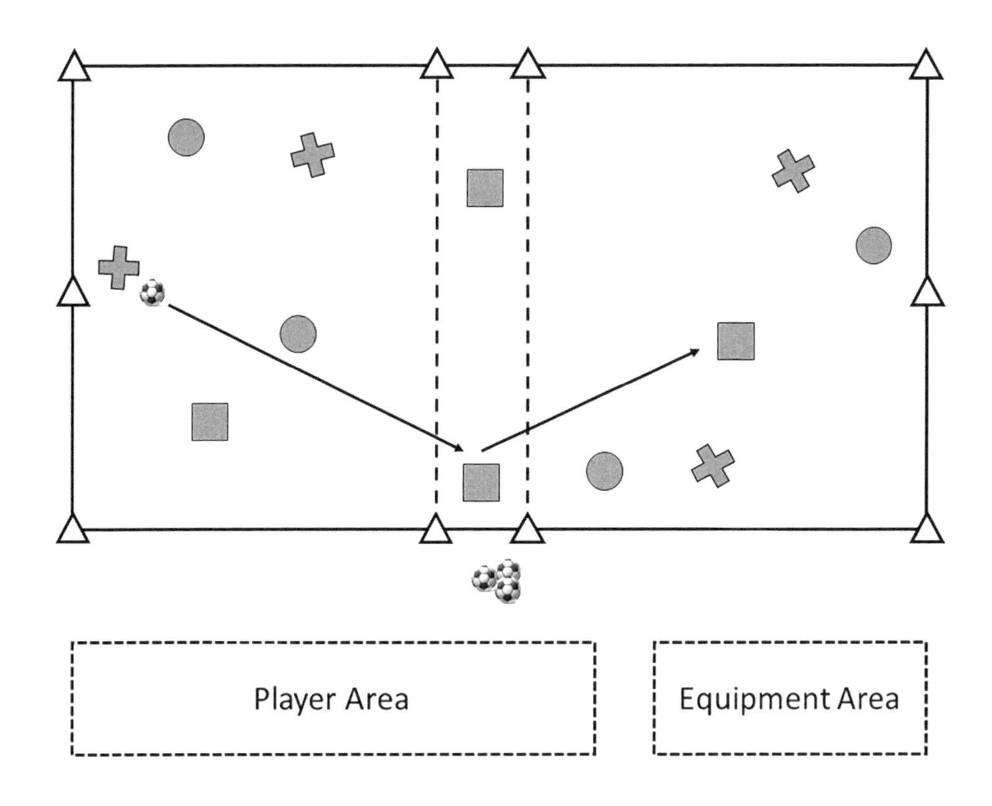

Practice Nine (b)

Within this practice a number of changes have been made to the original practice so that it is suitable for a different group of players. The three-versus-three situation in each zone has been reduced to a two-versus-two, so that the players on the ball have fewer decisions to make and a neutral player has been introduced in each end zone so that it is more challenging for the defending team to win back the ball. The set number of passes has been reduced; it could also be removed altogether. And in addition to this, the central zone now consists of only two neutral players to make it less complicated.

completing different types of 'skills' throughout the session. Or it could be that you link particular practices to well-known and popular soccer players. If you have a session that has a focus on 'passing' you might refer to a particular player who is known for their ability to pass the ball, or you may ask the players you are working with which players they think are good passers of the ball. Whichever way you decide to identify the players, you can then refer to them throughout the session, whether this is through imagery and questioning, such as by asking the players to imagine they are this player when they are in possession of the ball. What would they do in this situation? How would they do it? Or it could be that you and the players identify and list what these particular players do well and then refer back to them throughout the session.

Other ways in which you can be creative as a coach include adapting traditional 'playground' games to make them more relevant to the game of soccer. This can easily be done through introducing balls or other key characteristics of soccer, such as putting the players in teams or introducing direction to the game. Or it could be that you use 'scenarios' that inspire the players and encourage them to play in a certain way. This could be achieved by asking the players to play like a particular team, such as one that is known for pressing high up the pitch or is renowned for playing on the counter attack. Or they could be told they are playing against such a team and therefore they need to alter how they play. Alternatively, you could place your players in a specific match situation, for example, there is five minutes left of a Cup Final and you need to score a goal, what are you going to do differently? The opportunities to be creative as a coach are endless; the secret is to be fearless and to follow the advice that we are hopefully giving to the players – do not be afraid to try new things and do not be scared of making mistakes. Learn through your experiences and figure out what works and what does not work, whilst continuing to experiment and try out new ideas.

Enthusiastic and Inspirational

The role of a coach can be challenging and tiring and could even be described as an 'uphill battle'. Added to the everyday pressures of life, it is understandable that sometimes when a coach arrives for either training or a match day that they are not in the right frame of mind or it is not their number one priority at that time. However, the players will not be concerned to how you are feeling or what happened at work earlier that day and not because they do not care or because they are not bothered, but because they just want to play soccer and have fun with their friends. It is therefore important that at these times that you remember why you give up your valuable time and add to your already hectic workload. Whether this is down to your love of the game, wanting to provide opportunities for children or other adults to play soccer, because if you did not volunteer, then there would have been no one else and you just wanted your son or daughter to be able to play, or it could well be that it is all of these reasons or some other reason that is personal to you. Whichever reason it is that persuaded you to take on the role of a coach, you need to remind yourself of it and use it to motivate yourself whenever you need encouragement or a boost ahead of a coaching session that comes at the end of what has been a challenging day.

The players that you are working with will quickly pick up on your mood and therefore whatever mood you portray to your players will have a significant impact on the session.

This impact can obviously be positive or negative, so it is therefore well worth remembering that genuine, spontaneous enthusiasm is contagious. Consider a player that is anxious. It could well be that it is their first training session with this particular group of players, or it may just be that they are not looking forward to a particular session for whatever reason. The manner in which you greet them and then deliver the session will either make them more anxious or make them feel at ease and more relaxed, allowing them to enjoy themselves. However, more often than not, the players will arrive at training with endless amounts of energy and enthusiasm and therefore, instead of attempting to put a constraint on this energy, allow it instead to be infectious and look to channel it into the practices within the session. For instance, the set-up of *Practice Eight* encourages all of the players to be constantly active, either with the ball or attempting to win the ball, in a controlled and competitive environment. Therefore, instead of being restricted either in a line of players awaiting their turn to dribble around a set of cones or listening to a range of instructions on how to complete the practice, they are given the opportunity to expel their large resource of energy. Having probably spent the day in school where they have been restricted to a limited number of opportunities to get rid of some of their stored energy, they will look to training as an opportunity to go and play and use this energy. Children are naturally active and interested learners that are eager to interact, they just want to be given the opportunity to do this. Whilst playing, no one likes to be told to stop doing something, or to feel as if they are receiving negative feedback in the form of complaints or restrictions.

It could therefore be argued that it would be suitable to allow the players to just continue with their play without any interaction from the coach; however, the enthusiasm that they can bring to the practice is still very important. Providing encouragement to those players that are finding the practice challenging can be invaluable, as it can reassure them to carry on when they are close to giving up. Not only does this help develop resilience, it will also help to manage behaviour, as a player will often look to disguise what they see as failure or inability to do something by trying to deflect the attention away from this. This deflection can often be in the form of disruptive behaviour, which will not only affect the learning of that particular player, but it is also likely to affect other players within the session as well. The topic of managing behaviour will be looked at in greater detail in chapter 5, and within this, strategies to keep players engaged and on task will be discussed. As well as providing encouragement, enthusiasm can be shown through showing the players how much you are enjoying the time that you are spending with them, watching them play and actually coaching. How you project your voice and how the words are delivered can have a significant impact on the players. The use of words such as 'good' and 'well done' are always to be encouraged when working with players, especially young players, as they are encouraging words that can be used as positive reinforcement. The weight of this positive reinforcement, however, can be substantially increased very easily by using more powerful words and delivering them with energy and spirit. Replacing 'good' and 'well done' at the right time with 'outstanding' or 'fantastic' and exaggerating the delivery of the words can make a sizable impression on not just the player that it is aimed at, but on the whole environment. Also consider words that will have a big impact, words such as 'wow' or 'unbelievable', as using these words at the right time, and with high levels of energy, can be invigorating. Using these strategies when providing praise as well can boost the impact even further.

The importance of praise should not be underestimated; however, it can only be a powerful tool to help inspire players if it is used at the right time and in the right way. The impact that praise has can be reduced if it is overused by a coach, or if it is just used because the coach is unsure what else to do or say. Praise should be used to recognise that a player has done something that you have asked them to do, or when a player has attempted something that they have not tried before, or it could be simply that a player has done something really well. For instance, if you have asked a player to be more positive on the ball and they then attempt to dribble past a defender, you should praise the player whether they were successful or not. If a player does not usually use their right foot, but then during a practice they attempt a right-footed pass, then this should be rewarded with praise. Or it could be that during a practice that has a focus on defending, a player controls the ball really well, then this should be recognised by the coach and the player needs to be made aware that they have done something well.

How the praise is delivered is also important, if it is truly going to inspire a player to do it again or to continue to be adventurous in their play, then the coach needs to include a number of elements when delivering their praise. The praise needs to be specific in terms of the player who is receiving it and what it is specifically that they have done. In addition to this, it needs to be delivered with vigour and sincerity. Therefore, when providing a player with praise you need to ensure that you use the player's name, state exactly what it is they have done, whilst using words that express just how well they have done: *Connor that is an outstanding touch, a big well done*. But the praise should not end once you have recognised what the player did well; you also need to consider what happens next. After you have told the player what they did well, you then also need to challenge them to make it even better next time: *Sammy that is a fantastic pass, now next time can you think about playing it forward? Well done.*

Integrity

The start of this chapter emphasised the importance of improving the players you work with as 'people'. With integrity seen as the honesty and truthfulness of a person's actions, where the person has strong moral principles, it is a quality that must be adopted by all coaches. By demonstrating such a characteristic as part of their personality, a coach will be setting an example to the players – a quality, that hopefully they will adopt and can use in all aspects of their life, and that will allow them to exhibit a persona of trust and reliability. The fundamental element with integrity is ensuring that you are consistent with your choices and decision-making and that you uphold any statements that you make.

When working within grassroots soccer, hopefully the approach a coach takes is one of development and providing opportunities, which will be discussed in the next section of the chapter. A key component of both development and offering the players opportunities is the match day experience and a true test of a coach's integrity. If we are truly going to try to foster a learning environment and provide the players with opportunities, then we must give the players the same amount of time on the pitch whilst experiencing playing in all of the different positions you find within the game of soccer. If this is the approach that you choose to adopt and share with your players and other stakeholders, such as parents, guardians and fellow coaches, then to retain your integrity it is essential that you stay true to these values no matter what the circumstances. This can be a real test of character when certain situations appear to warrant a different approach. This could be during a match day when playing players in their favoured positions, or giving particular players extra minutes on the pitch will provide a greater opportunity of achieving a result that you believe will help improve the players' confidence. Though this may achieve an instant impact on their self-esteem and possibly their development, this impact will be extremely short-term, when the aim should be long-term development. Just as importantly, it will raise questions of your integrity not only as a coach but also as a person, the question could be asked and rightly so – if you have gone against your values and principles this one time, why would you not do it again in similar or different circumstances?

Another important aspect of integrity within coaching, especially when working with younger players, is ensuring that you keep your word. Children have surprisingly good memories and will remember most things that you say, especially when it is of interest to them. For instance, if they ask you if they can play in a certain position and you tell them that they can next week, do not be surprised when they ask you the following week if they are playing in the position you said they could. The first rule to remember before you make any promise is to ask yourself the question: Can I keep this promise? Is it something I will be able to follow through on? Even if the answer is 'I am not sure', then as a coach we should not be making any guarantees. If you are unsure, then be honest and tell them that, however, be prepared to be asked the question again a number of times until they get a definite answer. Again it is important that we do not give in to this pressure and look for the easy, short-term fix of agreeing to their requests. As in everyday life, saying 'no' to someone can be difficult and quite often an uncomfortable and unpleasant experience.

It is, however, part of life that people, children in particular, need to experience and accept. The process of saying 'no' can quite often be softened through either explaining why it is not possible or suggesting a compromise; what we do not get into, however, is negotiations. Of course, we want the player's experience to be enjoyable and that they are very much a part of the decision-making process in most circumstances, but in some instances the coach needs to demonstrate their authority. This does not mean that the method in which this is done has to be in anyway strict or aggressive. It just means that every so often as coaches we need to recognise that because of our life experiences and our role as the 'adult' within the group, we need to help the players recognise and understand what the correct decision is in these particular circumstances.

In every aspect of coaching we simply need to remain consistent in all of our actions and decisions. Whether this is in the form of the amount of time we give players on the pitch or the opportunities the players are given during training, the players' expectations and actual experiences of these events must remain constant. To achieve this, we must remain true to our values and beliefs and cannot allow any pressures, whether they are internal or external pressures, to affect these values and beliefs or worse still, encourage us to completely change them. The players will want and need our messages to remain consistent whilst being treated the same and fairly.

Equality

One of the key features of soccer is that it can be played by anyone, no matter their age, ability or gender. And as a coach it is your responsibility to ensure that any player you come into contact with gets the same opportunities and experiences as every other player that you work with. This can and should be both within the training environment and during the match day experience. When discussing integrity earlier in the chapter, the need for players to be given equal playing time in a range of positions was touched upon. Equal playing time is quite often the term that we refer to when we put soccer and equality together and rightly so, especially when the conversation is specifically about grassroots soccer or developing players. Grassroots soccer, in particular, is about providing people the opportunity to play soccer – no matter who they are – and therefore there is no real reason that one player should get more time on the pitch than another player. Of course what we do not want to do is change your role from that of a coach to that of a mathematician, and we should not become overly fixated on ensuring that every player has exactly the same number of minutes of playing time over the course of the season. What we can do, though, is take some time to plan to help ensure that during each specific game, the players that are available have approximately the same amount of time on the pitch. We can also take this a step further by ensuring that it is not just the playing time that is the same, considerations around which players start each game can also be made. By rotating which players start a game, we can help improve the self-esteem of a player and how they perceive themselves within the group. If a player constantly starts a game as a substitute and a coach starts a game with the players that they distinguish as the 'stronger' players within the group, then the other players will see their status as being less important. If, however, the players that start a game are rotated every week and alongside this all of the players get the same amount of playing time, then each player's status within the squad will also be equal.

Quite often we will play players in a certain position because the coach, the player or quite often both perceive it as the player's 'best position'. However, at a young age it is impossible to predict where a player will end up playing in the future, especially if they are given limited or no opportunities to play in different positions. And just because a certain position is seen as a player's strongest position does not necessarily mean that it is the position that they enjoy playing the most. Typical examples of these are the child who plays in goal and the child whose preferred foot is their left foot. If we take the goalkeeper first of all, this is a player that is often placed in this position because they want to play in this position, because no other player wants to play in this position, or they are categorised as a 'goalkeeper' by someone who they see as having more knowledge and experience, such as a parent, guardian, sibling or their coach. If this player is then restricted to playing this one position, then there is a distinct possibility that they will remain in this one position the whole time that they are playing soccer. Or if they do change to an outfield position later on, they will have limited experience to fall back on and will therefore be likely to be behind in their development compared to their teammates. Similarly, a player who is predominately left-footed will quite often be asked to play on the left-hand side of the pitch because of the fact that they are left-footed and proportionately there are considerably fewer left-footed players than right-footed players. These players are therefore less likely to have the opportunity to play in central areas or on the 'opposite' side of the pitch and experience all the different types of challenges that come with playing in these different positions.

To categorise or label players at such a young age will clearly have an impact on what type of player they become, as it will restrict their development. By deciding that a player is a 'goalkeeper' or a 'left midfielder' at a young age, we are choosing their future for them. How do we know that the player we have restricted to the role of goalkeeper could not develop into a gifted defender or forward if given the opportunity to do so? And on the flip side of this, by only allowing one player to play in goal, we are preventing the other players from having an opportunity to discover whether they would enjoy being a goalkeeper and if they have a talent for it. But it is not just a goalkeeper or a left-footed player that we restrict, quite often most players are restricted to just one or two positions from a young age because they are labelled as a specific type of player. Even if they are given an opportunity to play in a different position, quite often they will be quickly returned to their 'usual' position, as it is perceived they play better in this position. This, however, is to be expected if they are only given a limited amount of time to play in these different positions and, more importantly, we should be looking long-term, rather than short-term when it comes to player development and involvement within the game.

Providing players with the same opportunities should not just be restricted to a match day either; as coaches we should be looking to present all of the players the same experiences within training as well. If we refer back to *Practice Nine (b),* there are a number of different roles within the practice that ideally each player within the practice needs to experience. It would be tempting for the coach to put the players that they consider will need the most help within the practice in the central area. By putting these players in the central area, we may feel that we are helping them, as it will allow them to receive and pass the ball unopposed, therefore giving them time to complete the technique whilst under no pressure. We may also feel that by using these players within the central zone the practice has a better chance of 'working' and running smoothly. Similarly, the role of the neutral player within each zone could be seen as a key to the success of the practice, as they will need to support the team that is in possession of the ball and therefore the 'stronger' players will mainly be used in these positions. The focus, however, should not be on the aesthetics of the practice. Instead we should be concerned about whether the players find it both fun as well as challenging, and that it presents the same opportunities for all of the players. Therefore, we need to ensure that wherever possible every player is given the opportunity to experience all of the different roles. It may well be that for each of the roles we give different players different challenges or constraints that are relevant to them. For instance, when a 'stronger' player takes on the role within the central area, that area may no longer be an unopposed area and therefore players from the team out of possession can enter the area and put pressure on the players within it when they have the ball. This need for differentiation within practices will be looked at in greater detail within chapter 5.

Though the remaining chapters of the book will concentrate on the development of the players, the importance of this chapter should not be forgotten. Personality and behaviours form the foundations of what makes a successful coach and if these are not right, it does not matter how well we do everything else, we will fail as a coach. We will fail in helping the players achieve their full potential, we will fail in retaining the players within the game and we will fail in developing them as people as well. Having knowledge of the game is undoubtedly important, but not as important as understanding what young children need and how we as coaches can provide them with it. If we achieve this, then we will go a long way to maximising the impact we have on these young players in the small amount of time they spend with us.

CHAPTER 3
PRACTICE DESIGN

The planning and designing of a practice is one of the most important roles of a coach. Taking the time to carefully produce the practices that are to be used within the training session, not only will help maximise the players' development, it will also remove some of the concerns and stress from the coach during their delivery. A well-designed practice allows the coach to fully concentrate on the delivery of the practice and supporting the players. It will also allow the session to run smoothly, preventing the players from having opportunities to lose concentration and, furthermore, it will help you maximise the limited amount of time that you have with the players. The key outcome of careful planning, however, is the actual production of a practice that the players will find fun and challenging whilst being realistic and relevant to the game of soccer.

Outcomes: A Narrow Focus

There are a large number of elements in the game of soccer, and it is understandable that as coaches we want to help the players with all aspects of the game. But if we try to give them too much information on too many different topics they can actually end up not learning anything at all. At the end of the session we have done our job as a coach if every single player is able to take away at least one thing that they have learnt. For some players this will be the same thing, whilst for others it will be something individual to them. And though it is important that the players leave the session with a vital piece of information that is specific to them, it is just as important that there is a theme to this learning. To help achieve this, as coaches we need to have a clear learning objective to the session; there needs to be a clear objective that you want the players to achieve by the end of the session. For instance, it may be that you want the players to 'improve their forward passing', or it could be that you want them to 'retain possession', or you want the players to 'understand how to defend one-versus-one. Once we have decided on the topic for the session, we just need to ensure that our focus as a coach stays solely on the theme, in terms of both the planning and delivery of the session.

Once we have decided upon the narrow focus, we need to ensure that the practices we choose for the session provide the players with lots of opportunities to practice the outcome we have set for the session. So if we want the players to 'make a forward run', the practices within the session need to provide the players with lots of opportunities to make a forward run. It may also be the case that the practices we use actually force the players to make a forward run. We also need to ensure that during the practice every player has the same opportunities to make a forward run. This can be achieved by either regular rotation of player roles or by designing a practice where all players are constantly being given the same opportunities, which usually occurs in a game format.

Within *Practice Ten* the initial set-up of the practice is designed to encourage players to make a forward run into the second area, as it is only by doing this that the team can achieve a point. Rotating the teams around regularly will allow each player to have the same amount of opportunities to practice making a forward run. There are, of course, lots of other elements of the game happening in the practice, such as passing, receiving, dribbling, defending, as well as many more. Allowing these other elements of the game to happen within the practice lets the players rehearse making forward runs in a game-like situation and the design of the practice produces more forward runs than you would usually get in the same amount of time within a normal game. As coaches we just need to ensure when we deliver the practice we concentrate on supporting the players around the topic of the session and that we do not get involved in other aspects of the game. If a player is not defending correctly within *Practice Ten,* then we need to allow this to pass, as our focus is on the players who are trying to improve their forward runs. We only have a small amount of time within a session to help the players improve, and if we try to fit too much into this limited amount of time then no effective learning will take place. If, however, the feedback and support we provide to the players pertains exclusively to the session topic, then it is much easier for them to recall what they have learnt and for them to develop and improve during the practice. This learning can be enhanced further if specific restrictions and rules are added that increase the number of forward runs that are made within the practice. For this

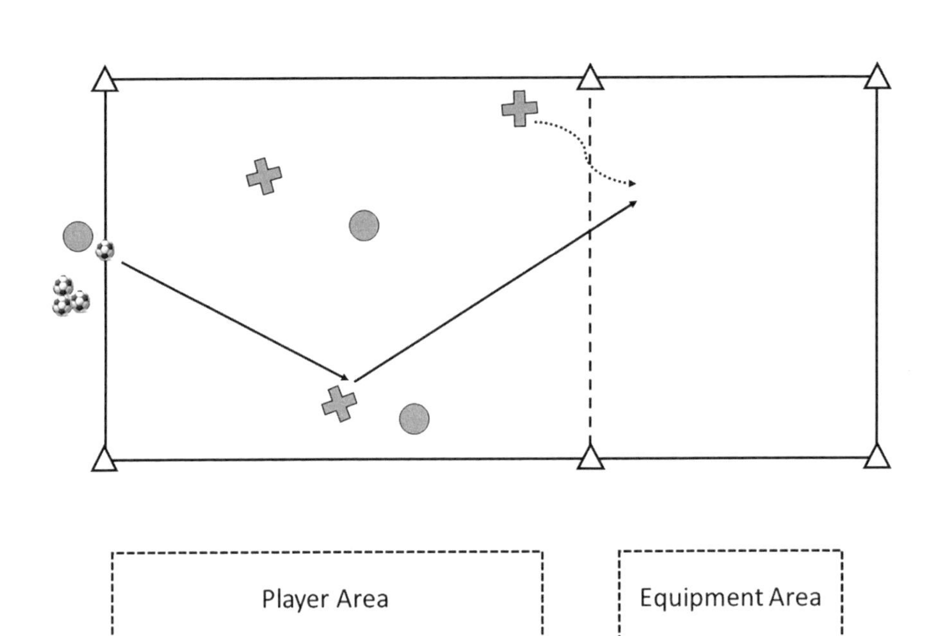

Practice Ten

Server plays the ball to one of the three attacking players who look to release a player into the second area by playing a pass over the line that divides the two areas. (Players cannot dribble the ball over the line.) Once this has been achieved, one defender can enter the area, and the attacking player looks to dribble over the end line. If needed, the attacking players can pass back to the server, and if the defenders win the ball, they look to pass the ball back to the server to achieve a point.

particular practice, a restriction could be put in place that stops the attacking players from being allowed to pass back to the server once the ball is in play, or a rule could be introduced that the pass into the next area must be completed within a set number of passes.

Quite often as coaches we will have a practice or a number of practices that we like to use and the players enjoy participating in. As coaches we can use these 'go-to' practices to achieve a range of different outcomes by making a small number of changes to the design of the practice. Earlier in this book we looked at *Practice Nine,* which was set up to encourage players to play through the thirds specifically by passing. By making slight changes to the dimensions, player positioning and tasks of the practice, the focus can be changed from passing to running with the ball. The important element is that the main principle and set-up of the practice remain the same. In this particular instance, the players are required to get the ball from one end third to the other end third via the middle third; however, instead of passing through the central third, the players are now required to travel with the ball. The central area is increased in size to replicate where on the pitch you would want a player to drive or run with the ball. Using a set-up that is similar to something that has already been used makes it easier for the players to understand and therefore allows them to concentrate on actual playing, rather than working out the actual practice. It is also a good strategy to help reinforce the principles of the game. These particular practices concentrate on the team being in possession of the ball, and if we look at the seven components of 'In Possession' that were discussed in chapter 1, then both *Practice Nine* and *Practice Nine (c)* focus on three of the seven components: depth, progression and penetration. Using a similar set-up for two different outcomes not only allows the players to easily understand the practice, it also helps them grasp some of the core components of the different phases within the game.

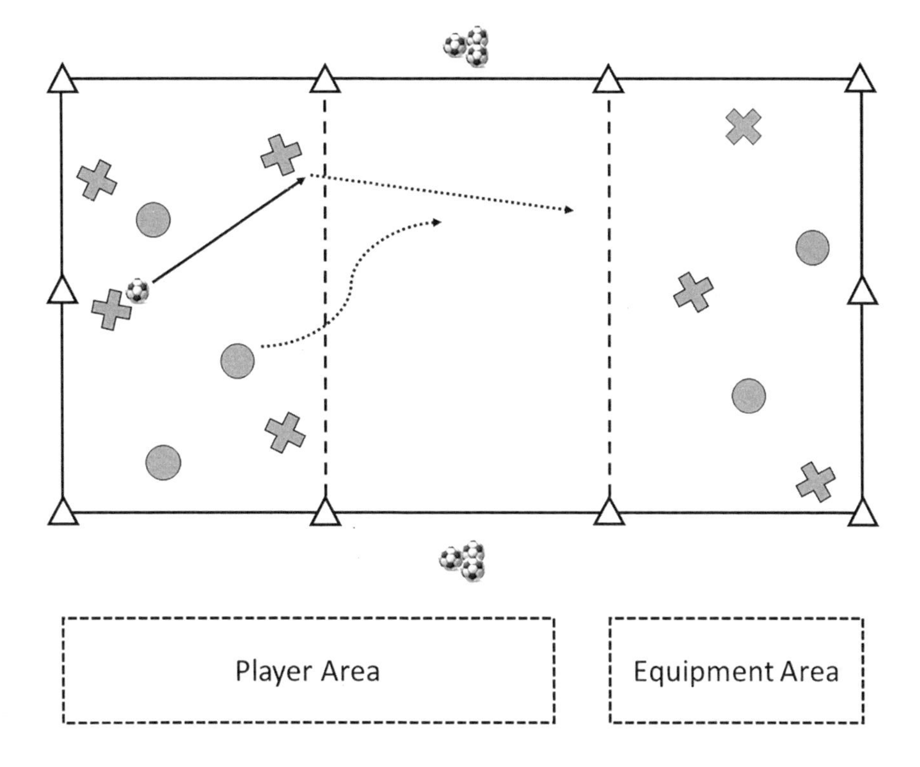

Practice Nine (C)

Players are split into two teams within the two end zones, with an overload for the team that is classified as the attacking team. The attacking team looks to complete a small amount of passes before they release one player into the central zone; the player must

(continued)

Practice Nine (c), continued

be in possession of the ball before they leave the end zone. They then travel to the other end zone where on entering they look to find a teammate. One defender is also allowed to leave the end zone and chase the attacking player 'running with the ball'. The practice then continues with the player that travelled with the ball and the chasing defender remaining in the end zone they travelled to. If at any time the defending team win the ball, they look to retain possession for as long as possible.

Replicating the Game

In chapter 1 we looked at invasion games in general and then the stand-alone characteristics of the game of soccer. It is important that we include as many of these features as possible within the practices that we design, so that the players are practicing in an environment that replicates their match day. Replicating match day scenarios allows the players to build up a library of pictures and memories that they can use when they come across similar situations during a match. They can then use these pictures and memories to help make a decision and come up with a solution to the problem they are facing. When designing a practice, we need to consider whether or not the content is something that the players would do during a game. And if the answer is 'no', then we need to ask the next question: If it does not happen in the game, should we include it within the practice? The first thought would be, no we should not and rightly so – why would we ask players to do something that they are not going to do in the game? And therefore do not need to practice? If, however, we never deviate from the game at all, then we will just basically be playing the game continuously, so changes do need to be made; we just need to ensure that these changes encourage the players to concentrate on a specific element of the game.

Practice Eleven is a common practice that is used to help players improve their passing by asking them to accurately pass a ball through a gate to a teammate who will then return it back. There are a large number of factors that occur within this practice that do not replicate what happens within the game of soccer. For instance, during a game of soccer, players do not need to pass a ball through a gate, nor do they pass a ball continuously to the same teammate and without any pressure from an opposition player. We do this as it allows the players to practice their passing and the design of the practice achieves this by providing the players numerous opportunities to pass the ball over and over again. It can therefore be said that the concept of this practice is realistic and relevant to the game whilst also being suitable for achieving the goal of improving the players' ability to pass. There are, however, further aspects of the practice that do not replicate the game and these factors can be changed so that the environment the players are in is a lot closer to the game, whilst still providing the same opportunities to practice their passing. In *Practice*

Eleven the players are passing the ball continuously over the same distance and at the same angle, yet in a game of soccer the distance that we pass the ball over is always changing, as is the angle between the player passing the ball and the player receiving it. The actual set-up of the pass within the practice is quite unrealistic for the game; how often in a game of soccer does a player pass the ball to another player who is standing immediately in front of them, i.e., at a ninety-degree angle? Especially over such a short distance? The other aspect that affects how realistic a practice is compared to an actual soccer game is that the players can complete the pass without having to make any decisions or without having to think about or consider anything else. Though we may not want to achieve this by introducing defenders, as it may make the practice too difficult for the players, there are other ways in which we can make variations so that the players are in an environment that is more irregular and unpredictable, therefore adding decision making to the practice.

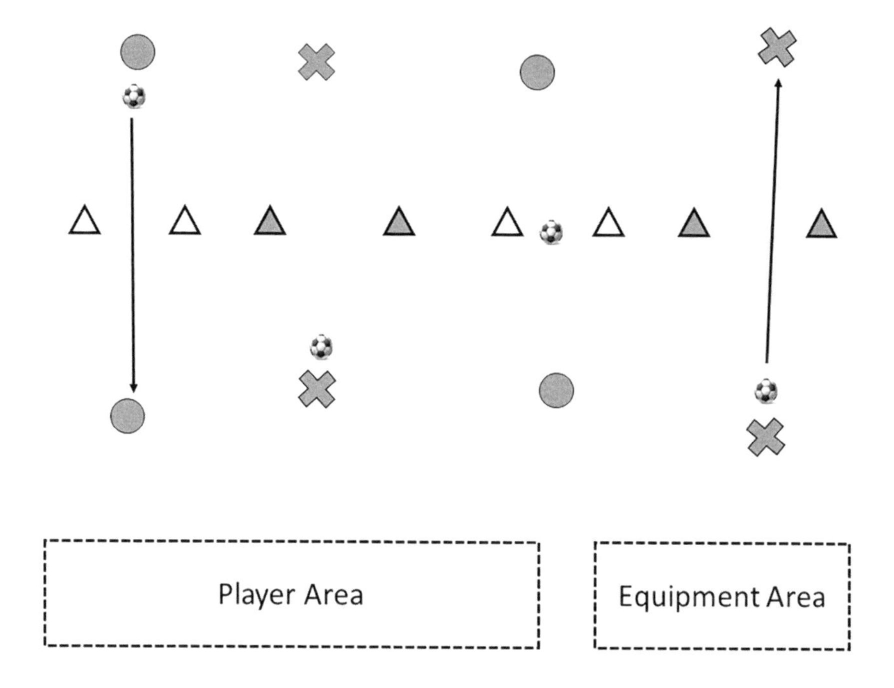

Practice Eleven

Players work in pairs and stand opposite each other and attempt to pass the ball through the gate formed by two cones. On receiving a pass, the player takes one touch to control the ball and then passes the ball back to their partner.

Practice Eleven (b) has the same principles as *Practice Eleven* whilst also providing the same outcomes, but by making a small number of changes to the lay-out of the practice, the returns that the players get from it can be significantly increased. By removing the restrictions of the players having to continually pass through the same gate, giving the players more freedom to pass the ball anywhere they want to within a designated area, the whole dynamic of the practice changes. The players will start to pass and receive the ball over various distances and angles; to achieve this they will experiment with a range of different techniques to achieve the desired outcome. And, just as importantly, whilst the players are attempting to pass the ball they will experience interference as they would during a game. The interference will not come in the form of opposition players, but through the movement of other players within the practice and the other balls being passed around the area. Players will now have to start to make decisions, such as when to pass the ball, the amount of weight they put on the pass, where they should go within the area so that they are in a position to receive a pass from their partner, etc. Along with this, the players are now also completing the task inside an area within specified parameters, which is an important part of the players' learning journey, as discussed in chapter 1.

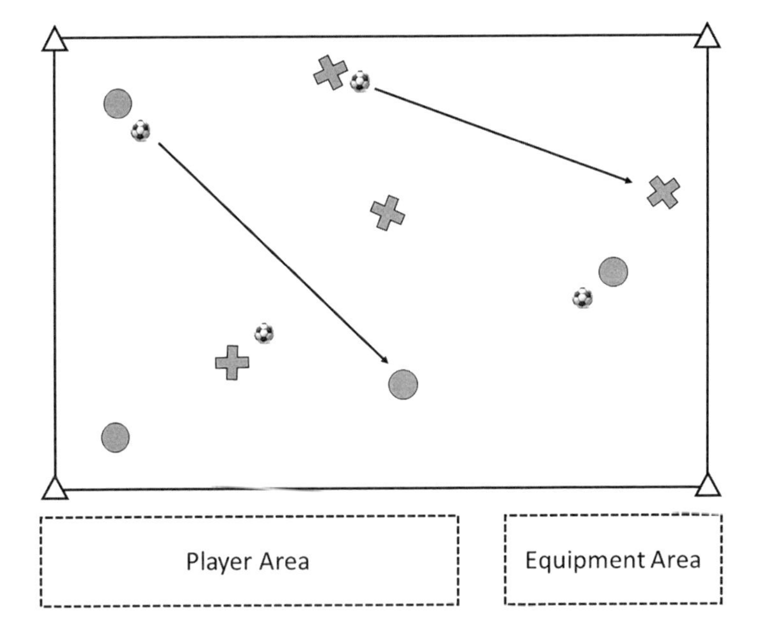

Practice Eleven (b)

Players work in pairs, passing the ball around within the area. Players are encouraged to use as much as the area as they can and are allowed to have as many touches of the ball as they want, passing the ball to their partner when they think it is the right time to do so.

It is these types of practices that we could describe as being 'messy', and as coaches we will probably feel uncomfortable delivering this form of practice at first. It is understandable that we think a practice is successful and that we are doing our job as a coach correctly if the practice is running smoothly and all of the players are doing exactly what they are meant to be doing and doing it correctly. And though it could be said that this form of practice where the players are completing a structured task successfully is a safe and controlled way for the players to learn, we have to ask the question: Are they actually learning if they are able to complete the task so easily?

These types of practices are often referred to as 'drills' and understandably so. If you were asked to describe a 'drill', more likely than not, you would use words such as: disciplined, repetitious, military, physical, tough and boring. Words that you would be unlikely to use would be words such as: enjoyable, educational, experimental or game-like. If you were to choose an environment to learn something, you would almost certainly choose the latter of the two environments described. We just need to move away from the preconception that, if the players are having fun and the practice looks a bit chaotic, then learning is not taking place. The reality is that they are learning considerably more and retaining the information more easily as they are enjoying themselves and being challenged. So though as coaches we may be uncomfortable with 'messy', we need to embrace it and encourage it within our practices, as it is the most productive and effective environment in which the players can develop. Another way in which the need for practices to replicate the game can be demonstrated through *Practice Twelve*, another common practice that is used to help the players improve their finishing.

It could be said that this practice design does provide an environment where the players can practice their finishing and allows them to concentrate solely on this technique. However, once more there are a number of elements of the practice that are far away from what the players will experience when they play the game on a Saturday or a Sunday. First of all, the pass provided by the coach is unlikely to replicate a pass that the players will receive during a game. The pass played by the coach is unopposed and therefore is made without pressure; the coach is also likely to have a different level of ability to the players. At the same time, it is also similar to *Practice Eleven* in that the angle and the way that the player receives the pass before they have a shot on goal is quite consistent and does not occur that often within a game. What we do not want to do is lose the number of opportunities that the players get to practice their finishing; we just want to make variations to the environment in which the players are doing it so that they are better prepared when they come across similar situations during a game.

The important part to remember when delivering *Practice Twelve (b)* and any other practice is that the set-up must allow for the players to have lots of chances to perform the focus of the session. Therefore, within *Practice Twelve (b)* we do not want the players spending too much time completing the set number of passes; therefore, we need to

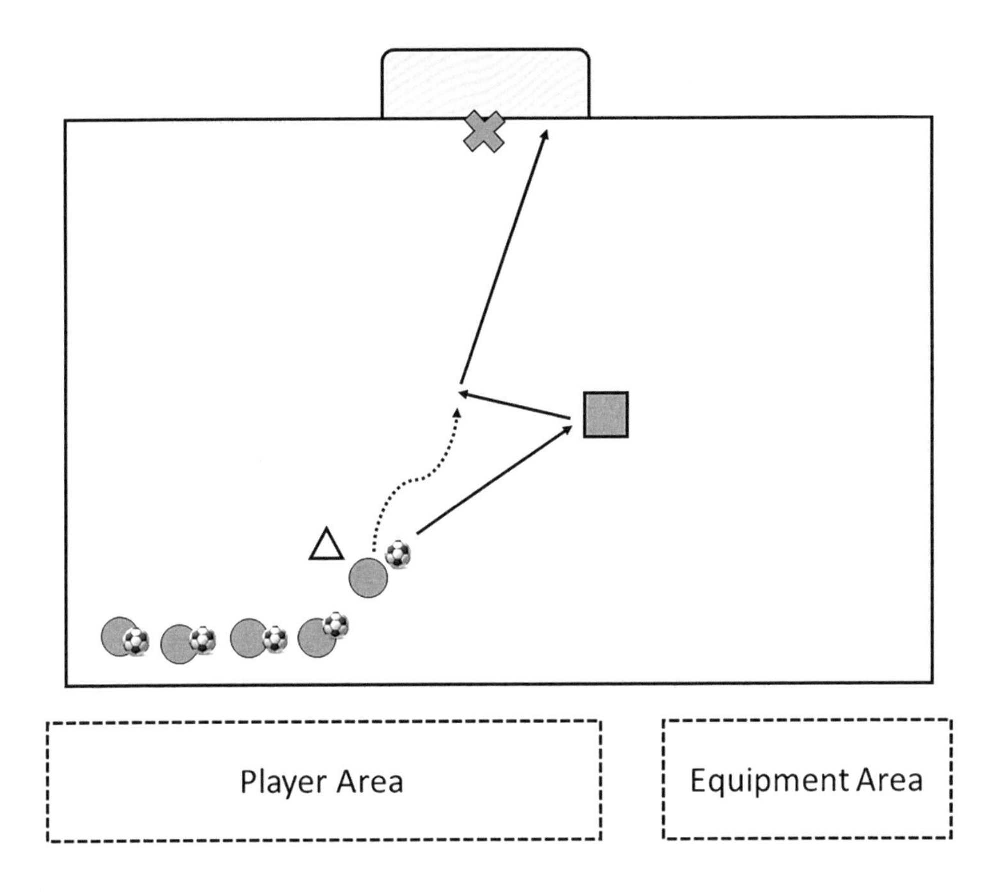

Practice Twelve

Players line up with one ball each and take turns playing a pass to the coach who then lays the ball off for the player to have a shot on goal. The player then retrieves their ball and joins the back of the queue.

ensure that the target is reached quickly, allowing the players to attempt a shot on goal. This can be achieved through a number of ways such as minimising the number of passes that need to be completed before a team is allowed to shoot (i.e., two or three passes), or by not allowing opposition players to tackle, but only to block or intercept passes and shots. In addition to this, having four goals within the practice it ensures that once a player receives the ball after the set number of passes have been completed they are in a position where they can have a shot on goal. Now the practice has been set up to allow the players lots of opportunities to have a shot on goal, and the way in which the players

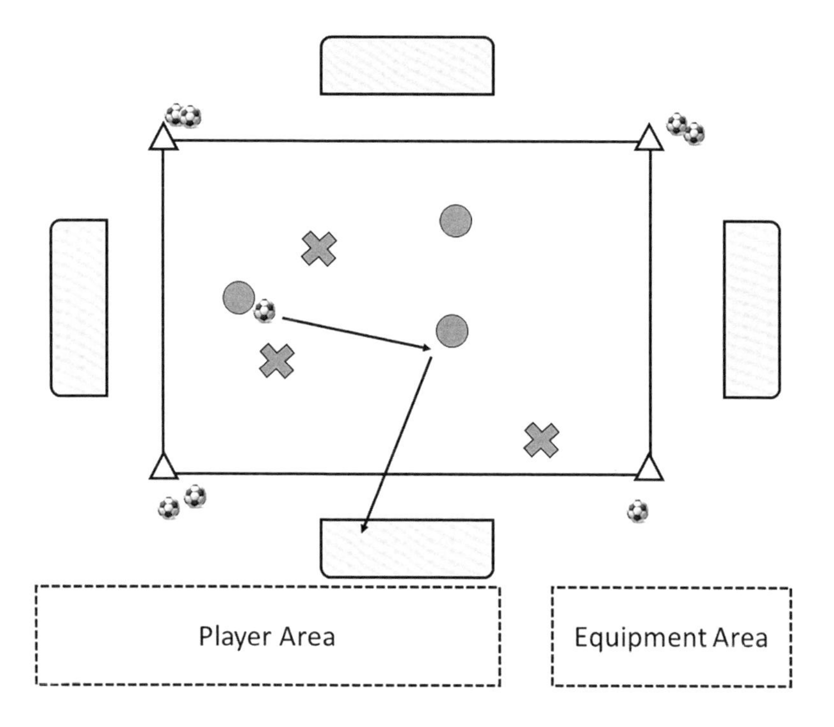

Practice Twelve (b)

Players are split into two teams and look to complete a set number of passes before they attempt to score in one of the four goals. (Players remain inside the area at all times.) Rules are put in place to ensure the players actually have a shot at goal and not just pass the ball towards the goal; this could be that the ball cannot touch the ground until it crosses the goal line. You could also have players positioned outside of the area that are used to help the teams retain possession until the set number of passes has been completed and then their roles change and they then become goalkeepers. Having the goals situated away from the playing area also helps to ensure that the players have to actually strike the ball towards the goal.

receive and then strike the ball will be completely different each time, just as it is during a game. Sometimes the ball will come to the player across their body; it could be played to them from behind or it could be that they set up the opportunity themselves by beating a player and then striking the ball. Similarly, how they strike the ball and their position on the pitch in relation to the location of the goal will always be different. In addition to this, there will be some form of pressure on the player as they are completing the strike; how much depends on how you have set the practice up.

Key concepts that can be found in both *Practice Eleven (b)* and *Practice Twelve (b)* are that they provide players with freedom and the necessity to make their own decisions, with the practice being carried out within an ever-changing environment, where nothing the players experience is ever the same. This is quite often achieved through the practices being completed within specified areas rather than players being told where to start, where to go next and where they finish, before completing the whole process again. There is also some form of interference, whether this is through direct opposition, where an opposition player or players are trying to stop you from completing the task, or through another player or players trying to complete the same task and inadvertently getting in the way.

As coaches we are still asking them to complete a task; we are just allowing them the freedom to complete the task in whatever way they want to. They can experiment if they so wish and try different ways or they may want to do it in a way that they find comfortable. So the task of getting from A to B may well remain the same, but instead of telling the players they must do it a specific way, they are allowed to work out the solution to completing the task themselves and they do not have to restrict themselves to doing it just one way. If we look at this in the context of a player attempting to get past an opposition player in a one-versus-one situation, it does not matter how they achieve this, as long as they get past the player. As coaches we might show them an exact way to do this and want all the players to use this particular skill to get past a player, but every player is different and what works for one player does not necessarily suit another player. Therefore, if we provide them an environment where they are able to find more than one solution that works for them, then hopefully we will not help just a small number of players improve their ability to get past a defender, but we will develop all of the players in this area of the game.

Putting the players in an ever-changing environment will challenge the players by asking them to complete the required task whilst experiencing interference and being forced to deal with different situations throughout the practice. If we replace players dribbling through a set of cones with players dribbling inside an area with a number of other players, then we will have produced an ever-changing environment. The interference will come from the other players dribbling in the area and will force the players to complete a number of actions that they will do during a game, actions that they would not do if they were just dribbling through a set of cones. For instance, if one player travels across another player's pathway, then this player may well have to completely stop or shift the ball into a different direction. And because the players are aware that there is 'traffic' within the area that they need to be aware of, they will automatically start to dribble, scanning and looking for a space that they can move into, something we will constantly ask them to do.

All of this will result in the players making decisions; because of all these extra elements that have been added to the practice, the players now have to make their own decisions rather than having everything prearranged for them. Soccer is a game where players are constantly having to reassess the situations they find themselves in and react accordingly as the picture in front of them develops and requires a different solution to the position they found themselves in a split second before. Eventually, once they have had a similar experience numerous times over a substantial amount of time, they will not only be able to recognise the situation and have a number of possible solutions, but they will be able to anticipate the situation before it actually happens. By putting the players in game-like situations as often as possible, they will be able to recognise triggers and patterns as they happen and then predict what will occur next, i.e., they are able to read the game.

Maximising Ball Time

Chapter 2 discussed the importance of a coach being organised, with one of the benefits of this being that it helps capitalise on the amount of time the players have to practice during the session. This time can be maximised further if we ensure that whilst the practice is going on that each and every player is active as much as possible. This does not necessarily mean that they have to have a ball to be deemed as being active; during a game of soccer, players spend most of the time without the ball, but they are still involved in the game. Therefore, during a session we ideally want the players to be active for as much of the session as possible, whether this is with or without a ball. If a session lasts for sixty minutes, then if possible we would want the players to be active for at least forty-five minutes (seventy-five per cent), leaving fifteen minutes for players to have breaks and for the coach to provide information and support. Therefore, the forty-five minutes they have left to practice needs to be fully utilised and no individual player can afford to be inactive at any time.

If we refer back to *Practice Eleven* and *Practice Twelve,* we identified that these types of practices lacked realism and prevented the players from making their own decisions. But in addition to this, these types of practices can quite often lead to the players being inactive for the majority of practice. This is particularly evident within *Practice Twelve,* where the players spend considerably more time waiting their turn than they do actually taking part. The amount of time that they spend being inactive within *Practice Twelve* could be reduced by having two identical practices going on at the same time, and the person playing the pass into the player taking the shot at goal could be another player instead of the coach. Ideally, however, if we change the format of the practice to that of *Practice Twelve (b)*, not only do we achieve all the benefits previously outlined, but we are now also increasing the amount of time each and every player is active within the session.

Another reason that players may become inactive during a session is due to extra unexpected players or because there is an odd number of players. Quite often as coaches if we have an extra player for the practice that has been produced, then we ask two players to rotate or take turns. For example, if we look back at *Practice Six* which consists of a one-versus-one situation, if there are seven players for training, one of the one-versus-one pitches would probably consist of three players with the players taking turns having a rest. The players on this pitch of three will therefore be less active than the other players in the session and they will lose opportunities to practice. Having a plan in place to accommodate this change in expected number of players will allow the session to continue without any delays, whilst also allowing all players to be continuously involved throughout the session. So, for instance, one of the pitches in *Practice Six* could be adapted to accommodate three players and this can be achieved in a number of ways.

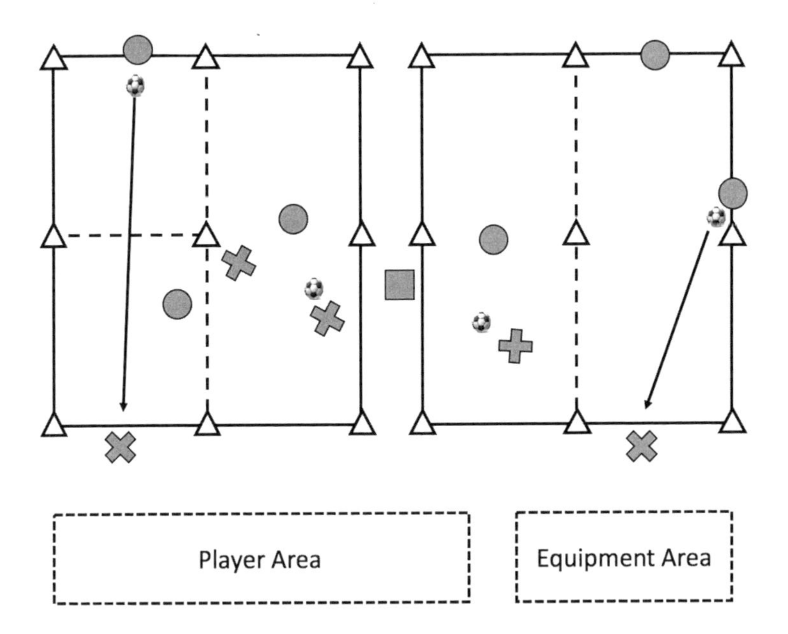

Practice Six (d)

Four different practices that have been adapted to accommodate three players. In the first practice the area has been split into two separate areas with a defender locked into each area, so the attacker has to go past two defenders in total to achieve their point. The second practice consists of two attacking players against one defender. The third practice has a support player on the outside that the attacking player can use if needed. And the final practice has the additional player acting as the server playing the ball into the attacker, they could also enter the practice to make it two defenders against the one attacking player.

When making these changes to a practice it is important to ensure, firstly, that you do not lose the narrow focus of the session. For instance, where there are two attacking players or an attacking player with a support player, that you do not get too much passing when the narrow focus is dribbling. Therefore, a rule may need to be put in place which limits the number of passes that the players are allowed to make; this would need to be as little as one or two. Secondly, it is also as important that the right players are allocated to the adapted practice, i.e., that it meets their needs. This will be discussed further in chapter 5.

STEP Model

The STEP model is used within physical education and coaching to support teaching and learning. By using STEP, practices can easily be adapted to allow for differentiation; it can also be used to either progress or regress the practice for the whole group. STEP is an acronym for Space, Task, Equipment and Players, where the concept is that changes are made to one or more of the four areas of the model to change the practice. For instance, a possession-based practice inside an area can be made more difficult by making the area smaller (space) or by changing the ratio of attacking players against defending players, i.e., from six versus two to five versus three (players). How this model is used to adapt practices will be discussed further in chapter 5, after showing how it can be used in the initial planning of a practice, something that the model is not usually used for.

When planning and setting out a practice, the space in which it takes place is critical to its success. If we consider a practice in the format of *Practice Six*, whether it has a narrow focus on attacking or defending, the set-up in which the practice takes place is crucial to whether or not it is beneficial for the players, and whether or not the players will be in an environment where they will be challenged but also have an opportunity to be successful. If we look first at the width of the area, this will play a crucial part in terms of who will be successful in the practice – the attacker or the defender. Should the area be too narrow and the practice is focused on the defending, then you will find that the defenders are finding lots of success, not because they are defending correctly but because the area is making it easy to defend. Similarly, if the focus is concentrating on attacking and the area is too narrow, the attacker will find it really difficult to find any success.

The size of the area also needs to reflect the situation where the topic would likely take place during an actual game. If we look at *Practice Six* again, the length of the area used is important as well. One of the key factors that influences whether or not a player decides to dribble in a game is the space available behind the defender they want to get past; there needs to be space beyond the defender for them to be able to go into. At the same time, the space available would eventually be restricted by the parameters of the pitch or by other players, whether these are opposition players or teammates. Therefore, the length of the practice needs to replicate this situation; it needs to be able to provide the attacking player space behind the defender, whilst also ensuring that this space is not too big, so that once they are past the defender they are close to completing whatever they need to do once they have gotten there, i.e., shoot at goal, pass to a target player or through a gate, dribble over a line, etc.

The actual shape of the area can also have a significant impact on the success of the practice and also the outcomes you will achieve. The majority of the time it would be expected that a rectangle would be used, as it replicates the shape of a pitch.

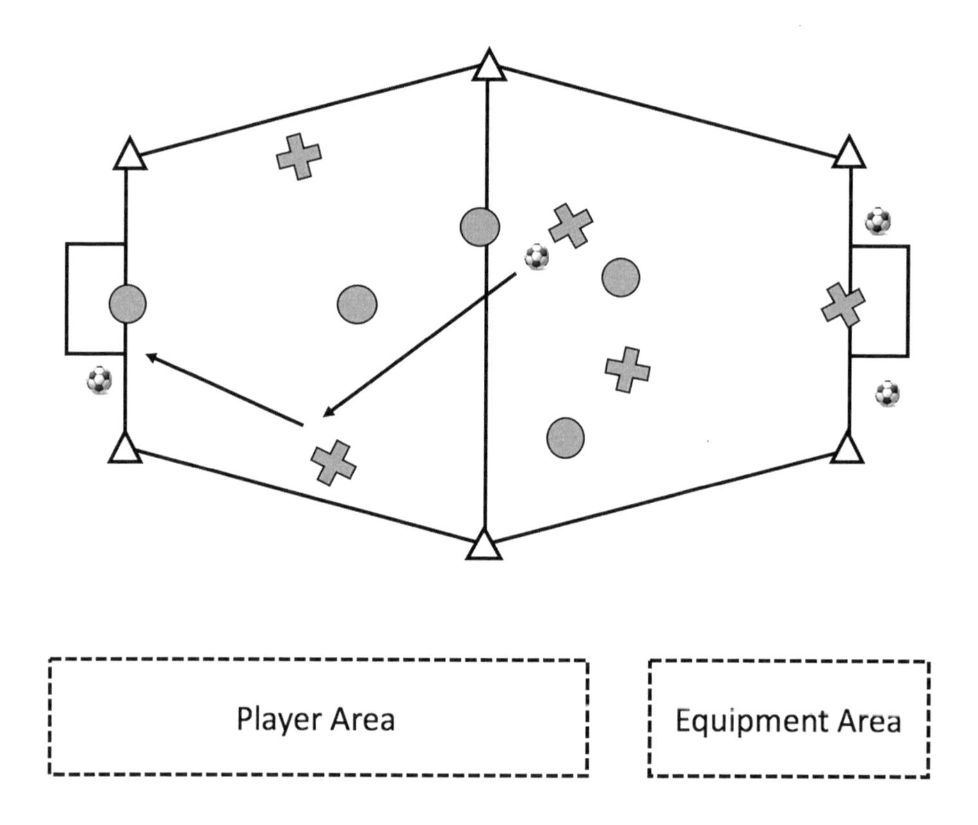

Practice Thirteen

A small-sided game with an emphasis on finishing. Pitch is in the shape of a hexagon to encourage players to shoot from most areas of the pitch. Different point systems can be implemented, such as extra points if you score from your own half or for a one-touch finish.

The narrow focus for *Practice Thirteen* is finishing. Therefore, you want there to be lots of opportunities for the players to be able to shoot. So if the size of the practice area is revisited first of all, then the pitch will be quite small, allowing the players to be able to shoot from most places or even anywhere on the pitch. Now if we look at the shape, the normal rectangular shape has been replaced by a hexagon. Using a hexagon forces the players to travel towards the goal and subsequently it will encourage players to have a shot on goal. Therefore, though the pitch itself does not fully replicate the pitch used for the actual game, it does represent the area of the pitch where a player is likely to try to score from, and it also helps generate more opportunities for the players to practice their finishing.

Finally, we can look at areas within the main area and how these areas are used to affect the practice and the outcomes you will gain from the practice. Just as with the main practice the size and shape of these areas are important, but just as important are how these areas are used. They can be used for a range of reasons. They could be used as 'safe zones' or 'no-go zones', or they could be used to lock players in, or players may be restricted to certain things within these areas, For example, they might be limited to a number of touches or they might not be allowed to do something (e.g., pass the ball). The important part is that whatever the areas are used for, they must be used to help the players practice the narrow focus of the session.

Practice Seven has been adapted by adding a square to the centre of the area. This square can now be used in a number of ways, all of which are linked to the narrow focus of the practice: passing. It could be that the attacking players are limited to a set number of touches within this area, possibly one or two, or it could be that instead of the attacking team needing to complete a set number of passes to achieve a point, they have to complete just one pass through the centre square. Another option would be to use the area as a safe zone for attacking players to receive the ball, where the defenders are not allowed to go. The key to the concept is recognising/understanding what you are trying to achieve with the practice, i.e., what is the narrow focus? And what do your players need during this particular practice? Will they need some support, to be challenged, guidance, etc.? And then use the areas to achieve this.

The task basically refers to what you are asking the players to do within the practice, but it can come in a number of formats such as rules or restrictions, or scoring systems. Again it is important the tasks that you set are directly linked to the focus of the session. If the focus of the session is to improve dribbling, then a restriction of two or three touches is counter-productive; instead a rule of a minimum of three touches would push the players towards having to dribble.

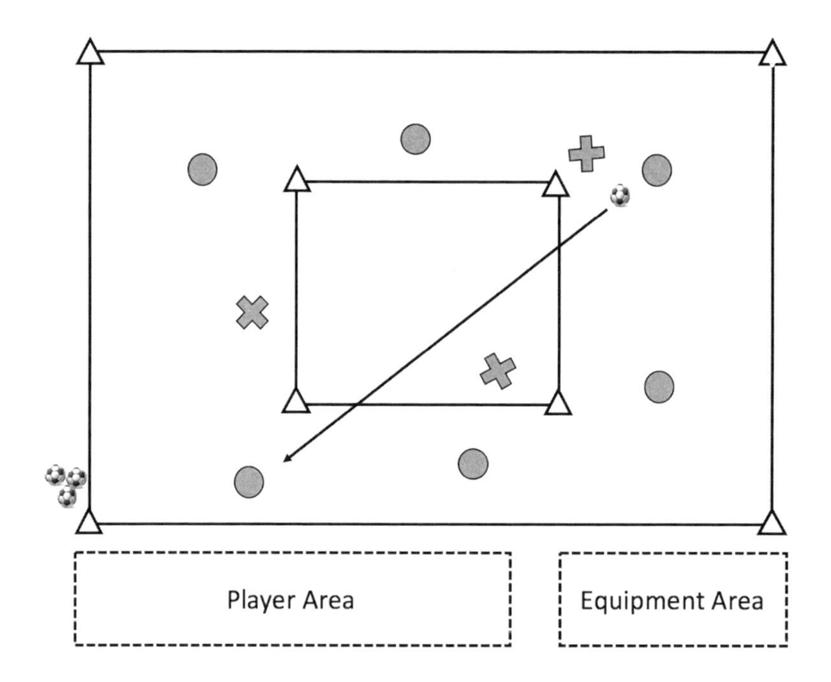

Practice Seven (b)

The attacking team look to complete a set number of passes to achieve a point. On doing so, they will gain a point and the practice will continue, should the opposition win the ball or if the ball goes out of play, the pass counter is reset and the practice continues. Rotate the role of the defenders regularly throughout the practice.

Restrictions are usually used to push players towards the session topic, particularly when it does not occur naturally to them, whether this is because they are not comfortable doing it or they prefer to do something else which they possibly find easier or more effortless. If we go back to *Practice Thirteen*, the game has a focus on shooting, which is encouraged by the shape and dimensions of the pitch. But if the players are historically reluctant to shoot, then you still may not get as much shooting occurring within the practice as you would like. Therefore, as well as the pitch design, restrictions could also be used to ensure that more shooting takes place. Putting a restriction on the number of passes that each team has within the practice will force players into shooting when they would not usually do so. It may be that they receive a pass and the team has used all of their passes up and therefore they have no choice but to shoot, or it could be that they are close to using up all of their passes and that they now recognise that if they pass, the player receiving the ball would have to shoot from a position that is less favourable to the position they could shoot from. The critical element when placing restrictions is that they should only be used for a short period of time; they should be removed to give the players an opportunity to achieve what you want them to do without being forced to do it. If needed, they can always be reintroduced again as a reminder of what they should be looking to do.

A scoring system can also be used to encourage players towards the session focus, with players or teams scoring a point by completing something that is related to the session focus, or gaining extra points by achieving something additional (also linked to the session focus) either before or after the main goal. If a scoring system is linked to the session focus, then applying it is usually a straightforward task and has already been implemented in a number of the practices that have been discussed in this and previous chapters. If we revisit *Practice Seven*, it is possible to see how different scoring systems can be built into practices to help achieve the session focus.

The original set-up of this practice includes the scoring system that is linked to the topic of the practice, which gives the players a clear goal to achieve, as well as a clear focus on the outcome of the session. In *Practice Seven (b)* an additional area was added to the practice that, as discussed, could be used for a number of reasons, including additional scoring systems. So after completing the set number of passes, the attacking team could then be given the additional task of having to receive a pass in the middle area. Adding this additional task to the practice provides the players with an extra challenge and it also brings the practice closer to the game as well. Usually, in a game of soccer you do not retain possession of the ball just for the sake of retaining possession. There is usually a purpose to it; therefore, adding an additional task at the end of the initial task provides both challenges and realism. Alternatively, this additional task could be achieved at any stage of the practice, with the players achieving 'extra points'. So the players could be given the task of achieving a set number of passes to achieve a point, but if one of these passes goes through the central area, they get double the amount of points; or they have to complete a set number of passes; or if they manage to achieve one pass through the central area before completing the required amount of passes they score a point and the practice starts again.

If we stay with the theme of passing, we can see how the final type of task can be used to help achieve the session topic. Rules are usually used to make it more difficult to achieve the main task. So the main task could be to score a goal, and if the topic is passing then a rule might be put in place where a set number of passes need to be completed first before a team can attempt to score or a pass must be played through a certain area first. We just need to be mindful again how these rules might affect the practice and the realism of it. If a rule is put in place where four passes must be completed before you can attempt to score a goal and then a player wins the ball close to the opposition goal, do we really want to prevent them from just going on and attempting to score? Therefore, quite often any rules we put in place require additional rules alongside them. So the rule that we put in place where a team must complete four passes before they can attempt to score might only apply when the team starts with the ball in their own half; if they win the ball in the opposition's half of the pitch, they can just go on and score. And then to compliment this, an additional rule might be put in place that if the ball goes out of play, the game always restarts with the goalkeeper, therefore forcing the team to start in their own half and having to make the set number of passes. When applying a rule, we usually do so to help achieve the session topic, but we do not always consider the possible side effects it may then have on the realism of the practice, so sometimes we need to consider possible countermeasures to keep the practice close to the game.

The final consideration in terms of 'tasks' is the players who are not working on the session topic. In *Practice Seven* the focus is on passing, but there are a number of players who have a different focus within the practice, i.e., the defenders. In the original practice, the task for the defenders is to win the ball and then to give it back to the attacking players. Not only is this task unrealistic to the game, when would a player who just won the ball in a game return it straight back to the opposition team? But it is also quite demotivating for the defenders, as they will soon work out that there is no point in winning the ball as they just have to give it straight back anyway. Therefore, a task that motivates the players, is realistic to the game, and links in to the topic is needed. A possible task could be that if the defenders win the ball, they gain a point if they then manage to make a set number of passes (this needs to be considerably less than the attacking players due to the overload of attacking players), or they could gain a point if they win the ball and then one of their players receives a pass outside of the area. This provides the defenders with a focus that allows them to work on the session topic.

The equipment part of the process is often used to help apply another one of the elements of the STEP model, mainly space or task. For instance, you may want to add an extra area within a practice, so you produce the area using cones; or you might use cones to create a gate that the players have to dribble or pass through. But you can also change the dynamics of the practice by adding or changing the equipment within it. The ball you use in a practice can be changed, so you may replace a normal ball with a smaller ball or even a tennis ball. This can have quite an impact. Consider how much harder it would be to dribble or pass a tennis ball compared to a normal ball. Or you may add equipment to a practice, such as another ball. If we revisit *Practice Seven* once more, think about how the practice would completely change if an additional ball were added? The intensity alone would increase significantly, if the attacking players now had to look after two balls. With just one ball there would be times within the practice when, as an individual player, you would not be needed; but if there were two balls that needed to be looked after, you would be needed as a player throughout the entire practice. The argument, of course, is that both of these will take the practices far away from the game itself, and therefore it should be noted that, as with restrictions, they should only be used for a short period of time to put a real emphasis on something within the practice. Or to give the players a challenge that they will need to find solutions to, which will then benefit them in the following practices, as these will probably be less challenging, due to them being taken back to being closer to the game, i.e., without the extra the ball or using a normal-sized ball.

The final element of the model are players, which is an element of the practice design we quite often forget about, when actually it is one of the most important parts of the session that needs to be considered. There are a number of decisions that need to be made; if it is a paired or small-group practice, who works with whom? If the practice has an overload for one team, how much of an overload does there need to be? How often do we rotate the players? Is this the role they are playing in the practice, or who they are working with in a pair or small group?

When deciding who should work with whom, we will usually match players up in terms of their ability. This is often the sensible decision, as it provides players with a suitable environment. In *Practice Six*, where there is a one-versus-one situation, matching players up that have similar abilities would provide them with an appropriate challenge. However, we must also remember that when it comes to playing a game, players will come up against a number of players with a range of abilities; therefore, they will come up against players that have similar abilities, but also players who are more and less advanced then they are. Therefore, if we keep matching up players in a session, how can they practice coming up against different abilities in a game? If we look at the attacking player in a one-versus-one situation, during a game they will try different ways to get past different players. Part of their decision-making process will be influenced by what they perceive the strengths of the player they come up against to be. But if we are to prepare them properly to be able to deal with these different situations within a game, then we must provide them with opportunities to experience these different situations within the training environment so that it is easier for them to deal with during the actual game. When *Practice Six* was discussed in chapter 2, the concept of a ladder league system was considered, where the player that wins moves up a pitch and the player who loses moves down a pitch. This allow players to compete against different teammates, all of whom will act and react in different ways when they are both defending and attacking.

Similarly, if we look back at *Practice Two*, we first of all need to consider how the target players are rotated so that the same players are not always doing that role. Certain triggers could be put in place that determine when the position is rotated. For example, it could be every time a point is scored that the role of the target player is rotated. With this type of strategy, we need to be careful that some players spend considerably more time in the role than others because of the different time frames between points being scored. To stop this from happening, the safer option would be to rotate the role after a set amount of time to ensure all the players get the same amount of time as the target player. The practice design also allows for players to be locked in zones or the two halves of the pitch – the diagram shows two-versus-two in each half of the area. At the start of the practice there can be some control over which players work together in the two different areas of the pitch by pre-planning and allocating which players work in which areas of the practice. Once the practice is up and running, then there will be a natural rotation of players working with different players as the role of the target player is rotated. Where in this instance there is no need for there to be any planning for the rotation of players so that they work with and against different players, other practices will require this detail of planning.

In terms of arranging the players so that there is an overload favouring one team, the exact number of players that are allocated to each team needs to be considered carefully. As with the size of the area, it can have a significant influence on how challenging the practice is for the players and the success they achieve within it. In *Practice Seven* the players are split to produce six versus three, an overload of three players in favour of the team looking to retain possession of the ball and achieve the set number of passes. If this were changed to seven versus two, the attacking players would be more likely to find success and they will probably find this success without having to be overly proficient at passing and receiving the ball. The considerable difference in numbers between the two groups of players just allows the attacking team to be successful. And again it would be quite demotivating for the two defenders, as it would be extremely difficult for them to win the ball. Similarly, if the groups were split to create a five versus four, it would be very challenging for the attacking players to achieve their target of successful passes. Identifying or finding the right balance of players in these types of practices is fundamental to their overall success.

Building a Session

The final element of the practice design process is linking the practices together to create an overall session. As previously discussed, a session should have a narrow focus and therefore each of the different practices needs to have the same focus. But in addition to

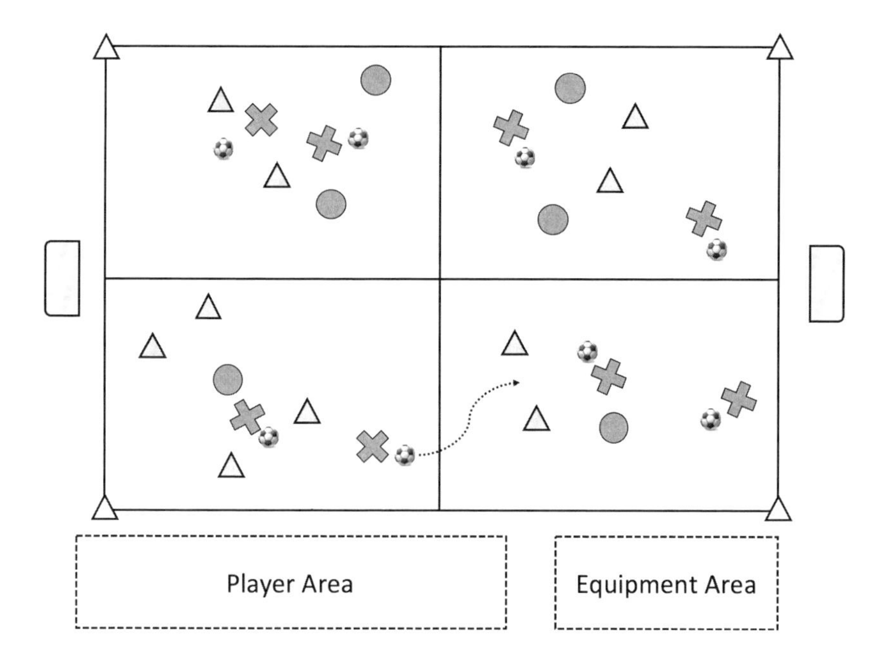

Practice Eight (b)

The area is split in four sections with the attacking players being able to travel with their ball between different areas, whilst the defenders are locked into their designated area. Attackers win points by travelling through a gate. If a defender wins the ball, they look to score in a small goal, from which the attacking player retrieves their ball.

this, they should also be linked together so that whatever the players learn or rehearse in one practice they can then transfer into the next one. This can be achieved in a number of ways, as shown with *Practice Two* in chapter 2; the same set-up/practice design can be used throughout the session and progressions are just introduced throughout. Alternatively, a number of different practices can be used to build the session.

The first practice, commonly known as an arrival activity or warm-up, should allow the players to go straight into the session as soon as they arrive at training. This first practice should be seen as an introduction to the session and needs to grab the players immediately, so that they are both engaged and active from the start. To achieve this, the practice needs to be easy for the players to understand and easy for the coach to set up. Being easy to set up will ensure that there is something for the players to participate in, either as soon as they arrive or shortly afterwards, depending on the circumstances and environment where the training takes place. Ideally, the coach will arrive and set up the session well in advance of the players arriving. This, however, is not always feasible due to the availability of the pitch beforehand or other commitments that the coach may have. Therefore, the selection of the first practice will often be dictated by how much time the coach will have to set it up and also how the players arrive at the practice, i.e., do they all arrive within a short period of time? Or is it over a longer period of time, meaning players will continually be joining in the practice at different times?

Practice Eight is an ideal first practice for an environment where a coach has a limited amount of time to set up and/or where the players arrive over a length of time. The initial set-up can be just four cones to provide a layout for the area (the central area does not need to be added at this stage) and the practice can begin with just two players, with other players joining in as and when they arrive. This initial practice could then be developed to become the second practice *(Practice Eight [b])* simply by using the STEP model.

Linking back to the STEP model, *Practice Eight (b)* can be set up however you want, so that it meets the needs of the players within the session. The number of defenders locked in each zone can be the same in each area or it can be random, so some areas could have two or three defenders inside them, or you could even have an area where there are no defenders, so that the attacking players get to go into an area where the intensity of the practice is considerably reduced. There is also the option of having one or two defenders which are not locked into an area who can go anywhere they want; this gives the attacking players a different kind of challenge, as they will need to be aware of these defenders at all times. It can be the same with the scoring gates with areas having different amounts of gates within them and there could also be a coloured scoring system in place, where different coloured gates are worth different points. Consideration just needs to be given to why some gates are worth more than others. Is it due to their size (i.e., are they narrower)? Or is it because of where they are situated (i.e., in areas where there are more defenders)? Or is it due to their location within the area, possibly towards the back, in the corner where it is more difficult to get to and then afterwards escape from? Finally, a task has been set for the defenders as well, with small goals or gates being added to two sides of the area, where the defenders must attempt to score or dribble through should they win the ball. Therefore, from the initial set-up of *Practice Eight,* which can be set up in a very short space of time with a very small amount of equipment, the session can then easily transfer into *Practice Eight (b),* which will become the main element of the session. The transformation takes place whilst the players are still active in the initial practice. This allows the session to progress to the next practice without the players needing to wait which can easily lead to behaviour issues, in addition to losing valuable time to practice. *Practice Two* requires more time to set up and more players to get the actual practice going. Therefore, as the first practice of the session it would only be suitable if the coach had more time to set up before the players arrive and if the players usually arrive within a small time scale.

There are some adaptations that could be made to *Practice Two* that would allow it to be more suitable to be the first practice that can also be applied to other practices. First of all, the practice could be split into two separate practices or games before being joined together to make one larger practice/game. Again, the key to this is that it does not take up too much time to organise and the players do not miss out on time when they could be practicing. So in this case, if approximately half of the players have arrived they could be playing the game in half of the pitch that has been set up, playing across the width of the pitch. As the other players arrive they could start the second game in the other half of the pitch, before the practice is just joined together and is played within the perimeters as shown within the diagram. As with *Practice Eight* this set-up can then be used for the next practice, with changes being made using the STEP model. The task would probably change from players using their hands and not being able to move when in possession of the ball to them using their feet and being free to move at all times. Other tasks could then be added, such as a set number of passes having to be completed before the pass into the target player can be made, or restricting the number of touches that players are allowed. Or it could be that the space is adapted; players could be locked into halves of the pitch or support players used around the outside of the area. The main point is that if the same area is used there must be some form of progression so that it becomes a 'new practice'.

Alternatively, the area or set-up used for the next practice is not the same as the first practice and the coach therefore sets up the next practice whilst the players are active and occupied with the first practice. Though the area is different, the focus must remain the same and there needs to be transferability from one practice to the other, so in the second practice they can use something they have been doing or practicing in the first practice. So originally *Practice Eight* was used as the first practice and then eventually it moved into *Practice Eight (b).* Another option would still be to use *Practice Eight* but then move it into *Practice Six*. So if the focus of the session is on dribbling, there are elements of what the players will be doing in *Practice Eight* that they can then use or transfer to *Practice Six*. The key elements of the first practice are that it allows the players to be active within the session immediately, and the activity that the players are performing links in to the focus of the session. Then, if required, it also allows the coach to complete other tasks that need to be done before the next part of the session, whether this is actually setting up the next practice, giving or obtaining information from parents and guardians or just greeting players as they arrive. The first practice needs to be a brief introduction to the session before they move quickly on to the second practice.

The second practice should be seen as the 'main practice' of the session. This is where the players will get lots of opportunities to practice the session topic whilst receiving support from the coach. Within this practice, the players should be given the opportunity to practice in an environment that replicates the game of soccer or a part of it. This then allows the players to transfer what they have learnt during training to the actual game more easily, as when they come across a situation within a game they can use their experiences from training to help solve the problem they are facing. For instance, *Practice Eight (b)* has already been identified as being suitable for the main practice. Within this practice the players will experience having to protect the ball from one or more defenders; whilst doing so they are also looking to identify space, i.e., the gates that they can travel through. They will come across a similar situation frequently during a game, where they are looking to protect the ball from an opposition player whilst looking to identify space on the pitch that will allow them to have more time on the ball and give them an opportunity to complete their next action, i.e., pass, shoot, drive with the ball, etc.

The main practice can be categorised into two different types: a technical practice and a skill practice, or unopposed and opposed practices. A technical or unopposed practice will allow players to have a feeling of success, to have lots of time on the ball and to be able to concentrate on the focus of the practice. In addition to this, depending on the design of the practice, players will also be able to develop their decision-making abilities and their perceptual skills. Of the practices that have been discussed so far, very few could be referred to as a technical practice. A good example, however, would be *Practice Eleven (b)* where the players are given lots of opportunities to practice passing or receiving the ball, with no pressure from any kind of opponent. They are also developing their decision-making and perceptual skills due to the other players completing the same task within the same area and all the different challenges that this brings with it and were discussed earlier in the chapter, such as when to pass the ball and the amount of weight they put on the pass. Another example of a technical practice can be seen with *Practice Fourteen*, which can also be described as a constant practice. Within a constant practice, the players repeatedly perform the same technique within an environment that does not change. Another example of a constant practice is *Practice Eleven* where the players work in pairs passing the ball between each other over the same distance each time and the same angle with no interference. As previously discussed, there are more effective ways in which we can support players to learn a technique, but there is a time and a place where a constant practice can be used, as they provide the players an opportunity to refine their technique in an environment where they have no other distractions and are unopposed. The key to a constant practice is that it is used sparingly and when it is used, it is only used for a small amount of time to ensure that the players remain focused and engaged.

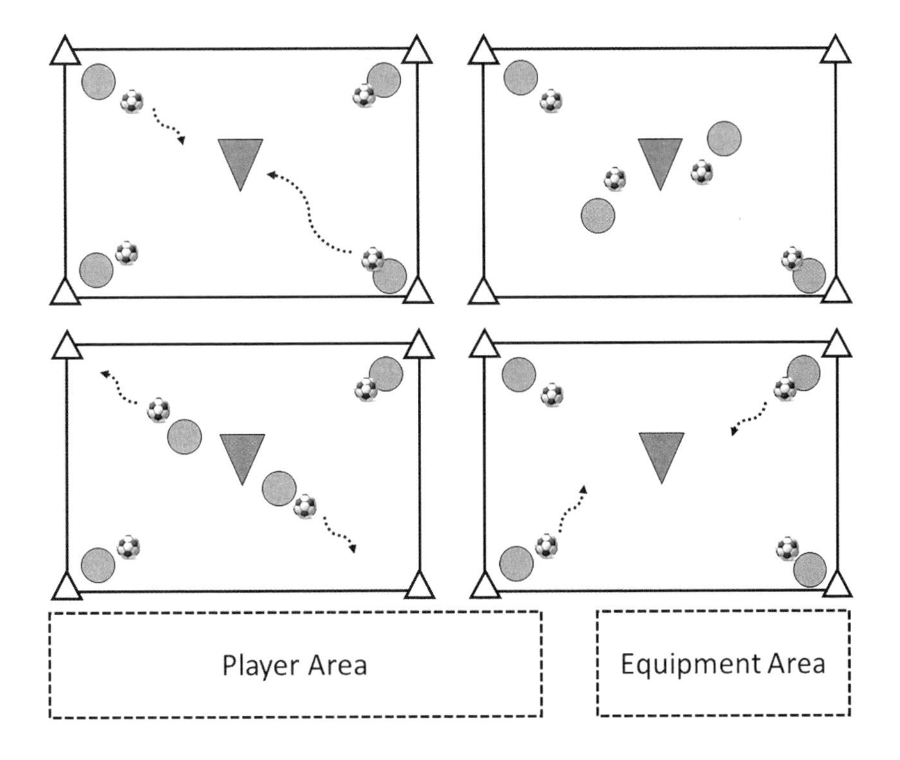

Practice Fourteen

Players work in pairs, with two pairs in each area. One pair at a time dribble towards each other and the large cone in the middle of the area. Once the pair gets to the cone, they complete a skill and go to an agreed side of the cone (i.e. right or left). After they have gone past the cone, they go to the corner of the area where their partner had started, and then the next pair starts and the practice continues.

The more appropriate environment for a technical practice is within a 'variable' environment which is more unpredictable and forces the players to have to make decisions whilst also completing the required task which has been set out by the coach. An example of a technical practice with a variable environment is *Practice Eleven (b);* it is further demonstrated by *Practice Fifteen.* In this practice, the players within the central area are asked to receive a pass within a tight area that is ever changing due to the movement of the other players in it, as well as the other balls that are constantly arriving and leaving the area. The angle at which the ball comes to the player each time will also constantly change due to the players on the outside and also the players within the central area changing their positions.

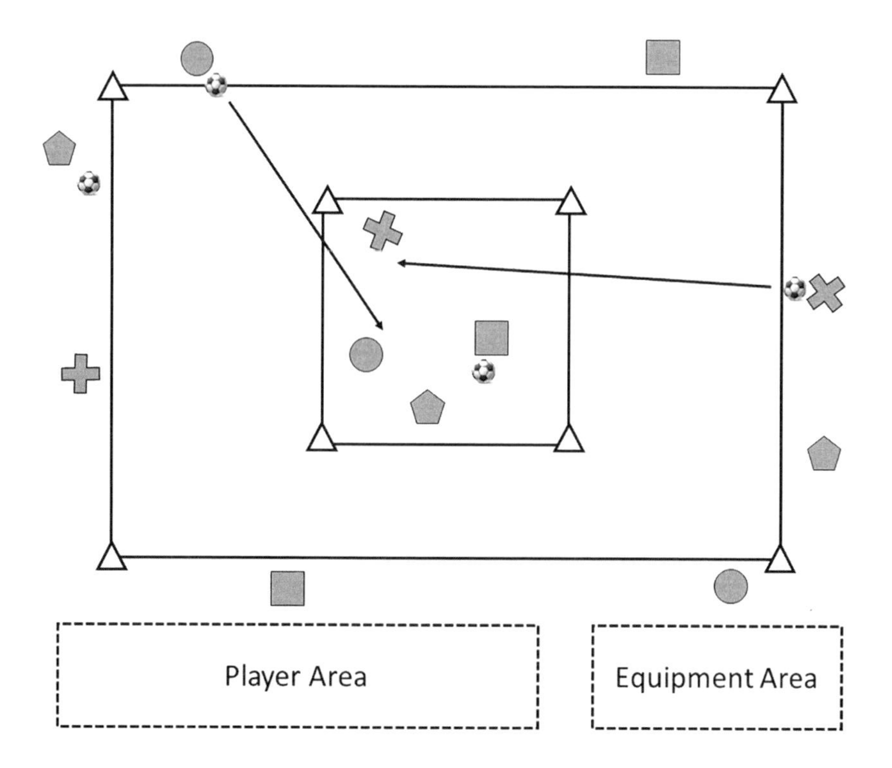

Practice Fifteen

Players work in threes with one player in the central area and the other two players outside of the larger area. The ball is played to the player within the central area who controls the ball before passing it on to the other player on the outside of the area. After the player on the outside of the area has passed the ball, they move to change their position to make it more difficult for the player in the central area to find them. The role of the central player is rotated regularly.

This form of technical practice is more challenging for the players in that they have a number of different things to consider, rather than just the actual technique of the pass or receiving the ball. It does, however, allow the players to practice a wider scope of skills that are linked to both the technique and the game of soccer, for instance, recognising and moving into space to receive the ball, or manipulating the ball to create a passing line to the player that has been identified for the pass.

The other form of practice that can be used at this stage of the session is a skill practice or opposed practice. This can be achieved in a number of ways, through small practices such as one versus one or two versus two (*Practice Six* and *Practice Eight*); overloaded practices such as four versus one or five versus two (*Practice Three, Practice Four* and *Practice Ten*); or small team practices such as three versus three or four versus four (*Practice Nine* and *Practice Seven*). Skill practices can be used on their own or as a progression for a technical practice. For instance, *Practice Fourteen* can be used to begin with to allow the players to concentrate on the technical aspect of dribbling, before progressing to an opposed situation using *Practice Six,* where they will then be able to develop their learning further by practicing their technique within a more variable environment. Any skill practice may be performed in either a variable or random practice. The main difference between a technical practice and a skill practice within a variable environment is that there will be a significant increase in variables within a skill practice which is caused by having opponents. Whereas a technical practice can have interference through just the movement of other players and other balls, a skill practice can have these as well, but also the increased interference of another player trying to take the ball off you. This brings a real unpredictability to the practice, as it is not possible for the players to foresee the actions of other players.

A skill practice remains in a variable environment, providing the players are still mainly focusing on the topic of the session and spending most of their time executing it. For instance, *Practice Six* can be classified as a variable practice because once the player receives the ball they will do nothing else but dribble with the interference or variance coming from the defender. Once the number of variances and actions are increased, the practice moves towards becoming a random practice. The best example of a random practice would be the game of soccer itself, due to all of the demands that come with it. For a skill practice to occur within a random environment, there needs to be an increase in the number of players within the practice and the players need to perform more than just an action that is linked to the session topic. For example, if the topic is dribbling, within a random environment the players will also need to do other actions, such as passing or shooting or both. The important thing to remember is that the topic of the session still needs to remain the main focus within the practice, in this instance dribbling. Therefore the players ideally need to be doing more dribbling than any other action, or they need to be doing more dribbling than they normally would, or the final focus, i.e., the way in which they score a point, is through dribbling. Though there are now a large number of actions taking place, the emphasis must remain on the session topic. An example of a skill practice with a random environment can be seen within both *Practice Two* and *Practice Twelve (b)* where the players have to deal with a wide range of interferences and are asked to complete a wide range of tasks.

A practice which will always have a random environment is a game practice. This is the final stage of the session in which the players get an opportunity to practice everything they have learnt within a game situation. With the need to keep a focus on the session topic, the game needs to be a conditioned game, where the condition or conditions are linked back to the focus of the session. When planning a conditioned game, the starting point should be the normal game of soccer and then features are either added or taken away from it. However, certain aspects of it should remain in place: two teams (could still use support players), direction, a perimeter and goals. This can be seen in *Practice Thirteen* where the shape of the pitch has been changed and the length reduced, both to encourage more shooting within the game.

A common set-up for a conditioned game is a 'thirds practice' (*Practice Sixteen*) – as the thirds can be used in a number of different ways – which can be used for almost any session topic. For instance, players can be locked into specific zones and the ratio of players in each area can be adapted to suit the needs of the session. Other restrictions that could be put in place include how the ball has to be transferred from one area to another. Does a player have to pass it? Does a player have to travel with it? Or it could be that the players are restricted to certain actions within certain areas, such as in the middle third? Or players are restricted to two touches only? Or the team can only pass the ball once? A point scoring system can also be introduced for each area, for example, if the session has a focus on pressing, teams can be awarded extra points if they win the ball in the final third and go on to score a goal. Or if a team scores a goal it is worth the number of passes the team completed before it reached the final third.

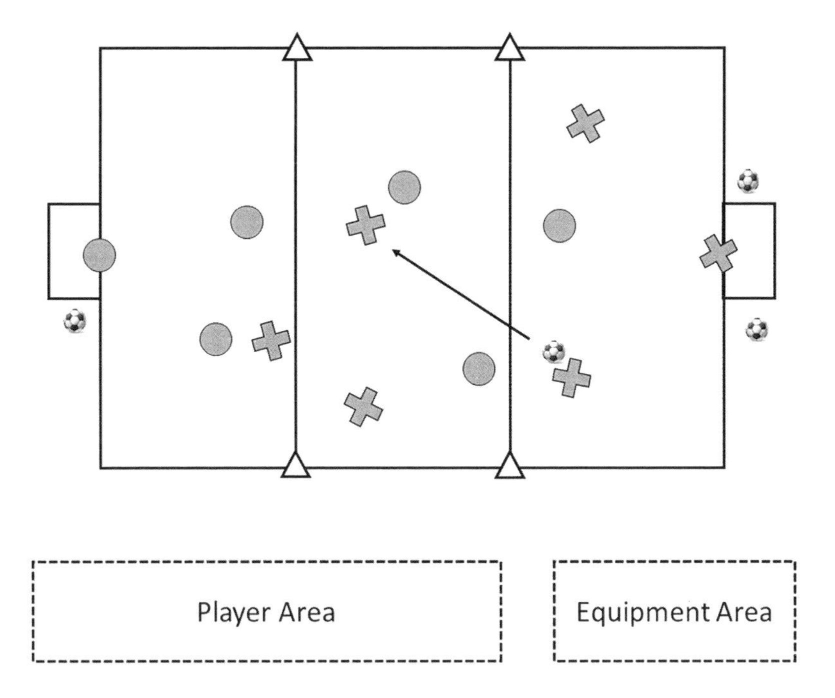

Practice Sixteen

Pitch is split into thirds; these do not have to be equal. Game is played as normal but with relevant rules, restrictions or conditions that support the topic of the session.

Alternatively, the pitch can be split vertically instead of horizontally as shown in *Practice Sixteen (b)*, which again can be used in a number of ways to support the session topic. For instance, if the session was on dribbling it may be that only one player at a time from each team is allowed in the wide channels, thus creating a one versus one in the wide areas. Or if you are looking to help your players create space, a rule could be introduced that when your team has possession of the ball there must be at least one player in each of the wide channels. Or support players could be used but are restricted to the wide channels only.

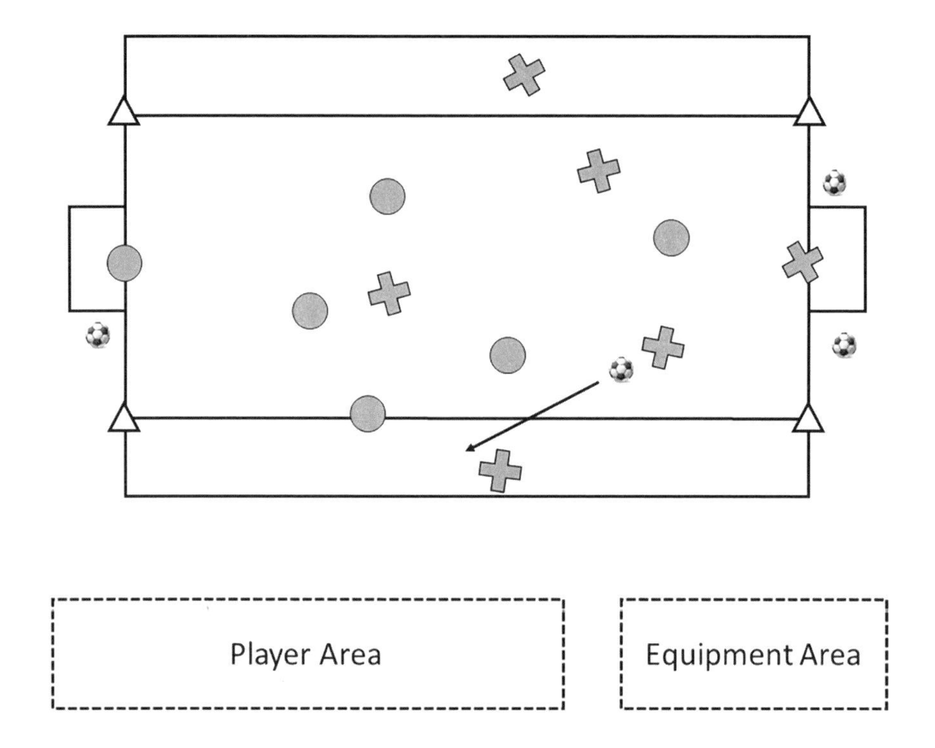

Practice Sixteen (b)

Pitch is split into thirds; these do not have to be equal. Game is played as normal but with relevant rules, restrictions or conditions that support the topic of the session.

As the session enters its final moments, the conditions can be removed from the game and it can move into free play where the players can just experience playing the game. Subconsciously they will be applying everything they have learnt previously in the session and also the sessions before. It is important at this stage that they are just given the opportunity to play and enjoy actually playing the game without any stoppages or interruptions.

Using this format provides structure to the session and also helps ensure that there is a clear and narrow focus throughout, by linking the practices together. The first practice should be a short introduction to the session that is easy for the players to understand and allows them to be active and engaged as soon as they arrive. This then moves into the main practice, which provides the players with a step-by-step process on how to improve in terms of the session topic. The main practice can consist of a technical practice that moves into a skill practice or just a skill practice, but either way there should be some form of progression to challenge the players whilst also keeping them motivated and engaged. Finally, the session moves into a conditioned game that lets the players apply their learning in an environment that is close to the actual game before they enter into free play.

The purpose of this session format is to provide organisation and structure to a session, it will also add progression, meaning the players will be challenged further as they move through the session, which is a key element of learning. This, however, does not mean that this format has to be followed every time; other formats or structures can be used and can be equally effective, depending on the context in which training takes place. The first practice for when the players arrive is essential to ensure the players are engaged and active when they arrive; therefore, usually an arrival activity would be designed to allow players to begin with a minimal amount of players and so that it is easy for extra players to join in as they arrive. But in situations where the players mainly arrive together, there is an opportunity to start the session with a game and then finish as usual with a conditioned game leading into free play, with the main practice sandwiched in between. Starting with a game, especially a conditioned game, provides the players with something recent to reflect back on later on in the session. They can then use what they experienced in the first game and what they learn in the main practice to help them solve problems they will face in the conditioned game at the end of the session. Of course, in addition to this, the players will enjoy the novelty of starting a session with a game, removing the inevitable question of 'when are we going to play a game?' Another option could be to slightly extend the arrival activity and then move straight on to a conditioned game, leaving out the technique and/or skill practice. To do this, the first conditions of the game need to be quite restrictive so that they reduce the level of the challenge facing the players. A number of additional progressions would then also need to be used to keep the players engaged and challenged. This method, however, can be particularly challenging for the coach due to the length of time the players will spend in one practice.

Overall the session structure needs to suit the players, the environment and the coach. Ideally, it will follow the layout of the first practice moving into the main practice and then a conditioned game to provide structure, progression and player engagement. However, there is also nothing stopping the coach from being creative and changing or adapting this process occasionally. Whether it is the topic of the session, the requirements of the players, or just the need for something different that prompts the change to the format, there is no reason why the session could not start with a game or a number of small games. Or it could even consist of just one game, provided the coach is able to add a number of progressions that will keep the players engaged and motivated, whilst also helping them learn and develop. Provided the session has been carefully planned and it is relevant to the game and for the players, then we cannot necessarily say there is a right or wrong way that it should be structured. The key message from this chapter should be that the planning stage of the session is just as important as the actual delivery of it.

What Will They Learn?

When considering whether or not a session was successful, one of the questions that should be asked is: What exactly did the players learn? If we were to ask the players at the end of the session what they learned, they should all be able to provide similar information to each other. The importance of providing the right environment for the players to flourish cannot be understated, but once the players are within this environment they still need support from the coach to help them with their development. If we look at the comparison between a training session and the classroom environment, we would definitely want our children to learn in a lesson that is both fun and engaging and that provides them with an opportunity to experiment and work out solutions to the problems they are facing. This is exactly the same type of experience they should have whilst they are within the training environment. However, at some stage the players will not be able to work it out themselves and they will need some help. In the classroom, if a child continues to get their sums wrong they will receive guidance from the teacher. In coaching terms, this guidance can come in a number of different formats and strategies that will be discussed in future chapters, but the support that we give the players should actually start during the planning process.

At the start of this chapter we looked at giving the session a narrow focus so that the coach and the players have an objective to work towards, such as to make forward runs or improve passing. To help the players achieve the focus of the session, we need to break it down into smaller chunks that make it more manageable and easier to understand and we can do this by identifying the 'coaching points' of the session topic. Coaching points are essentially the step-by-step process of how to complete the focus of the session. So if we look at *Practice Sixteen*, the focus of the session could be on forward passing. We need to break this action down into two or three key actions that the players will need to perform to help them to be able to pass the ball forward. So in this particular instance, the coaching points could be:

1. Find space – can you find an area on the pitch to receive the pass and that will allow you to play a forward pass?
2. Look forward – before receiving the ball, can you identify where you will look to play your pass?
3. First touch – on receiving the ball, can your first touch go forward to make it easier to play your pass forward?

The coaching points produced within the planning process should be used in each practice to provide the players with a clear and consistent message throughout the session. Each coaching point can be introduced and revisited in each practice, or some of them can be held back until later on. There is usually a logical order in which they are performed and therefore they can be introduced by the coach in the same sequence. This can be seen within the example used above. By completing the coaching points in the order that they are set out, the players are more likely to be successful in being able to play a forward pass. If they were to leave out one of the coaching points or do them in a different order, it would make the task much more difficult. If they did not look forward before they received the ball, it would make it very hard to identify a potential pass, or if they did it after they had received the pass and had their first touch, then it would slow the whole process down and therefore the opportunity to play forward could disappear before they have the opportunity to do so.

Exactly the same process can be applied to any other practice and should be used to ensure that the players get structured support for their development, through a 'building block' approach to learning. This can be seen again in *Practice Fifteen* where the players within the central area will need to complete specific actions within a particular sequence to give themselves a greater chance of completing the task successfully. Here the coaching points could be:

1. Adjust your position – can you find a position in the central area that will ensure there is a clear passing line between you and the player passing the ball?
2. Identify your next pass – whilst the ball is traveling to you, can you identify the position of the teammate you are going to pass to next?
3. First touch – when you receive the ball, can your first touch take you in the direction in which you are going to pass the ball and also allow you to make the pass with your next touch?

The amount of information produced in the planning process does not have to be as detailed. It can simply be: (1) positioning, (2) identify the pass and (3) first touch. The important part is that you have thought through the process of what is needed to complete the topic of the session successfully and that you have produced a clear, logical method for the players to learn the topic of the session.

Now, at the end of a session it is probable that the players would be able to recall some information that is key to the topic of the session. It would not be expected that the players can remember all of the information or that it would be completely accurate, especially if the topic is new to them. But if each player is now able to recall one or two key pieces of information that were important to the focus of the session, then this will be integral to their learning and development in terms of the topic. This information can then also be used in future sessions, particularly when there is a link between the topics or there is some similarity in the content of the coaching points. By adding a small number of these coaching points, the fun, engaging and realistic environment that we have created has now been enhanced even further by bringing a structured learning process to the practice that will aid the players in their development.

The difficult element of this stage of the planning process is being able to identify what the coaching points are for the session topic. First of all, there is not any one rulebook that states what the coaching points should be for each topic. Soccer is a game of opinions and even with these technical points, there will be different opinions about what should or should not be included and, in some cases, in what order they should occur. As with everything in the planning process, the selection of the coaching points needs to meet the needs of the players and therefore it should be the case that different coaches will use different information for their coaching points. What is imperative, though, is that the selected coaching points are technically correct, and it is this component of planning that can be challenging. There are a number of strategies that can be employed to improve our knowledge about this area of the game.

We can of course study the topic, through reading or any other form of research and this will definitely help improve our understanding of our technical knowledge of the game.

This increased knowledge gained from research is really important in developing our understanding of the game and is essential in underpinning the information that we will be passing onto the players. Once we have this information, it is important that we build upon it through more practical-based learning. We could fall back on previous experience, whether this is through playing or watching the game. We can use what we had to do or what we observed in similar situations to that of the session topic. Coaching courses are also a valuable source of knowledge where learners can gain important information, not just from the tutors but from the other candidates as well. The final strategy that can be used by a coach in identifying the key coaching points of the session topic is to visualise or perform it themselves, as doing so allows you to experience it and break it down into its key components. Once we have this underpinning knowledge, the most effective way to enhance it is through experience, not just through delivering sessions ourselves, though this will undoubtedly help enhance knowledge, but by watching games and other coaching sessions which can also increase our understanding of the game and individual requirements for different aspects of the game.

There is, without a doubt, a lot to consider in the planning stage of a session and it can be quite daunting to begin with. It can also be quite a time-consuming process that is not achievable for everyone due to other commitments and demands placed upon them. However, if we can increase the planning that we do by any amount, it will have a significant impact on the quality of the session that we deliver. Not only will it provide the players with a clear focus for them to concentrate on and learn, it will also allow them to do this within an environment that puts them in realistic and relevant situations that are linked to the topic and the game of soccer. In addition to this, it is more likely that the session will be well organised, with practices that are linked together. This will help maximise the small amount of time that both the players and the coaches have within the session. Planning can also have a positive impact on the players' behaviour and the amount of time that they have on the ball, whilst also supporting the coach in providing essential structured information to the players. Therefore, though it can be difficult to find the time to plan effectively, the rewards that you will gain from doing so are invaluable.

CHAPTER 4
PLAYER-CENTRED APPROACH

As coaches we can often be guilty of expecting too much too soon from the players and trying to teach them aspects of the game that they either do not currently need or are not ready to learn yet. If we first have contact with a player when they are six or seven years of age, then there is a possibility that we could be working with that player for more than ten years. Similarly, when we are teaching a new skill or topic, we are often keen for the players to grasp it straight away and therefore we forget about the long-term learning process that they need to go through before they can be deemed as being competent. We need to be aware of the importance of this long-term learning process in the player eventually becoming an expert.

In chapter 1 the importance of competition was discussed with the acceptance that the players will always play the game and try to win, and that the format of soccer makes it naturally competitive. However, the role of the coach is to step back from the competitive element of soccer and understand that their part in the process is not to help the players to win, but to help them get as close to reaching their full potential as they can. The role of the coach in this process can be compared to that of the builder when building a house. Before you see the final result, a lot of work has taken place that no one will ever see, work that is integral to the success of the building and the final product. If a coach is to do this when building or developing a player, then a player-centred approach needs to be taken.

Within a player-centred approach there is a need to give the players autonomy to make their own choices and decisions within training, during a game and – just as importantly – outside of soccer as well. The coach supports the players by using a range of strategies that will help develop their decision-making ability and also to become effective reflectors, reflecting not only on their own performance, but also on the performance of their teammates and opponents, as this will help in their decision-making process. The coach will need to understand where the player is currently situated within their learning journey, allow them to have freedom within the practices, and support them in reviewing performance. This chapter will set out how to adopt a player-centred approach by outlining the role of the coach and the role that the design and delivery of the practices have in the process.

Player Development

When you first learn maths, you start with the fundamentals and then you look to hone these skills before progressing to the next stage. What you do not do is jump straight to trigonometry or algebra, nor do you start to attempt to do this level of difficulty until you are ready to do so. And when you do finally attempt it, you use different aspects of your previous learning to help solve the new problems you face. Therefore, the fundamentals that are learnt at the very start are used, such as adding, subtracting and multiplication, and these are essential to everything else that we learn.

Soccer is exactly the same, in that certain underlying skills need to be learnt, developed and refined first, as they will become fundamental to everything that a player does throughout the time that they play soccer. Therefore, within the early stages of their development it is essential that as coaches we concentrate on these skills, because if we do not, it will restrict what they can do in the future. Take the young player who always plays as a defender who is discouraged from dribbling and instead is encouraged to clear the ball quickly and is praised when they do so. This player's ability to be able to complete certain skills is now being restricted; what they are doing now as a young player is what they will always do from that point until they finish playing the game.

We need to ask ourselves the question: Does it matter that as a young player they lose possession of the ball near their own goal whilst they are attempting to dribble past an opponent? The argument, of course, is that they need to understand that sometimes it is not the right decision to dribble or there are better or even safer options. However, there is plenty of time for them to learn this and they can do this further down the line of their development pathway. What we need to do as coaches is, first of all, provide them with all the tools that are available, so that they can then be in a position where they have choices, rather than be in a position where they only have the one option available to them. What we therefore need to understand is: What are the priorities for the players at the very early stages of their development? What are the addition, subtraction and multiplications of soccer?

In addition to this, the different areas of a player's development also need to be identified and understood. It is now widely accepted that player development within soccer encompasses four key attributes: physical, technical, psychological, and social elements. Developing all four of these areas helps children to develop more than just their soccer skills, such as helping them to gain confidence, build self-esteem, learn to work as a team and improve their decision making. The remainder of this chapter will discuss each specific component of the player's development, explaining why it is important and how as coaches we can support the players with their learning in each of the four different areas.

Technical Development

There are key technical aspects of the game that players need to develop and master that will then underpin all of their other learning going forward. If a player is comfortable and confident when they are in possession of the ball, then it will make it easier to learn and develop other technical aspects of the game, whilst also supporting them within the other three areas of player development. Focusing on the fundamental techniques of the game during the early stages of their development will not only provide them with a number of different options to choose from when they are in possession of the ball, it will also significantly increase their enjoyment of playing the game of soccer. The whole reason children choose to play soccer is because of the joy they get from playing with 'the ball', so surely we should support them to develop a range of techniques that help them to keep the ball?

These key fundamental techniques are basically anything that allows a player to retain possession of the ball, whether this is retaining possession themselves or passing the ball to a teammate for them to keep the ball for their team. This will include receiving or controlling the ball, dribbling, turning, running with the ball and passing. Arguably the most important technical element of the game for players to learn and develop is dribbling, yet quite often it is the one that the players are discouraged from doing. Dribbling can be seen as being selfish and risky, yet if successful it can often bring great rewards. Beating a player in a one-versus-one situation will force another player to leave their position and therefore open up space on the pitch for the player on the ball and their teammates. Therefore, alongside a number of the other key fundamental techniques such as turning and running with the ball, possession should be seen mainly as an individual task rather than as a team challenge, with each individual player needing lots of time on the ball. Therefore, the early stages of a player's development should focus on promoting ball contact. This can be achieved through small-sided practices such as one versus one. Other practices can also be used such as two versus two or small overloaded practices such as two versus one or three versus two, where there are still lots of opportunities to work individually, but now a passing option is also available, but only if needed.

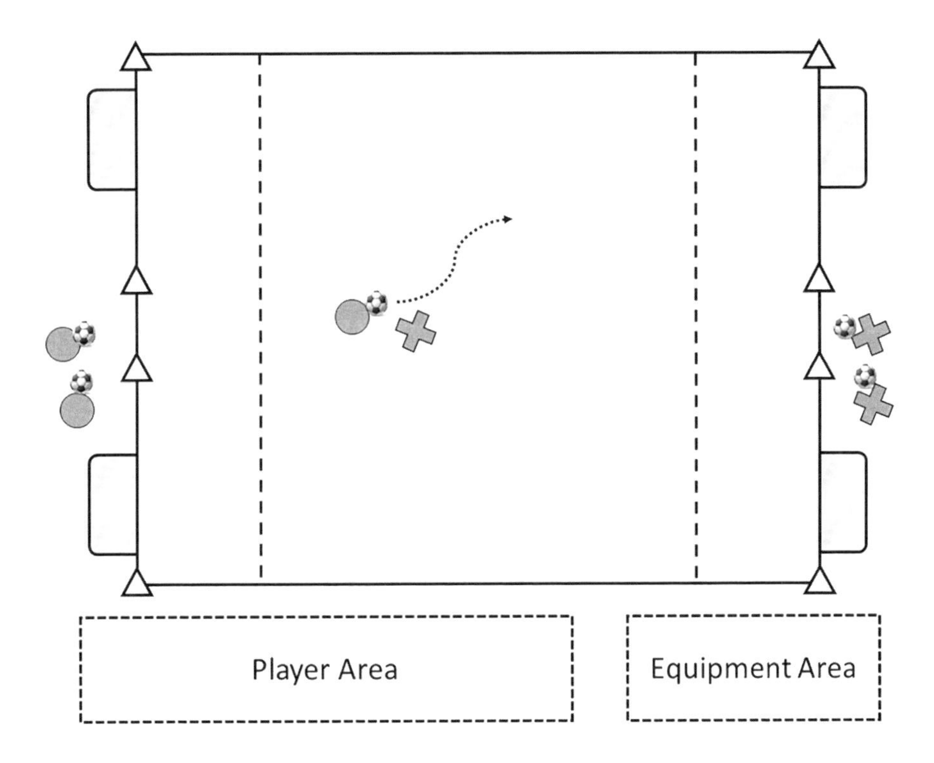

Practice Seventeen

One player enters the pitch through the central gate and attempts to pass into one of the two small goals. They can only attempt to pass into one of the goals once they have entered the 'end zone'. As soon as the player attempts to pass into a goal, a player from the other team enters the pitch and attempts to pass into one of the opposite two goals; the player who was just an attacker becomes a defender and looks to stop the new attacker from passing into the small goals. This rotation of roles continues. Players enter the pitch as the attacking player, then transfer to becoming the defender, then exit the pitch, before entering the pitch as an attacker again.

Practice Seventeen is an excellent example where players are given an opportunity to be creative and to experiment, whilst having to complete a range of the fundamental techniques that are needed within the early stages of their development and they will need to work out when each one is required. So, for instance, if they are able to enter the pitch quickly and get ahead of the defender, they should run with the ball and get to the end zone quickly before the defender has an opportunity to recover and get back goal side. Or if the defender does get goal side, the attacking player will have to dribble and/or turn to get past the defender. Finally, once they do enter the end zone, the decision first of all needs to be made when to attempt the pass and into which goal? This is before actually having to execute the pass. Progressing the practice to a two-versus-two game provides the players with a 'passing option'; the key is to not allow the focus to shift away from individual possession to a passing or possession practice. Introducing a maximum one-pass rule provides the player starting with the ball an option to pass it to their partner, but they know if they do pass it on, then their partner will have no option but to retain the ball. Therefore, over time they will develop their decision-making skills and only pass the ball when they really need to, which in turn will increase their ball contact time again.

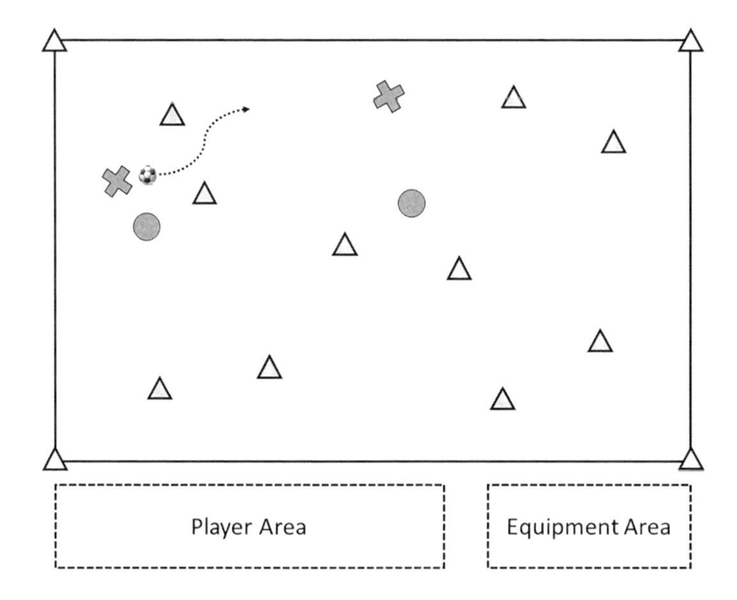

Practice Eighteen

Divide into two teams of equal players (two versus two or three versus three). Teams can score a point when a player dribbles successfully through any of the gates. On achieving a point, the team retains possession and can continue to try and win another point.

Similarly, *Practice Eighteen* provides the players with a passing option, but by matching the teams in numbers and by not providing an overload it makes the pass to a teammate challenging and when they do receive a pass, it will again involve a number of the fundamental techniques discussed earlier and the need for 'individual possession', as they are likely to have an opposition player close to them. In addition to this, the scoring system forces the players to dribble if they want to win points. This could be increased even more by introducing further incentives to dribble, for instance, if a player dribbles through one gate and then another gate without being tackled or passing the ball, they could achieve an extra bonus point, so they would achieve three points for dribbling through two gates.

Later on in their development, once the players are more experienced and have a much older 'playing age' (i.e., the number of years they have been playing the game), the benefits of focusing on individual technical ability will start to show. This can be seen as a really exciting time for both the coach and the player, as it will demonstrate the confidence and ability that can develop from all of the hard work that took place during the early years of their development. Once this stage has been reached, it is important that we continue to challenge the players by putting them in situations where they will encounter tactical problems and by involving them in increasingly realistic situations where they can use the fundamental techniques and skills they have developed to help find solutions.

Within *Practice Nineteen* players will have to solve the problem of getting the ball into an area of the pitch where they can attempt to score in one of the three goals before the 'blocker' can get to that goal and block it. To do this, they will need to use all of the fundamental techniques they have already learnt to quickly move the ball from one area or side of the pitch to another and give them a better opportunity to score a goal. Whilst doing this, the players will develop their tactical understanding of the game. For instance, they will quickly work out that when their team is in possession of the ball they will need to have players or 'options' on both sides of the pitch so that the blocker is unsure which goal to protect. Basically they will need to make the pitch big by using its full width, something they will be asked to do when they have the ball in a game.

Width, as discussed in chapter 1, is a key element in one of the three principles of the game. And it is these key elements of the three principles that can start to be introduced to the practices so that the players begin to gain some knowledge about these. At this stage they do not need to be introduced to specific tactics or strategies; they just need a simple understanding of what the specific element means and what it looks like during a game. In *Practice Nineteen* players will work out how they use width – by making the pitch as wide as possible they are likely to achieve more success. If the practice is then adapted slightly,

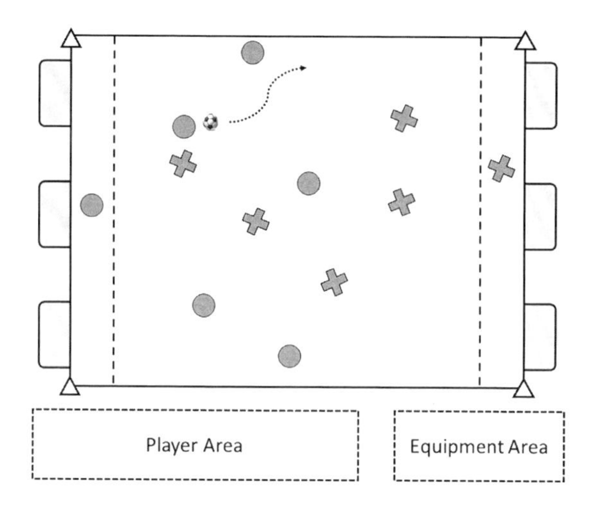

Practice Nineteen

Small-sided game with six small goals. Each team has a 'blocker' that is restricted to the small end zone; the blocker is free to move up and down the end zone. Teams cannot score in the goal that the blocker is standing in front of.

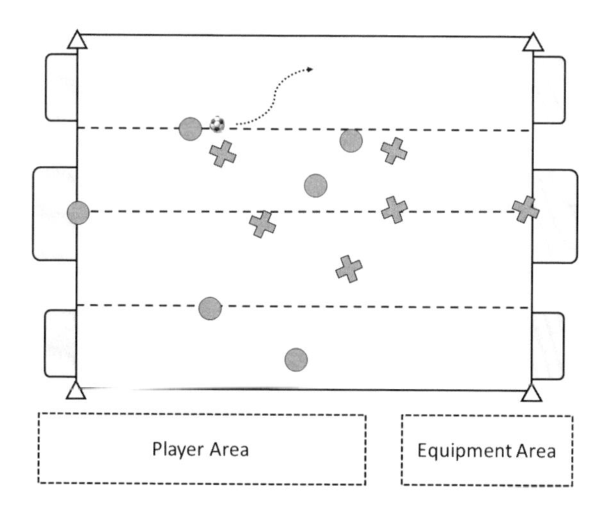

Practice Nineteen (b)

Small-sided game with two large goals and four small goals. Teams can earn three points by scoring in the central (large) goal or one point for scoring in one of the two small goals. The pitch is also split into four channels and the team that is out of possession are challenged to only have players in only two of the channels at a time.

as in *Practice Nineteen (b)*, they are then provided support and guidance on how they can stay 'compact' as a team and by doing so make it more difficult for the opposition to score.

The channels within *Practice Nineteen (b)* provide the players with some guidance and by challenging the team out of possession to only be in two of the channels at a time, it also provides them with a picture of what it looks like to be compact as a team. Ideally, when the ball is in one of the two central channels, the team out of possession will only have players within the two central areas. When the ball is in a wide channel, they will fill that wide channel and the adjoining channel. And in time, the players will start to understand where they need to be on the pitch in relationship to the ball, without the need for the channels as guidelines.

To summarise, players need to be given lots of time and opportunities to master the fundamental techniques of the game, as they underpin everything that they need to do with the ball. There is no rush to propel them to the full game and expect or ask them to play in the same way as adult players. Allow them to concentrate on retaining possession of the ball as an individual rather than doing so as a team, which they can do further on in their development. Reducing the number of players within practices can limit the options that they have available to them in terms of being able to pass possession on, and they are often forced to retain the ball themselves.

Physical Development

Children are meant to be active and this usually occurs through some form of play, during which time they will learn and develop a wide range of movements that they will then continue to use throughout the rest of their lives. These movements can be as simple as crawling, walking and jumping, or they can be more complex movements such as running, climbing and landing. When a child develops and improves these skills, they are more likely to participate in physical activity. They are also more likely to do well within these physical activities or sports if they excel in these movements. In fact, it is not uncommon to see a young child that excels in one sport also excel in other sports. A young child that does well in a sport such as rugby will quite often find it easy to switch to other sports such as soccer and hockey. Then as these children get older and progress through school, they will become a popular choice for most, if not all, of the school teams. This is because most sports require the participants to be physically competent and within invasion games it is a vital component of a player's performance.

If we look at the modern game of soccer, we associate it with physical requirements such as power, strength, muscular endurance, stamina and speed. Players that possess these physical attributes within the eleven a-side version of the game will definitely have an advantage over players that do not. However, we need to understand when these physical qualities should be developed and enhanced. Though they can be improved in the early stages of a child's life, their ability to build them up is very restricted as they have limited cardiovascular capability and their bones don't stop growing until late adolescence. Therefore, similar to the player's technical development, we can leave these specific areas of a player's physical characteristics until further down the line. Instead we can concentrate on the key fundamental physical attributes that need to be developed and enhanced within their early years, before their bodies begin to change. Once they enter adolescence and their bodies begin to change, it becomes much more difficult to have any impact on these fundamental physical features.

The main fundamental physical attributes that need to be prioritised at a young age – not just for soccer but for a child's overall physical development – are agility, balance, co-ordination and speed, or the ABC's. And it is these physical attributes that usually make a child good at all sports. If they are highly competent across these four areas of physical characteristics, they will usually be high achievers across most sports. Therefore, quite often we can use other sports and games to help players develop and improve their ABC's, just as we can use other invasion games in the development of players' understanding of the principles of the game.

Agility is described as the ability to move and change direction quickly and effectively whilst being in control. In addition to this, players with good agility are able to stop and start suddenly. Agility is particularly important in one-versus-one situations, and especially for the player on the ball, as well as for players when they find themselves within tight areas or they need to change the direction they are facing whilst under pressure. Therefore, it can be said that the need for players to have good agility coincides with their ability to retain possession of the ball individually. By being agile, players have a greater chance of eluding the opposition and moving into space.

As with the other key fundamental physical attributes, agility can be developed within soccer-specific practices, using other sports, or through fun games. Ideally, we would always go to a soccer-specific practice, as it will allow the players to practice mastering the ball, whilst also developing their agility. Within *Practice Twenty*, players will find success if they are able to attract the defender to one gate and then get to the other gate quickly. To achieve this, the player on the ball must first of all change the gate they are attacking unexpectedly, and then they must catch the defender by surprise. To do this, they would need to be able to stop suddenly before turning sharply and accelerating away.

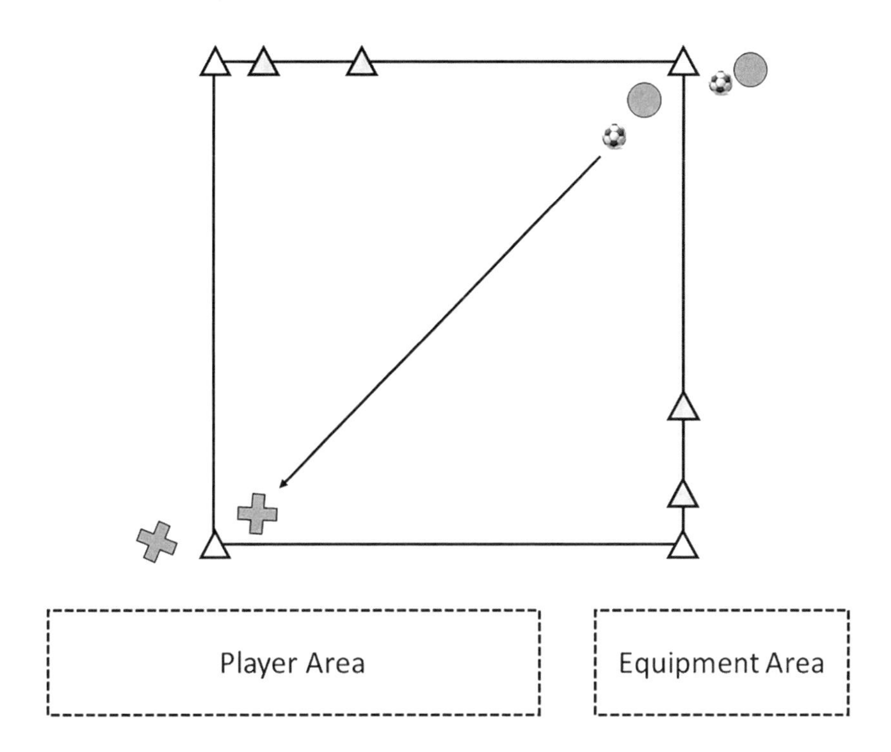

Practice Twenty

Set up a small square with two gates, positioned as shown in the diagram. A defender plays to the attacker who then looks to dribble through one of the two gates; the attacker must have the ball under control as they travel through the gate. If the defender wins the ball, they become the attacker, and they must then attempt to dribble through one of the gates.

Alternatively, as a coach there may be times when you want to solely focus on improving the player's agility and therefore a practice may be used where there is an even greater requirement for the players to demonstrate an ability to change direction quickly and to be able to stop and start unpredictably. This is when a game or elements of a different game can be used. Within *Practice Twenty-One* the players need to convince the players blocking the gates that they are attempting to get through one set of gates before trying to get through the other set of gates whilst avoiding being tagged. With the two sets of gates being close to each other, players will also still need to avoid being tagged, even if they have managed to fool the blocker. Alternatively, players can attempt to accelerate quickly through a gate if they can see a blocker is occupied by another player.

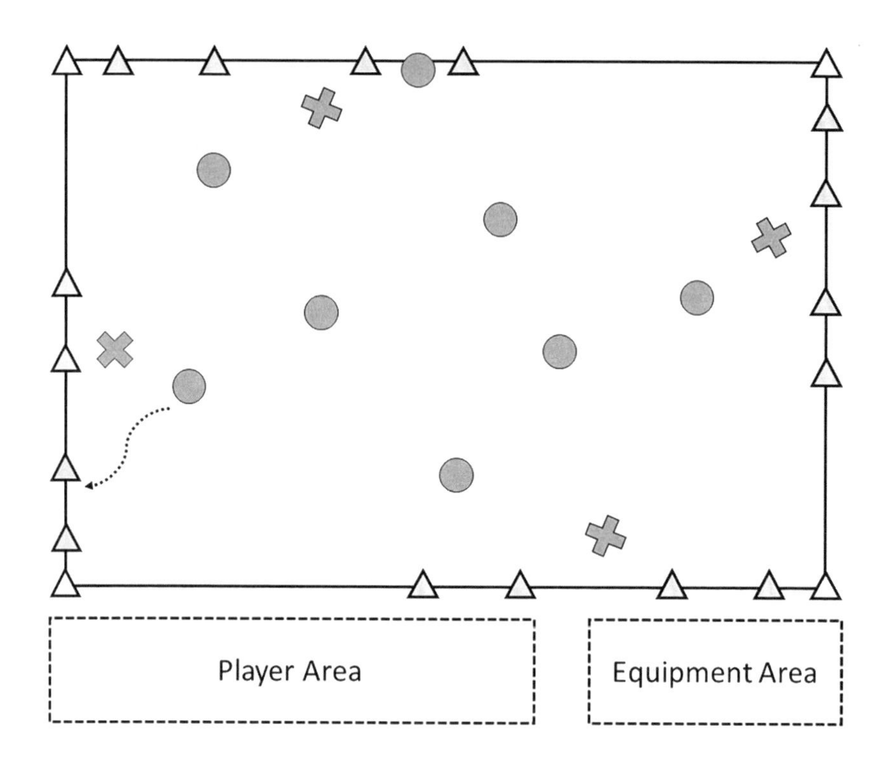

Practice Twenty-One

Players are given the roles of blockers. They are given two gates to protect, which are near each other. Blockers are only allowed to move sideways. The other players look to get through any gate without being tagged by a blocker; if they do, they earn a point. If they get tagged, then the blocker earns a point. Once through a gate, a player can re-enter the area and look to win more points.

Finally, a game can be used that incorporates other sports that require high levels of agility, sports such as basketball or rugby. Earlier in the book we looked at *Practice Two* and how it can be used as an introduction practice with the players having to pass the ball with their hands, gaining a point if they manage to get it to their target player. One of the main rules within the game was that players were not allowed to move when they were holding the ball, similar to the rules in netball. Therefore, if we want there to be a focus on agility, we need to move away from netball and get closer to basketball or rugby. So when players are in possession of the ball they would now be allowed to move with it, but if they are tagged by an opposition player, they lose possession and must pass the ball to the other team. To avoid being tagged, players will need to change direction unpredictably, whilst also changing their speed, i.e., slowing down and accelerating quickly. The level of agility required within the game can be extended further by forcing players to retain the ball longer than they may want to. For instance, players may be required to have possession of the ball for a minimum amount of time before they can pass it onto to a teammate. Or you may only allow the team a maximum number of passes. Therefore, when they receive the ball that player may not want to waste a pass until they are farther up the pitch or there may be no passes left and therefore they must keep it until they are in a position where they can attempt to pass it to the target player.

The key element to a practice that looks to develop a player's agility is that it has some form of 'avoidance', so that the players need to change both direction and speed quickly and unexpectedly. Therefore, some form of tag game is usually used, the difficulty of which can be increased by reducing the size of the area and also by changing the shape of the area. The difficulty can be increased by adding further areas within the main area that can be used as 'no-go' areas. Therefore, when approaching these areas, the players will be forced to change direction, whilst also reducing the amount of space they have to avoid being tagged. By participating in these types of practices, the players will not only develop their agility but they will also start to come up with strategies to avoid being tagged, which they can transfer to the game of soccer and use to avoid being tackled.

The need for players to have good balance within soccer is quite often underestimated, though it is needed when executing any technique or when a player is travelling with the ball, especially at speed. When completing any technique, a player will only be standing on one foot and if they are unbalanced it will affect how they execute this technique. Probably the best example of this is when a player is having a shot on goal, especially when they are trying to generate power. If the player is off balance, they will find it really difficult to strike the ball in the correct area and also to perform the technique accurately. It needs to be done from a stable base, which can only be achieved through good balance. Similarly, when a player is travelling at speed and attempting to go past a player, they will look to change the direction they are travelling quickly and in doing so, they are looking to throw the defender off balance. To take advantage of the defender being off balance, the player must remain balanced, as it will allow them to maintain their speed and stay in control of the ball.

Simple tasks can be added to practices that will incorporate a small amount of work regarding balance. When using tag games to help develop a player's agility, additional tasks can be added to work on their balance as well. For instance, if a player is tagged they could be asked to balance on one leg for a set amount of time or until another player releases them. These tasks could also be added to some practices when players have a small amount of waiting time before their turn, such as *Practice Twenty* or *Practice Two* where the servers could be encouraged to balance on one foot whilst they are waiting for the ball to be played to them. Or practices could be adapted so that they can be used to develop balance. If we return back to *Practice Twenty-One* that was used to help improve the agility of the players, increasing the distance between the gates it will make it easier for the attacking players to get through them; however, we can then increase the difficulty again by having the players hop through a gate. This can be set as a rule where they have to do it, or they can be encouraged to do it by rewarding them with extra points if they do so.

Ideally, the practices will incorporate the players having to maintain their balance whilst moving at speed, where movement could be straight-line running, changing direction or adjusting their body position, for example going from standing to crouching down. This can be seen within *Practice One* where players need to be able to crouch down and collect a cone whilst running quickly and also changing direction. For a player to be able to collect a cone successfully and avoid being tagged at the same time will require a good level of balance. They will need to be able bend down and probably stretch out to collect the cone, therefore changing the position of their centre of gravity and making it more difficult to remain balanced. This is also replicated within *Practice Twenty-Two* where the players are avoiding being tagged, therefore moving at speed and changing direction, where balance will be required to help them be as quick as possible during these changes in direction. The real challenge, however, comes first when a player has to place the ball down inside an area whilst being chased and then again when they have to collect the ball from the floor. Again, this will need to be done at speed and possibly with a change of direction, as they need to avoid being tagged straight away.

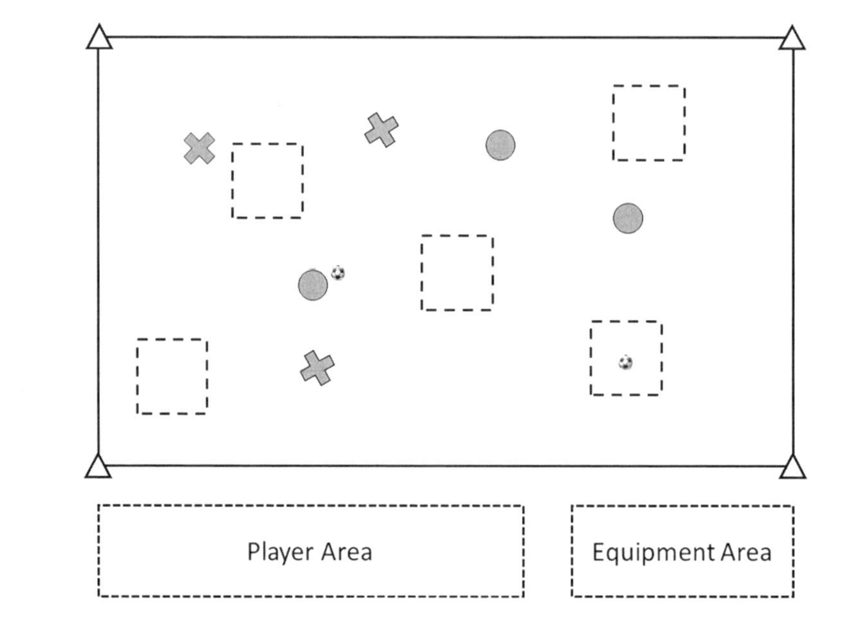

Practice Twenty-Two

Players are split into small teams, ideally three versus three. Using two tennis balls, teams pass one ball between themselves using their hands. If they get tagged whilst in possession of the ball, then possession changes hands. The other ball is left inside one of the five scoring areas. Teams win a point if they are able to place the ball down in one of the five scoring areas (cannot be placed down where the other ball is situated). Once this happens, a player then picks up the other ball, and the practice continues.

Co-ordination is a key physical component that is transferable across most, if not all, invasion games. It can be seen as the ability to move two or more body parts under control, smoothly and efficiently. There is also eye-hand or eye-foot coordination, which is the ability to do activities that require the simultaneous use of the hands or feet and eyes. The element of being able to move two or more body parts whilst under control will be developed through most practices that the players are involved in. To be able to pass and dribble with the ball will require co-ordination from the player, as a number of body parts will be required to complete the action. Therefore, the players will be working on this element of co-ordination most of the time. So as coaches we need to consider how we can provide further support for hand or foot and eye co-ordination.

The importance of foot and eye co-ordination can be fully appreciated once we understand that vision controls the movement of the foot. Refining this part of a player's physical performance allows them to be in full control of how and where they make contact with the ball. This will then allow a player to make pinpoint passes, to strike the ball cleanly or be in full control of the ball whilst dribbling. It also helps a player to perform the techniques of the game whilst keeping their head up, which in turn will allow them to scan and make decisions at the same time as performing the technique.

The development of co-ordination can be achieved in a number of ways; it can form part of a practice that has a different narrow focus or through practices that are specifically designed to improve co-ordination. For example, if we revisit *Practice Eight* where the players are working in pairs, with one player attempting to keep the ball away from their partner, this is mainly used to develop the player's ability in either dribbling or defending, but by making a few small adjustments, co-ordination development can also be achieved as a by-product. First of all, reducing the size of the area will make it more likely that players will come across other players more often and therefore there is a greater need to dribble with their heads up, meaning they are spending less time looking at the ball. Or by changing a rule so that the players are no longer working in pairs and any player without a ball can tackle any player with the ball. The players with the ball will need to constantly scan all of the area and be aware of any player without a ball, therefore again they will spend less time looking and concentrating on the ball. Forcing the players to have to dribble whilst looking away from the ball will help the development of their eye-foot co-ordination, as it will increase the need for the player to have full control of their foot, so that they can concentrate on other aspects of the practice, i.e., scanning for other players and space. Having increased control over their foot movements will then allow the players to strike the ball more accurately when performing other techniques such as passing and shooting.

Another practice that can be adapted to help improve co-ordination is *Practice Two* where the players pass the ball between themselves using their hands. Replacing the ball with a tennis ball will put extra demands on the player catching the ball. First of all, due to the size and weight of a tennis ball compared to that of a soccer ball, it is much easier to throw and therefore it can be thrown with greater power, generating more speed in the pass. Obviously, the quicker a ball is traveling the more difficult it is to catch and the need for good hand-to-eye co-ordination is increased. Secondly the smaller size of the ball makes it more difficult to catch, plus it also allows a player to catch the ball one-handed rather than two-handed, which again requires increased levels of hand-eye co-ordination.

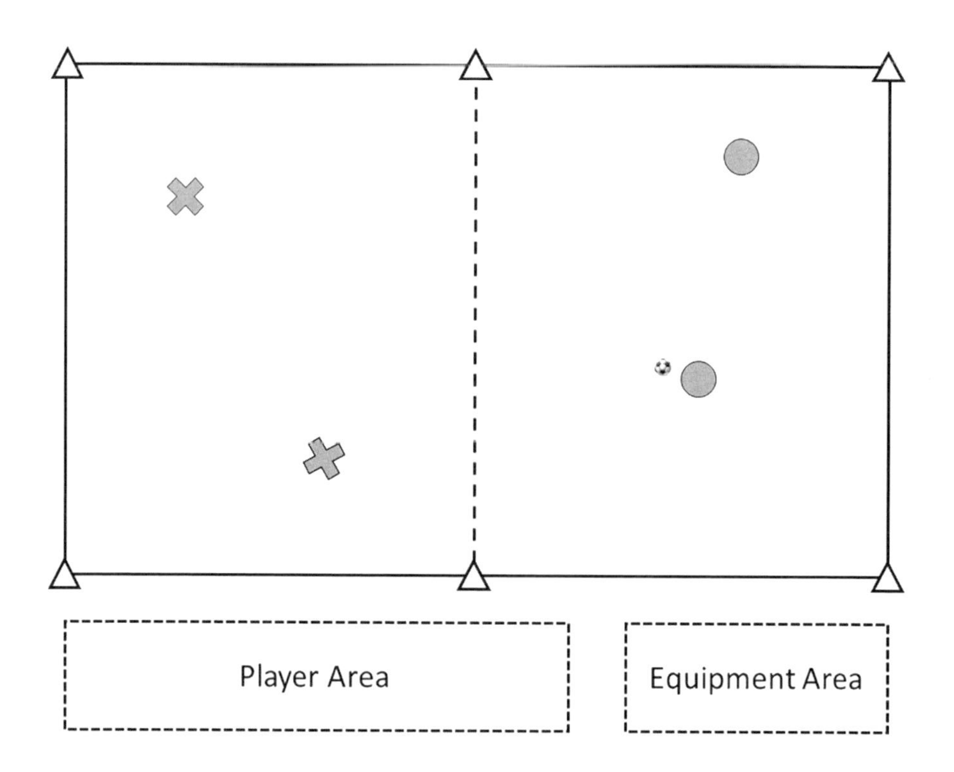

Practice Twenty-Three

Teams of two players work in a small area split in half, with the players locked into their halves of the area. Using a tennis ball, players attempt to throw the ball (underarm) into their opponent's half with their opponents looking to prevent the ball from bouncing by catching it. If the ball does bounce, it is a point to the team throwing the ball; if, however, the ball lands outside of the area, the point goes to the other team. If the ball is caught, then the game just continues.

Alternatively, a game that solely focuses on co-ordination can be used as the first practice of the session. Though it might not have a direct link to the rest of the session, there can still be some kind of link to some session topics and therefore they just need to be used at the right times. In *Practice Twenty-Three* the design and set-up of the practice allows the players to work on their co-ordination in a number of ways and though there is no direct link to any aspects of the game of soccer, some aspects have a closer connection than others. For instance, with the players trying to accurately throw and also catch the ball over short distances there are some links to both passing and receiving. The main element of the practice is, however, to improve co-ordination through the need to catch the ball and throw it into a very small space, i.e., an area where the opposition team cannot reach it.

Speed, though being similar to other physical attributes such as strength, power and stamina, in that it develops much quicker during and after puberty, also differs, as there is a time frame during a child's early years when it can also be improved alongside agility, balance and co-ordination. Having speed has always benefitted a player within the game of soccer, but in the modern game it is becoming more and more important in all positions. The ability to get away from a player, whether with the ball or running onto a pass, or to be able to recover quickly when you are out of possession, is a real asset and can provide a significant advantage over players who are not as quick.

The speed of a player can be broken down into different parts: with and without the ball, top speed and acceleration, with each one being as important as the other. Practices can be designed where the players can develop just one of these parts, a number of them or all of them. How a practice can develop all parts of speed can be seen in *Practice Seventeen* (b). Forcing the player to run the ball past the same line where the player entering the pitch starts provides the player entering the pitch with a few yards' advantage straight away. By having this advantage, the player on the ball just needs to concentrate on staying ahead of the recovering defender whilst keeping the ball under control. The player who has just scored the point, and therefore changes to becoming the defender, needs to catch the attacking player up before they score their point. So this practice can be used for a number of different focuses, such as running with the ball or recovery runs, and the coach would concentrate their support and their feedback on the session topic, but whilst this is happening the players will also be getting high returns in speed development.

Alternatively, a practice can be put on by the coach where the focus is solely on speed development; however, it must be stressed that this focus should be for one practice only

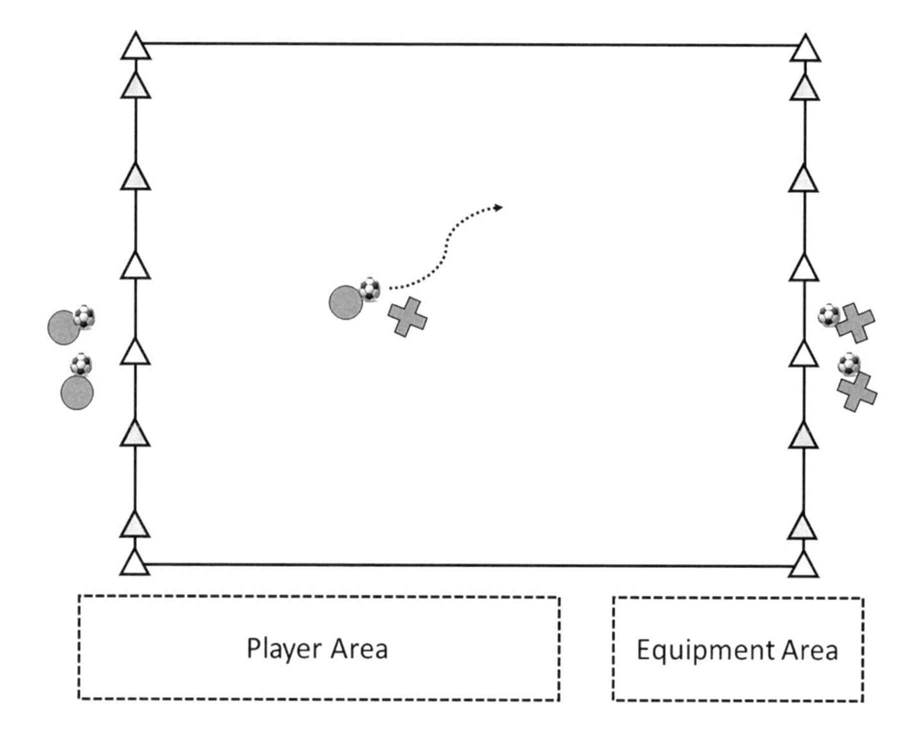

Practice Seventeen (b)

One player enters the pitch through the central gate and attempts to run the ball through one of the two small gates. As soon as the player drives through a gate, a player from the other team enters the pitch and attempts to drive through one of the opposite two gates, the player who was just an attacker becomes a defender and looks to stop the new attacker. This rotation of roles continues constantly. Players enter the pitch as the attacking players, then switch to become the defenders, then exit the pitch before entering again as attackers.

and not the whole session. Therefore, it should be used as the first practice only and when it can be linked to the topic of the session, for instance, a practice that concentrates specifically on developing players' speed can be used at the start of a session that has a narrow focus on running with the ball, forward runs without the ball, counter attacking etc. Or it could be an element of the game where speed over a shorter distance is needed (i.e., acceleration), and this could then be linked to a session focus such as turning or pressing.

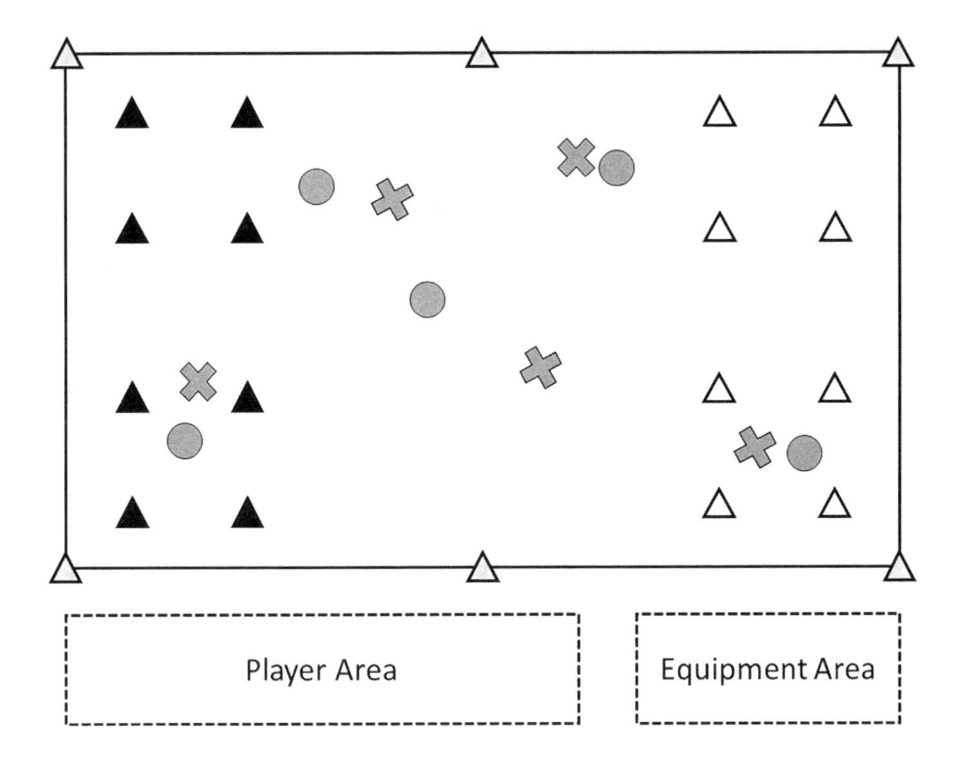

Practice Twenty-Four

Working in pairs, players attempt to travel from one area to another without being tagged by their partner. Players can only be tagged when they are outside of the small areas (i.e. travelling between areas), and the player attempting to score the point decides when to leave the area, with the tagger having to react and chase their partner. Players can get additional points if they travel to an area of a different colour (greater distance).

The set-up for *Practice Twenty-Four* can be changed and different rules applied so that it can be used for all the different types of speed. For acceleration, the different scoring areas can be situated close together or more could be added. Also, the two players can both start near to each other by both players starting anywhere inside an area. To then change this to support top speed, the scoring areas can be situated farther apart and the tagging player has to start on one of the cones that is chosen by the player who is trying to avoid being tagged. This then gives the player a few yards' head start, but a greater distance to travel; therefore, their top speed becomes more important. Balls can then be added to the practice to help develop speed with the ball; a ball could be introduced to just the player being chased or to both players, and this does not need to be the same for everyone within the practice. Those quick players on the squad may have to have a ball, whilst their partner, who is not as a quick, might not. For another pair within the practice, both might have a ball, as the player being chased is not as quick. The key element to the success of the practice is that the player being chased has the possibility of reaching a scoring area without being tagged, to encourage and also allow them to reach and maintain their full speed.

The key to the player's physical development during the early stages of their player pathway is to concentrate on the aspects that they can develop and will not be able to develop later on. The focus therefore must be on their agility, balance, co-ordination and speed, not just because of the limited time frame of when you can have a meaningful impact on these particular physical attributes, but also because they are essential to all invasion games, soccer included. They will also play a vital role in all of their future physical activity, including any other prospective sports they may want to participate in, but also the simple everyday activities that they will undertake throughout their lives. Ideally, these physical attributes will be developed as additional returns from practices that have a narrow focus on a topic that is a lot closer to the game of soccer. For example, if we are using *Practice Six* to help develop dribbling, can we also have an impact on their speed development by increasing the length of the area, so that once the attacker gets past the defender they need to accelerate away and then also maintain their speed, to ensure the defender does not have an opportunity to recover. Or a specific practice that concentrates on physical development can be used at the start of the session as the introduction practice.

Social Development

Children need to develop a range of things at a young age if they are to keep playing in the long term, and one of these is a passion for the game of soccer. It could be argued that the majority of players start playing soccer with this already, having acquired it by watching the game and playing it with their family and friends, before they even joined a team. If this is the case, then it is just as an important that this hunger for the game is not extinguished. It should be that the players have so much fun at training that at the end of a session they are already looking forward to the following week.

The social element of training will play a significant role in whether or not the players enjoy their experience and therefore key social skills should not only be developed but also encouraged and allowed to flourish. These skills will not only contribute to their enjoyment and love for soccer, but they will also influence both their working life and also the connections and bonds with those people that they have their closest relationships with: family members and close friends. Social skills such as empathy, decency, communication, teamwork and ownership. The development of these skills can be promoted through practice design, but the biggest impact is usually achieved through how the practice is delivered.

The first social element that we should promote within training and on match days is the need to behave decently. Decent behaviour is simply doing the right thing or being a good person and, ideally, doing it without being prompted or persuaded to do so. An example within the environment of soccer could be a player being well-mannered and polite or helping with the training and match-day environment, i.e., collecting the equipment at the end of the session without being asked or engaging with their teammates and coaches both politely and respectfully. The key role that a coach plays in this process is not punishing players if they do not do it, but instead praising them if they do. As coaches we should always be looking to catch them being good.

In chapter 2 the key characteristics of a coach, such as integrity and equality, were discussed along with the need to display these on a constant and consistent basis. By demonstrating these qualities, a coach will not only set the right example for their players, but will also support them in becoming good people. For instance, if on a match day we ensure that every player has the same number of minutes on the pitch, this demonstrates equality and it is also the right thing to do. The purpose of grassroots soccer is to provide everyone with the opportunity to play; therefore, some players do not deserve more time on the pitch just because they are deemed as being a better player. Similarly, a coach can demonstrate integrity by ensuring that if they say they will do something then they do it. So, if they promise a player they can play in a certain position in the next game, or they can take on a certain role in the session, such as being a 'floater', then they need to ensure that this does happen – again, it is the right thing to do. This behaviour can then be transferred to the players. If the players have been asked to help collect in the equipment, then every player should help to do this. If the players are working in small groups and taking turns at having a go at a certain role, then they should all have the same number of turns. It is critical that the coach fully understands their role in this process, in that it is not about punishing those players that do not do this; instead it is about rewarding and praising those that do. The coach needs to concentrate on 'catching them being good', a strategy that will be discussed further in chapter 5.

Empathy, or the ability to understand and share the feelings of someone else, is an important ability for every child to develop and demonstrate. As with most other aspects of life, the players will come across a range of different personalities and characteristics within the training and match day environment, and they must therefore learn how to build relationships with all these different people. If we look at a squad of ten players, then within this squad there are ninety different relationships and then if another player joins the squad there will be an additional ten new relationships that need to be built. It could therefore be said that the social bubble that a soccer squad exists within is extremely complex and ever changing. It is also not unusual for small friendship groups to be formed or they may well have already been in place beforehand, for instance, in school or as pre-existing friendships. It is therefore important that as coaches we encourage and promote the players spending time and interacting with all the other players on the squad. This can be achieved in a number of ways, both through random selection and careful planning.

The partner who players work with can be changed regularly within practices such as *Practice Six* and *Practice Eight*. Whilst in practices where the players are working in small groups, such as within *Practice Fifteen*, then the allocation of players to each specific group can be selected ahead of the session, with careful consideration, putting players with other players that they do not usually work with. This can also be replicated when they are working in teams and can even be extended to the match day, where the players on the pitch and those off of it can be varied each week. It is important to emphasise at this point that players should not be kept apart from their usual friendship groups or never allowed to choose who they work with, we are just looking to vary who the players are grouped with in each session, rather than them working with the same ones every week. Once the players are within these pairs or groups, it is then how they interact and work together and through this they will be able to start to develop their empathy. Players need to understand that everyone should have an input and that not everyone will agree with their opinion. In a similar way that they find hard to learn to share from a very young age, whether this is their toys or whose 'turn' it is, they now need to learn to share and accept opinions and ideas.

For *Practice Two (b)*, the teams have to make a choice at the start of the practice whether or not they want a goalkeeper. If they do not want to have a goalkeeper they will then have an extra outfield player within the main playing area, possibly giving them an overload, depending on the decision made by the other team, which they will be unaware of until the game starts. Then within certain times during the practice, there are breaks, where the teams will have opportunities to discuss how their choice whether or not to have a goalkeeper is going and whether or not they want to change their decision. During all of these discussions it is the role of the coach to help ensure that every player on each team is given the opportunity to put forward their thoughts and that their opinion is considered by their teammates. Then the coach should support the players in coming to a final decision. Small tasks such as these will support the players in being able to compromise and to take other people's feelings and views into consideration and not just their own.

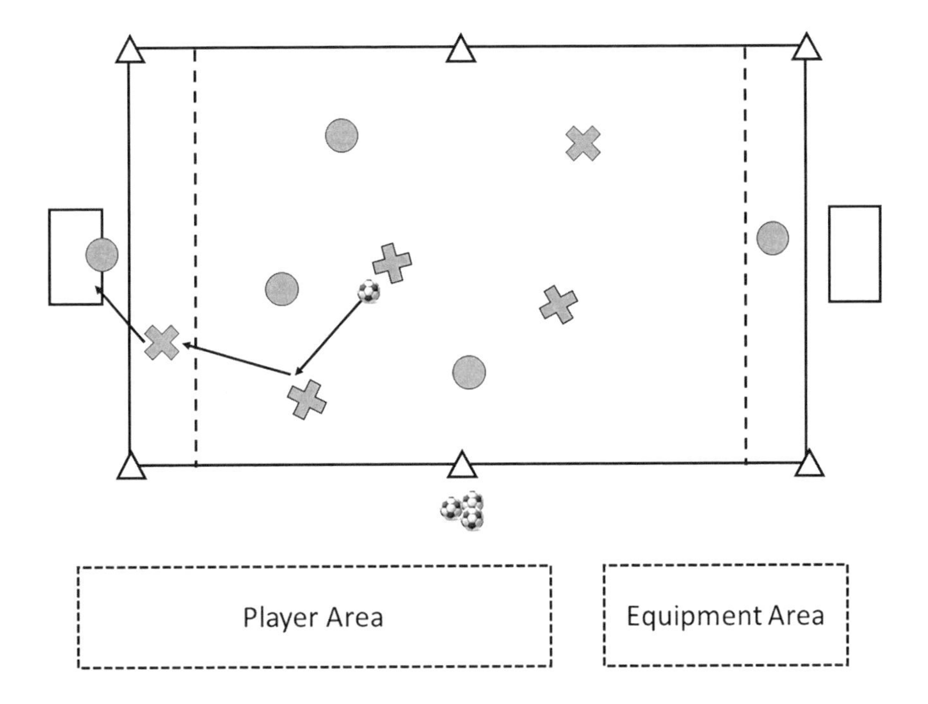

Practice Two (b)

Players are split into two teams, with each team having a target player in an end zone. Teams look to play the ball into their target player who then has a maximum of two touches to get a shot on goal. Once the ball has been played into the target player, one player from the opposition team can enter the target area and put pressure on the target player whilst they are attempting to score.

Communication is a word that we use a lot within soccer. We are always encouraging players to talk to each other, to ask for the ball or to give information as they pass the ball on to a teammate. And communication becomes increasingly important later on in a player's development, when the need to work with other players in critical partnerships, such as two centre backs or a fullback and a wide player, or in their units – defensive, midfield and forward. This is particularly pertinent when the team is out of possession and there is a need to stay compact as a team. However, at the beginning, what the players are actually saying to each other and the accuracy of the information, is not necessarily important. The important part is that the players have the skills and confidence to communicate to their teammates; this includes both talking and listening, and also the ability to take information on board and then apply this newly obtained knowledge.

It is not uncommon for a coach to be perplexed when they cannot stop the players from talking off the pitch, but then cannot get a word out of them on the pitch. But rather than asking the players to simply talk more during practices, they can be given tasks throughout the season that will provide them with the confidence to talk to, and in front of, their teammates. These tasks can come in a variety of shapes and sizes and can be imbedded into sessions, rather than being the main focus. If we look back to *Practice Two (b)* and the element where the players need to decide whether or not to have a goalkeeper, this task immediately promotes discussion, which in itself stimulates all aspects of communication. Setting similar tasks throughout the season can help players develop their communication skills and become more effective communicators.

Another effective strategy we can use as coaches to develop the players' communication skills is by giving them more responsibility and putting them in situations that they are not used to. For example, as the players arrive, their new habit at the start of the session is now to find out the information that tells them what to do in the first practice. This information is probably usually obtained by asking the coach, or by looking at the tactics board where there could be a diagram and instructions. However, sometimes one or two players could be given the responsibility of explaining to their teammates what they have to do, i.e., they become the assistant coach. This does not mean that they cannot take part in the activity themselves or that they have to stand on the side watching the practice. They can continue to take part as they would usually do, but as new players arrive it is their responsibility to explain to these players what they have to do within the practice before returning to taking part again. This approach may only work for some players though – those that arrive early for the session. The players that, for whatever reason, struggle to arrive on time will not get the opportunity to take on this role.

A practice design that has not been considered yet is a carousel format, where the players rotate around a number of small practices. This form of practice design is usually used at the start of the session as the first practice. An example of a carousel format can be seen within *Practice Twenty-Five* where the players spend a few minutes in each practice before rotating around to the next practice, visiting all four. Whilst rotating, one player from the group stays to explain to the new group of players what they need to do within the practice, before joining their group in their new practice, where one of their group members will need to pass on the information they had received. The coach can also be creative at the start in how they give the first group in each practice the information they need to understand what they actually need to do and then pass on to the next group. This information could be written down for one group member to read out to the rest of the group; they could just tell one group member for them to then relay it back to the rest of the group. Or they could even get the group to choose or make up the content of the practice themselves, which would create a lot of communication within each group.

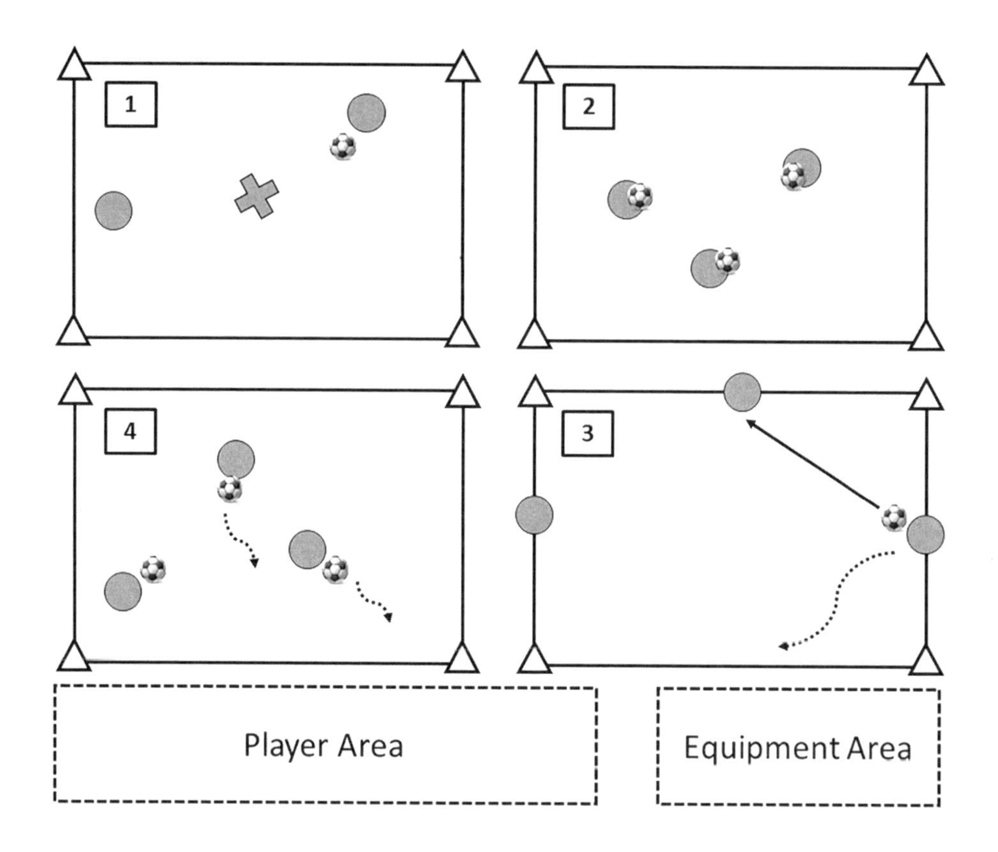

Practice Twenty-Five

Within the first practice, two players look to retain possession against a defender. If the defender wins the ball, they swap roles with the player who lost it. In the second practice, the players look to complete keepy-ups, and in the third practice, the three players each stand on one side of the area and pass the ball between themselves. Once they have passed the ball, they move to the side of the area that is free. Finally, in the fourth practice, the players each have a ball and dribble around the area, completing any skill of their choice.

Teamwork or working together is a particularly important social skill that the players will need whilst playing the game of soccer and also in most aspects of life. Teamwork is seen as a collaborative effort of a group of people to achieve a common goal or to complete a task in the most effective way and therefore it is basically the main feature of soccer. The test that grassroots soccer coaches can face when they try to promote teamwork within their team is that some players will quite often dominate, whilst others can find aspects of the game a lot more challenging. This can result in some players being viewed as being less important to the team than others, by both by themselves and their teammates.

Coaches will often look to resolve this by promoting teamwork within some of their sessions and this will sometimes come in the form of practices where every player has to touch the ball to achieve a point or before the team can attempt to score. Though these types of practices must be applauded for their intentions in trying to help to keep all of the players involved and made to feel valuable, they can often have the reverse effect. For instance, the player who is responsible for losing possession of the ball may feel they have let their teammates down, especially if they are the last or nearly last player who needs to have touched the ball. Usually, this player is also a player who is seen as being less important to the team and therefore the result of them losing possession of the ball can have a significant impact on their confidence, an area which will be discussed in greater detail later on in the chapter. The other consideration that needs to be made in regard to these types of practices is that they reduce the level of realism, as the opposition players will begin to defend unrealistically, i.e., they will not be too concerned about protecting the goal. Instead they will look to stop the last couple of players who need to touch the ball from receiving it, or they will put them under a lot of pressure once they have received it. On the flip side, it can also be unrealistic for the team in possession of the ball, as they could have a player on the ball who, under normal circumstances, you would want to have make an attempt on goal, but instead they need to go away from the goal and seek out the player who has yet to touch the ball.

The actual concept of these types of practices should not be disregarded. Instead, they just need to be adapted so that all the players have more of an opportunity to have an impact and feel they are valued members of the team, rather than feeling the pressure of having to contribute. Instead of every player having to touch the ball, players and teams could be encouraged to include every player by being rewarded if they do. Goals could be worth the number of different players that touch the ball in the build up to the goal, with extra bonus points if every player touches the ball. Or if we look back at *Practice Sixteen*, where the pitch is split into thirds and players are locked into their designated areas, we could look at imposing a rule that every player must touch the ball. But only when the team starts with the ball from their goalkeeper (the game always restarts with the goalkeeper; there are no throw-ins), if a team wins' possession off the other team they can go on and attempt to score a goal whenever they want. The key to this is the allocation of the players. The players that may require further support will probably need to be allocated to an area which is not as challenging to achieve success compared to the other areas. These areas could be less challenging as they have an overload of players in favour of the team in possession or the players allocated to each area are closely matched in terms of ability. By doing so, all players have a realistic opportunity to contribute to the success of their team.

Other strategies that can be used to promote teamwork include point-scoring systems where teams can achieve different points depending on the difficulty of the task. If we return back to the thirds practice again, instead of players being locked into the different areas, teams could earn points for each area they advance into and then more points for actually scoring a goal. Again this provides all of the players an opportunity to gain points for their team and contribute towards their possible success. Another strategy that can be used by the coach is to put the players in situations within their teams where they have to come up with strategies and allocate roles and responsibilities. This can be seen within *Practice One* where two teams look to invade each other's territory and capture a cone before returning to their own half of the area. Here teams may decide to allocate specific roles to each player, i.e., some might stay and defend their cones, whilst the other players look to grab their opponent's cones, with each role being as important as the other in the context of the game. The coach just needs to ensure that if teams do decide to allocate roles, then players are not allocated the same role for each game.

This form of teamwork can also be found in other practices such as *Practice Seven (c)* where, similar to *Practice One*, teams have something to protect and something to attack, which is basically the main principle of the game of soccer – a team looks to protect one goal whilst trying to score in the other one. In this particular practice, though players may well be given specific roles to begin with, as the game develops these roles will basically become redundant and instead players will need to react to the situation that they face. Working together as a team will become particularly important when they are in possession of either both or none of the balls. To win this particular practice, all members of the team will need to play some part.

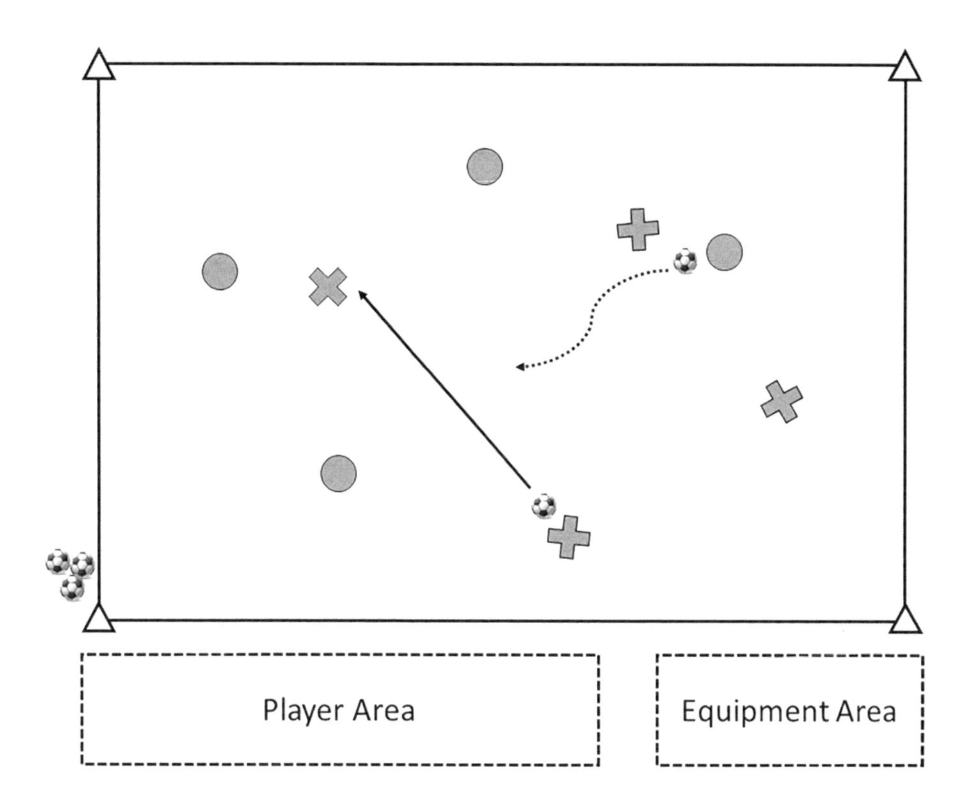

Practice Seven (C)

Players are split into two teams and are given a ball each. The teams then look to retain possession of their own ball whilst also looking to gain possession of the other team's ball. A team wins the practice if they are able to retain possession of both balls for a set amount of time.

Ownership, or being accountable, is another social skill that is equally important both within and outside of the environment of soccer. As players progress along their development pathway, the need to take ownership or responsibility becomes increasingly important. This is even more important outside of soccer where, as they get older they need to become more and more independent and eventually take responsibility for all aspects of their life. This is quite clearly a mammoth undertaking that everyone has to go through, and though as coaches we will probably only have a small impact, the impact that we do have will play an important part in their journey to adulthood. However, any impact that we do have on developing their ownership within their personal life will have a much greater impression on their ability as a soccer player. Encouraging and supporting players to take ownership and to be more independent will also allow them to become decisive decision makers and problem solvers. Key skills needed for a sport that is played within an ever-changing environment where the players will never come across the exact same situation. They will however face similar situations that they have come across before and therefore need to take ownership in these circumstances and find a solution to them.

The first steps that we can take as coaches to develop ownership within players are to reduce their dependence on us. Instead, they look to find answers to their own questions first and only look to get the answer from the coach as a last resort. This will begin as they arrive to training, where the first practice will be ready for them; they just need to know what they have to do. As part of this new habit, players need to go to a new source to obtain this information. Instead of asking the coach, they might need to get the information from a tactics board or they may need to seek out another player and get the information from them. The information could even be sent to the parents or guardians beforehand and it is then the players' responsibility to remember what to do as they enter the pitch. The coach just needs to choose whichever method best fits their and the team's circumstances, or they may even decide to regularly change it to make it more challenging for the players.

This particular method of developing ownership is done alongside other social skills. For instance, gathering information from a teammate will also include developing both players' communication skills. This is not unusual when it comes to ownership and the other social skills as well; quite often when you are supporting the development of one particular aspect of the social side of the game, you will inadvertently help support at least one other one as well. We can see this if we look back at empathy, where the players were given the task of deciding whether or not they wanted a goalkeeper or an additional outfield player. Though the main purpose of this task was to encourage the players to get their views across to their teammates whilst also considering the opinions of others, the players will also be developing their communication skills as well as giving them ownership. Usually, the coach will tell the players what formation they are playing or the position of individual players, but instead they are given the responsibility of doing this themselves as a team. Then they also take ownership of making any necessary changes to their selection when given the opportunity to do so.

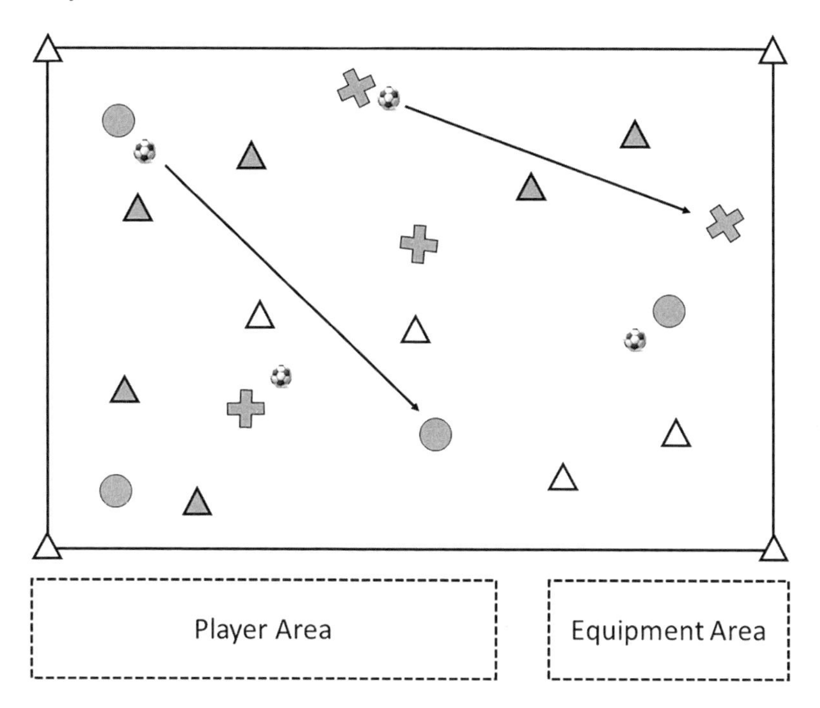

Practice Eleven (c)

Players work in pairs passing the ball around within the area. Players are encouraged to use as much of the area as they can and are allowed to have as many touches of the ball as they want. When passing the ball to their teammates, they look to do so through one of the gates situated around the area.

Other ways in which the coach can introduce or encourage ownership are through simple tasks that may look straightforward or do not even look like tasks, but can be just as effective. In *Practice Eleven (c)* cones have now been added to the area and the players are asked to try to pass the ball to their partner through a set of cones before moving on and looking for another gate that is available. Instead of the coach setting out the gates and deciding where exactly they should go within the area, and what exact size they should be, this is left to the players to determine. This task of just putting out the cones may well be seen as giving the players ownership, as they are being given the responsibility of completing the set-up of the practice, but the ownership that they have been assigned goes much deeper than this. When the players are setting up a gate, they are making a decision around their learning; they are taking ownership of their development. Where they position the gates within the area, and how wide the gates are, will influence the difficulty level of the task. Further into the practice the players could be asked to reposition the gates or change the width of them to make it more challenging. Again they are being given the ownership and input into their own development.

This form of ownership can be used across most practices in a range of formats. Players can be given the responsibility of setting the different scoring systems within a practice, or they could be asked how a practice could be progressed. So within *Practice Twelve (b)* the players could decide how many points are awarded for each different way of scoring. They may, for example, decide to award more points for goals that are scored with a first touch finish or with a player's non-preferred foot. Players can also be given the responsibility of deciding how a practice should progress in terms of making it more challenging, or they could even decide to regress the practice if they feel it is currently too difficult. If we look at the same practice, the players could be allowed to make any change they want to it, or the coach could give them a number of options to choose from. They could, for example, be given the option of moving the goals farther away from the area, or instead, when a goal is scored, the goal that it is scored in is then locked, reducing the number of goals available to score in.

The importance of social development should not be undervalued, it plays an important role in the overall growth of a player, helping them to become independent and less reliant on the coach. Developing skills such as ownership, communication and teamwork will allow the players to be able to react to new situations, alone or with the help of their teammates. This removes the need to wait to be told what to do by the coach, by which time it will be too late. In other words, we are providing the players with leadership skills and encouraging them to become leaders on the pitch. By helping them obtain these type of characteristics and qualities, players will be able to cope and even excel within the ever-changing environment that is a game of soccer, whilst also guiding or even leading their teammates through the game.

Psychological Development

The final area of a player's performance is often seen by coaches as being the most important aspect of a player's development, but not always for the right reasons. When the psychological side of the game is discussed by coaches, areas such as having the right attitude, determination and commitment, are often at the top of the list. And though these traits are undoubtedly great qualities to have, they are extremely difficult to instil in a player. Players are, however, likely to self-improve within these particular areas if they play and train in the right environments. If they are in an environment where they enjoy playing, and are given lots of opportunities to improve and take an active part in their own development, then they will naturally become more motivated and determined to get better. This will be achieved if we follow the approach of everything that has been outlined in both the previous and upcoming chapters, allowing the coach to concentrate on more essential psychological elements of a player's development, which in turn will contribute to creating the right environment.

The psychological demands of the game of soccer are extremely high and will play a significant part in the level of ability that a player can achieve. Confidence, positivity, creativity, problem solving and decision making are psychological skills that you would want any player to demonstrate. As with the fundamental physical requirements that were discussed earlier within the chapter, it is just as important that these psychological skills are also introduced and encouraged early on within a player's development. For instance, if a player lacks confidence in the initial stages of their introduction to the game and this is not addressed early on, then this is unlikely to change and it will become a feature of the player's game. As coaches we need to reverse this characteristic and also any of the other key psychological attributes that a player needs but does not currently possess.

Players with high levels of confidence will naturally find the other important psychological traits easier to come by and therefore this particular area of development would be the logical place to start. Within chapter 2 the importance of a coach being enthusiastic and inspirational was outlined and this plays an important part in the growth of the player's confidence. However, this support arrives to the player externally and there is therefore a limit on the amount of influence this has on their growth in this specific part of their advancement. Therefore, it is essential that coaches also influence how the players feel about themselves; they need to have an impact on their internal feedback, they need to help them grow their self-esteem. To achieve this, the players need to experience success, they have to see that they are improving and to understand their own capabilities.

To enhance a player's self-esteem, the coach may need to provide a helping hand within the practice designs. This does not mean that the practices should allow the players to find success easily, as this would be detrimental to their development; players will not improve if they are not challenged. Therefore, the practice needs to be challenging, but with options to make it slightly easier for the players when they need it. In *Practice Eight*, players look to keep the ball away from their partner, whilst looking to gain points by dribbling through the scoring zone. There could be players on the squad that find this task too difficult or might need support sometimes, possibly depending on which other player they are partnered with. Further areas could be added to the practice which could be used as safe zones for the players that are in possession of the ball.

Careful consideration needs to be made regarding these zones to ensure they achieve their purpose. Their size and shape are particularly important, as they not only need to provide an area where the player in possession of the ball can have a break from being chased, but they also need to give the players an advantage as they exit. What they do not want to do is just allow the defender to be able to wait for them on the outside. A reasonably sized square will allow players with the ball to either travel through whilst the defender has to go around, or stop in the square and then exit the opposite side to where the defender is waiting. The safe zones also need to be in a position where they provide the player with the maximum number of exit opportunities, as well as a chance to gain a point shortly after exiting, i.e., they need to be away from the corners of the main area and quite close to the scoring zone. In addition to this, the safe zones need to be there to just support the players and not provide them with the 'easy' option. Therefore, only a small number of safe zones should be made available and then additional rules added to ensure that players cannot constantly use them. This could include only one player at a time being allowed within a safe zone and/or a player only being allowed to use a safe zone once until they get a new partner and then they can use it once more. The important part is that the player is not simply provided with an option that completely removes the challenge or makes it much easier. Instead, they need to be provided opportunities to receive support, but only when they really need it, giving them more chances to experience the feeling of success and lift their self-esteem.

Another example of how this can be achieved can be seen within *Practice Twenty*, where players were awarded points for dribbling through one of two sets of gates, with the emphasis on turning. There is no reason why a third gate cannot be added to the practice that is situated in close proximity to where the attacking player starts the practice. Adjustments would just need to be made to the scoring system within the practice, with the original two gates worth considerably more points than the new gate. The players will still be encouraged to travel through the original gates because of the high rewards they will receive in doing so. But they will also have the option, if they feel that they need it, to gain some success by traveling through the extra gate. So, for instance, if they feel the defender is closing them down quickly, or if they were not happy with their first touch, they may choose the gate that offers them a greater likelihood of success.

Boosting a player's self-esteem within the environment of soccer has the same effect as increasing it in any other circumstance. Anyone who has an increased level of confidence in their ability to complete a certain task is more than likely to be able to complete the task successfully. They often just need support and reassurance at the start to build up this confidence, before they can fully trust themselves. Probably the best example of this would be a child learning how to ride a bike. To be successful at this task, they just need the confidence in their own ability to be able to control the bike whilst remaining balanced. To begin with, they need the safety net of knowing someone is there to support them in completing the task, i.e., there is someone there to help them remain balanced and upright. Gradually this support is reduced, quite often without the child knowing it, until it is completely removed as the child gains more confidence and belief in their ability. The support mechanisms that a coach puts in place within the practices act in the same way, providing the players with the help they need, until they have enough self-esteem where they no longer need them.

In a similar way to which we want players to be confident on the ball, we should also want them to be positive and direct in their play. Too often a coach will encourage players to take the 'safe' option and not to take risks, to pass to a teammate rather than attempt to go past an opposition player or to 'clear' the ball when they are in their own defensive third or under pressure, rather than try to retain possession. This goes back to what we believe the priorities are for the players in the early stages of their development. Is it to provide them with the fundamental skills needed to play the game, which if they are not developed, will limit their abilities for the remaining time that they play the game? Or is it to fast forward their learning and try to get them to play the same way as the full version of the game? Encouraging young players to be positive and to take risks will undoubtedly result in them losing the ball, conceding goals and losing games. But at this stage of their playing pathway, does any of this matter? Especially when these actions actually form part of their learning and their development.

The restrictions and conditions that we often include within a practice design can actually have the effect of quashing players' positive play. Enforcing rules, such as players having a maximum number of touches or a set number of passes to be completed before a team can score, can restrict or remove the opportunities for players to be positive and direct when they have possession of the ball. There are definite times when such rules could and should be enforced, i.e., when it supports the focus of the session, for instance, retaining possession or build-up. Otherwise, these rules should not be introduced to a practice, but instead the opposite could be added to a practice. The maximum number of touches could be removed from a practice and instead the players could be forced to have a set minimum number of touches, giving them more time on the ball, during which time they should be encouraged to go forward, away from their own goal and towards the opposition goal. As with any rule or condition that we introduce, we need to contemplate how it affects the realism of the practice. The key consideration for this particular rule would be the effect it has on the player who has the attempt on goal; before they can do this they will need to have a set number of touches first. This has a significant impact on the realism of the practice, particularly when a player is in a position to have an immediate attempt on goal, for example, from a cross. Having an attempt at goal is also a positive action, and therefore we do not want to prevent the players from doing this. An exemption to the rule should therefore be put in place so a player would need to have a minimum number of touches of the ball, unless they have an attempt at goal. Similarly, instead of having a minimum amount of passes before the team can have an attempt a goal, a maximum number of passes could be introduced, therefore pushing the players to keep the ball for longer and only passing it when they really need to.

Other ways in which we can encourage the players to be 'positive' in their play includes asking them, when they can, to play forward. This may be by dribbling, driving with the ball, passing or even just running forward to be an option ahead of the ball. Again, simple rules or conditions that encourage the specific element of positive play can be added to practices. If we look at encouraging players to make forward runs ahead of the ball, all we need is a condition that will get the players in the mind set to make runs that take them farther up the pitch than where the ball is situated. Within chapter 3 we looked at a thirds practice, and specifically *Practice Sixteen*, where the pitch is split into three sections. This practice can be adapted slightly by adding further sections and then a condition can be added where once a player has made a pass, they must move into a section that is ahead of the section the ball was passed to. Or gates could be added to a normal pitch and similarly the player has to run through a gate that is ahead of the ball, after they have played the pass. As both games progress, the rules can be removed and the players can move into 'free-play' with the coach observing to see if there is still an element of forward runs. If the players have returned back to their normal play, then the rules can be reintroduced for a short period of time. However, it needs to be remembered that it will take the players a long time to learn any new skill; therefore the process should not be rushed, but instead revisited over a long period of time.

To enable players to be creative, we must provide them with freedom. Within chapter 1 this need for players to be given freedom was first introduced and then within chapter 3 it was put into context through practices that allowed the players to make their own decisions and to experiment with possible solutions to the problems that they come across. And by doing so we are basically encouraging the players to be creative; by not providing the players with the answers, they will need to try out different ways to find success. This includes not just working out how to solve the puzzle in front of them, but also finding the method that works best for them. As each player is an individual with different characteristics and qualities, we cannot provide a 'one-size-fits-all' approach to our coaching and the information and support that we provide the players.

Within *Practice Six* the players are given the task of getting past the defender and dribbling the ball over the line that they are protecting. To do this, the player with the ball is given the freedom to come up with the solution themselves about how to do this, whilst the coach provides support. This support, however, does not need to come in the form of showing them a specific skill, as one skill will not always be suitable for the situation that a player faces –where the space to dribble the ball is situated, the defender's body position, and the location of the other players, including teammates, opposition players and the actual defender they are facing, etc. Instead the support provided by the coach could be aimed at the foundations needed within any skill. To get past a defender, the attacking player will need to use some form of feint or trick to transfer the defender's body weight one way, before shifting the ball in a different direction, whilst the exact timing of when they complete the skill is integral to its success. Once they have done this, the need to accelerate away or execute the next technique, such as a pass or a shot, is also essential to the overall process. The specific skill used by the player could be a skill they have practised at home or one they have seen someone else use. This particular form of learning has become a lot more common and is widely used by players, due to the ease of its accessibility through a range of different platforms, such as social media, online videos and television. The important part of the process is that the players are given the licence to be creative when coming up with possible solutions to the situation that they are facing. So that when they come across the vast range of different situations that will undoubtedly occur within a game, the players are used to being creative and creating a solution themselves with the coach providing support on how the player could possibly improve the solution that they have fashioned.

Other examples of allowing and encouraging players to be creative can be seen within most of the practices used throughout the book. For example, *Practice Two* is a game-like practice where the players can be creative in the different ways they look to get the ball to their target player. In a technical practice, such as *Practice Fifteen*, the player in the central area can be creative in how they receive the ball and then how they pass it on to their teammate. For instance, they may choose to allow the ball to roll across their body or produce some type of turn, before trying out a range of passes, such as a driven pass along the ground or a lofted pass to their teammate for them to receive aerially. This can then be developed further within *Practice Fifteen (b)* where the two players working together in the central area can be really creative in how they combine with each other.

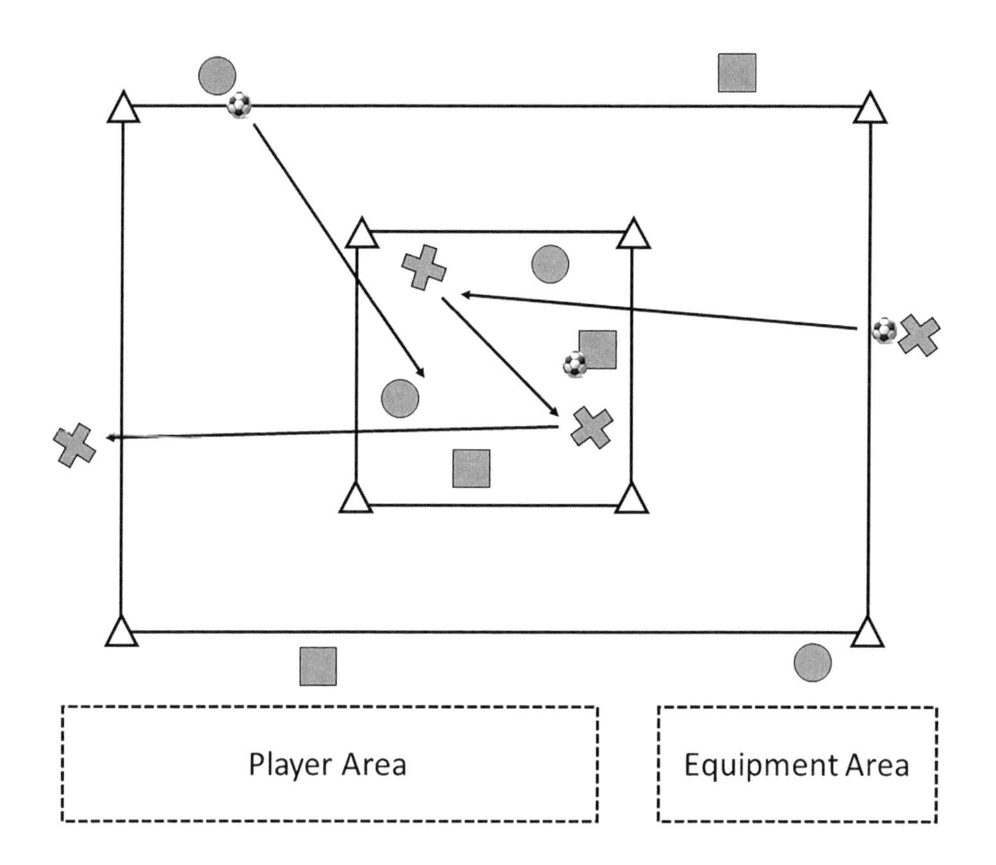

Practice Fifteen (b)

Players work in groups of four with two players in the central area and the other two players outside of the larger area. The ball is played into the pair within the central area who combine before passing it on to the other player situated on the outside of the large area. After the player on the outside of the area has passed the ball, they move to change their position to make it more difficult for the players in the central area to find them. The role of the central players is rotated regularly.

In *Practice Four* and *Practice Ten* the players have to come up with different ways in which they can either find a teammate within the target zone or be the player receiving the ball. This will involve the players being creative in different ways, ranging from the initial build-up and retaining possession to the more difficult task of finding the pass into the target area. These types of practices, in particular, require players to be creative in their play as they represent some of the more difficult elements of the game. To be able to penetrate the opposition and create goal-scoring opportunities can be extremely challenging, as ultimately this is what the opposition are trying to prevent. This is particularly prevalent within the eleven a-side game where tactics become more important and the players have a greater understanding of the game. A well-organised team can be extremely difficult to break down and therefore creativity is usually the key to unlocking goal-scoring opportunities.

As with positivity, we should not try to subdue the player's natural impulse to be creative; children are naturally creative and this is evident within their 'play'. And the more that they play or experience, the easier it is for them to be creative and the more creative they become. Creativity is seen as the ability to make connections between previous experiences. People who are creative cannot always explain how or why they did something, it just seems obvious for them to do it and they do it without the need for any thought process, they just picture something and apply it. They are able to connect previous experiences and fuse them with new things. So with children they may use something they have watched on television, learnt at school or seen someone else do and then integrate it into their play. Therefore, the more different opportunities we can offer and, more importantly, allow the players to experience, the more creative they will become. This means not being preventive or discouraging them from trying things, no matter what the circumstances or how as coaches we might not be entirely comfortable with them doing it in that particular instance. For example, if they are in possession of the ball close to their goal and they are under pressure from an opposition player, they should not be discouraged from being creative in how they get out of that situation. As mentioned right at the start of the chapter, it does not matter if this leads to the team conceding a goal; it is more important that we are allowing the player to have this experience and to be creative in trying to work out a possible answer to the problem they face. The more times that they come across this or similar situations, the more experiences they will be able to connect together to come up with effective solutions.

This then links into the players developing into effective problem solvers. During a game, players will constantly come across problems that they will have to solve without the direct support from anyone else. Yes, they will have teammates that can provide support, for example, by being available for a pass, as they will then help to provide one option to the problem, but it is down to the player on the ball whether this is the correct option or whether there is a more suitable one. These problems can come in all shapes and sizes: it could be a one-versus-one situation where the defender is particularly difficult to get past or finding a pass to a teammate who is being closely marked. It could even be being through on goal and having to beat the goalkeeper. Players need to have the know-how to solve the problem that they face. They will not always be able to execute it well enough or accurately enough, but hopefully they will know what they should do.

Similar to creativity, problem solving will be naturally developed in the majority of the practices that are used throughout the book. Again, by providing the players with freedom, the coach is almost forcing the players to have to solve the problems themselves that they come across within the practice. This can be seen even within an unopposed technical practice, such as *Practice Eleven (b)*, where the players are organised into pairs and they pass the ball between themselves and their partner, along with all of the other players. The players will immediately need to solve the problem of how they pass the ball to their partner successfully without it being blocked by another player or another ball. They will begin to recognise that they will need to look first before they play the pass to ensure the pathway is clear. Then, if required, they will come up with further solutions, such as delaying the pass or altering the type of pass. For example, they may use a chipped pass rather than a pass driven along the ground. Removing the rigid constrictions that you find in more traditional 'drill' practices, provides the players with the freedom to make their own decisions, rather than the coach or the practice making the decisions for them.

The need to be able to solve problems can be seen throughout most practices used within the book. If we look back at *Practice Four*, the two attacking players have to work out how they can get past the defender and win a point by one of them receiving a pass in the target zone, before the second defender has time to recover and support their teammate, which would make the task for the two attacking players a lot more difficult. The topic for this particular practice can also be flipped so that the focus is on the players out of possession and, in particular, the first defender. The main problem that the defender will need to try to solve is how they delay the two attacking players long enough to give their teammate a sufficient amount of time to recover and help them defend. Either way, the practice provides the players with realistic and common problems that they will encounter and need to solve during a game. Similarly, within any of the formats of *Practice Two*, the players will need to work out the best way in which they can get the ball to their target player. Whilst doing so, they will be taking a number of factors into consideration. For example, how do they retain possession of the ball until the opportunity arises to play into the target player? How do they play the ball into the target player so that the target player can control it well enough for the team to achieve a point?

Even within *Practice One* where the players are working in two teams to try to take each other's cones back to their own half of the area, they are constantly having to make decisions. When to stop helping defend their own area and attack the oppositions area instead? Which specific cone should they try to take? Once they have got one of the other team's cones, which route do they take back to their own half to avoid being tagged? Though there is no actual ball involved within this practice, and it is primarily aimed at developing the player's ABC's, it provides the players with similar tactical problems that they will come across in a game of soccer. For example, how do you attack the opposition whilst ensuring you retain the right amount of balance to protect your own territory? The situations that players come across in a game will constantly be changing. This could be the score line, the amount of time left in the game, different players for both teams (i.e., substitutions), or how the opposition are playing. Therefore, players will need to be equipped so that they are adaptable and not perturbed when during a game they are constantly facing new and different problems.

The challenge that we will face as coaches is that once we have set the players these problems, we must not set our expectations too high in terms of the players being able to solve them. What we cannot do is take the opportunity away from the players to solve the problem themselves; we cannot step in too soon and provide the answer for them. We will never get the opportunity to do so in a game, and therefore they need to learn to solve problems themselves. Players will find success easier to come by within *Practice Twenty-Six* if they receive the ball on the back foot with an open body, so that they can move forward more quickly and, hopefully, get in front of the defender so that they are protecting the ball with their body, as well as creating a clear pathway for the pass to be played into the goal. As coaches we will have this knowledge already and we could share it with the players at the start of the practice. But if we do, we are not even giving the players a chance to face the problem, so they will find it more difficult to recognise a similar problem when they are playing in a game. We will cause similar problems if we wait until the practice has started. Though we may now be giving the players a chance to experience the problem, we still might not be giving them the chance to solve it themselves. Instead, the players need to be allowed the time to try to solve the problem themselves, with support from the coach when needed in the form of questions. The starting point for this could be: When you receive the ball, what do you want to do straight away? This allows the players to still be the ones that are solving the problem, with the coach just providing relevant prompts, when needed, that help the players come up with the solution.

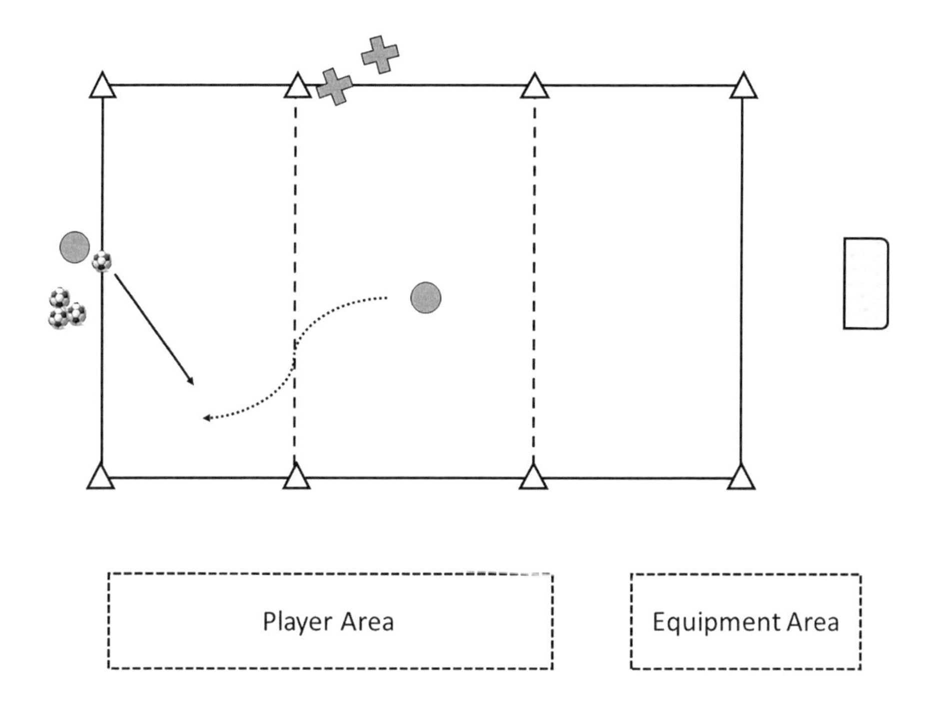

Practice Twenty-Six

Attacking player drops in to receive the ball from the server and then looks to drive towards the third zone where they can pass into the small goal. The defender can go and defend once the player has received the ball.

The final piece in the jigsaw with regards to the psychological development, and in fact the whole development of the players, is decision making. With them developing a range of different skills across all four elements of player development that they can use in all areas of the game, they now need to be able to decide or select which to use in each given circumstance. When in possession of the ball do they drive and accelerate into an area of space? Do they look to be positive and confident and go past an opponent by dribbling? Or do they have the awareness to see that there is a teammate in a more favourable position and pass them the ball instead? Whichever decision they make will have a knock-on effect on what happens next. Does their team retain possession of the ball? Do they create a goal-scoring opportunity? Or do they actually lose possession of the ball? It is therefore imperative that they we constantly put the players in a situation where they are having to make decisions, so that it becomes easier for them to make the right decision.

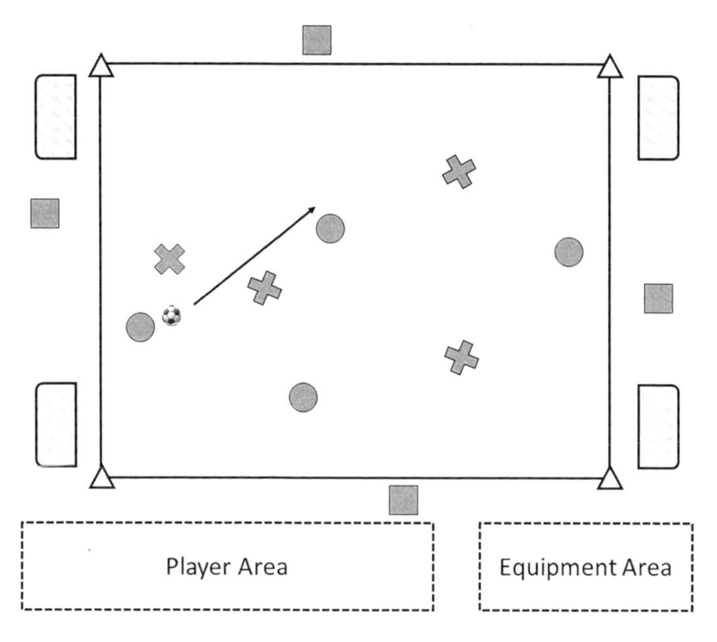

Practice Twenty-Seven

Teams are split into three teams, with two teams within the area and the other team acting as support players around the outside of the area. One of the teams in the area looks to complete a set number of passes before they can attempt to score in one of the small goals. The other team looks to win the ball and in doing so they can look to score immediately, without the need to complete any number of passes. The team that needs to complete the set number of passes can use the support players to help them retain possession, but if they do, then the number of passes they have completed resets to zero. The role of the three teams can be rotated each time a point is scored.

Practice Eighteen had a focus on dribbling where teams won points by dribbling through a gate. They can also pass the ball between their teammates, but to achieve a point a player is required to actually dribble. If we then want to add decision making to this practice, then we just allow the teams to achieve a point by either dribbling or passing through a gate. We can still achieve the focus on dribbling through the scoring system by awarding more points if a player dribbles through a gate, rather than passing the ball through. Players are now being asked to make a decision. When is the right time to dribble and when is the right time to pass? The need to make this decision existed within the practice beforehand as players were able to pass to their teammates to help retain possession of the ball, but by adding it to the scoring system it gives it more of a focus. Provided that we are giving the players freedom within a practice, then they will always have to make decisions and this can only be beneficial to their development, as it will give them a better understanding of the game. But then, in addition to this, we can make decision making a more essential element of the practice, but only when it is the right time for the players. With decision making, arguably the most important but also difficult element of the game, it is important to introduce it to the players, but slowly and in stages of difficulty.

The main focus for *Practice Twenty-Seven* could be passing or retaining possession, with an end product of making a pass into one of the small goals to give having and retaining possession a purpose. To begin with, the team in possession can use the support players to help them achieve the required number of passes. This still provides the players on the team that have possession of the ball with a number of different decisions to make. This includes when and who to pass the ball to, and also once the number of passes has been achieved, whether the player on the ball attempts to pass into a small goal to win a point or pass to a teammate, as it may be a difficult opportunity or the teammate may be in a more favourable position. If at a later stage the rule is introduced that the pass counter is reset if one of the support players is used, then this puts a greater emphasis on the need to make the right decision when a player is in possession of the ball. Players will need to make the important decision of whether to keep the pass counter moving up so that they can be closer to having a chance to score a point, or to just look to retain possession to ensure the other team do not win it. This decision gets more important the closer the team gets to achieving the required amount of passes, as the chance of winning a point increases. This can be linked to the game and how the level of importance of decision making increases as the team in possession of the ball gets closer to the opposition goal.

As with possession, decision making when a player or a team is out of possession is extremely important, and the more players are involved, the harder it is to make the correct decision, as there are more options to choose from. So if we look at a one-versus-one practice, the decisions that the defender has to make are limited to those that are associated to being the 'first defender' or the defender that 'goes to the ball'. These would include their body shape and where they are trying to force the attacker to go and when to attempt to actually win the ball. As soon as we add an additional defender, the number of decisions to be made increases significantly; straight away a decision has to be made as to which player goes to the ball and which defender acts as the 'second defender' providing cover and support. This can be seen within *Practice Ten* where the two defenders are looking to prevent the attacking players from achieving a point by one player receiving a pass in the target zone. Obviously the best way to stop the attacking players from winning a point is to get the ball off them, so the initial decision that will need to be made is when to try to win the ball and when to just protect the target zone. A number of additional decisions will need to be made by the defenders throughout the practice and these decisions alongside the decisions made by the attacking players will have a significant influence on the outcome and which team is successful.

Other ways in which decision making could be added to a practice is through providing players or teams scenarios within game practices. For instance, a team may be given the scenario that they are winning a game with just five minutes left, and therefore if they make sure that they do not concede in that time, they have won the game. The other team will then obviously be given the scenario that they need to score. The first few times that this approach is used by the coach may not have the desired affect that they are looking for, i.e., the team who are defending their lead makes less risky decisions, and the team that needs the goal does the opposite. But over time they will learn to make 'different' decisions compared to what they might usually make, because of the situation they face. As coaches we can also influence the decisions that players make by giving them restrictions or challenges. These types of individual interventions will be looked into in greater detail in the next chapter, but touching upon them now will provide insight into how as coaches we can have an influence on a player's decision making. If we return to *Practice Eighteen*, we have now provided the players with two options to score a point, by either passing or dribbling the ball through a gate. Despite having the option and being given the licence to make a decision about how they can score a point and, hopefully, making that decision based on what they see in front of them, some players will still not make a decision; they will carry on doing what they prefer to do or what feels more comfortable to them. A player may, for instance, prefer to pass the ball rather than dribble and usually makes the decision to pass when they receive the ball, even if there is an opportunity to dribble and score a point. Here the coach may need to support the player in making them consider their options and not just choosing their preferred choice. Giving the player the challenge of having at least three touches before they can pass the ball will help the player consider dribbling with the ball rather than just passing it.

The other key support that a coach can provide in helping players develop their decision-making skills is by, first of all, allowing the players to actually make a decision and then, if needed, to provide support for the decision that they made. Quite often as coaches we are too eager to provide the answer before the player even has the opportunity to make a decision themselves. And this usually happens in two different stages. The first stage happens 'in play', where we provide the player with instructions or basically tell them what to. How often do you hear a coach tell a player to 'pass the ball' or to 'shoot'? By doing this, we are taking away the chance to make a decision from the player. We need to let whatever is happening play out, so that we can see what happens. It may be that instead of passing, as we wanted them to do, they dribble past a defender before passing it on to a teammate who is in an even better position than the player we wanted them to pass to. Therefore, not only have we taken the option away from the player to make their own decision, but we have also stopped them from making a better decision on their own. If we do this, not only are we stunting their decision-making development, we are also possibly affecting their self-esteem. Consider being in that player's shoes, having the confidence and positive mind-set to want to take the defender on, but then hearing their coach telling them to pass the ball. Do they go against their coach's instructions? Or do they follow their instructions and pass the ball? Either way it is putting the player in an uncomfortable position.

The second stage where we as coaches can sometimes provide the answer before the player is given an opportunity to decide themselves is in the support we provide afterwards. This can happen in two ways: either we just give the information or answer to the player, or we may ask them a question but give them limited time to make a decision themselves. For example, on receiving the ball, a player makes the wrong decision in terms of the teammate they chose to pass to. Rightly, as a coach we want to support and help the player make a different decision the next time that they find themselves in a similar situation. The first mistake that can be made in such circumstances is that we just tell the player what they could or should have done. If we do this, we are denying the player the opportunity to reflect on the decision that they have made and to consider a different choice that they could have made. If we do not allow the player this reflective process, then they will find it harder to develop their decision making. By just giving the player the answer, we are removing them from the learning process, but by asking them a question and therefore encouraging them to select a different choice, we are putting them at the centre of the process. Allowing a child to be involved in their own learning gives them a feeling of responsibility and therefore a sense of achievement when they find the answer themselves. The player will also be more motivated and eager to learn if they are allowed to be involved or have a say in the process.

However, errors can still be made, even if we include the player in the development of their decision making. The player may be given the opportunity at the start to be involved, but then often the coach is still too eager to provide the answer and does not let the player finish the learning process. If we consider the same scenario of the player making the wrong choice of pass, a coach may ask the player what they might do differently next time. And the player correctly identifies that they would choose a different option to pass to. Quite often at this stage the coach will correctly praise them, but then instead of continuing the learning process the coach will provide the final part of the answer along with their praise: 'Well done. That's right, you could have passed it to so-and-so, as they were in a better position to receive the pass.' So though the player has identified that they have could have chosen a different teammate to pass to, they have not been given the chance to decide which teammate. Quite often as coaches we need to follow up our first question with a second – and possibly even a third – question to ensure that the player is involved in the whole process.

This chapter has just touched upon the vast and foremost topic of player development. Due to its complexity and the amount of material to deliberate, it would not be possible to do it justice here. However, there are some key take-home messages that, if we follow, will have a huge impact on the advancement of the player's development and the type of player that they become. When they first begin their journey, and for the majority of the time, if not all of the time, that they spend with us as a coach, they are children, not small adults and they are not ready to play the full version of the game. The process to prepare them for this final form of the game is a long process that should not be rushed, because it does not need to be. As coaches we should not be in a hurry to get them to the next phase of their development. Let them enjoy and experience the stage that they are currently in, as once they leave it, they are unlikely to return back to it. We should concentrate on what the players need to learn and practice at their particular stage of development and then use these as building blocks to allow the player to move on to the next stage and eventually form together to make the finished article. Finally, we need to remember that there are four aspects to a player's performance and they are all equally important. Often as coaches we might concentrate on or only be aware of two of the four aspects, these being the technical and physical sides of the game. The psychological and social elements, however, are just as important and can easily be added to practices by simply giving the players both freedom and responsibility. What we cannot do, though, is treat all the players the same. We need to recognise that the team is made up of individual players and, therefore, they will all have different needs across all four aspects of their performance.

CHAPTER 5
UNDERSTANDING YOUR PLAYERS

Possibly the greatest challenge we will face when coaching soccer is that it is a team game and therefore when planning and delivering a session, it is aimed at a number of players, yet all of those players will have different levels of ability, will be at a different stage of their development and will have different needs. So a practice that is suitable for two or three players on the squad could be too easy for some players and too difficult for the rest of them. This can also change from session to session, with a player that found the previous session too difficult finding the current session too easy. We also have to take into consideration the four different aspects of performance that were discussed in the previous chapter which can then increase the range of differences between the players even further. Figure 1 shows how two players on a squad can easily have a range of abilities across the four aspects of the performance. The first player has good social and psychological skills, but struggles a little technically and more so physically. Whilst the second player is very good technically and has good physical attributes, they are not as strong psychologically as player one and they find the social aspect of the game really difficult. Therefore, the experience that these two players have in a practice will be completely different.

These differences across the four aspects of performance are not just restricted to different players; there can also be a variance in the same player's ability, depending on the topic of the session. Figure 2 represents how a single player's ability could differ within two different sessions. It could be that within a session that has a focus on passing they have good technical ability, as well as a good understanding of when and where they should pass the ball, and because of this high level of ability they have high levels of self-esteem. And with passing not needing as many physical requirements, compared to other elements of the game, such as running with the ball or finishing, their physical ability could be described as being average. If we then put this player into a session which has a focus on dribbling, technically they are not as comfortable as they are when passing the ball, and because of this they are not as confident and positive on the ball. But their physical attributes are more noticeable in this type of practice. Therefore, a player could quite easily look like two completely different players in the space of just two sessions.

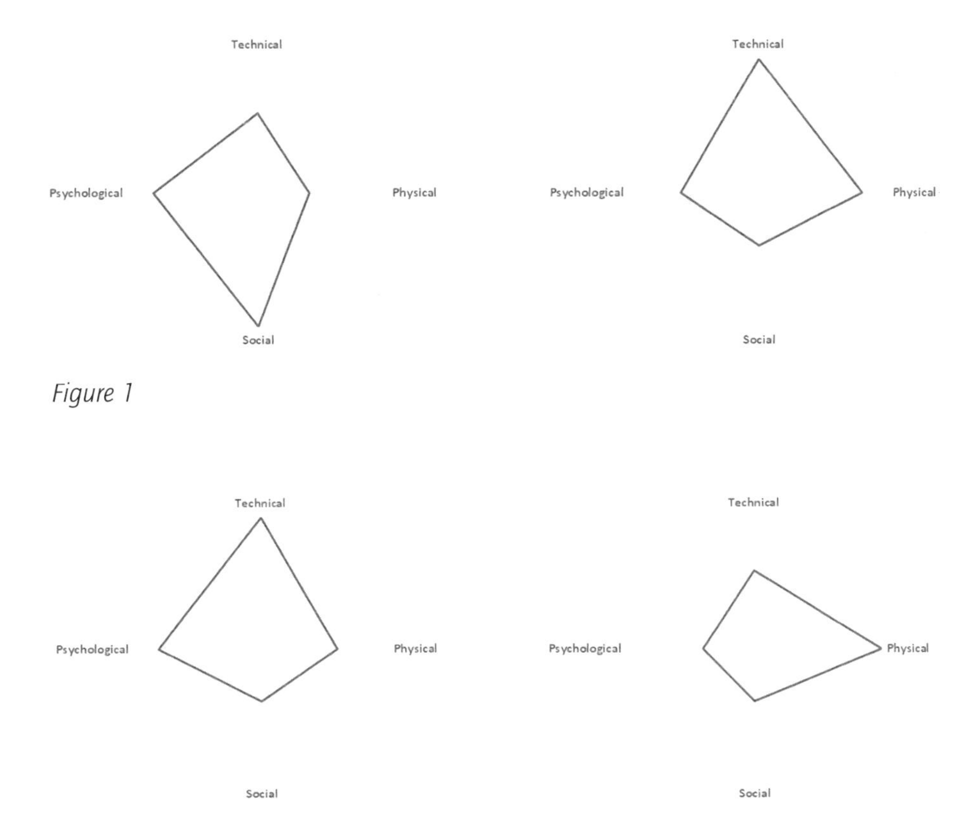

Figure 1

Figure 2

At this stage it should be made clear that it is not expected, nor is it realistic, to think that a practice should be adapted to meet the needs of every individual player within it. However, it is feasible to make changes or additions to a practice that can make it more suitable for all the different players within it. Doing so will allow the coach to help support the development of all the players rather than just a few. By first of all understanding that there will be different types of players within every practice and then recognising which exact players will need more help than others, and which will need to be challenged more, plans can be made to accommodate the differentiation that will occur within every session.

In chapter 3 the STEP model was first introduced as a tool that can be used within the initial planning stage of a session. By using one or more elements of the model, a practice set-up could be changed to ensure that it is relevant to the topic of the session. However, the STEP model can also be used to adapt a practice to allow for differentiation; this can be done from the start, with the players split into separate practices. The model can then be used to create slight changes in the set-up of the different areas. Or if there is just one practice area, the model can be used to provide different rules or challenges just for certain individuals or small groups of players. It can also be used throughout a practice to progress it and make it more challenging. Again, this can be for individuals, small groups or every player. The main thing to remember when introducing these progressions is that they must be relevant to both the topic of the session and the player or players.

Differentiation Within Mirrored Practices Using STEP

When we split the players across a number of practices that are set up the same, this is referred to as 'mirror practices'. This is shown within *Practice Six*, where the players are put into pairs and are all working in exactly the same area, trying to achieve exactly the same task. *Practice Six (d)* shows how these mirrored practices could be adapted slightly to meet the need for extra players, with the players now working in threes instead of pairs. The same principle can be applied to bring differentiation to the practices, so that players can be challenged in a way that meets their specific needs for the particular focus of the session. When applying differentiation to mirrored practices, you are basically using a number of progressions that you would normally use within a practice, but you are just fast-tracking some players through the progressions, allowing them to start where some of the other players are looking to progress to. This also links back to the player's psychological development of self-esteem. In chapter 4, the need for players to be able to achieve success within a practice was essential to keeping them motivated and to building self-esteem. Therefore, we need to put them in a practice where it is possible for them to find success, but then if we want them to develop, we need to progress the practice to make it more difficult.

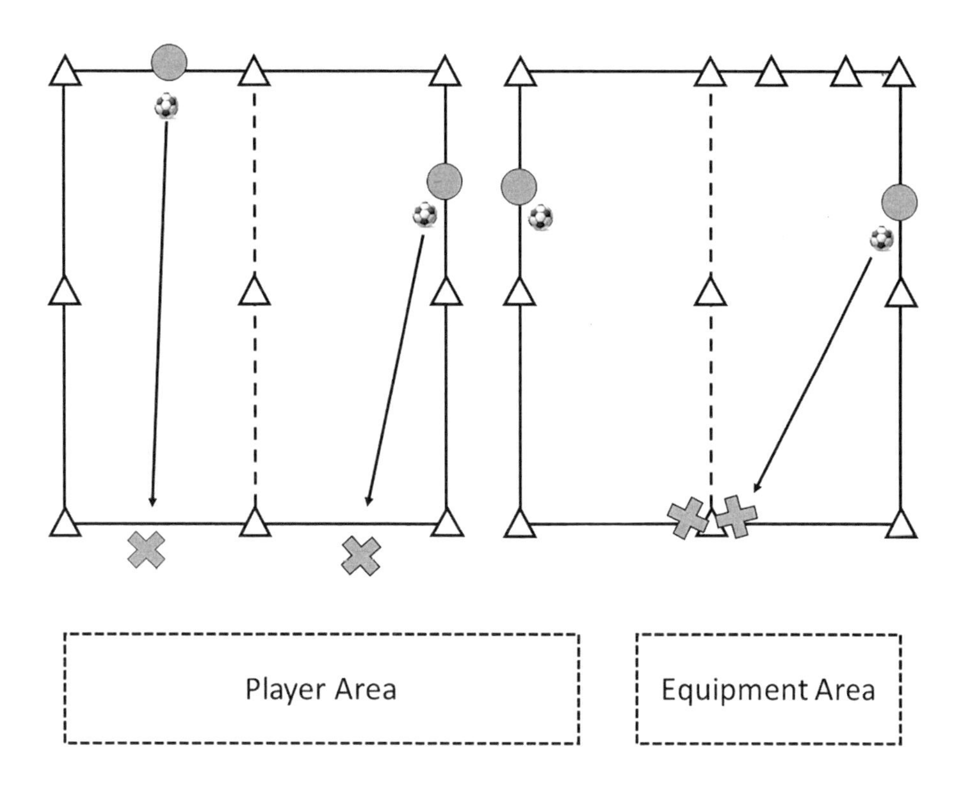

Practice Six (e)

The defender plays the ball into the attacker who looks to dribble the ball over the defender's line. If the defender wins the ball, they look to dribble over the attacker's line. After each go, rotate the roles of the players.

The four practices within *Practice Six (e)* get progressively more difficult and challenging for the players. But that does not mean that all of the players have to start at the first practice and work their way through the different progressions; they can start at different places and then look to progress from their starting point. If we know our players, we will be able to identify which players will be more successful than others and which may find it particularly difficult. Once we have done this, we can then allocate players to specific practices within the planning stage. The first practice involves the attacking player receiving the ball from the defender and then looking to dribble over the far line where the defender started the practice. The second practice is exactly the same set-up, but using 'player' from the STEP process, the defender has been positioned closer to the attacking player, providing them less time before they are closed down by the defender. The third practice also uses player elements from STEP. Now, along with the defender starting closer, the attacking player starts in the corner rather than the middle of the area, giving them less space and options once they have received the ball. Finally, the fourth practice uses tasks and equipment from STEP, with the attacking players now also being asked to dribble through one of two gates instead of the whole line being available.

It is important to remember that we cannot start any player within the fourth practice unless there is another progression that has been planned so that the players can progress, should they be ready to do so. It is also important to remember that just because there are a number of progressions within the practice that every player needs to work their way through every one. A player should only move on to the next progression when they are ready to do so, i.e., if they are finding regular success in the current format of the practice and they now need to be challenged further. Other options available for this particular practice to advance it and challenge the players further could be to alter the 'space' by making it narrower to reduce the space to get past the defender, or to lengthen the area to increase the distance to get to the end line. Or through equipment, by reducing the size of the ball or by using bibs as a 'tail' on the attacker, with the defender now just needing to grab the bib, instead of actually winning the ball.

Similar adjustments can be made to other one-versus-one practices, such as *Practice Twenty*. For instance, some of the changes that were made to *Practice Six* can also be made to *Practice Twenty*. Changing the starting position of both the defender and attacking player can increase the difficulty of this practice, as do reducing the size of the ball and decreasing the size of the area. Or the STEP process can be used to make similar changes that are relevant for this particular practice. The positioning or the size of the gates can be adjusted or the attacking player could be given the additional task of once they have travelled through a gate, can they turn back into the area? The format for providing differentiation within mirror practices is to just make slight adjustments to the practices that move the practice up a level in terms of difficulty. At first glance, the practices would all look the same and the players would look as if there are doing exactly the same thing, but the small changes made to each of the individual practices allow the players to be challenged at a level that is relevant to their specific needs for the session topic. This means that the progressions that have been planned do not have to be followed in a set order, they can be introduced to meet the needs of the players. For instance, players may start in the first practice for *Practice Six (e)*, but then for their next

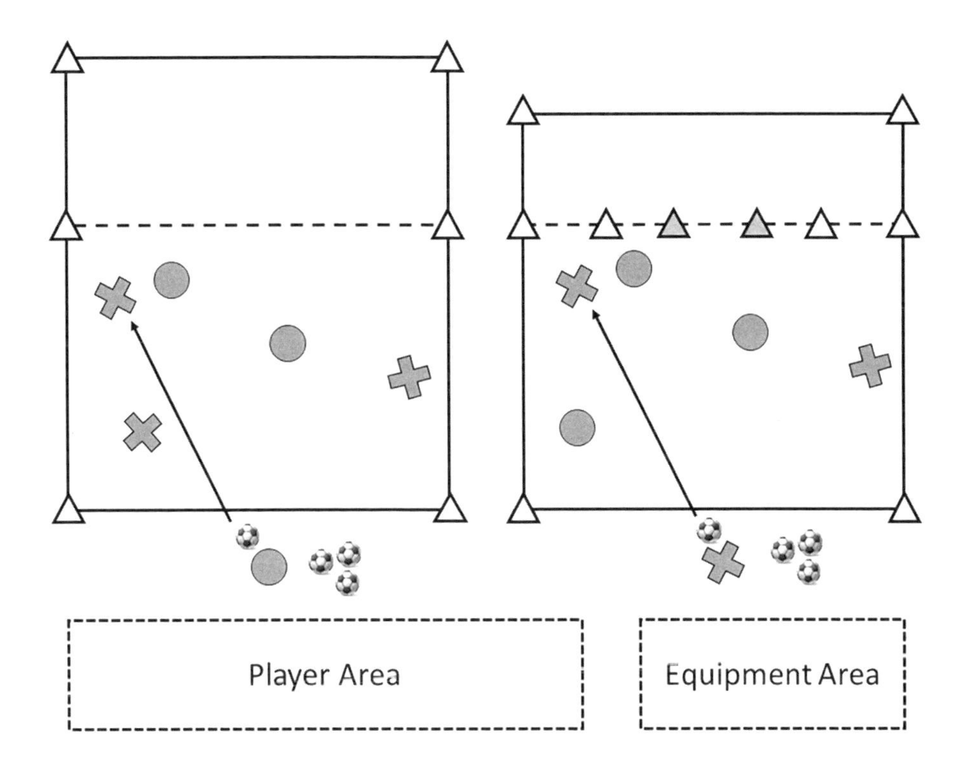

Practice Ten (b)

Server plays the ball into one of the three attacking players who look to release a player into the second area by playing a pass over the line that divides the two areas (players cannot dribble the ball over the line). Once this has been achieved, one defender can enter the area and the attacking player looks to dribble over the end line. If needed, the attacking players can pass back to the server and if the defenders win the ball, they look to pass the ball back to the target player to achieve a point.

progression the defender starts from the same position but the attacker moves to their new starting position. The reason for this is that the players in this particular practice still need an adequate amount of time to receive the ball and control it; therefore, they still need the current distance between them and the defender. However, once they are dribbling they are having a lot of success by using the same skill. If we reduce the space on one side of the grid by starting the player on that side, they will find it very difficult to execute a skill that takes them to this section of the area; therefore, they will need to use a different skill instead to get past the defender.

So far, we have only looked at mirror practices being used in one-versus-one practices, but they are also used in 'small-numbered' practices such as three versus one or four versus two, where the squad of players has been split into two or three groups. Not only do these types of practices allow more ball contact time for the players compared to practices that involve the whole squad (squad practice), they are also quite often less challenging for the players as the reduced amount of players means there are fewer decisions to make. Using these types of practices also allows for differentiation between the two or three different areas that are being used, just as we would for the one-versus-one practices.

A number of changes have been made to the second practice within *Practice Ten* (b) that will challenge the players more in a variety of ways. All of these changes should not be implemented in one go, but they demonstrate how two groups of players can be working on exactly the same topic in nearly identical environments, but with different levels of difficulty to meet their needs. If we go through the STEP process stage by stage, we can see how each element of the model can be used to bring differentiation into a session. In terms of space, the size of the second area has been reduced, and it could be argued that this makes it easier for the attacking players to score a point once they are in the area, as they have less distance to travel to get across the end line. However, the focus of the practice is the pass into the second area for a teammate to receive, and by reducing the depth of this area, there is more emphasis on the weight and accuracy of the pass being right. With regard to the task element of STEP, a number of different rules could be added to the practice to increase the level of difficulty. This could include the pass that releases the player into the second area having to be a player's second or even first touch. This is particularly relevant to the practice, due to the situation it is trying to replicate in a game. Other tasks that can be added to the practice could be setting the attacking players a set number of passes to complete before they can make the pass that releases the player, or flipping this and only allowing the attacking players a set number of passes. This would depend on what was occurring beforehand within the practice. Are the players finding it too easy to make the pass and so keep doing it almost straight away after receiving the ball from the server? Or are they finding success, but only when it is an obvious and simple pass? In terms of players, the role of the 'server' has been switched, so there is now a three versus two in the area in favour of the defending team. Different rules could be applied to this to affect the level of difficulty this adds to the practice. The server could be allowed to enter the area as soon as the pass has been made, or they might be made to wait until a certain number of passes have been made, or they may have to remain outside of the area and just act as a support player. Finally, cones have been used to create three gates which the attacking players must pass through when passing into the second area. The two gaps between the three gates represent opposition players and therefore the pass has to be made either between or around these two 'defenders'.

Differentiation Within Squad Practices Using STEP

The more difficult task for a coach can be introducing differentiation within a squad practice, where all the players are involved in the same practice. Therefore, whatever changes are made to progress the practice and make it more demanding usually has an impact on every player, which is obviously not ideal, as not every player will be ready for whichever progression is introduced. However, that said, it is possible to achieve this and a number of strategies that can be used have already been discussed within some of the previous chapters. First of all, we can look at the allocation of players and areas, and how these can be literally separated, so that the players are situated within areas that meet their needs in terms of the session topic.

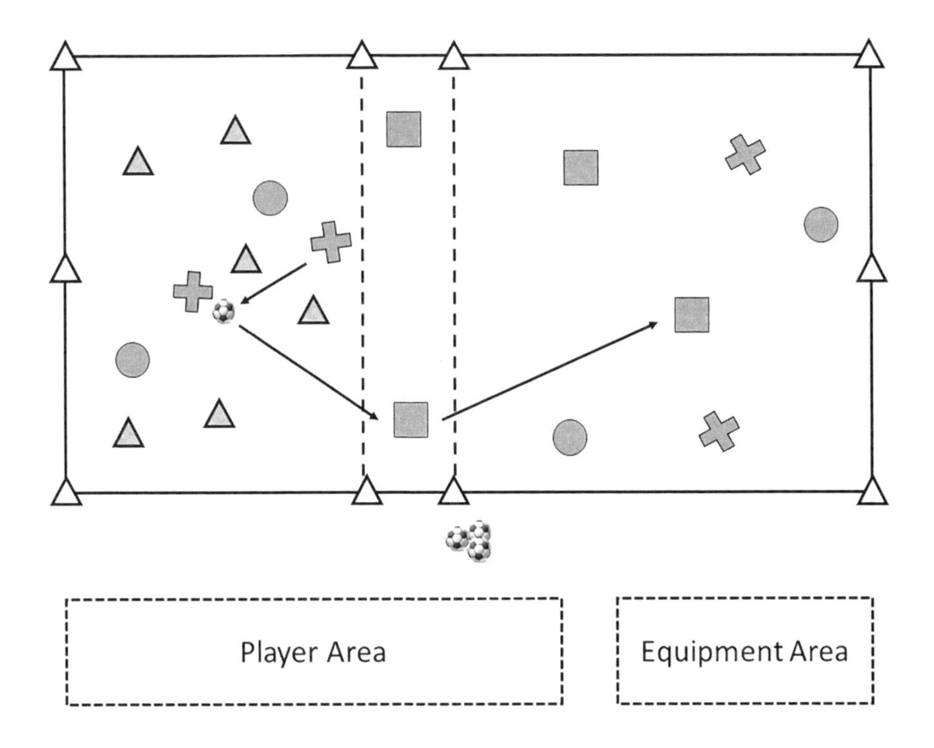

Practice Nine (d)

Players are split into two teams with the teams split between two areas. In between the two zones there is a central zone where there are two support players. Teams have to complete a set number of passes before they look to transfer the ball from one zone to the other via the central zone using one of the two support players.

With *Practice Nine (d)* there are a number of differences between the two areas. Again, it is important to stress that not all of these differences need to be in place and probably should not be, as any one of them will make it more difficult for the players in that particular side of the practice. As coaches we sometimes think that there is a written rule that if we split an area in half, then each half of the area needs to be exactly the same size. Having one area slightly larger or smaller than the other area is a quick and easy way to introduce differentiation to a practice and quite often the players will be unaware that there is any contrast in the two sizes. Other differences between the two halves of the area, however, are more noticeable. One half of the area has 'floaters' which make it easier for the team in possession to retain the ball and then transfer it to the other side where there are no 'floaters' and instead there are a number of gates, with the teams having to pass through at least one gate before they can attempt to send the ball across. Other possible options that could be used are having one side of the area having to complete a set number of passes before they can pass the ball across or 'floaters' who could be added to both sides, but on one side they support the team in possession, whilst on the other side they support the team out of possession. The key factor to differentiation within these types of practices is obviously the allocation of the players which, to ensure the session runs smoothly and with a high percentage of ball rolling time, needs to be organised beforehand. This is where our understanding of the players is essential, as is knowing which players would be most suited to each specific area.

Another strategy that we have already discussed, and which can be used within a squad practice to add differentiation, is to adapt a scoring system so that there are different levels of scoring, which the players can then choose from during the practice. By doing so, it would be expected that the more advanced players within the practice would try to attempt the harder way to win points to get the higher reward. In *Practice Twelve (b)* players win points by scoring in one of the four goals on the outside of the area. Within the last chapter, different scoring systems for this practice were discussed. For example, more points could be awarded for goals that are scored with a first touch finish or with a player's non-preferred foot. This could be extended further by using differently sized goals, with more points being awarded for goals scored in the smaller goals, or the goals could be positioned at different distances from the area. Goalkeepers could also be added to protect some of the goals, or targets could be added to some of the goals, such as placing a ball on top of a cone and awarding bonus points to players who hit it with their shot. Despite any of these options being available to every player within the practice, it still provides differentiation to the practice. If we take the targets within the goals, the players who are not as strong as the other players at finishing will just concentrate on trying to score a goal, whilst the stronger players will not be happy with just scoring – they will want the bonus points. Therefore, positioning the targets in an area of the goal where you want players to aim their shots, i.e., in the corners, will help the players with more ability progress from just shooting into the goal to placing their shots in the corners. This type of strategy of introducing differentiation can sometimes also provide the added bonus of encouraging the players that we consider as having less capability to have a go at the more challenging aspects of the practice, something that they might not get the opportunity to do in a mirrored practice.

Squad practices can also be unopposed, i.e., a technical practice and these too can be challenging for the coach to incorporate differentiation. But with careful planning and organisation it is most definitely achievable. In *Practice Eleven (c)* gates were introduced for the players to pass the ball through within their pairs and these gates can be used in a number of ways to challenge players. By using different colours, the players can be given a range of tasks that meet their particular needs. The first way in which the different colours can be used is by using them to identify the size of the gates. For instance, if three different colours are used, one colour can represent 'small' gates, another 'medium' and the final colour would be for the largest-sized gates. It is then the choice of the coach whether or not this information is shared with the players. The decision as to whether or not the information is shared will probably depend upon how the differently sized gates are used. First of all, pairs could be told to use specifically coloured gates only, with the stronger players being allocated to the smaller size gates, etc. In this situation, the coach may not choose to share with the players that there is an assortment of sizes; it is then likely that the players will not notice that there are any variations and will just presume everyone is doing exactly the same task. Alternatively, the players may be allowed to pass through any gate, but are informed that each colour represents a difference size. Players will then approach the practice in a range of ways. Some will treat each type of gate the same, some will actually avoid the small gates, whilst others will give the smaller gates more respect and will take more care with their pass through these particular gates.

Another way in which the coloured gates can be used is by giving the players a specific route to follow. Again different pairs can be handed different routes, with the higher level players given more complicated routes, which can be achieved by increasing the distances that they have to travel and the number of times that they have to change direction. As before, the players do not need to be told about the range of routes and so the practice will look identical to those taking part and to anyone watching it, but underneath, due to the careful planning involved, the players will be receiving an individual experience that is relevant and appropriate to them. The different colours could also represent different tasks, for example, the type of pass that the players have to complete. This could be a specific foot that they have to use or a certain part of their foot; for example, they may have to complete a disguised pass using the outside of their foot. Again, the players may avoid certain coloured gates or approach them differently.

Other ways in which differentiation can be added to a technical practice includes using similar strategies that are used in other types of practices. However, these strategies can be less discreet and are more noticeable to the players, compared to the ones we have just discussed. This is another key element of knowing your players. Depending on the individuals in the squad, a coach will need to decide which type of strategy to use when introducing differentiation to their practices. Most players will be aware of all of the other players and they will compare themselves to these other players and will subsequently rank where they see themselves within the squad. When doing so, some players will be comfortable with where they see themselves and some will not, in that they may believe some players have what they perceive as a greater level of ability, but do not want others to see this as well. In addition to this, they will also analyse where they think you as a coach see them and the other players within the squad. Though as coaches we will not be classifying the players in order of their ability – we are just identifying what level of support they need – some players will not see this and may see the support they are being given as an indicator of where the coach ranks them within the squad. Therefore, we need to be able to recognise how adding differentiation to a practice could impact the players and then choose a strategy that is suitable for them. So in *Practice Eleven (c)* we could give the players who are doing well a smaller ball, to make their task more difficult. This, however, will be a clear indicator to the rest of the group that these players are currently doing better than them and therefore we need to be sure that they are unperturbed by this.

How players perceive differentiation within their training, however, can be changed so that they do not see it as a ranking process, but as a development tool that will support them in their learning and is personalised to meet their individual needs. This will mainly be achieved through the environment that we create as a coach, by using the qualities and characteristics discussed within chapter 2. However, the process can be quickened and enhanced further by demonstrating to the players that you understand each of them as a player and that all players on the squad are equally important and each will receive the same amount of support. This can be demonstrated to the players through the use of 'individual challenges' which can be used in any form of practice and in different ways that will control the level of difficulty.

Differentiation Using Individual Challenges

Before we look at how to use individual challenges within our coaching, it is important first of all to understand what they are and what they are not. When giving a player an individual challenge we are asking them to try something, we are not telling them that they have to do something; it is not a rule or an instruction. Therefore, the wording we use when giving a player a challenge is essential to its success as a development tool. If we look at a player that is predominantly right-footed and does not like to use their left foot, telling them that they can only use their left foot within a practice will only result in them probably not wanting the ball first of all, and then if they do receive it, they will most likely lose possession. Therefore, not only will we probably have no effect on the development of their left foot, we will probably cause a loss of self-esteem and confidence in themselves. The other thing to consider when we restrict players to using just one foot is that the environment then becomes completely unrealistic to them. One of the main reasons that we encourage players to be able to use both feet is so that when it is the right time to use their non-preferred foot they feel comfortable using it and it feels natural to them – they do not need to think about it, they just use it. If a player is restricted in a practice to just using their left foot, when the ball comes to their right foot, they will have to readjust their positioning or use their left foot to try to control it in an unorthodox manner. Yet in a game we would want them to use their right foot. Therefore, we are forcing them to do something that we would not want them to do in a game. So instead of giving them an instruction, we should provide them with a challenge.

When providing a player with a challenge, key phrases such as 'can you' or 'how many times are you able to' should be used to let the player know that they are not being restricted in any way, but are just being asked to try to do something. By doing this, not only are we making it a more realistic environment for the player, we are also providing them with freedom and helping them develop their decision making. So if a player is challenged to 'use your left foot where possible', they will look for opportunities within the practice to use their left foot and over time they will recognise when they should use it. To help them with the challenge, the coach can provide praise when they actually use their left foot, no matter what the outcome is, as they are receiving praise for just attempting the challenge. We can also provide further support as a coach by making the player aware of any missed opportunities that they had to achieve the challenge, so if the player receives the ball with their right foot when they should have used their left foot, the player could be asked: 'What should you have done there?' or 'What might you do differently next time?' This prompts the players to reflect on what they just did, whilst also giving them a gentle reminder of their challenge. Though a restriction of having to use your left foot might lead to that player having more touches with their left foot compared to using an individual challenge, these touches will be unrealistic and therefore it will not support them in developing their non-preferred foot. If, because of the individual challenge, the player has just one more touch with their left foot compared to what they would usually have, this will have a much greater impact on their development and will be much more beneficial to them in the long term.

It is also important that when we are planning or setting challenges we not only consider the individual needs of the players, but also the focus of the session. If a player needs support with their dribbling, but the session has a focus on passing, then we need to keep the focus on passing. We cannot provide a challenge such as, 'Can you have at least five touches of the ball?' This could actually reduce the number of times they pass the ball, as they might lose possession trying to achieve the five touches. Though the player needs this type of challenge to help in their development of dribbling with the ball, we must only use it when the focus of the session is about or linked to dribbling. Similarly, we need to ensure that the challenge will develop the player in a way that's related to the topic of the session. If a player is doing well within a passing practice, quite often we will revert to limiting the player to a small number of touches. But if we limit them to two touches, for instance, we are challenging their first touch rather than their ability to pass the ball, because if their first touch is not quite good enough it may result in them losing the ball or not being able to execute the pass correctly. The challenge needs to make the actual passing of the ball more demanding, so we could ask the player to try to always pass the ball forwards, as a forward pass usually requires more accuracy than a square pass or a pass back.

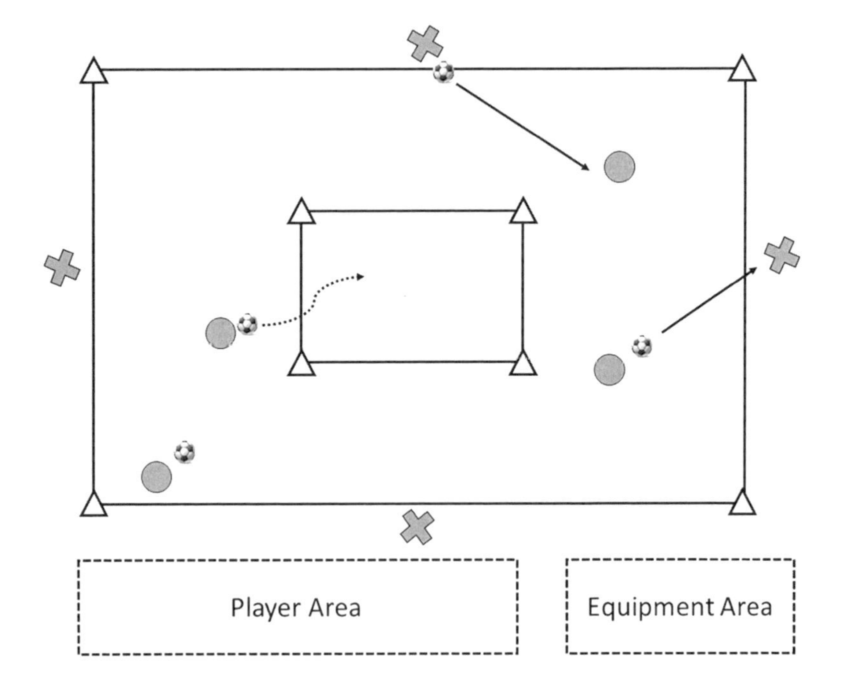

Practice Twenty-Eight

The players are split into two groups, with one group working within the area and the other group spread around the outside of the area, acting as servers. Players within the area receive a pass from a server and then must travel through the centre square before passing the ball to another server who does not have a ball. The player then receives another ball and repeats the process. The roles of the two groups are rotated regularly.

The focus of *Practice Twenty-Eight* is receiving to play forward, because the player always has to travel through the central square before they can release the ball; they are having to travel in the opposite direction from where they receive the ball. The environment created within the practice looks to replicate a midfielder receiving the ball from a defender and then playing forward. Therefore, there is an emphasis on the player in the central area receiving the ball with an open body and on the back foot. So the type of challenges that could be used within this practice could start with: 'Can you control the pass with the foot that is the farthest away from the player passing the ball?' and 'Can your first touch take you towards the centre box?' This is for the players that need extra support. Whilst the players that need a more difficult task might be challenged with: 'Can your first touch take you into the centre box?' or 'Can you receive on your back foot and then use your other foot to take you into the centre box?' All of these challenges are linked to the focus of the session and provide different levels of challenge for the players. Once the coach has planned these possible challenges, their next task is to observe the players within the practice and identify which player requires which challenge. It is likely that the coach will have a good idea before the practice begins of the requirements for each player, and it is probably possible to present them with the challenge before the practice even starts, but it is important to provide them with an opportunity to demonstrate what they can do first and give them a chance to surprise us. This need to allow time to just 'observe' will be discussed further in the next chapter.

It is also possible to affect the level of the challenge by the way in which we deliver it to the player, specifically within opposed practices. Within *Practice Twelve (b)* a player who is doing well within the practice could be given the challenge of 'scoring with their first touch'. How this challenge is presented to the player will determine the level of difficulty for the player. The player could be given the challenge away from the other players so that only they know what their challenge is. If we do this, we need to be mindful that their teammates will not be aware and there is a possibility they could get frustrated if they see this player keep trying to score with their first touch. They could also unknowingly make the task harder for them as the pass that a team-mate plays into them does not allow them to have a first-time shot. Therefore, it is often the case that a player is given their challenge in front of their teammates or they are instructed to let their teammates know about it. To increase the level of difficulty for the player, the most effective way of giving them the challenge is in front of all the players, so that the opposition is aware of it as well. Allowing the opposition players to have knowledge of the challenge gives them the opportunity to prevent the player from achieving it. So as the ball is travelling to the player, opposition players know they will be looking to strike the ball straight away and therefore they can defend against this appropriately. Whereas if they are unaware of the challenge, they may not be expecting it, providing the player more time and opportunity to execute the first time shot.

Another good example of how the delivery of the challenge can have a major impact on the level of difficulty can be found in any version of *Practice Two*. If a player is dominating within this practice, i.e., they are the player that is seeing a lot of the ball and are often the player that makes the pass into the target player, then as a coach we need to make the experience a lot more difficult. Providing the player the challenge of having to try to touch the ball before it is played into the target player would probably have little effect on their development, as they are probably achieving this already. However, if we provide the player with the same challenge, but make the opposition aware of it, it becomes a completely different experience for them. Now that the opposition are aware that this particular player is looking to receive the ball, they will probably decide to play in a different way. It is likely that they reduce the space that this player has when their team are in possession of the ball; this could be in the form of being man-marked or just being closed down more quickly as the ball is travelling to them or once they have possession. This is particularly relevant to this player, as if they are dominating in this type of practice then they will more than likely do the same in a game, and if they do, then it is also likely that they will be defended closely. So we are therefore preparing them for the environment they will find themselves in within a game. The other return we will get from this challenge, in addition to the player that was given the challenge having to work harder to find space to receive the ball and having to retain possession under pressure, is that the other players on the team will also now find the task more difficult. Beforehand they would probably look to pass the ball to the player that is dominating the practice; now if they choose to do this they will need to take more care with the pass or they will now have to look for a different option – are they now going to be the player that passes into the target player? Also as the dominating player is now expected to have less of the ball, their teammates will subsequently have an increased amount of time on it.

These individual challenges can be expanded to group challenges and are applied in exactly the same way, but are used when a number of players – rather than just one – need challenging or supporting in some way. Realistically, we cannot keep providing each individual player within a practice an individual challenge throughout the entire session. Plus, providing the players with a group challenge helps develop some of the social skills that were discussed in the previous chapter: communication, teamwork and ownership. So if we use *Practice Two* again, but this time with the scenario that one of the teams as a whole are doing well, a group challenge could be used instead of setting a number of individual challenges. For instance, the team could be set the target of completing a set number of passes before they can pass into the target player or they could be challenged with trying to use a limited number of touches. The more difficult part for the coach would be to provide the team that are not doing as well with a suitable challenge. The key to this is identifying why it is they are not scoring points – is it the fact that they are just not able to get the ball? Or is it that they can get possession of the ball, but they are just unable to get it to the target player? Whatever the reason, the challenge needs to provide the players with a gentle nudge towards what they are struggling to achieve. So if they can get possession of the ball but they are struggling to get it to the target player, they could be set the challenge of passing it to the target player within a set number of passes. Reducing the amount of passes prevents the team from just keeping possession and puts the focus back on getting the ball to the target player.

When planning these challenges, it can be helpful for the coach to write them down on small cards or pieces of paper and use them within the actual session. Not only do they provide a helpful prompt for the coach to give the challenges out to the players, but they also are a reminder of the different challenges that are available to use as well. It is much easier to consider the range of challenges that can be used whilst planning, rather than when you are in the frantic environment of the session. The small cards are also an effective way of passing the challenge on to the player; the player can be called over and handed the card for them to read, before passing it back to the coach. Getting them to read the card will help ensure that they digest the information. If we remove the player from the practice and give them the challenge verbally, quite often they will be distracted by the action that is continuing without them and therefore may not be fully focused on what is being said. The players usually also enjoy receiving the challenge in the form of a small card, especially if they get to keep the card whilst they share the information with the rest of the team, before returning it back to the coach.

Individual challenges can be a really effective tool for turning a practice that is generic for the whole squad into a more personal experience for the player where they can work on a specific area of the session topic that is particularly important for their development. In addition to this, providing individual challenges to some of the players can also have a positive effect on other players within the practice. Challenging some of the stronger players within a practice can make the environment more suitable for the other players, i.e., it is now challenging for them, but not so difficult that they are not able to find any success. The key to the success of the challenge is in selecting the right challenge that is not only relevant to the topic of the session but also meets the needs of the player. This can be achieved through careful planning and understanding the individual needs of the players. But, just as importantly, it is by simply having a go and gaining further experience and finding out what works for the players as individuals and as a group.

Managing Behaviour

Before we leave the topic of understanding the players that we are working with, a subject that comes up a lot is how to deal with disruptive behaviour. But before we look at how we can manage the session – not necessarily to deal with disruptive behaviour, but to put measures in place that will help prevent it in the first place – it is important to remember who we are working with and that we need to manage our own expectations. Within chapter 2, we touched upon the fact that they are children and not small adults, and as such we cannot expect them to behave in the same manner that we do or act in a way that is similar to how we want them to. The main motivation for a child to play soccer and to come to training is to have fun and spend time with their friends. To improve and develop as a player will not be very high on their list of priorities. And it was also noted that children will become disengaged quite easily if they are finding something too difficult or too easy, or if they become bored with the activity. In addition to this, other general characteristics of children that we need to be aware of include: needing frequent reassurance, being sensitive to what others think, they are eager to please and be liked by both their peers and also adults, their moods can change quickly and they are usually very talkative. All of this knowledge is imperative, as it will help us to understand who we are working with and why they behave the way that they do.

From the outset the players need to be given rules. Providing children with limits and boundaries allows them to think in an orderly way and get along with other children and adults. Children actually want a structured environment, despite their protestations to the contrary. If as adults we are permissive and inconsistent, it can be unsettling to a child and provoke uncertainty. However, they will also look to test the limits of these boundaries, as it is in their nature to do so. They will often do this to see how the people that they see as their caregivers will react. They will also do it to test the limits, to see what they can get away with and to try to assert their authority. We therefore need to first of all anticipate this behaviour from them, so that when it does happen, it is not unexpected or comes as a shock. This is particularly important, as we are more likely to react without fully thinking if the behaviour is unexpected. It is not enough for players to just learn and follow the rules that we have put in place. Instead we need to help them learn to set boundaries for themselves, whilst also respecting those of others. For them to be able to do this they need to be able to recognise what others want and need, but at the same time express what they want and need as well. So when we talk about boundaries, it is about identifying and understanding our own needs and then respectfully understanding the needs of everyone else.

The introduction of the equipment and player areas allow a session to be organised and safe for both the players and the coaches. Rules are put in place that nothing can be removed from the equipment area unless the coach says it is okay to do so; this ensures that the players are not able to use anything unsupervised. To begin with, the players will undoubtedly test the boundaries on this rule. They will see whether or not they can take a ball from the area and play with it before they are given permission to do so. We need to therefore foresee this behaviour and be prepared for it, and this does not include having some form of punishment or consequences in place. Instead we need to help the players first of all remember what the rules are and then also why they have been put in place. By doing so we are supporting the player in their development of understanding rules and other people's boundaries. So if we see a player remove a ball from the equipment area before they are given permission to do so, instead of punishing the player, we can ask them two simple questions. Can you remind me what the rules are for removing anything from the equipment area? Which is then followed up by: And why do we have this rule? Once they have answered the questions, we can then politely ask them to put the ball back and then thank them once they have.

This strategy of reminding players of the rules that are in place and the reasons why can be used throughout a session and it can be made to be even more effective if the players are part of the process that produces the rules. It is first of all easier for them to remember them and then also easier for you as the coach to remind the players of the rule and to help them understand that what they are doing is not the right thing to do. Instead of a coach asking the player: What is the rule about taking things out of the equipment area? The coach can ask: What is the rule that you made about taking things from the equipment area? This then puts a more personal meaning on the question and also on the action of the player. They are now basically breaking their own rules and not those of the coach. When producing these rules, the players will probably need some guidance; plus there will also be some specific rules that you will definitely want to be included. So we might need to provide them with a gentle nudge towards selecting the right rules. Again by asking the right questions we can support the players in finding the solutions: What rule could we put in place about taking items from the equipment area? Though we may have pointed them in the direction that we wanted them to go, it will be the players that produce the actual rule.

Once the rules have been created they can be made available to everyone through a 'code of conduct'. This can be shared with both the players and parents at the start of the season and, if possible, displayed somewhere permanently where they are always on view. They can then be used throughout the season whenever they are needed to remind the players about the rules that as a group they produced. If there is a specific rule that the group is no longer following, for instance, all players help collect and put away the equipment at the end of each session, they could be reminded that at the start of the season they decided that they would all work together to gather it in. This could be just a verbal reminder or a visual reminder by bringing a copy to training, or if some form of social media group is available it could be sent out electronically. Whichever method is available and the most suitable for the group should be used and it should be done so as to provide the players with a reminder and not used as part of a punishment.

If a player is not demonstrating the correct level of behaviour, the go-to strategy is quite often to punish the child. This could be that they sit out of the practice for a while or they do not get to play in the game at the end of the session. However, we need to remember that they are there to play and train, not to sit out and watch. As mentioned earlier within this section, children look for frequent reassurance and are eager to please and be liked by adults. A player will sometimes behave in the wrong manner, as they want some form of recognition from either their team-mates or the coach, but whenever possible we must try to ignore this type of behaviour. Of course this is not always possible, especially if it is having an impact on other players or if it is putting someone at risk. In these circumstances we need to intervene and try to redirect the behaviour through reminders of the expectations that we have of them and also the rules and guidelines to which they agreed. In most other cases we should not provide them with what they were aiming to achieve from their behaviour: the attention of the coach. So instead of acknowledging bad or poor behaviour, we should look to ignore this and in its place we can recognise and reward good behaviour. This strategy is often referred to as 'catching them being good'.

If a player arrives to training and immediately takes a ball from the equipment area without looking at the instructions for the first practice and then proceeds to just kick the ball around, we can ask them to remind us of the rules about what they do when they first arrive at the session. Once they have returned the ball to the equipment area and then checked to see what they have to do, we can provide them with praise for doing so. But then, more importantly, the next time that they arrive at training we need to monitor their behaviour, not to try to catch them misbehaving but to try to catch them being good. If the next time they arrive they follow the rules that have been put in place, i.e., they read the instructions first, then collect anything they need from the equipment area before joining in with the first practice, then we must recognise this and let them know that we have seen them do this through praise. This strategy of catching them being good can be applied throughout all elements of the session and for any type of behaviour, with the aim of changing their behavioural habits so that if they do want to get the attention of others they do so through good behaviour rather than bad behaviour.

Other reasons that the players may misbehave can be because they are either bored or they are finding something too difficult. Both of these can be prevented through practice design and set-up of the session. Boredom usually occurs because players are either finding a practice too easy or they are inactive for too long. Players can become inactive if there is a gap between practices caused by the coach having to set up the next practice or if the coach is talking for too long. Therefore, the organisation and communication skills discussed within chapter 2, and the need for planning that was emphasised with chapter 3, become important tools in a coach's strategy in preventing boredom and possibly poor behaviour. Keeping the players constantly engaged and active prevents them from becoming bored and keeps them focused on a specific task.

The next step is to then ensure that they do not become inactive within the actual practice or lose focus. Players will become inactive if they are forced to queue and wait their turn. We need to ensure that all players are always involved in the practice, even if this means they take on the role of a server and support player, so that they have a focus and need to concentrate on the practice. Then these roles need to be rotated regularly to ensure the player's involvement increases after being the server or support player. A player can also become disengaged if they are finding the practice too easy or if the practice goes on for too long. Children want to be challenged. One of the factors that make video games appealing to them is the challenge of working through different levels that become increasingly more difficult. Using a similar format within our practices by introducing progressions and/or individual challenges can make the environment more stimulating. The flipside of the players finding it too easy is that they may also find a practice too difficult and this too can lead to poor behaviour. If children find something too challenging, they will either lose interest or, more commonly, they will try to mask that they are unable to do what they have been asked to do by distracting their teammates and coach from noticing. They will look to do this by moving away from the task and engaging in something else, and quite often this will involve trying to distract other players from the task as well. In these circumstances we need to recognise that the task is too difficult and make adjustments that will allow the practice to be less demanding, or provide the player with an individual challenge that they can focus on.

Other considerations that we may need to factor in when we are looking to prevent poor behaviour are: Who they will be working with and where will they be doing it? In terms of whom they will be working with, not only does this impact on the level of difficulty of the practice for the player, we must also consider the social implications it can have and the subsequent knock-on effect on their behaviour. Players will obviously behave differently depending on whom they are sharing a practice with. The different relationships that they build with each player on the squad, both inside and outside of the environment of soccer, will influence how an individual behaves when they are allocated with specific teammates. Therefore, when planning which players work with whom, the coach will need to consider how they interact with each other. This does not mean that certain players should always be kept apart. As we looked at earlier, it is important that players get to spend time with all players on the squad, as it is beneficial to their social development. But what we can do as a coach is carefully select when particular players are put together within practices. So these could be practices where there are fewer opportunities for them to be distracted or lose focus, which could then lead to poor behaviour.

Sometimes the location of particular players within the session can also have a direct impact on their behaviour. If we use any of the formats of *Practice Six* as an example, a number of small pitches will need to be used with just two players using each area. Therefore, some consideration might be needed in allocating certain players to the area that they are going to be working in. As well as keeping specific players away from each other by ensuring they are not working in the same area, we may also need to ensure they are not working in the area directly next to each other. In addition to this, putting players in one of the 'end' pitches may provide some of them opportunities to go 'off task' when the coach is not nearby, i.e., at the other end of the practice set-up. To reduce the chances of this happening, the players that are more likely to engage in disruptive behaviour can be allocated to the areas that are situated centrally, so that no matter which pitch the coach is visiting, they will remain in close proximity to the ones in the middle of session.

Overall, instead of considering what we should do if someone does misbehave, we should look at what we can do to prevent it from happening in the first place, i.e., we need to look to prevent bad behaviour rather than punish it. By understanding what specifically triggers a change in behaviour for individual players, strategies can be put in place that will reduce the likelihood of these triggers occurring. So if putting one player with another particular player encourages a change in behaviour in one of or both of the players, then at times these players should be kept apart. But the most effective strategy that we can use is by putting on practices that will not give the players any opportunity to misbehave, but more importantly produce an environment that they will find fun and engaging and stimulating, so that they have no thought of behaving badly. And just as importantly, we need to remember that they are children and as such they are still learning what is right and what is wrong; they are still gaining an understanding of rules and boundaries and will look to test how far they can stretch these. Our role therefore is not to penalise them, but instead help them remember what are the expected levels of behaviour and what they should and should not be doing. Doing so will help to create an environment where every player feels both safe and valued.

CHAPTER 6
REFLECTION DURING THE SESSION

Arguably one of the most difficult aspects of coaching is reflecting on an on-going session and understanding what exactly is happening and more importantly why. Too often as coaches we will look to blame the players if we believe the practice is not working as we had imagined or they are unable to do what we wanted them to do, rather than looking at the practice design and set-up, which is usually the cause of the problem. Similarly, when we do identify that there is a problem, we are reluctant to make any changes, because we see it as admitting that we made a mistake and we do not want to admit this to ourselves or anybody else who may be watching, whether this is other coaches and/or parents. This is a natural reaction for anyone to have, as making a mistake can be hard for people to digest and as a result we will often choose to 'double down' rather than actually face the fact that we have made a mistake. As a result, confirmation bias kicks in, which makes us seek out some form of evidence to prove what we believe is right. So as coaches we look for evidence that proves it is not the fault of the practice, because when we planned the practice we obviously thought it was suitable and relevant for both the players and the topic, otherwise we would not have planned it that way. Therefore, there must be another factor that is causing the issue, and the only other factor that we can envisage is the players, so we look to them to do better, when in a number of instances this is not possible, as the practice does not allow it.

The first problem therefore that we must overcome as coaches is to be comfortable and confident enough to hold our hands up and recognise not that we have made a mistake but what we had planned is not working as we had visualised. As soon as we can overcome this hurdle, then we can concentrate on supporting the players within the practice by making any necessary changes that need to be made. Not making these changes will likely result in the value of the practice being drastically reduced or lost altogether. Once we are at ease in making a change to a practice, the next step is being able to understand and recognise why exactly it is not working and what alterations need to be made. This is no easy task and will take some time to master and can only be achieved through practice and experience; however, by following particular guidelines it is definitely attainable. This chapter will therefore cover not only reflecting on a session as it is happening and the art of observation, but also the process we can go through to help pinpoint what it is that is preventing the practice from materialising the way we had planned.

As coaches we sometimes believe that we need to be constantly involved in the session. Whether this is through providing instructions or motivation to the players, there is a belief that the players need to hear our voice or that they need to be aware of our presence, otherwise they will not perform to their best standards. However, this continuous need to be immersed within the practice can often be counterproductive in supporting the players. Not only does it produce an environment in which the players effectively have to rely on the coach to provide additional motivation and encouragement, it also prevents the coach from concentrating on their main role of helping the players improve. Taking a step back from the practice not only allows the players to just get on with the practice – which gives them the freedom and opportunity to solve problems themselves, which has been advocated throughout the book – it also lets the coach transfer their focus to the practice and whether it is allowing the players to practice the topic of the session in realistic situations. To help with this, sometimes it is beneficial if this step back from the practice is an actual physical step back. If we can position ourselves a couple of yards farther away from the practice than usual, it will not only help remove the temptation to go in and get involved, it will also provide the coach with the space and time to concentrate fully on what specifically is happening within the practice and whether it is suitable in terms of the session focus and the development of the players.

Reflective Process: Realism

The first step in the reflective process is to identify or define what exactly success and failure look like within the practice. At first glance this may seem obvious, but it is not necessarily that simple. For instance, if we look at *Practice Seventeen*, we are looking at creating an environment where the players can practice playing quickly or counter attacking in a one versus one, before producing an end product of a forward pass. The obvious indicator as to whether the players are finding success within the practice or not is if the players are completing a successful pass into one of the small goals. But this will not tell the full story of whether the practice is successful in terms of putting the players in the correct environment for practicing the session topic. The first picture that we need to consider is the entrance of the attacking player and the relationship between them and the player who is transferring from being the attacking player to becoming the defender. What is the common picture that occurs? Is the defender in a position where they are already in the correct position defensively or are able to get themselves between the ball and the goal? Or are they too far out of position? Which therefore provides the attacking player a free run at the target zone. If the attacking player keeps getting a free run at the target zone, then it is defeating the object of the practice, it is turning into 'running with the ball' rather than one versus one. So not only are they not practicing the session topic, this will also have a knock-on effect on the next practice, which would be set up to continue with the session theme of playing quickly in a one-versus-one situation. Other possibilities that may occur are that the area between the two target areas is either too big or too small, which can then lead to a number of different outcomes, such as the distance that the attacking player has to travel is too far, the area size is too small, making it too difficult to get past the defender or it could be that the area is not long enough, so there is limited space behind the defender for the attacker to attack. There are numerous ways in which the practice may not succeed, but only one way in which it can. Therefore, the first step of the reflective process is: Does the practice generate a realistic situation for the session topic? For example, are the players completing the session topic in a similar situation to that in which they will find themselves during a game?

Reflective Process: Opportunity to Practice

The second step within the process is to identify whether or not the players are getting plenty of opportunities to practice the topic of the session. As touched upon within chapter 3, the players should be doing more of the topic then they would usually do in another practice or a game. They need to be given lots of opportunities to practice the session topic, so that they have the best possible chance to improve. If we go back to *Practice Seventeen*, the obvious reason as to why the players would not get as many chances to practice the topic as we would like is that there are too many players within the practice and therefore they are spending too much time waiting for a go. If this is the case, then it would just mean that an additional practice area is needed. However, there can be other reasons that prevent the players from practicing the topic, one of which can be the task that they are asked to complete before they get to the main element of the practice. An example of this can be seen within *Practice Ten*, where the main focus is the attacking team trying to play a pass into the target area for a teammate. Before they attempt this, they may be given an additional task that they have to complete, such as completing a minimum of three passes. This additional task helps make the practice more realistic. Without it, the players may look to complete the pass into the target area as soon as the ball is played in by the server, rather than waiting until the right time. Because the practice would have been live for a period of time before the three passes have been completed, it will make it more difficult to attempt the pass into the target area immediately, and therefore it is more likely that on completing the third pass the attacking players will need to make at least another pass before they try to achieve the final pass. However, it is possible that the attacking players are finding it overly difficult to complete the three passes and therefore rarely get the opportunity to attempt the pass into the target area. Once this has been identified as being the problem, the coach needs to decide whether the issue can be rectified or whether it needs to be eradicated from the practice. The players may just need some support and this could be achieved by increasing the area size or reducing the number of passes they have to complete. Or, if needed, the rule could just be removed. Though it was stated earlier that the rule was in place to make the practice more realistic, it is better to lose some realism if it means that the players get a good amount of opportunities to practice the session topic. So once the coach has observed the realism of the situation, the second step of the reflective process is to check that the players are getting plenty of chances to perform the focus of the session.

To help complete these first two steps of the reflective process and the remaining steps as well, there are certain strategies that can be used that will help make it not just easier but more accurate as well. The first approach that can be used is to adopt a number of positions around the practice area. Observing the practice from a range of positions will provide the coach with more and also better opportunities to identify anything that needs attention. It will also give the coach a better chance to work out what the cause of the problem is as well. The topic of the session can also influence the most suitable place from which to observe the practice. For example, if there is a session topic that is related to playing forward, this could include forward passing, running with the ball, receiving to play forward, etc. Therefore an ideal position for the coach would be to observe from behind the play, as it will enable them to see the same or similar pictures as the players. Seeing the same thing as the players will make it much easier to relate to them and understand what they are experiencing within the practice.

Another strategy that can be used by the coach to improve the quality of their reflection is not to just rely on their own observations, but to use those of other people as well, such as the coach they are working alongside. This can be particularly useful, as quite often we will not see things that are quite obvious to other people. This can be linked to observation bias, where people have a tendency to see what they expect or want to see. So if we are the one who has created the session, we will want to see what we had planned for and can therefore sometimes miss something that is blatantly obvious to others. In addition to this, another coach can be used as a sounding board to discuss your observations, the outcome of which could be them agreeing or providing a different point of view. Either way it will help you decide on what it is you are seeing, as well as the solution, if one is needed.

Reflective Process: Level of Difficulty

The last remaining step of the process, before we are able to move our attention to supporting the players, is to assess the difficulty of the practice and identify whether it is at a suitable level for the players. Within chapter 5 we discussed how within our planning we can accommodate the different types of players that we will have in the squad, so that they are all challenged in a way that meets their individual needs. This next stage of the reflective process is used by the coach to establish whether or not the level of difficulty we had planned has materialised or whether the players are performing unexpectedly, And, is this above or below the expectations that we had?

The main difficulty with this part of the process is knowing how long to continue to just observe and when to act upon the observation and make relevant changes. The simplest decision that can be made is to make a change when the players are finding the practice too easy and need to be challenged further. This is usually relatively easy to identify, as the indicators are quite obvious, in that the players will be finding a lot of success and this success comes quite easily to them. The trickier part of this comes when we have to work out what exactly it is they are finding easy and therefore needs changing to make it more difficult. To achieve this the coach will need to break the practice down into the different elements that the player or players have to perform to be successful. Once this has been identified, the coach can then introduce the relevant progression or individual challenge that will increase the level of difficulty for that particular area of the performance. Or alternatively, changes can be made to the set-up of the practice that again will have an impact on how challenging a particular area of the performance will be.

The more difficult element of this part of the process is when it appears that the players are finding the practice too testing. It is not necessarily identifying that the practice is too hard or making relevant changes once this has been identified, which is the same process as when the players are finding the practice too easy. The difficult part is the timing of the intervention by the coach, in that they do not make changes too quickly, as it may be that a short amount of time later the modifications to the practice are not needed. The question that we need to ask ourselves is: Are the players finding it too hard or are they still in the process of working out how to solve the problem they are facing? What we do not want to do as coaches is to step in too early and provide the players with help in the form of making the practice easier, when there is still a chance that the players can work out themselves what they need to do to find success. If we do, we are taking an important learning opportunity away from the players that would contribute to the development of their problem-solving and decision-making skills. There is no quick solution to learning when to step in to make the practice easier for players and when not to; it just comes from experience and time on the pitch, getting to know and understand the players, and recognising signs that indicate they need support. One rule, however, that can be used at the beginning of the learning journey is that we should ignore our first instinct to go in and help the players. To begin with we will be too eager to go into the practice and help the players because we feel uncomfortable seeing the players struggle and also watching what we see as the practice not working. But this tricky element of the practice is usually the most important part of the learning process and we therefore need to be very careful not to end it too early.

There is a lot for the coach to reflect upon at the beginning of the session and we need to be mindful that this process does not take too long and take us away from our role of supporting the players. Though this reflective process is an extremely important task that needs to be completed at the start of each practice by the coach, we should not get side-tracked by it and allow it to take too long. It could be that the conversation with the other coach, about what they have seen and what you have seen, turns into an in-depth discussion and then starts to distract us from the task at hand, which is deciding whether or not anything needs changing. Stepping back from the session provides the coach with an invaluable opportunity to check that the practice is providing the players with the best possible environment for learning and developing the topic of the session. As soon as this has been established and any necessary amendments have been made, the coach can then fully focus on providing direct support to the players.

Observation: Supporting the Players

Once we have finished reflecting on the practice to ensure that it is suitable both for the players and the topic, we now need to observe the performance of the players and identify whether or not they require support. In chapter 3 the benefits of adding coaching points to the planning process were urged and now that we have entered the delivery stage of the session, the need to have these can be highlighted further. We can now use these coaching points to bring some structure to our observations, as they provide clear indicators as to whether or not the players are performing the topic of the session correctly. They basically make the observation of the players' performance easier. –

Within *Practice Twenty-Nine* the coaching points could be:

1. Check your shoulder: – is there space behind you so that you can play forward?
2. Open your body – can you open your body shape, so that you can see both the ball arriving and also where you want to play?
3. Back foot – can you receive the ball on the foot furthest away from the player making the pass, so that your touch can go forward?

Therefore, the first coaching point provides the coach with a specific focus for their observations. There is no need to consider the other coaching points until the players show an understanding of the first one. The observations can be concentrated on the players within the area and the team that has possession of the ball. This again makes this part of the observation process easier for the coach, as they now only have a small amount of players that they need to focus on and they are just looking to see whether or not they complete a specific action successfully – in this instance, do they check their shoulder before they receive a pass? No other elements of their performance matter at this stage and therefore the coach can just give this particular action their full attention.

When observing a coaching point, the coach is just looking to see whether or not the player is executing it correctly. If they are, it is just a matter of providing the player with direct specific praise and encouragement, as outlined within chapter 2; 'Fantastic Connor, I saw you check your shoulder then before you received the ball – can you do that every time?' This demonstrates to the player that you have recognised that they have done what you have asked them to, whilst also providing them with a reminder to continue to do it. If, however, the player is not executing it correctly, the first question that the coach needs to ask themselves is: Are they attempting to do it or just not doing it at all? If they are just not doing it, they just need a reminder of what they should be doing: 'Sammy, what should you do before you receive the ball?' Once they have provided the answer, it is just a matter of praising them and encouraging them to keep trying. If they are attempting to do it but not quite doing it correctly, then as a coach we may need to go in and provide some form of support. This can be in any form that the coach sees as being appropriate at the time, such as a demonstration, question and answer, or direct instruction. Once this has been completed, it is really important that the observation process of this particular player continues as we need to 'check learning'. Quite often after working with a player, we will immediately move on to another player to work with them. This is understandable, as we want to provide support to all of the players and

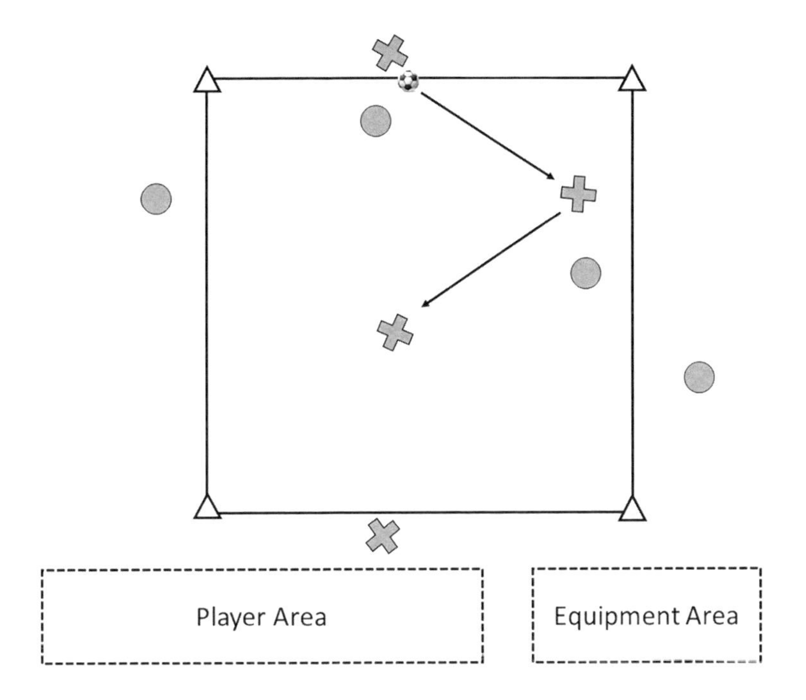

Practice Twenty-Nine

The area is set out as a square, and the players are split into two teams. Each team has two target players facing each other across the square, with the two teams playing in different directions. A point is awarded if a team gets the ball across the area from one target player to the other without the opposition touching the ball. To achieve the point, at least one player in the area must touch the ball (i.e. it cannot go directly from one target player to the other). If a team wins a point, they retain possession of the ball and look to transfer the ball across the area to the other target player. The target player role should be rotated regularly.

spend the same amount of time with each player, but that small amount of extra time we spend watching a player after supporting them is essential to their development. There is little point in supporting a player if we do not check their learning afterwards. Once we have supported a player, we should follow the same observational process that we did when first observing them. If, however, they require continued support we cannot persist in helping and observing them or we will be neglecting the other players. Once we have supported them on a couple of occasions, it is then time to allow them to continue to work out the solution themselves. We can, however, still observe from afar and provide praise when they find the answer or whilst they continue to try.

During this observation of the players, the coach may well discover that for one of the coaching points the players do not need any support as they are completing the action correctly already. This could be before the coaching point is even introduced by the coach and if this is the case, then we should not waste time still working on this particular action if the players are already capable in this area of the topic. It is, however, still worthwhile mentioning the coaching point to the players, as it plays an important part in the process and though they are completing it successfully they may not necessarily realise they are doing it or understand the importance of it. Therefore, the players should be informed of what they are doing and praised for doing it, with the praise including an explanation as to why it is important that they do it, but given quickly and briefly, so that the next coaching point can be introduced and practiced.

It is likely that these coaching points are introduced in either the first or main practice, and it could be that they are all introduced one after the other in the same practice, or the latter points could be presented to the players after a progression or in the following practice. Whichever method is used, the coaching points should be a common theme during the whole session and should be revisited and reinforced throughout. If we revisit *Practice Twenty-Nine* and the three coaching points of (1) check your shoulder, (2) open your body and (3) back foot, the same coaching points could also be used for *Practice Twenty-Eight* and therefore they could be put together to make a session. So during *Practice Twenty-Eight* all three coaching points could be introduced and then when we get to *Practice Twenty-Nine,* it is just the matter of reinforcing them at the right time. There is no need here to go through them again in the logical sequence that we identified in the planning process; instead we need to observe the player's performance and if they are not doing what we have asked them to do – receive to play forward – then it is a matter of identifying which of the coaching points they are not completing correctly (it could be more than one). Once it has been identified, the coach just needs to intervene as outlined earlier. Adopting this process allows the coaching points to be introduced and practiced separately in the first part of the session and in sequence, allowing the player to put them together like building blocks before they are used in context in the concluding parts of the session.

Allowing some time to just take a step back and not fully immersing ourselves in the session lets us fully concentrate on watching what we have planned on paper materialise in front of us and seeing if it pans out as we had hoped. Using the different steps that were introduced within this chapter provides the coach with clear indicators as to whether or not the practice is effective in terms of providing a realistic and challenging environment to practice the session topic. At this stage we must not be afraid of making changes to the practice, as these slight amendments can have a major impact on the effectiveness of the session. If we do not make these changes when they are needed, then it is likely that the session becomes almost pointless in terms of being a tool for learning. Once we are satisfied that it is appropriate, we can then switch our focus from observing the practice to observing the players and providing them with the necessary support to develop and improve their performance in relation to the focus of the session. And using the coaching points identified within the planning process provides not only the players, but the coaches as well, with a clear and specific element of the performance to concentrate on. Which essentially is what we are there to do: to create an environment where the players can learn through self-discovery and then to provide support when they require it.

CHAPTER 7
REFLECTION AFTER THE SESSION

Once we have completed a session and everything is packed away and the players have left, the final stage of the coaching process begins. Whether we do it deliberately or unconsciously, we begin to reflect on the session and what went well and what we possibly would do differently next time to improve it. Any coach will tell you that there is no such thing as the perfect session; there is always something that can be changed that will improve it further. As coaches we reflect so that we can improve. We are always striving to be better and to learn new things, and reflecting allows us to do this by gaining a greater understanding of not only ourselves in our role as coaches, but it can also help us gain an improved insight into the players we are coaching, as well as the game itself.

However, just reflecting is not enough on its own to be an effective tool for personal development. Quite often we will reflect upon a session and identify specific areas of it that we were really happy with or felt did not go as well as we had hoped, but then do not action these, in that we do not use them to help direct our coaching going forward. If we do not act upon our findings from our reflection, are we actually reflecting or are we just remembering what happened? Therefore, even though we are taking the time to reflect back on the session and we are doing it for the right reasons, in that we want to advance as a coach and improve the experience for the players, if we do not actually action the conclusions that we make, then the reflective process that we just went through will be wasted. It is therefore really important that as a coach you find a way to reflect that works for you, so that it becomes an effective process that adds value to your coaching.

Why Reflect

Before we look at how we can reflect effectively, it is important to understand exactly why we should reflect. It has already been identified that we do it to improve ourselves and though this is the end product, there are a number of other benefits that we might not be aware of which we get from reflecting and therefore make it even more valuable as a process. We first of all need to see reflection as a process where we can extract learning and if we are able to do this, it is seen as learning to learn. The ability to be able to learn how to learn can be achieved if you are able to continuously persist in learning, organise your learning, be aware of your learning needs, and identify the opportunities that are available to you that will provide the necessary support that you require. A large proportion of this comes from reflecting. Just by engaging in regular reflection we are committing to lifelong learning and within the reflective process we are attempting to identify the areas that as an individual we need to improve. Finally, by actioning these areas that have been identified as requiring development, we are seeking the support that we need to gain the necessary knowledge to improve and develop. Doing this allows us to build upon our prior learning and experiences and apply this newly obtained knowledge to further challenges that we come across. To be able to commit to learning to learn, we have to be motivated to do so, whilst also having the confidence in ourselves to remain within the process.

Over time our reflective practice will also reveal patterns of behaviour in both ourselves and the players, and these patterns could occur in any stage of the coaching practice: planning, delivery or review. These behaviours could be either positive or negative, and it is important that we do not just concentrate on the negative behaviours and ignore the positive ones. If we can identify something that we are doing well or that the players enjoy, then we can continue to use this strategy within our sessions to support the players, being mindful not to overuse it as it could start to lose its effectiveness if it is used too much. Similarly, if we identify a pattern in terms of a specific area of session planning or session delivery that could have been better, then we can put something in place to improve this. For example, if we notice that the players continually struggle to understand the practice set-up in terms of the rules, the boundaries, etc., and it takes too long for them to work it out, we can see that it is a common theme and prioritise it in terms of an area for development. Whatever the specific reason is for the players not being able to understand the practice, it could be that the design of the practices needs to be simplified or that that we need to change how we communicate to the players. Now that it has been identified, a plan can be put in place to improve this area of our coaching.

Reflective practice also enables a coach to provide the safest possible environment for the players. Using past experiences allows a coach to assess potentially difficult situations more effectively to ensure the safety of themselves, the players and anyone else attending the session. On previous occasions we may not have been completely happy with how we dealt with the situation, or we may not have had the required knowledge which was needed to deal with the matter at that time and it is not until afterwards, when we reflected and identified a need for development in this area that we searched for and obtained the required knowledge. We will also seek to find the answers to the questions raised within our reflection, and to find these answers we will often engage in discussion with people who we see as specialists in this area of knowledge. In this instance, it would likely be a welfare or safeguarding officer and therefore it has encouraged us to engage with people we would not usually have many dealings with. This can often lead to gaining further knowledge in addition to what we originally sought. This can only be beneficial to our development as a coach. Even if we use just some of this new knowledge, if we only take one piece of information from these conversations, then it has been both worthwhile and advantageous to our progress.

It has also been shown that self-reflection can increase a coach's self-efficacy, in that it increases the belief we have in ourselves to be able to execute actions and solve problems that we face. Whilst this can be confused with self-esteem, self-efficacy specifically relates to a particular task at hand, whereas self-esteem or confidence can be a lot broader and can actually include negative feelings as well, for instance, a player can be confident that they will not get past a defender in a one-versus-one situation and therefore they will decide to pass the ball instead. Basically, the biggest difference between the two is that self-esteem allows for failure, but self-efficacy concentrates only on succeeding in the current task. If we put this into a coaching context, the task at hand could be planning a session or providing feedback to a player. By reflecting back on previous experiences where we have either been successful or where we have made mistakes, we can now have an understanding of why we made these mistakes and what we would do differently next time, and we are able to approach the task with improved levels of self-efficacy. By having these enhanced levels, we can approach a task with the belief that we can perform it well and we are therefore more likely to view the task as something which can be performed and completed successfully, rather than something that we want to avoid. So if we refer back to the planning, when we go through the review process after a session, we should include the effectiveness of the practices in terms of the set-up, its realism in relation to the game, and the focus of the session, the level of challenge it provides the players, etc. By reviewing our planning, we will start to identify what is working and going well and what needs to be changed and improved. Then as the number of positives increase and simultaneously the number of areas for improvement decreases, then our self-efficacy in relation to planning will escalate and therefore we are likely to continue in the process of planning rather than looking for excuses to avoid it.

By engaging in self-reflection, we will start to understand ourselves better when we are in the role of the coach, as it allows us to understand our own needs as well as our own habits. Basically, it allows you to understand all of the different pieces that, when put together, make you the coach that you are. And the more that you know about yourself as a coach, the better you are at being able to adapt to changing situations or new challenges. Self-reflection enables us to pinpoint the areas of our performance that are either strengths or areas that need to be changed and/or improved. The areas for improvement can then be prioritised in terms of learning and development, whilst the areas of strength can be used to increase confidence and self-efficacy. Quite often reflection is seen as the least important element of the coaching process, with greater value put on both planning and delivery. But engaging in self-reflection and then acting upon the findings from it can be just as important, as it can help us improve in the other two areas of the process. Therefore, we should look, when possible, to spend as much time reflecting as we do planning and delivering, whilst also treating it with the same amount of respect.

What to Reflect Upon

The greatest challenge that we can face when reflecting is knowing what exactly to reflect back upon. Because of this uncertainty, we can often find ourselves just pondering over what happened, rather than pinpointing specific outcomes. For a coach to fully utilise the reflection process, they must be able to identify and then work with specific evidence. Therefore, we should not try to look at too many things; instead we should identify a small number of focuses that we can concentrate on. To do this, these areas of focus will usually need to be chosen beforehand, so that it makes it easier to think back on afterwards. This, however, is not always feasible, as a key event may occur within the session that needs to be added to our reflection. Nevertheless, the majority of the time the area of focus should, where possible, be confirmed before the session, and this identification of what exactly the coach will reflect upon after the session can become part of the planning process. So alongside planning what the players will learn and how they will do this, the coach can also plan their own learning through pinpointing their areas for reflection.

If we are to fully utilise the process of self-reflection, then when selecting the area of focus for our reflection we must look beyond the usual guidelines we use to decide whether or not the session was successful and look deeper by analysing the reasons why and the subsequent outcomes. For instance, a common benchmark we will use is whether or not the players enjoyed the session. It should be noted at this stage that this is an excellent indicator as to whether or not the session was successful and should not be ignored, especially as children will usually be very honest in their responses and therefore the information we get back from them will be accurate and reliable. However, we cannot solely rely upon the initial feedback that we receive from the players. Just being told by the players that they enjoyed a session is not enough for it to be used as evidence within our reflection and for it to be categorised as a positive. We need to look deeper and identify the specific reasons why the players enjoyed it. The reasons that they enjoyed themselves could have little to do with the actual session, they might have just liked playing with their friends or events prior to the session were less enjoyable and therefore in comparison just getting to play soccer would be much more exciting, no matter how it was delivered by the coach.

So if we use this example of the player's enjoyment as a traditional guideline that we use within our reflection, we now need to take this further and deeper, if it is to be an effective guide to the success of the session. So what specifically did the players enjoy about the session? Was it that we started the session with a game? Is it because there were different scoring systems within the practices, so that it provided the players with different options? Did the players enjoy the use of scenarios within the game at the end of the session? Identifying specifically what it is the players enjoyed about this particular session will allow the coach to pinpoint what went well and then when it is the right time to do so, it can be used again within a future session. And the same can be done with the parts of the session that the players did not enjoy, provided they are not crucial elements, i.e., if it affects the safety or development of the players, they can be removed from any future sessions. This understanding of the players is critical if we are going to provide them with the best possible environment for their specific needs.

Further guidelines we usually use within our reflection include how the practice looked and how the players performed within it. So we will look back on at how the practice looked to the eye: Were the players finding lots of success? Were the players doing exactly what they were meant to be doing? But this initial picture that we see does not provide the full story. When we see that the players are finding lots of success, we should not automatically place this into the 'what went well' category. Rather than looking for how much success they were getting, we should be looking at how much they improved from their starting point at the beginning of the session to their position at the end of the session. If they are finding lots of success, it is probably an indicator that the practice is too easy for them and therefore it should actually be seen as an area that needs to be changed. Whereas if they are progressing throughout the session, then this is probably a sign that the environment is allowing the players to practice and find solutions to the topic of the session and therefore can be seen as a definite positive and something that we have done well in the planning and delivery process.

If we then look at whether the players were doing what we wanted them to do? This can have a number of different elements to it and we need to be careful that we are looking at it through the correct lens. Is it because the practice design is simple and easy to understand? Or that the practice design allows the players to concentrate on practicing what they have been asked to learn? Or is it down to how it was communicated to the players? All of these can be seen as a positive and are excellent findings to come out of the session. The difficult part is to identify which was the single factor that allowed the players to carry out the task correctly. Or it could be that more than one of these points, that when they were put together, contributed to the players being able to do what they have been asked to do. However, we can also be blinded by this and see something that we want to see rather than what is actually happening. Are we seeing a practice that the players are executing correctly or is it a practice that tells the players where they have to pass the ball to, where they have to move to etc., and therefore removing all the elements of freedom, problem solving and decision making – which, as we have shown, are all key elements in a player's development? Instead, we want to see a similar picture to what we see with a player's success within a session: a steady improvement from start to finish, so the practice may well look messy and disorganised at the start, but this is hopefully part of the learning process and not because the players do not know what they are doing. Then as the players begin to work out solutions, it goes from being messy and disorganised to a practice that flows and has clear patterns.

The key is to look beyond what we see or what we want to see and go into greater detail, not just accepting what we see as being a positive or an area for development, but asking ourselves the 'why'. By doing this we will get a more in-depth answer and the real reason as to why this element of the session was successful or something that can be improved upon. It could, in fact, change our opinion as to whether or not it was a positive. If we refer back to *Practice Eight*, for instance, the players work in pairs trying to keep the ball away from each other, with an additional area in the centre of the practice which the player with the ball can travel through but the defender cannot. After the session, the set-up of the practice could initially be seen as being a positive, as the players had lots of opportunities to dribble and the central area allowed the players that might be struggling to escape their partner. So at first glance the practice design was a success. However, when we look deeper, the players are not spending as much time as we think dribbling. Because of the size of the central area, the players are actually driving with the ball to get away from the partner and then wait for them to catch up, before they then drive through the central area again. So, in fact, the players are spending most of their time driving with the ball or standing still with the ball. By identifying this, we know next time that we need to reduce the size of the central area and add a rule where players are limited to the number of times they can use it. Looking deeper and more closely at the session during our reflection will enable us as coaches to identify exactly what did happen and why to ensure that we continue to develop and improve and provide the best possible environment in which the players can practice.

Up until now we haven't touched upon philosophies, which have become increasingly recognised as being a critical factor in how we coach and the impact that our coaching has on the players. When it comes to philosophies, it is important that we recognise that there are two types: playing philosophy, i.e., how we want the team to play, and our coaching philosophy, which is more of a definition of our beliefs and values which is formed by our behaviours. Hopefully, by reading this book you have either been able to confirm that the way in which you coach is the right way – in that you are putting the players first and that your focus is on helping the players develop as both soccer players and people through a holistic and player centred approach – or you may have now made the decision to make some slight adjustments to your coaching, so that your coaching philosophy aligns more closely to this. Obviously, it is important that we recognise that everyone has an opinion and it cannot be expected that as coaches we have exactly the same coaching philosophy, but whatever philosophy we do adopt, we must remember that we are working with young children and that it is a long term process rather than attempting to fix everything straight away.

The same can be said with regard to a coach's playing philosophy; soccer would not be the same if every coach and team approached how they play a game exactly the same way. Part of what makes the game so interesting is watching what unfolds as two teams with completely different approaches play each other. However, we must remember that this relates mainly to the adult game, where the main or only thing that matters is the result. It could be argued here that as this is where we are aiming to get the players to, then we should expose them to this, so that they are fully prepared for it. There is definitely some plausibility to this – it is just a matter of deciding when exactly we do this. The answer to this is simply when they get close to playing the adult game and not when they are just being introduced to the game. In the early stages of playing the game, i.e., when they are children, the playing philosophy of coaches should be very similar, which is based on players being comfortable and clever in possession of the ball. A 'want the ball, love the ball' approach. Whilst out of possession, players should be attempting to win the ball back efficiently and intelligently. But this does not mean that there is no room for flexibility or variety in a coach's playing philosophy when working with young soccer players. For instance, different formations may be favoured or used, or different ways in which the ball can be retained and then progressed from a team's own territory to the opposition's.

However, our philosophies as coaches can quite often be idealistic in that we do not always practice what we preach. There can often be inconsistencies between what we say we are going to do and what we actually end up doing. We may have the right intentions and want to deliver our sessions with a player-centred approach, but then once we are in the thick of the session and it is not going the way that we had hoped, we can easily find ourselves forgetting our beliefs and putting these to one side and replacing them with a 'quick fix' approach. The same situation can also occur with our playing philosophy; we may say that we want the team to play a certain way that encourages the players to be brave and positive on the ball, but once the players start to lose the ball, we can quite often go against these beliefs and urge the players to play 'safe' instead. Therefore, including our coaching and playing philosophies within our reflective practice plays a critical part in our development as a coach. Reflecting on our philosophies allows coaches to not only check to see if they are practicing what they preach, it also lets them see if the philosophy that they have adopted is actually right for them and the players. As we move along our coaching journey and the players progress through their own development, it may well be that the philosophies that we first adopted are no longer appropriate.

If we look at reflecting on our coaching philosophy, first of all, for us to be able to do this we need to identify particular behaviours that we can then measure against our perceived philosophy. So if we use a player-centred philosophy as an example, we would need to identify specific behaviours that we would expect to see with this type of coaching. When using a player-centred approach, it would be expected that a coach allows plenty of ball rolling time, so that the players have lots of opportunities to practice and problem solve; that they limit the number of whole-group stoppages; and when they do stop, they use a question-and-answer technique with players rather than giving them the information; and that the stoppages are also quick and short to allow the players to return to practicing. Other behaviours that we would expect to see are the regular use of praise, individual interventions and the use of 'silence' to give the players sole responsibility for their learning. Our perception could be that we do all of these, because that is what our coaching philosophy is all about, but when we reflect back on a session it materialises that we stop practices a lot and for too long, and before we give the players an opportunity to provide an answer or find the solution, we give them the information. By regularly reflecting on our behaviours during a session and their links to our coaching philosophy, we can make sure that not only are we being consistent in terms of what we say we will do and what we actually do, but it will also help ensure our philosophy is continually evolving and meeting the needs of the players.

It is a similar situation with our playing philosophy, but instead of measuring our behaviours, we may need to recall the behaviours of the players and our subsequent reactions or non-action. For instance, if we refer back to a playing philosophy of wanting the players to be brave and positive on the ball and a player decides to just 'clear' the ball under no real pressure. How do we react to this behaviour? Do we ignore it? Do we praise them for not taking a risk? Or do we ask them what could they do differently next time? If we are being true to our playing philosophy, then the answer, of course, is to ask the player what they could have done differently. Without looking back on situations like this and thinking about what our response was, we cannot truly say whether or not we fully follow our philosophy of how we want the players to play the game.

We can also reflect upon our playing philosophy through the design and delivery of our practices. For instance, if within our playing philosophy we want to use winning the ball as a springboard to attack the opposition, we need to ensure that this is what we are replicating within all of our practices when it is available to do so. If we use any of the formats of *Practice Six* as an example, where we are replicating a one-versus-one situation, what we ask the defender to do when they win the ball becomes crucial in terms of our playing philosophy. If we say they win a point by just winning it or clearing it, then not only are we removing the opportunity for them to practice how we want them to play, we are also sending them mixed messages. But awarding a point to the defender only if they win the ball, and are then able to drive or dribble the ball over the opposite line they were defending, removes any possibility of the players being confused about how you want them to play and provides an extra opportunity for them to practice. The main area of the coaching process where we should be making sure that there is a strong link between the practices and the playing philosophy is, of course, within the planning phase. However, it is very easy to miss these tiny details, especially when they might not be linked to the session focus, and therefore it becomes increasingly important that we do include it within the reflective process.

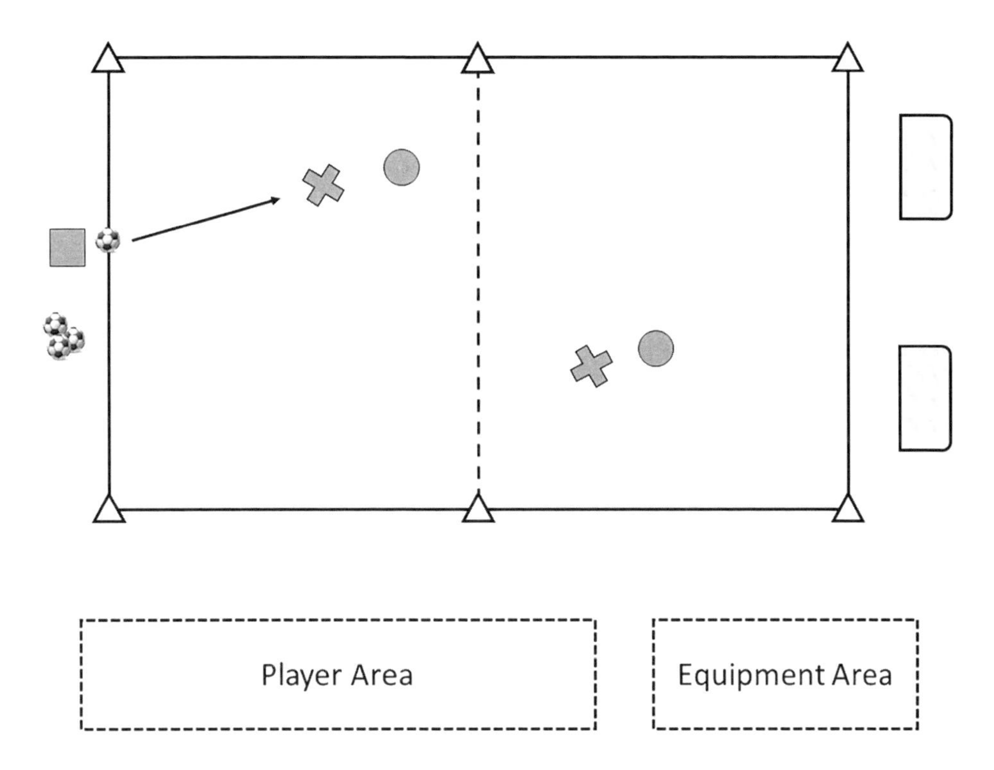

Practice Thirty

The area is split into two, with an attacker and defender in each half. Server plays the ball to an attacker who then looks to transfer the ball by passing or dribbling into the next half. Once in the next half, the attackers look to pass the ball into one of the small goals. At any time, the attackers can leave one half and move into the other half, whereas the defenders are locked into their designated areas. If the defenders win the ball, they look to play it back to the server to win a point.

If we take a look at *Practice Thirty*, there is a focus on players being able to receive the ball and play forward. In terms of the actual set-up and rules, the practice ticks a number of boxes: it is game-related, the players will get lots of opportunities to practice the topic, it provides the defenders with an incentive to win the ball and if they do win the ball it allows for transition to occur. So when it comes to reflecting on the session afterwards, it is likely that we would see that practice as a success and with good reason. However, what we may not have considered is how it links to our playing philosophy. So if our playing philosophy included wanting the players to be comfortable on the ball and able to receive a pass under pressure, then it may not have been as successful as we had first thought. Allowing the attacking players to have full freedom of the area but locking the defenders into their designated halves will probably encourage the attacking players to both occupy the same half and therefore create a two-versus-one overload. This will then have the additional knock-on effect of the player that the server chooses to play into being the player that is in space or farthest away from the defender. Similarly, if the playing philosophy out of possession is to win the ball back quickly and to press the opposition players, then we are also stopping the defenders from doing this, as we are not allowing the defender to be able to follow the attacker when they drop in to receive the ball or to support their teammate.

This does not mean that this practice could not be used with this set-up and these rules; we just need to ensure that we do so at the right times and for the correct reasons. It could be that we want to work on rotation, so when the attacking player does drop in and they receive the ball, the other attacker now needs to recognise that they need to move forward into the next area to be an option ahead of the ball, or it could be that it is used for the players to practice finding space. Or it could be that we are just allowing the players to experience receiving the ball under less pressure, as this will likely happen during some point in a game. The important element is that when we are reviewing the practice we are not only measuring how effective it was in terms of allowing the players to practice the topic, but also how we want them to play in relationship to the topic.

Another example can be seen within *Practice Six (b)*, which is a one-versus-one practice. On beating the defender, the attacking player looks to play the ball into a small goal to the side of the area, replicating the attacking player crossing the ball. So again an effective practice which allows for the players to practice in game relevant situations. The only consideration that we may need to make is: Does the final task replicate what we want the players to do in this situation? It could be that if a player does go past a player in a wide area, we may want them to drive into the box and therefore the small goal needs to be replaced by a gate which the player has travel through with the ball. Or it could be that we want the player to cut the ball back in these situations for players situated near the edge or in the middle of the box. If so, the position and angle of the small goal would need to be adjusted to replicate where the player needs to be aiming their pass or cross.

Identifying key areas of the session that we want to reflect upon, before we actually deliver it, will provide us with a clear focus when we go through the reflective process afterwards. It will make it much easier to identify specific events and subsequent outcomes, as well as making sure that our reflection does not turn into just thinking back about what happened and there being no real conclusions or action points to take away.

The reflective section of the coaching process can be just as important and effective as the planning and delivering components, provided that we actually reflect and not just think things over. So how exactly as a coach do we reflect? And what can we do to ensure that it is an effective process, to make sure that we do not waste this valuable time?

How to Reflect

The first important message in regard to the question 'How do we reflect?' is that there is no wrong or right answer, it is just whatever works for you. Doing so will help to ensure that we actually engage in the process rather than try to evade it, as it will be much easier to complete and its benefits will become much clearer. In addition to this, it will also help to ensure that we not only reflect, but we also act upon these reflections so that we can improve as a coach. In the next part of this chapter, a number of different strategies that can be used as part of the reflective practice will be discussed. Not all of these strategies have to be used, nor should a coach try to use them all at the same time, but they can be used at different times to provide a range of viewpoints that will allow a coach to get a full 360-degree examination of their coaching. Alternatively, just one of the options may be used, as this is preferred by the coach, because it is seen as being the most suitable and relevant to them and how they like to work.

The first option that is available to a coach is to find someone who you can trust to critique your coaching but more importantly to give accurate feedback. To do this, it is vital that the person you use has some kind of knowledge and a good understanding of what it is you are trying to achieve, not just in the session that they are observing but overall, i.e., the long term development of both yourself and the players. To achieve this, the discussions beforehand with the observer are just as important as the conversations that take place after the session. This pre-session conversation with the observer should be used to provide them with a clear picture of what it is you are trying to achieve, i.e., your coaching and playing philosophy as well as the session topic. Once this has been communicated to the observer, the specific areas that you want to be observed can then also be passed on to them. For example, you may want them to concentrate on the topic and whether it was relevant for the players and if it was achieved within the session. Or it could be that you want them to look at your interventions with the players. Do you intervene at the right time? Do you ask the players the right questions? Providing the observer with these specific elements of the session for them to concentrate on will help ensure that they do not get side-tracked by everything else that is happening, and therefore allow them to provide accurate and precise feedback at the end.

Once the session is completed, the next decision that needs to be made is how this information is given to the coach. It could be face-to-face, or it may be that it is written, or it could be a discussion over the phone. Again there are no right or wrong answers; it is just the most suitable for both the coach and the observer. Some people may prefer written feedback, as it is easier for them to take the information on board and, if needed, they can keep it to refer back to and remind themselves of any particular part of the feedback they were given. But a discussion, whether it is face-to-face or over the phone, allows the coach to ask further questions and, if needed, get clarification about the information that is being given. This form of feedback will therefore be more in-depth and so it could be argued that it is more valuable. It also allows the coach to provide further information to the observer, such as the decisions behind some of their actions, to give the observer more of an insight into the coach's performance, which may then result in them making changes to their feedback.

The obvious choice for the person to observe and provide feedback is any other coach that you work alongside. A relationship with this person would have already been built, so they will have a good understanding of you and also the players, which can be very helpful during the process as they will have a better level of knowledge of what the players like and need, and whether the behaviours that the coach is adopting, and the reactions and actions that they have, are normal or unusual. Having already built the relationship also makes the feedback process much easier, as the other coach will feel comfortable in providing it, whereas someone with less of a relationship with the coach may feel awkward or uncomfortable giving the coach feedback that is possibly not positive. Therefore, they might not provide everything that the coach needs to know and could possibly give them the wrong impression of where they are in terms of their coaching.

There are, of course, also advantages to using someone other than the person you are coaching with, such as a parent, another coach at the club or a coach from outside of the club. Though the coach may not have as close of a relationship with these people, they will observe the session from a different vantage point and with a different set of eyes. In doing this, there is an opportunity for them to see things that are not obvious to the coach and whoever they are working with, simply because they looking from outside of the practice, rather than inside of it. They may also have some areas of knowledge and experience that the coach currently does not have, which can be used to identify specific elements of the session that other people would not see, as well as helping to provide possible solutions to some of the areas that have been identified for improvement.

The other option in terms of obtaining feedback is to get it from yourself, which of course is the usual source that we go to. However, this source can be very unreliable in that what we remember about the session can be inaccurate, with studies showing that a coach can only accurately remember a small percentage of the events that occurred within a game or a session. Then with the information that we do not recall correctly, we will often see events how we want to remember them, whether this is in a positive or negative way. For instance, if we believe that we are not very good at communicating with our players, then our recollection of how we provided the players with information, whether this was verbal or non-verbal, will be quite negative, even if it was quite effective throughout. Similarly, if we have planned a session on finishing, we will want to recall that the players had lots of chances to have a shot at goal and they were better at it by the end of the session. Our memories of what actually happened can often be blinded by what we wanted to happen or what we just presumed happened.

To reduce this inaccuracy in the review process, a video of the session could be taken if possible. This does not mean a video has to be taken every session, but recording it from time to time will allow the coach to have a more accurate picture of what actually happened. By watching a recording of the session, not only will the coach be able to see exactly what did occur, they will also be able to observe actions or characteristics of themselves that they were unaware of. So if we look back at the previous examples of a finishing session and the communication skills of the coach, what we thought happened and then what we see when we watch it, could be two completely different things. Instead of thinking the players got lots of opportunities to practice their shooting and improving as the session evolved, we actually see the players waiting around a lot for their go or not having many shots because the task they have to complete before they can shoot is too difficult. Or it could even be that they are shooting a lot, but the shots are unrealistic to the game, i.e., they are too close to the goal or there is no goalkeeper so there is not much need for power or accuracy. When we observe our communication with the players, we see that they are actually able to understand and follow the instructions quite easily and therefore it is quite effective. In addition to this, it will also reconfirm some of our thoughts, which until we see them, we may be unsure are accurate. Watching a recording of a session will help ensure that the reflective process is not only much more accurate, but also considerably more effective.

In addition to making the process more accurate and effective, watching a session can also make us aware of things that we were previously oblivious to. Whatever the behaviour might be, watching yourself coach can be a real eye-opener and really helpful in your development process. This could be anything, from spending too much time talking or stopping the practice too often, to focusing our praise and support on just certain players. And, as with any part of the reflective process, the positives and strengths of our coaching should also be identified and appreciated. For instance, we might not realise that our manner with the players is excellent, or that the practices are really effective in keeping the players engaged and on task. Because we are so occupied with the session, we can often miss a lot of what is happening around us or misinterpret what we see or thought we saw. Watching a video of the session enables us to stop the footage, as well as watch it over and over again until we are one hundred per cent sure of what we have seen. A recording of the session can also be used in conjunction with other reflective strategies; for instance, it could be used alongside obtaining another person's feedback. Sharing the recording with someone allows them to watch it on their own time and as with ourselves, it lets them stop the footage and also watch it again.

Because recording a session has such a large number of positives attached to it, it is the one strategy that, if possible, should be used by all coaches within their reflective process. The unique outcomes that are attached to this form of reflection allow a coach to see and review aspects of their coaching that are not possible to see with any other strategy that is available to them when they are reflecting. It is also the only type of reflecting that can be trusted to be completely accurate, with little chance of any other factors clouding our vision or influencing our thought process. Watching a recording of a session will provide you with the clearest picture of who you are as a coach; the strengths that you bring to your sessions; the areas of your coaching that you would like to develop; how your coaching philosophy materialises from what you state it to be; how it looks on the pitch; and how your session planning transfers from paper to the training environment. It is by far the most effective way for a coach to reflect.

The strategies that we have looked at so far are mainly subjective in that they are someone's opinions, whether it is your own opinion or those of someone you have asked to provide you with feedback. These opinions can be invaluable, especially when they are different to yours, as they will provide you with a different perspective on things. It does not mean that you have to fully agree with these opinions or with any aspect of them, but if you do, then you have probably learnt something from the experience. However, the greatest benefit that you will get from these discussions is that they will be thought provoking, which in turn will encourage you to be more inquisitive, not only to gain further information, but to ask yourself questions about your own coaching and whether changes can or should be made. To complement these opinions, actual facts and figures can be really beneficial and can either support opinions or provide an argument against them.

The first way in which we can use facts within our reflection is by using timing – by timing how long it takes us or the players to do something. The best example of this would be ball rolling time – how long are the players active during the session? This does not necessarily have to be with a ball. It could be they are a defender in a practice or it is the first practice of the session and there are no balls in the practice, such as a tag game.

What they cannot be doing, though, is standing around waiting their turn or listening to the coach or waiting for the next practice to be set up. The English Football Association (FA) states that there should be a minimum of seventy per cent ball rolling time in a session, so during a sixty-minute session, the players should be active for a minimum of forty-two minutes. By timing how long the players are active, we can check to make sure that we are maximising the time that they have the opportunity to learn. If it is not as long as we would like it to be, then we can look at the timing of other elements of the session to see if they are taking too long. These include the length of the stoppages – is it taking too long to get information across to the players? Or explanations of the practice – are we spending too much time telling the players about the set-up and rules of the practice? By identifying such issues, we can either look to resolve them within the planning phase or introduce strategies that will help prevent them from happening whilst we deliver the session. This could be, for example, limiting the amount of time that our stoppages last by instructing the other coach with whom we are working to get the players back to playing once the time is up, regardless of whether we have finished talking to the players or not.

Another way in which we can use facts and figures within the reflecting process is by counting the number of times something happens within the session. As well as lasting too long, it could be that we stop the session too many times. As with the length of the stoppages, strategies can be put in place to restrict the number of times that the practice is stopped in order to help ensure the players spend more time being active. At the start of the session, a coach could be limited to a set number of times they are allowed to stop the practice, and once they have reached this number of stoppages, they cannot stop the practice again. Not only does this increase the ball rolling time for the players, it gives them more opportunities to solve problems themselves. It also forces the coach to carefully select when to stop the session and, with time and practice, they will only stop it at key times when there is a need to get an important message across to the players.

Counting within our reflection can also be used to analyse the effectiveness of the practices in relation to the session topic. *Practice Thirty-One* has a focus on counter attacking: by forcing one team to complete a set number of passes in the other team's half, it provides the defending team opportunities to not only win the ball but then break quickly, as the other team are likely to commit players forward as they try to complete the set number of passes. Therefore, on paper, the practice looks to be suitable for a session with a focus on counter attacking, but it can only be seen as being successful if during the practice we witness a lot of 'counter attacks'. As discussed earlier in the book, the session topic needs to occur more often than would usually happen in a normal game. Therefore, keeping an actual count of the number of times each team counter attacks or has the opportunity to counter attack will help provide a clearer picture of whether or not the practice was correctly set up to allow the players to develop their ability to counter attack. The same approach can be used for sessions with other topics. For sessions on possession, the number of passes made can be counted or the number of shots can be noted within a session that has a focus on finishing.

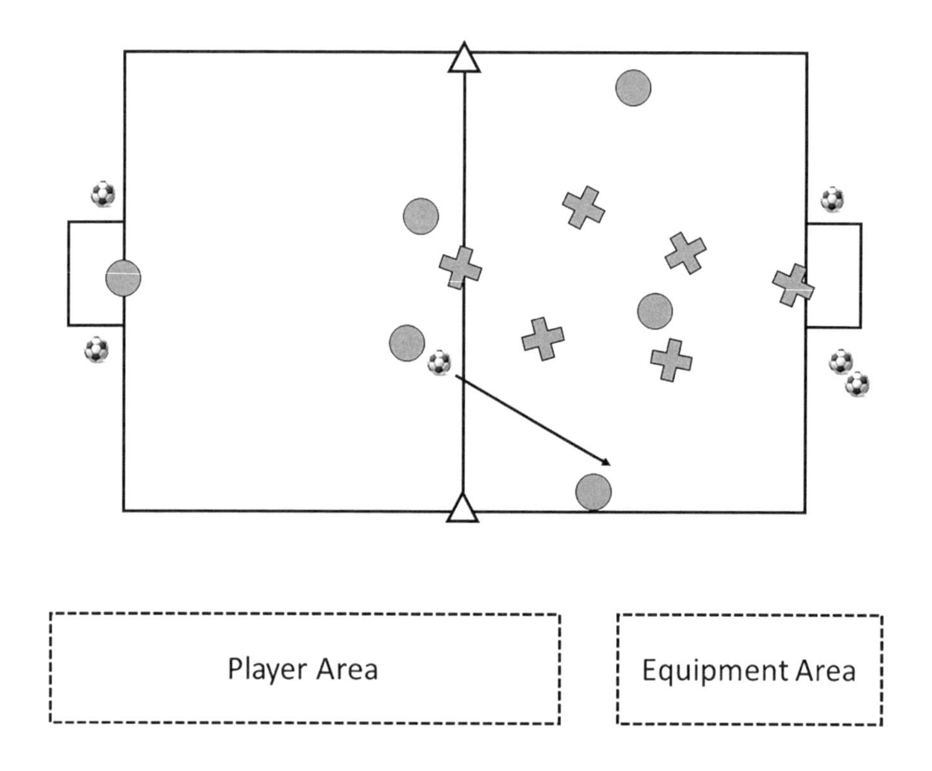

Practice Thirty-One

A small-sided game that always restarts with the goalkeeper whose team has possession of the ball, with the opposition having to retreat to their own half. The team in possession of the ball must then complete a set number of passes in the opposition's half before they can attempt to score a goal. If the opposing team wins the ball, they can just attack without the need to complete a set number of passes.

How any of these facts are collated can be done in a number of ways and both during and after the session. Collecting the data whilst the practice is going on can obviously be challenging for the person who has been asked to do it, as it is easy to miss something or be unsure whether it classified as the action they are being asked to count. However, it can be used to help build closer relationships or make someone become, or even just feel, more involved. This is a strategy that can be used particularly with parents, as it not only allows them to get involved, it also helps you as a coach to communicate to them what it is you are trying to achieve within the session. This can then prevent parents from providing the wrong type of encouragement during the practice. For example, if the session had a focus on dribbling and they are now aware of this, they are less likely to promote passing the ball to the players. Alternatively, it can also be used when the session has been recorded, as counting the actions whilst watching the session again will help ensure the data that we collect is more accurate, especially as we are able to watch it again or pause the footage if needed. Whichever method is used to collect the data, the evidence that can be obtained from it can be used to either confirm what the coach thought happened within the session or provide them with an alternative perspective, something that they would not have seen or considered without the facts and figures.

Once we have actually gone through the reflective process, it is then essential that we record our findings. If we do not do this, it is likely that it will lose its value. By not recording our findings, they can soon be lost and forgotten about, as we are unable to go and look back over them. A good example to demonstrate the importance of this can be seen within the design of a practice. Following the delivery of a session, it was identified within the reflective process that one of the practice designs was unsuitable, as it did not allow the players to practice the topic enough. If we do not record this anywhere or make the necessary changes to the session straight away, the next time that we come to deliver that session, it is likely that we would deliver the exact same practice as before, which would result in exactly the same outcomes.

Using some form of reflective journal, whether this is an electronic or hand-written version, allows a coach not only to record their findings, but to be more engaged in the process. Writing down our thoughts about the session or the findings from discussions that we had about the session can help provoke further analysis, which results in a deeper thought process. In addition to this, it allows a coach to create a story of their coaching journey, so they can track how they are developing, whether they are achieving their goals, if there continue to be specific areas of their coaching that could be improved or are going well, or if their coaching philosophy has changed. Any number of stories could unfold from the journal and they can support the coach in any way that they choose. However, this can only happen if we are honest with ourselves when we are completing the journal. We need to remember the purpose of completing the journal, in that it is all about you and it is there to support you. It is not about keeping a record of how well things went, it is about helping to identify how we can improve as coaches and provide the players with an environment in which they can develop, whilst enjoying their soccer.

The structure and the content of the journal is entirely up to the coach, it just needs to be in a format that works for them and does not discourage them from completing it. It could be that it is quite structured in that you choose specific aspects of coaching that you review each week, such as session organisation and practice design, learning outcomes and interventions. Or it could be more flexible in that you just write down whatever is on your mind when you are writing or whatever stands out from the session. There is an argument that the more structured approach allows for more of a focus and makes it easier to track the coaching journey. The aspects of our coaching that are reviewed can be changed, so that more areas can be reflected upon; however, it is important that we do not alter these too often or too quickly, as we cannot expect any changes that we make, to happen immediately – we need to allow time to implement new ideas and practice new skills. By reviewing the same parts of our coaching over a number of weeks or months, we can track the development of these specific areas, and when we are happy that we are performing consistently or there have been clear levels of improvement, we can then look at other aspects that we want to reflect upon.

Opportunities to Develop

Once we have reflected and areas of development have been identified, the next step is to work towards improving these parts of our coaching. A lot of the time this can be achieved just by actually identifying that it needs to be changed and then putting it into practice, either in the planning stage or on the pitch. A number of learning models have suggested that seventy per cent of our learning comes from 'experience' – where you can discover and then practice and refine the specific skills needed to be successful in that particular role. Other benefits that it brings to the learning process is that it allows you to make decisions and then observe the outcomes of these and whether they were the right ones to make, making it similar to the environment we are trying to create for the players. Again, similar to the environment that we want for the players, it allows you to face challenges and interact with other people, who could be fellow learners or someone who you see as an influence. It also provides us with the opportunity to be creative and innovative and, of course, reflective (during the session). But there are times when we cannot just rely on experience and we need further support, to help with our understanding and development.

One place where we can find this support is within our own club and all of the coaches working with other teams. It is often believed that we can only learn and gain ideas from coaches that are more experienced or have more qualifications than ourselves, but this is a long way from being right. Of course there are definitely things that we can learn from these coaches, but we can learn just as much from coaches who may have only just started their coaching journey or have less formal education. If we refer back to chapter 2, the qualities that are needed to be a successful coach were discussed, as well as how we may already possess a number of these through other aspects of our lives. This could be through our work or upbringing or any other parts of our lives, and therefore the same can be said about any other coach. As a coach we might be very well organised, have really good levels of patience with the players and are always positive and enthusiastic throughout every session, but we may not be as confident with our communication skills and creativity when it comes to session planning. We could, however, find coaches within our club who are really strong in these areas of their coaching. For instance, a coach that is at the start of their coaching journey could be working with a squad of very young players and therefore they quickly need to work out how they can communicate quickly with the players to avoid them becoming distracted and also to ensure that the time they have with them is maximised in terms of opportunities to learn. By observing this coach, it might be possible to identify and then use the strategies that work for them. Or if it feels that these would not be suitable for the players that you are working with, they could at least stimulate ideas of what would work for them. Similarly, a coach who has been working with the same group of players for a number of years may not have numerous qualifications, but they may be very creative with their session planning as they have to be, to keep the players engaged and motivated. They have also had to develop their session planning as the players have gotten older, as their needs have changed in terms of what they need to learn and practice.

Giving ourselves the opportunity to stand back and watch other coaches deliver a session and work with a different group of players can be very rewarding. Not only will it provide you with possible ideas that you can use within your own coaching, but it can also help reinforce or confirm all of the really great things that you are doing so well. And, just as importantly, it can reignite your enthusiasm and love for coaching. There will be stages on your coaching journey where there are a number of challenges and the enjoyment you get from the experience is reduced or even non-existent. Watching another coach, collecting new ideas and watching the enjoyment the players and the coach get from the session, can reignite our passion and excitement and provide a much needed boost for all of the elements of our coaching. No matter what level we are working at, coaching is highly demanding and at times can be quite draining and it is therefore imperative that we find strategies for ourselves to help revitalise our appetite and refuel our energy levels.

The favour can also be returned by inviting other coaches to watch your sessions, which can also be very beneficial to you, in that it can provide an opportunity to develop and grow as a coach. Delivering a session in front of other coaches that we do not know very well or have a limited relationship with, can take us completely out of our comfort zone and can be quite stressful and nerve wracking. But doing so will help increase your self-esteem and you will feel proud of yourself for achieving a new accomplishment. Also completing one challenge will make it easier to complete the next one, and you will also find it easier when you return back to the normal training environment where the only people watching are the players' parents. In addition to this, the conversations that take place afterwards, which differ to those when you have asked someone to specifically observe your session and provide you with feedback, can be very educational. You will find that the conversations usually begin with the observer highlighting what they enjoyed and what they will take away from the session and use themselves. This is then usually followed by the observer asking questions about what they have just viewed to help their understanding and to gain further knowledge. By having to provide this information, we are developing not only our own communication skills, it also helps us to reinforce and strengthen our knowledge of the session in terms of our thought process in relation to the planning process and actual delivery of it. These conversations will also usually lead to the observer providing information on their coaching and some of the ideas and strategies that they use, which can then be adopted or adapted for our own use.

Though actual formal training is now seen by some as only shaping ten per cent of our learning, the importance of this type of learning should not be underestimated and should definitely not be discounted. The key to this form of learning is to approach it with an open mind and to enter the process with the mind-set that you will gain new knowledge and even if you take just one thing from it, then it has been beneficial and worthwhile. A common issue with formal coach education is that we often approach it from the standpoint that it is just a mandatory requirement that must be completed to achieve the end goal of a recognised qualification. This standpoint has usually been formed from the belief that the content of the course is a standardised curriculum that is based on what a high-level coach should look like and do and that the learners are then expected to mimic them. Therefore, this form of learning is seen as being ineffective in that it is not personalised and instead is a 'one-size-fits-all' approach. Coaches quite often are unable to see the link between the content of the course and the reality of their experience of being a coach.

Though the knowledge of the course tutors and the information that is provided can be quite high level and possibly unsuitable for the environment within which the learners are working, it is unlikely that this is the case for all of it. There will undoubtedly be some 'golden nuggets' that you will be able to take away from the experience that will have a big impact on your coaching and on you as a coach. There will also be other information that may not be as relevant but can still be used in some way to improve your coaching, whether this is by using only parts of what we have seen or by adapting it to make it suitable for your own environment. In addition to this, these courses provide opportunities to engage in other forms of development that have already been outlined within this chapter. They provide a chance to have a discussion with the other coaches attending the course, where ideas and experiences can be shared and relationships formed, creating new support mechanisms that can be continued beyond the end of the formal learning process. They also allow those attending the course to observe other coaches delivering, whether this is the experts delivering or in some cases, the learners themselves getting the opportunity to put on a practice. When this occurs, it provides the learners a chance to see coaches similar to themselves delivering a session and also the opportunity to deliver a session themselves, where they are likely to receive feedback afterwards.

Coaches can look to improve and develop themselves in a number of different ways and there is no particular way which is more effective than the others. Quite often a coach will choose the one that is most accessible to them, for example, if they are working alongside another coach, they will look to obtain feedback from them. Or they will select the option that they are the most comfortable doing. It can be a lot more stressful delivering a session whilst others are observing, compared to gaining new ideas through watching a coach. They may even select the one that they see as the most beneficial or worthwhile. This could be observing or talking to a coach that they see as more experienced or qualified, as they would have greater knowledge of the game. There is no right or wrong choice in terms of what coaches should do to improve themselves. The fact that you are engaging in some form of development, with the overall goal to get better at what you do, is enough and needs to be applauded.

At the start of the chapter, the topic of lifelong learning was touched upon, with it being suggested that if you can get into the habit of reflecting after each session, then you are engaging in a form of self-initiated education which is the basis of being a lifelong learner. By continuingly reviewing our performance as coaches, both in the planning and delivering stage of the process, we are accepting that we will never be a finished product and that there are always areas of our coaching that can be improved. This commitment to personal development can then be enhanced further by engaging in activities that could improve not only yourself but also others, such as observing or being observed by others. This engagement in personal development, whether it is through formal or informal learning, will not only help you grow as a coach, but it will also have an additional return, in that if your coaching improves then it would be expected that your players will improve as well. The 'plan, do, review' model is widely recognised within the coaching industry, as is the importance of this process. But if we can add a further stage to it – 'act upon' – it then enhances it even more. Adding on the 'act upon' stage reminds the coach that once they have reflected they have not quite finished, and therefore encourages them to do something about their findings from the reflective part of the process, which then stimulates growth and development.

CHAPTER 8
PRACTICE INTO MATCH DAY

Match day is always surrounded by anticipation and excitement by everyone involved – the players, family and, of course, the coach. It is the main reason that most people are involved in the sport and understandably so, as it is where the most enjoyable elements of the game are heightened and it is therefore essential that as coaches we do not get caught up in this excitement, but at the same time not take any of it away from the players. Now is a good time to remind yourself that your role as a coach, especially within the grassroots game, is about providing players with the opportunity to play the game that they love and to help these players to develop and get as close as possible to their full potential. Therefore, winning games of soccer should be very low on our list of priorities. We should take more pride as coaches in winning games and winning trophies when a team is reaching the end of their journey as youth players, rather than when they are just starting it or are in the middle of it, because this surely shows that we have done our job as a coach. Not only have we provided the players with an environment and experience that makes them want to stay in the game, but we have also developed and improved them to an extent that their development is much greater than those teams who they have grown up alongside but have now surpassed – or increased their distance from – in terms of level of ability. To do this, we must prioritise learning over winning games and therefore as coaches we may need to change our mind-set in that we approach it not as 'match day' but as another training session and therefore another opportunity for the players to learn and develop.

When doing this, it does not mean that we have to do the same for the players. As mentioned in the opening of this chapter, players look forward to playing a match and it plays a major part in why they initially start playing and then also stay involved in the game. So the trick is to allow 'all the players' to still enjoy the day as much as they usually would, whilst also increasing the learning that takes place. This is much easier to achieve than it sounds, by fully utilising every aspect of a player's match day experience – before the game begins, during breaks, at the end of the game and when they are a substitute, we can turn match day into an extension of the previous training session, whilst not taking away any of the enjoyment that the players get from playing a game and instead, actually adding to it.

The Warm-Up

This is quite often the longest amount of time during the match day experience that the players spend not actually playing the game, and therefore it can be the time that we take advantage of the most. It is also the time when we as coaches often make the most mistakes and also revert back to bad habits, in that the activities that we put on for the players are inappropriate or they are everything we said we would not do during training. The first mistake that we usually make is that we allow the players to revert back to their own bad habits that we have worked hard to remove from the training environment. When the players arrive for the game, we allow them to organise their own activity, which unsurprisingly involves them taking turns at taking a shot at goal, exactly the same activity that we did not want them doing at training. The advantage of using an arrival activity and the effect it can have on the development of players at the start of training was highlighted during chapter 3 and it can be argued that they are equally, if not more important, to use on a match day, as this is when the players are more likely to arrive sporadically and spend more time away from the close attention of the coach who is often occupied with a number of tasks in preparation for the game.

Using the same arrival activity that was used in the last training session prior to the game can be an effective strategy to get the players active immediately and also build upon the learning that took place during training. Because the players have just participated in the activity a few days previously, it is easy for them to remember what to do and also to recall their experiences within it; therefore, they are able not only to be active and engaged as soon as they arrive, but they can also learn from their previous time in the practice and either try something new or practice something they found difficult the first time around. A match day arrival activity can be set up exactly the exact same way in which the training session started, or it could be set up so that it replicates how it looked at the end, i.e., where it progressed to and it could then be progressed further. For instance, *Practice Thirty-Two* is an arrival activity that is primarily used for sessions that have a focus on dribbling, but can also easily be adapted for other topics such as running with the ball and passing. The initial set-up would be what the players are first introduced to when they arrive at training and also on match day, should the coach choose to use this approach. The practice could then be progressed by adding 'taggers' inside the area, where they have to dribble the ball and try to tag the other players travelling through the area. Points can then be awarded to the taggers for every player they tag and to the players for every time they travel through the area without getting tagged. The other option for the coach is to then use this progression as the starting point for when the players arrive on match day and then add a further progression, such as adding two players on the outside of the area (one on each side) that have to pass a ball to each other through the area, gaining a point each time they do so, whilst providing an additional obstacle for the other players to avoid.

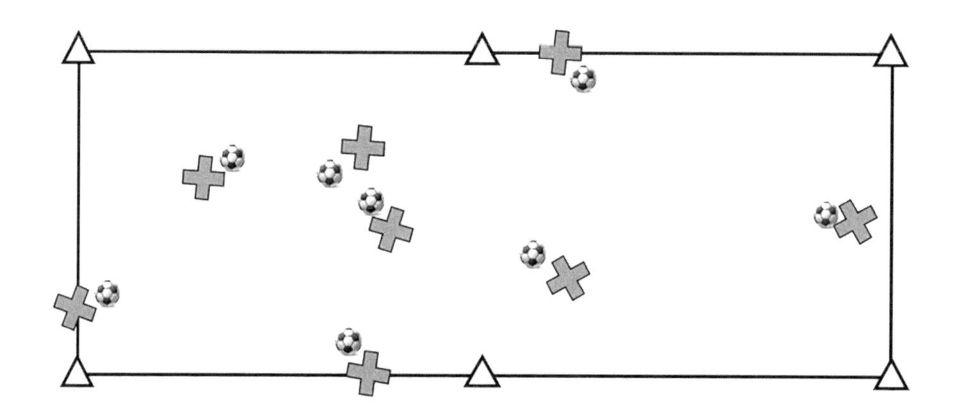

Player Area

Equipment Area

Practice Thirty-Two

Players dribble up and down a long narrow area. When travelling from one end to the other, players must visit each of the two long sides of the area at least once. Once they have reached the end of the area, they turn and travel back down, again visiting each long side at least once. The practice continues in this fashion, with an emphasis on the players scanning and manipulating the ball to avoid the other players.

Another mistake that we often make is that we forget that children are not small adults and therefore use warm-up activities that we see professional or adult teams do, which are not relevant or appropriate for young players. The best example of this is the use of stretches within the warm-up and, in particular, static stretches. When is the last time you saw a young child pull a hamstring? Or when did you see a child perform stretches before playtime at school or before they have a kick about with their friends? Not only are they not needed, but as they are usually performed using a regimented instructional method, they conflict with the message that we need to promote – freedom and play in all aspects of their training and development. Small children are quite flexible and the activities that they participate in are dynamic in nature and therefore performing static stretches will not benefit or prepare them for the upcoming activity they are about to take part in. There could be an argument that dynamic stretches could be used, as this form of stretching is a closer match to the activity ahead and that we should be getting them to do some form of stretching, as it teaches them good habits. But this good habit can be taught when they do need to begin to stretch or just before they do, or if a coach still persists that young players need to stretch, they can be disguised in a form of play. When performing a stretch, it is highly unlikely that they will complete it correctly anyway, and therefore getting the players to perform the relevant movements in some form of play can be much more effective and beneficial.

The use of tagging games in a player's physical development was promoted earlier in the book and, in particular, how they can be used to improve agility and also speed. But through small adjustments they can also be used as an effective warm-up activity ahead of a game. In *Practice Thirty-Three* a number of cones have been added to the area where a normal game of tag takes place. Various rules can now be added that will allow the players to complete a range of dynamic stretches in the disguise of play. For instance, the players avoiding being tagged can now earn points by touching a cone with their hands, if they do get tagged, they lose a point and the tagger earns a point. The key to this particular version of tag is the ratio of taggers to those avoiding being tagged; if there are not enough taggers, it will make it easy for the other players to touch the cones. By increasing the number of taggers, the remaining players are then likely to have to try to touch the cones whilst on the move and therefore stretch down to reach a cone as they run past it. Another option is to use the cones as bases and the players earn points by transferring from one base to another without being tagged; again if they are tagged they lose a point and the tagger earns a point. Here the players can be given a range of different movements or 'dynamic stretches' to complete between the bases. For example, they may have to complete heel flicks or karaoke steps, therefore completing stretches once more whilst playing. On this occasion, the number of taggers would need to be reduced to allow the players plenty of opportunities to move between bases, and the positioning and number of bases will also be important.

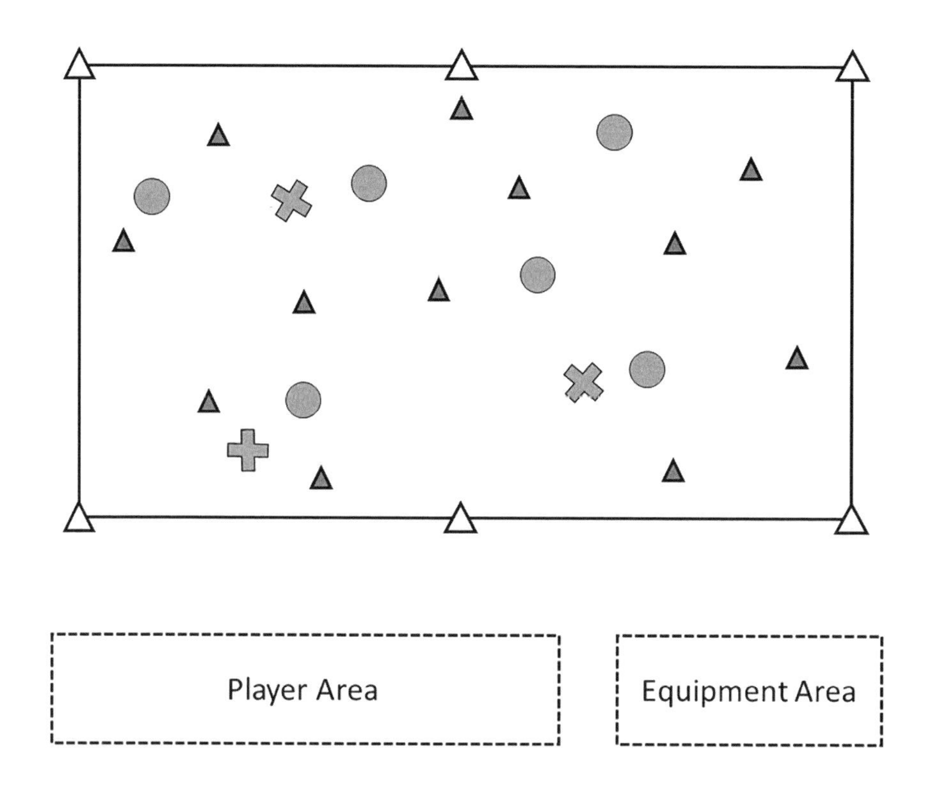

Practice Thirty-Three

This is a game of tag where the taggers gain a point every time they tag one of the other players. The players who are trying to avoid being tagged can win points if they are able to run between two cones, but they lose five points every time that they are tagged. The role of the taggers is changed regularly, and players only take on the role of a tagger for a short period of time.

The other mistake that we make during the period before the game is putting on a practice that we would no longer use within a training session. If we refer back to *Practice Twelve*, where the players were queuing up, waiting for their turn to have a shot on goal, it was noted how this does not represent what the players will experience in a game. In addition to this, the players spend long periods of time waiting for their turn. Therefore, this practice that we often see before a game actually goes against everything that we are trying to achieve within a warm-up; we are getting the players to practice something that they are highly unlikely to actually do within a game, whilst also spending most of their time stood still waiting for a go, having just spent a considerable amount of time 'warming up'. Surely it would be more beneficial for them to spend time being active, whilst practicing something that they are likely to come across once the game starts?

The most effective solution would be to allow the players to play in small-sided games, such as two versus two or three versus three, depending on the number of players on the squad and the resources and space that are available to the coach. Firstly, doing so allows the players to be constantly active, as within a game with these numbers the players are always involved, whether their team is in or out of possession of the ball. Secondly, it provides the players an opportunity to practice a lot of the things that they are about to do in the game within a realistic environment. Players in these games will be passing, dribbling, controlling the ball, tackling, etc. – everything they will do shortly in the main game. These small-sided games are also a good representation of what will happen in the game. When you watch a five-versus-five or seven-versus-seven game, or even a full-sized game, a lot of the time you will see small-sided games within them. For example, in a seven a-side game, a lot of the moments within it involve a small number of players, such as one versus one, or two versus one or three versus two – exactly the same pictures that you will see in a three-versus-three game. There is also another way in which we can use small-sided games during match day and this will be discussed later on within the chapter.

If it is not feasible to set up a number of small-sided games before the game, there are two further other options available to the coach. First of all, a practice which is easy to set up and easily adaptable can be used for every game. This gives the players the continuity of having the same activity, which then helps contribute to the players having a routine as they arrive on the day of the game. It also allows the players to get active and playing quickly. And by being easily adaptable, it can be altered when required to give the practice a different focus, whilst also providing variety for the players so that they remain motivated and engaged and do not become tired of participating in the same activity each week. Ideally, the practice will also incorporate many of the actions that the players will perform in the game afterwards. If we look back at *Practice Two* where two teams are looking to transfer the ball from one target player to another target player, this is a good example of a practice that has all of the elements needed within a warm-up activity that can be used regularly on a match day. It involves most of the actions that the players will perform within the actual game; the only component missing is shooting or finishing. It can be set up quickly, with only a small number of cones needed to set out the area and it can be easily adapted to provide variation and different outcomes. For instance, a number of small gates can be added within the area, with players needing to pass or dribble the ball through one of the gates before they can pass it to a server. Or another area could be added inside the main area which could be used in a number of ways, with teams having to complete the task before they can pass into the server, such as a player having to receive a pass inside the area or the ball having to be passed through the area.

Other practices that could be used in this way include *Practice Twenty-Nine* where the number of players used in the central area can be increased to accommodate the number of players, or additional servers could be placed on the outside, so each side has two servers instead of just one, which can represent two defenders or two centre backs, playing out from the back into the midfield area. Again, a number of different rules or tasks can be added to provide variety and a variety of challenges. *Practice Twenty-Seven* would be another option that could be used. To make it easier to set up, the small goals could be removed and instead, after the set number of passes have been achieved, a player has to dribble out of the area straight away, i.e., as soon as the set number of passes has been completed, the player receiving the last pass is not allowed to pass the ball and therefore must try to dribble out of the area without any support from their teammates.

The other option available to the coach is to extend the previous training session by using one of the practices from the session as the warm-up activity. This warm-up format can be used all the time so that it becomes the norm for the players, or it could be used if and when the coach feels it is needed. It could be that you feel that you did not get through everything you wanted to within the training session and therefore the time before the game provides an opportunity for the players to spend some further time practicing and learning. And because they would have done the practice just a few days earlier, it will be easy for them to remember what they are doing and therefore they are likely to get 'active' quickly. Taking this approach also links into another way in which the whole match day experience can be improved and used to support the players' development and speed up the learning process. This is achieved by linking training to the match day.

Linking Training to Match Day

At the beginning of the chapter, the idea of approaching match day as another training session was put forward and one of the most effective ways to do this is by continuing the focus from the previous training session into the match day. Doing so allows you to lengthen the time that the players are learning and developing their understanding and ability in relation to the topic. By extending the amount of time that the players are practicing and learning, it would be expected that they would improve more quickly and be more likely to reach their full potential. It can be a challenge for a coach to adopt this approach during a match day and it will undoubtedly feel uncomfortable and unnatural to begin with. It is also possible that you may receive some form of objection to this approach, as understandably most people will just see it as a game of soccer and will not want it to be an opportunity for the players to learn. But with a bit of planning and a little patience, it is possible to find the right balance of maximising learning, whilst allowing the players to experience and enjoy match day for what it is: a chance to try to win a competitive game of soccer.

The first option available to a coach has already been discussed within the chapter. Using a practice from the training session prior to the day of the match for the warm-up provides the players with an opportunity to continue their learning of the chosen topic. It could be that the coach picks up exactly where they finished off the practice in the training session. This is probably the point during the session after a number of progressions have been added to the practice and the coach has decided to end it and move into a game. Or the coach could revisit a certain part of the practice, such as the very start or after the first progression. The other option would be to carry on the theme of the previous session and use a practice that was not used within it. This could be a practice the coach had planned to use, but did not have enough time to introduce during the session, or just a practice that allows the players to work on the same topic that was the theme for the previous one. If this approach is chosen, then it should be done with real caution, as the danger of doing this is that it takes too long to get going, in terms of explaining it to the players and them fully understanding what they need to do. If this happens, then the main emphasis of the practice is lost, in that it is not fully preparing or 'warming up' the players ahead of the game. It is important that we do not forget the main reason for the players participating within the practice is to prepare for the game, so this must remain the priority, but if we can include some form of learning within it as well, then it can only be beneficial for the players.

The next opportunity for the coach to link their training session to the match comes just before and during the actual game. This is done by simply putting a 'focus' on the game, in the same way in which we have one for the training session. Having the same focus as the training session that preceded the match day gives the players a really good understanding of how what they do in training transfers to the game. So, for instance, if the training session had a narrow focus on dribbling, the game that follows this session could also have a focus on dribbling. This could include having the information that the players are given before the game focus on dribbling. For instance, players could be asked: When during the game will you look to dribble with the ball? What will you try to do whilst you are dribbling with the ball? This is all that needs to be discussed with the players; there is no need to overload them with additional information, as giving them too much will likely lead them to them not being able to recall any of it. By giving them just one element of the game to focus on, it is much more probable that they will retain what they are being asked to do and also attempt to apply it.

It is then possible to take this a step further by giving the players a challenge during match day. Just as we do during a training session, individual players or the group as a whole can be given challenges that are linked to the theme of the focus. If we continue with the example of dribbling, once we have completed the discussions with the players about when we might dribble with the ball during the game and what we might need to do whilst we are dribbling, we could then provide some or all of the players with some challenges that are linked directly to it. So, this could be that we ask particular players that prefer to release the ball as soon as they receive it, to have at least three or four touches before they look to transfer it to a teammate. Doing so will almost force the player to retain the ball for longer than they usually would and therefore it is more likely that they will be closed down by an opposition player, which will lead to the player having to dribble. It is really important that if we do use these challenges during the match day that we do not impose these challenges on the players for the whole of the game, but instead that they are used for a small amount of time or for one period of the game. If we do ask them to do this for the entirety of the match, then we are likely to take away some of the enjoyment that they get from playing the game. By asking them to do it for just a small amount of time, we are giving the players a chance to apply what they were practicing during the session in the match. If we do not give a player who prefers not to dribble this challenge, then it is possible that they do not attempt to dribble at all during the game.

The argument against taking such an approach is that whilst attempting to complete the challenge, the player loses the ball and the team concedes a goal, or that the player achieves little success and therefore loses confidence. If we consider the first point about how it could affect the outcome of the game and that it could cause the team to lose, the response would be: So what? Does it really matter? If along their learning journey players make mistakes that lead to their team conceding a goal or losing a match, does it really matter? When we consider the whole context of the amount of games that they will play throughout the length of time they are involved in the game and then also the low level of importance attached to these games when they are so young, the answer must surely be that it does not matter. In fact, these mistakes are an important part of the learning process, as they allow players to work out what works and what does not work. If we create an environment where it is accepted that players will make mistakes and that it does not matter if they do make them and it is just seen as part of the learning process, then any mistakes that are made in training or a game will pass by without even a thought.

With regard to the lack of success affecting a player's self-esteem or confidence, this again can be controlled by the environment that we create. If we can provide praise and congratulate the player for attempting the dribble and do not put any emphasis on the outcome, we can actually help them grow their confidence around this particular aspect of the game, as well as their overall self-esteem. The player has earned this praise for being brave enough to make the decision to retain the ball and then for attempting the dribble as well. Further pressure can be removed from the player if during the pre-match talk we explain to the players that by asking them to take extra touches of the ball before they release it, or by asking them to dribble more during the game, that it is your fault if they get tackled, it is your fault if they lose the ball and the opposition then go on to score a goal.

This support for the players can then be taken a step further by getting the parents or guardians involved as well. Quite often a coach will do their pre-match talk away from everyone else, as this could be done for a number of reasons, such as they find it easier for the players to concentrate or it is just down to the set-up of the pitch in terms of where the coaches and spectators have to stand. But if we are able to complete the pre-match talk close to parents and guardians, there are a number of benefits that can be gained from doing so. First of all, it helps create a closer relationship between you and this group of people who obviously have a major influence on the players' development, but more specifically they are an external influence on the decisions that the players will make during that particular game. Positioning ourselves in a place that allows them to listen to what is being discussed with the players allows them to feel they are part of the process. Instead of being on the outside looking in, trying to work out what is happening, they can now be a contributing factor in supporting the players' development. They are therefore more likely to help you in implementing a long-term player-centred approach, rather than unknowingly inserting possible obstacles into the process, such as taking away the decision-making process from the players by telling them what to do.

This then leads to the second way in which the parents or guardians can become involved in supporting the players. If we discuss with the players before the game that the focus is on dribbling and that we want them to try to dribble with the ball as much as possible during the game and the parents and guardians hear this, then once the game is up and running, they are then likely to support the players in achieving their task. Instead of telling a player to 'pass the ball', they are now more likely to encourage the player to stay on the ball and praise them for attempting to dribble and hopefully going past an opposition player. By doing this we are not only helping create the right environment for the player, but we are also getting a buy-in from other key stakeholders in the player's development: their parents or guardians. By including them in the process, by communicating the key messages to them at the same time as the players, allowing them to know what we are thinking and what our plan is, we are bringing them in from the outside – where they have just been looking in and observing – to the inside, where they now feel like an important cog in the wheel of the player's development.

The final way in which we can link the match day experience to training is by providing the players with exactly the same environment. So everything that we have identified that we want the players to encounter and feel during a training session also needs to be replicated during match day. Therefore, we want to ensure that we facilitate the match day with a player-centred approach, where every player gets the same opportunities and the focus is on fun and development. As with a training session, if we are going to create the right experience for the players during a match day, we need to accept the importance of the planning stage and then on the day we need to remember that the players are children and will therefore behave like children and will want to play and have fun. It is our responsibility to allow this to happen, whilst also incorporating some form of learning and development at the same time.

A player-centred approach during match day is very much similar to how it looks during training in that it involves the players being given the opportunity to find their own solutions to the different problems that they face, whilst receiving support that is specific for their individual development needs. When the players are training, this environment is produced by giving all the players the same amount of time and the opportunity within the practices to try to solve the problems they come across themselves. When providing support, the coach does not provide the players with the answers, but instead uses a question and answer technique, which helps them come up with the answer on their own. Individual challenges or restrictions are used to help the players with their own exclusive needs, whilst ownership and responsibility are also promoted by allowing them to make their own decisions in relation to themes such as the positioning of gates within a practice, how practices will progress, the position they will play in during the game at the end of the session, and the formation that they will use within this game. It is therefore quite easy to replicate this on the match day.

Ownership and responsibility are particular elements of a player-centred approach that can be implemented quite easily and with some high returns. If we take the team talks before the game or during intervals, for instance, these are usually led by the coach and the decisions made within these are also often made by the coach. We can change this by allowing the players to contribute and even make some or all of the decisions during these talks. So, instead of the coach deciding what formation the team will play and who will play in which position, can this be handed over to the players themselves sometimes? During the intervals when we are reviewing the period that just ended and are planning for the next period, can we again pass the responsibility of doing this on to the players from time to time? As coaches we may have to be brave in allowing this to happen and it will definitely feel uncomfortable doing this and will take you outside of your comfort zone, but discovering what they can be capable of and listening to the ideas that they come up with, can be extremely rewarding.

Using a question and answer technique can also be easily introduced during a match day as well, and its use during games is just as important as using it within the training environment. If we use question and answer during training, but then revert back to providing the players with information and the answers when they are playing a game, then we will lose the impact that this strategy has on the development of the players. If instead we continue to use this process on a match day as well, it will actually speed up their development, particularly within the psychological area of the game. Again during talks before and during the games, using question and answers can help the players work out solutions to the problems they are facing, allow the coach to check learning, possibly from the session prior to the game, and help to promote the players to reflect upon and analyse their own performances. Introducing this technique whilst the game is actually in progress can, however, be more challenging for both the coach and the players, but it is more than achievable if we trust in the process. Instead of telling a player they are standing in the wrong position and directing them to where they should be, we can simply ask them if they are happy with where they are standing. Could they stand somewhere that would help them protect the goal better? Instead of telling a player to 'pass' or to 'shoot', give them the chance to make the decision themselves and if they make the wrong decision, instead of telling them what they did wrong, ask them what they might do differently next time.

The most challenging aspect of using question and answer during a game is that if it is to be truly effective, then we need the full attention of the player whilst we are asking the question and they then provide a response. This also needs to be done immediately after the action has taken place, so that it is easier for the player to remember what happened and to help ensure what they do recall is accurate. This does not necessarily mean that we have to actually remove them from the game, but it does mean that their involvement in the game will need to be put on hold temporarily, whilst the discussion between yourself and the player takes place. This can obviously be difficult for the player, their teammates and the coach and also for those watching. Especially if whilst this is going on the team concedes a goal or they miss out on a goal-scoring opportunity because the player is not standing where they would have been if they were not speaking with the coach. But it goes back to asking: What exactly do we want to achieve? Do we want to sacrifice a valuable learning opportunity for that player, one that will benefit them not only in the game that they are currently playing in, but for all future games as well because we are worried it 'might' have an impact on the team conceding or missing an opportunity to score a goal in a game that is not important in any way? By having a long-term strategy to our coaching and player development, we will need to accept that there will need to be sacrifices along the way, but these are insignificant when compared to the returns that we will gain throughout the journey and the final product that we help the players reach.

In terms of providing the players with the same opportunities and promoting equality, this would need to include not only equal playing time for all of the players, but also rotating which players start the game and the positions that they play. If we are truly going to implement a long-term approach to the development of the players, then this needs to include providing them with a range of experiences and not just during training, but also when they play games as well. If we continuously put the players in the same positions, then they will miss out on facing a variety of situations, which they will not experience in the position that they always play. For example, if we always ask a player to play as a defender or centre back, how often will they find themselves in a wide area with the ball against an opposition defender? How often will they be in a position to cross the ball or have an attempt at goal? We also need to ask the question: How can we tell at such a young age what a child's best position is? And how can we lock them into a position that we think they should stay in for the rest of the time that they play the game? By providing each and every player the same chance to have a go at being a striker, to be a defender or to play in the wide areas, then we are giving them all the same learning experience, whilst also giving them the opportunity, as well as the time, to discover where they enjoy playing and where their own unique qualities and skills as a soccer player are best suited.

When we are considering rotating the positions that the players play in, we should always look to include the goalkeeper within this process. Of all the positions within soccer, the goalkeeper is, of course, the most unique and requires a completely different set of skills compared to those of an outfield player. From their first introduction to some form of physical activity, we should encourage children to play a range of different sports.

By doing so, they can transfer skills they learn in one sport to other sports that they play; they can also 'sample' these sports to find out which ones they enjoy the most or are most suited to and it prevents 'burn out' in that they do not get bored farther down the road, due to playing the same sport from a young age. In the same way, we should encourage and allow young players to sample and try a position that is completely unique to the game. And if we cannot tell at a young age whether a player is going to be a striker or a defender in the future, how can we possibly tell if they will or will not be a goalkeeper? Especially when you consider that as the game changes and gets closer and closer to the full version, i.e., eleven-versus-eleven, the skills and characteristics needed to be a goalkeeper change quite significantly compared to when they first play the game. Therefore, if we rotate who plays in goal, it will benefit the player who enjoys playing in goal, as it will help them with their footwork and to experience playing outfield, which they might find they enjoy. It will also allow other players to try out this position, which they may discover they enjoy or are good at or both.

Linking the match day to training is one of, if not the most, challenging aspects of transforming our approach to coaching with a long-term, player-centred approach. It can be uncomfortable at first for a coach to implement and it can be challenging to get the buy-in from additional stakeholders: other coaches, players and parents. Quite often they find it difficult to look beyond what is directly in front of them, which is basically just a game of soccer and are therefore unable to see that it can also be a further opportunity for the players to learn and develop. And because there is this resistance against this form of approach from the start, it can be difficult to continue to introduce and persevere with this new concept. However, if we can persist and educate the other stakeholders by explaining why we are adopting this particular approach, then the rewards can be endless. And if we do make these changes and make the match day experience similar to that found within our training sessions, it does not mean that we have to lose everything that the players enjoy about playing the game. It can still be competitive and fun and the players can still approach it with a mentality to try to win the game; it is then just adding a hint of opportunity for the players to develop and learn at the same time, with the message that though it is nice to win, it does not matter if we lose.

Substitutes

Once a match has started, as coaches we understandably concentrate mainly on the game and supporting the players within it. As a result of this, we often forget about the players who are not involved in the game and are waiting patiently for their turn to play. This time that the players spend on the sidelines, waiting to get on to the pitch, is another opportunity that can be utilised by the coach to provide them with another chance to learn and develop. This can be achieved through either giving them a task to complete whilst they are watching the game or by putting on an activity that they can participate in. Which one we choose can often be influenced by external factors outside of our control. For instance, the weather can have a major impact on which strategy we choose for that particular day. If it is a particularly hot day, we may not want the substitutes to be involved in an extra physical activity and therefore instead a task they can complete whilst watching the game would be more suitable. And if the weather is cold or wet, then a physical activity to help keep players warm would be more suitable, plus a written task in these type of conditions may not be possible. Other factors that can have a bearing on which approach we take to provide further learning opportunities for the substitutes will include the space that is available next to the pitch – is there enough to put on an activity for the players? The equipment that the coach has available – is there enough, or the right type, to put on specific activities? The number of substitutes that we have can also almost make the decision for us in terms of what we provide for them. Either way, by providing a task or a physical activity, we can improve the experience the players have when they are not playing in the actual game.

At the start of the chapter we discussed using small-sided games as a warm-up activity for the players. They were put forward as ideal activities to prepare the players for the main game as they allowed players to be constantly active and they involve most things that will happen in the match that follows; basically they are a realistic representation of the full game. Therefore, not only are they a good warm-up activity, they are also ideal for the substitutes to play whilst they are waiting to play in the match. Players turn up on match day because they want to play in a game of soccer; they do not want to be standing and waiting their turn, so if they cannot be involved in the main match, then surely the next best thing is to play in a small game with their friends. Their experience could be enhanced further if we can involve the substitutes from the other team as well, so that they get the opportunity as well and so that they are all playing against players that they do not usually play against. These players will be different to the teammates that they usually play with and therefore will have different strengths and have different ways of doing things, meaning new challenges and new problems to solve. Overall these small-sided games will produce a stimulating and enjoyable learning experience for all involved and are clearly a better use of the time for the substitutes compared to just being stood watching the match.

Of course, the activity that we put on for the substitutes does not need to be restricted to just a small-sided game. First of all, the games do not have to have goals, especially if small goals are not available. Different forms of games can be put on that are simple to set up and do not need much equipment. *Practice Thirty-Four* just consists of an area and two teams, and in this particular instance the teams win a point if a player is able to dribble the ball over the opposite team's line. Other variations of this small-sided game could be that teams are awarded a point if a player receives a pass on the other side of opposition's line, i.e., off the pitch. Another option would be that the teams have to complete a set number of passes before a player can drive out of any side of the area, or it could be that two cones are used instead of actual goals. Any of the options are more than suitable, especially when they are compared to what the players were doing before.

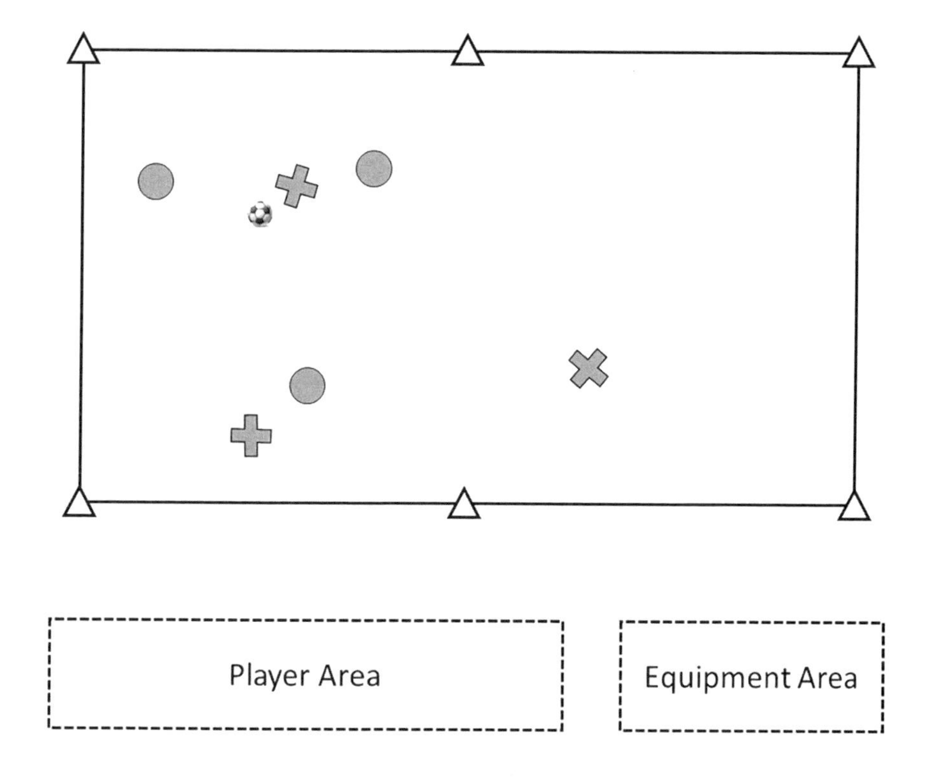

Practice Thirty-Four

A small-sided game consisting of whatever players are available to play. Teams win a point if one of their players dribbles the ball (under control) over the opposing team's line.

The other option is to move completely away from actual small-sided games and just provide some form of activity that the players can do whilst they are waiting to play. So, for example, they could play soccer tennis, have a keepy-ups competition or participate in some form of rondo. These particular activities are suitable if the area available is restricted or if the number of players taking part is also limited. As with the small-sided games, the rules and the size of the area can be changed to meet the needs of not only the players in terms of their ability, but also the outcome that you want to achieve in terms of levels of intensity and/or difficulty. Do you want to use it just for the players to enjoy or do you want it to be an environment where they challenged and taken out of their comfort zone? Again there will be factors that influence our decision making. The weather could affect how intense we want the activity to be, as could the length of time that they are expected to be doing the activity until it is their turn to go and play in the match.

Overall it can be quite difficult to plan an activity for the substitutes, as quite often we can never be sure exactly how many players we will have until the actual day of the game and we do not always play the games at the same venue and therefore it is not always possible to know what space, if any, is available to set up the activity. Therefore, it is recommended that a coach use just two or three activities that are quick and simple to set up and cover all of the different situations that are likely to occur throughout the season. For example, one activity could be used for when there is a limited amount of room, another for when there is a small amount of players and the last one, which is likely to be the small-sided game, for when there is the 'usual' amount of players and sufficient room to set up. By putting on any kind of activity for the substitutes, we are helping to improve all of the players' match day experience, with the possibility of some learning and development also taking place. This can only be a good thing and therefore it does not matter what format it comes in, as long as the players are active and enjoying it.

The other option is to give the substitutes a task to complete whilst they are waiting for their turn to play. This can be really beneficial for their development, as it can be a different way in which they can learn compared to how they usually learn within training. These tasks can be based on the individual players completing the task for themselves, or they can be aimed at helping and supporting the whole team. Providing the substitutes with these tasks encourages them not to just watch the game but to start to explore and consider what is actually happening within it as well. This then helps the players to start to analyse, a valuable skill that can play an important part in their development. If they can start to get in the habit of analysing their own performances, they will be able to identify what they do well and what they could possibly work on to get even better. So by not only providing a further opportunity to learn whilst the match is going on, it can also enhance their development going forward, by promoting deeper learning through the players becoming critical thinkers and possibly self-directed learners.

The first option is to provide the players with tasks that are directly related to them. It could be that you inform the player of the position they will play in when they come on and then they have to try to identify what they will try to do when it is their turn to play. This might include identifying what the player who is currently playing in that position is doing really well and/or what they could do that they are not currently doing. It could also include analysing the player they could possibly come up against and again identify particular areas about their performance that could benefit them when they go on to play. Other possible options for individual tasks could be that the players are asked to provide feedback to a specific teammate that they have been assigned to watch. So during the break, before the usual group team talk takes place, the substitutes could be given a minute to give feedback to the teammate that they were observing. Another option would be to ask each individual substitute to watch every player, including players from the other team, on the pitch and identify one thing that they see a player do that they will then try to do themselves when they come on to play. This could be a particular skill, how they press a player on the ball, how they receive the ball – it can be anything they want, they just need to make sure they try it when it is their turn to play.

Alternatively, we could ask the substitutes to work together and gather information from the game that could be beneficial for the whole team. This could be that we ask them to count the number of successful and unsuccessful passes that the team makes during a period, or it could be the total number of shots that they have and how many of these are on target. The information that they gather could then be used during the interval to provide the players with both feedback and also targets for the next period. Ideally the tasks that we give to the substitutes are directly linked to the training session that took place before the match, so if the focus of the session was on passing or possession, then the task of counting the number of passes would be relevant and suitable. If the session had a focus around dribbling, we could set a task to identify where players like to try to dribble with the ball, so we could split the pitch into sections for the players completing the task. This could be as simple as the two halves of the pitch, the attacking half and defensive half, or it could be slightly more complicated and split into more sections, either vertically or horizontally or even both.

Once the information has been passed on to the players during the interval, a specific target for them to try to achieve for the next provided can be set. So if we return to the task that is based on passing, we could ask the players to try to achieve more successful passes in the next period or we may ask them to not try to pass the ball as much when we get in the final third of the pitch, so can we concentrate on passing the ball in the defensive and central third. The task of collating the data to see if the team is successful in achieving this target can then be given to the substitutes for the next period. The information can then be gathered again and used in the next interval or at the end of the game. Using this particular strategy of all of the substitutes completing the task together helps develop other skills as well as their analysing and observational skills. To complete the task successfully, the players will have to work as a group and organise who will be responsible for each element of the task and then be able to put it altogether. If we refer back to chapter 4 and the different areas of a player's development, then this form of task is really beneficial for supporting the players with their social skills, skills that they can use both on and away from the pitch.

It is easy to forget about the players who are not are on the pitch, as we fully concentrate on the game and those players participating in it. We feel it is our responsibility to provide these particular players with all of our support and guidance, because if we do not it may affect the outcome of the game, or that they cannot do it without our support, or because that is what we are expected to do and that is what everyone who is watching expects. But we need to remember that every player gets the same support and receives equal amount of your time. It can, of course, be argued that they will all receive this equally if they spend the same amount of time on the pitch and this is true, but why limit it to the time when they are playing the game? Can we utilise the full time that they are with us on a match day? And by carefully planning either tasks or physical activities for the substitutes, they will not need much support or help and therefore whilst doing whatever they have been asked to do, they will also be developing skills related to ownership and responsibility, something that can only be beneficial and a positive for their long term development.

The Role of the Coach on Match Day

The final piece of the jigsaw in creating the right environment is the role that we take on as the coach and changing this from a controlling, managing role to a facilitating, supportive role. This will include letting go of some or all of the responsibilities and decision making that takes place throughout match day and passing these on to the players. Once we have done this, we then just need to provide them with some guidance and also the confidence to work out and apply their solutions. The hardest part of this process is letting go and allowing the players to have more ownership of the day, particularly during the actual game and also the team talks that take place before, during and after the match.

We can find it difficult during the game not to give the players instructions or to provide a commentary on what is happening. When we see them struggling with something, we naturally want to help them and the quickest way in which we can do this is to directly give them the information. We can find it difficult and uncomfortable to stand back and watch it happen and not step in and provide them with support. But if we continue to do this, how can we expect them to find the answer themselves? How can they become independent thinkers and problem solvers? They will always be dependent on us providing them with the solution. Therefore, it can be difficult to step back and just watch as they attempt to work out what they should do. This, however, is essential if we are going to fully promote a long-term, player-centred approach to our coaching and we can still, of course, support the players in a number of different ways. We have already spoken about using question and answer with the players whilst the game is still in progress and this is probably the most effective way in which we can support the players during the game. We can, of course, also provide large amounts of praise and encouragement, especially when we can see that they are trying to do the right things but they just cannot quite pull it off, such as the execution of a pass or an attempt to go past a defender. By praising them for making the right decision and/or for just attempting this particular skill, we are sending a message to them that what they are doing is the right thing and that they should continue to do what they are doing. This will help increase the player's self-esteem and provide them with clarification that they are making good decisions and identifying the right solutions to the problems they are facing. Though we might not be providing them with an instant fix, we are providing them with the guidance that they are on the way to solving the problem themselves, which is much more rewarding for both you and them, rather than just giving them the answers.

The other area of match day where we can pass on responsibility and ownership is during the talks that we have with the players before, during and at the end of the game. Some of the different ways in which this can be achieved have already been touched upon within the chapter. Passing on the responsibility of selecting the team formation and the playing position of the players is a great example of passing on ownership to the players, but it is what we do in our role as facilitators during this time that will determine how effective this task is in terms of providing an opportunity for learning to take place. Facilitating it does not mean that we just step away from the situation and allow the players to make all of the decisions. The first step of the process is how we actually deliver the task to the players. If we just ask them to choose any formation that they want, then they might come up with all kinds of different variations, which might not only be unsuitable but will also make it difficult for everyone to agree upon the formation that will be used. Therefore, the task set by the coach could be to provide two possible formation options that the players have to choose from and if the players are unable to decide which option they want to use, the role of the coach is to facilitate a discussion in which the players get to say why they think their choice of formation should be used. Ensuring that the task does not offer the possibility of it moving away from its main purpose and become too open in terms of where the players can take it will help to make sure that the opportunity for learning to take place does not get lost within unstructured discussion. So whilst facilitating the task, the coach needs to ensure that the discussions stay on the task and that there is an agreed-upon and quick conclusion.

Also previously discussed within this chapter was the option of giving the substitutes tasks to complete whilst they are waiting to play in the game. Some of these tasks included gathering data, such as the number of successful passes or the amount of shots on target. On gathering this data, we can then allow the substitutes themselves to present it back to the rest of the players, along with any additional information they want to add. Again as coaches we are then responsible for ensuring that the conversations that take place stay on task and that there is an endpoint, so that the players who are going on to play have a clear focus on what they are trying to achieve. Once more this can be really difficult for a coach to allow to happen, as there will be other things that they have seen within the game that they will want to talk to the players about and try to fix. But it goes back to that long-term approach. Trying to resolve problems that have literally just happened is very much a quick fix approach that will not allow the players to learn the crucial skills they need to develop at this stage of the journey that will be crucial later on. And constantly changing our focus on what we want to work on with the players can also really hinder their development.

The discussions that take place after the game can also follow the same format in that they are player-led, with the coach overseeing and providing direction, if or when the discussions move away from the focal point. After the game, the players could look to identify what went well and what could possibly be improved; this could be in relation to their own individual performance and the team as a whole as well. This then presents another opportunity to pass on ownership to the players, this time in relation to their willingness to learn and practice away from the time that they spend with you and the other players. Based on the areas that they identified in which they could have done better, players can come up with suggestions for what they can do to work on these areas of their game before the next training session or game. Here the players are now starting to take ownership for their own learning as we encourage them to become motivated learners who are actively seeking the knowledge and solutions that they need so that they can become better in the area that they want to develop. By encouraging the players to take more ownership of their own learning, we are directing them towards the process of lifelong learning, which does not just improve knowledge, but also enhances social inclusion, personal development and self-sustainability. These are skills which can only benefit them in their personal lives as well as in their professional lives.

The biggest concern that we have with this approach of passing on ownership and responsibility is that the players are not ready or capable of taking on this responsibility and coming up with the right solutions. We see ourselves as the experienced adult that has all of the knowledge and therefore we should be helping them by giving them the answers to the questions they are being asked. But we need to give them the opportunity to surprise us. How can we possible know that they are not ready or do not know how to solve the problem, if we have not given them a chance? When a child brings their homework back from school, we expect them to attempt it on their own first and then if they are struggling to complete it, then we provide them with some support and try to help them to work out the answers. We wait and see what they do know and what they can do, before we even consider providing support. What we do not do is just tell them the answer, because we know this is not how they will learn and that they need to understand the process themselves, so that in the future they do not need any help. So why would we change this approach to a child's learning, just because the subject is now soccer? Just because it is a sport, and possibly something that we enjoy ourselves, does not mean that the process of how a child learns changes. We know what is right for a child in terms of how they learn and therefore we should not allow ourselves to be distracted or blinded from what we know is the right thing to do, just because it is soccer that they are learning.

Allowing the match day to become an extension of the players' training and learning is one of the most difficult things that we can commit to in our coaching. It is easy to get carried away with the whole match day experience and the fact that it is a game of soccer. Naturally we want to try to win the game – it is one of the main reasons that we enjoy being involved in this particular sport. But we need to remember that this is not the reason we got involved in coaching in the first place. The most likely reasons for starting our coaching journey are to provide the players with an opportunity to play the game, to teach them how to play it and to help them to become as good as they possibly can at playing it. Therefore, in the exact way in which we plan and deliver our coaching sessions, we should approach a match day with the same objectives that we had when we started our coaching journey: to produce an environment which allows the players to play a game that they love, whilst being able to learn and develop along the way. We are in a unique and privileged position where we can have a major impact on the lives of these young children and it is essential that we respect this privilege by ensuring that they are in an environment where they feel safe and can just enjoy playing the game that they love, and this includes both the training environment as well as the match day environment.

CHAPTER 9
BUILDING SESSIONS

Throughout each chapter, different practices have been used to provide examples of how we can produce the ideal environment for the players to be able to enjoy their soccer. They will be given the freedom and opportunity to be creative, so that they can attempt to work out different solutions to the many problems they will face in practices that they will find both challenging and fun and where the environment they are playing in is chaotic and ever-changing, just like the game of soccer itself. With these specific examples of practices that will put the players in such challenging situations, you should get a clearer picture of how coaches can create the perfect 'classroom' for learning the game of soccer, whilst also fuelling players' love for the game, keeping them motivated to stay involved both in the short and long term. This chapter puts all these practices together in one section, basically as a library of practices, so that they can be referred to quickly and easily and can help with the planning of your sessions. In addition to the practices that have already been used throughout the book, a few more practices have also been added to increase the support provided within this crucial part of the coaching process.

As discussed in chapter 2, coaches will naturally look to implement sessions that are used by other coaches, those practices that we think the players will enjoy and that we basically like the look of. Or we may use practices that are used by those we see as more experienced and successful coaches, because it is presumed that they must be effective, if they are being used by these 'higher level' coaches or teams. But we must remember the message from chapter 2, which is that when we are looking to use these other practices, we cannot assume just because they are suitable for one group of players that they will be suitable for others, or more specifically for the group of players that we are working with. Therefore, the practices outlined in the rest of this chapter are not meant to be taken straight from the book onto the pitch, but rather they are there to provide initial ideas and concepts which can then be altered and developed to meet the specific needs of the players. A number of possible variations are provided with each practice to help stimulate ideas of how the practice can be varied. Most of the time, we will not know whether these ideas will work until we actually implement them on the pitch. And if they do not work, we should not be discouraged, but rather see it as a further opportunity to learn in terms of both our coaching and also what does and does not work with the players.

As well as possible variations for each practice, a recommendation is also provided on which element of the session they can be used for: first practice, main practice or game practice. It is then possible to select a number of practices than can be put together to create a full session. Quite often a practice can be used for more than one element of the session and can be used in whatever way is required for each particular session; how they are used will be influenced by a range of factors, including the topic of the session, the other practices that are being used, the players' current understanding of the topic and the space and time available in terms of the set-up and delivery. However, what will not be provided is the focus that the practices can be used for, as each one can be used for a range of different topics.

When selecting practices for a specific topic we just need to remember two key things in both the planning and delivery of the session that were discussed in chapter 3. First, whatever the topic of the session is, there must be lots of opportunities for the players to do it within the practice. Remember they should be doing it more often than they would usually do in a normal game, especially if it is a key part of how they win points. For instance, if it is a topic on passing, they might need to complete a set number of passes. This then either wins them a point or it allows them to then go on and win a point. Therefore, when making alterations to vary the practice, not only should we be considering the needs of the players, but also the focus of the session. Do the changes that we make encourage or even force the players to do a lot of whatever the topic of the session is? Are they getting lots of opportunities to practice the topic?

The second key factor we need to remember is that when we actually deliver the practice, all of the support we provide the players is focused specifically on the topic of the session.

It is important that we try not to help the players with too many elements of the game in just the one practice. Though it is great and understandable that we want to help them learn as much as possible, the learning that takes place will be much more effective if it has just one clear aim: to improve passing or to improve dribbling, or whatever we have selected the topic to be. If we start adding additional information for the players to process, the key messages we are trying to get across and focus the practice around can easily get lost.

If we can remember these key messages, then these practices can be used throughout the development of the players. They will provide the players with the right experience and the right environment to learn and develop, no matter what stage of development they are at or what format or level of the game they are playing. Any player will enjoy taking part in them, provided they are suitable and relevant for those particular players.

Practice One:

First Practice / Main Practice / Game Practice

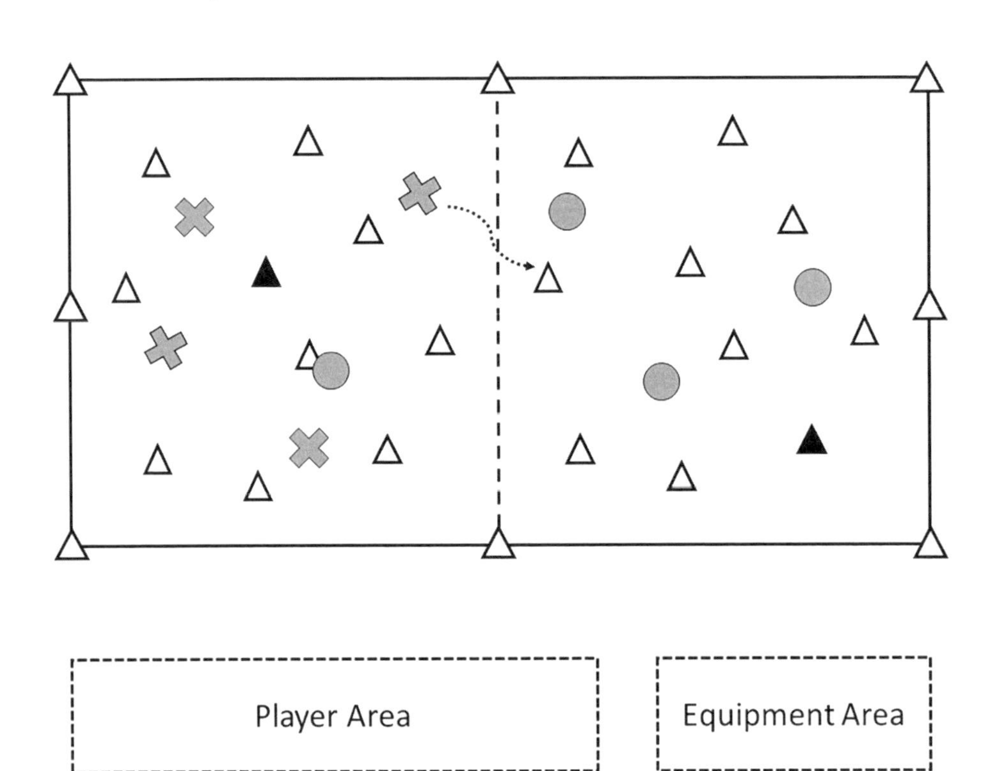

Practice One

Players are split into two teams, with each team defending the cones in their half of the pitch whilst also trying to steal the cones from the other team's half of the pitch. Players can stay or leave their half of the pitch when and as they please. If a player is 'tagged' in the opponent's half whilst in possession of a cone, they must drop it where they were tagged and return to their own half and touch the far end line before returning to the game. Each cone is worth one point apart from a number of 'bonus' cones (these are a different colour to the rest of the cones), which are worth extra points (the exact number can be decided by the players). After a set amount of time, the game ends, and the team with the most points in their half wins.

Possible Variations

- Consider the width and length of the area to meet the needs of your players; each half of the area does not have to be identical in size or shape.
- Allow the players to choose the location of the cones on their half of the area.
- Players can only move by hopping.
- Use a number of different coloured cones, with each colour worth a different point.
- Keep as a team game, but players are paired up and can only tag each other.
- Change the cones for balls, with the players having to dribble the balls back to their side of the area.

Practice Two:

First Practice / Main Practice / Game Practice

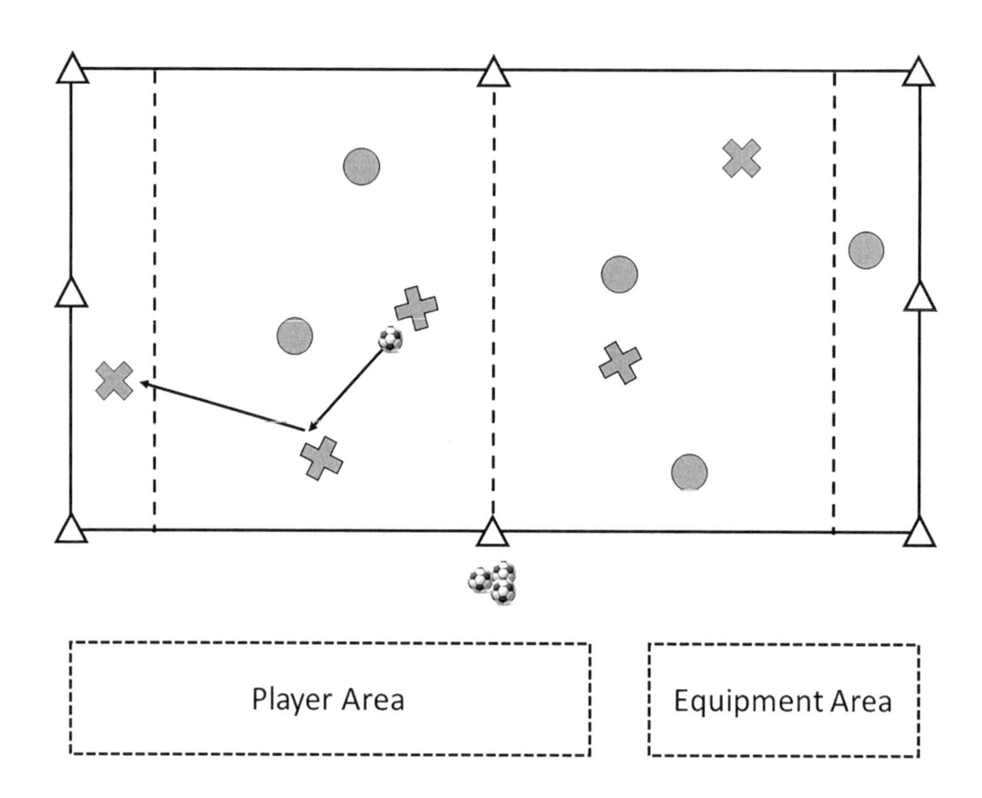

Practice Two

Players are split into two teams. Each team has a target player in an end zone. Teams win a point by playing the ball to the target player. Players use their hands only to receive and pass the ball (similar to netball, when in possession of the ball, they cannot move). If a target player receives the ball, it is a point, and they pass the ball to the opposition.

Possible Variations

- Players can move with the ball but if tagged, must hand over possession.
- The ball cannot touch the ground. If it does, possession gets handed over to the other team.
- If a team wins a point they have to retreat into their own half before play restarts.
- Teams are split in half with half the team restricted to one half of the pitch and the other half to the other side of the pitch.
- A set number of passes must be completed before the ball is played to the target player.
- Have an extra task once the ball has been played to the target player. For example, another player has to go into the end zone and receive a pass off the target player, or the target player has an attempt at goal.
- Instead of using their hands, players now use their feet.

Practice Three:

First Practice / Main Practice / Game Practice

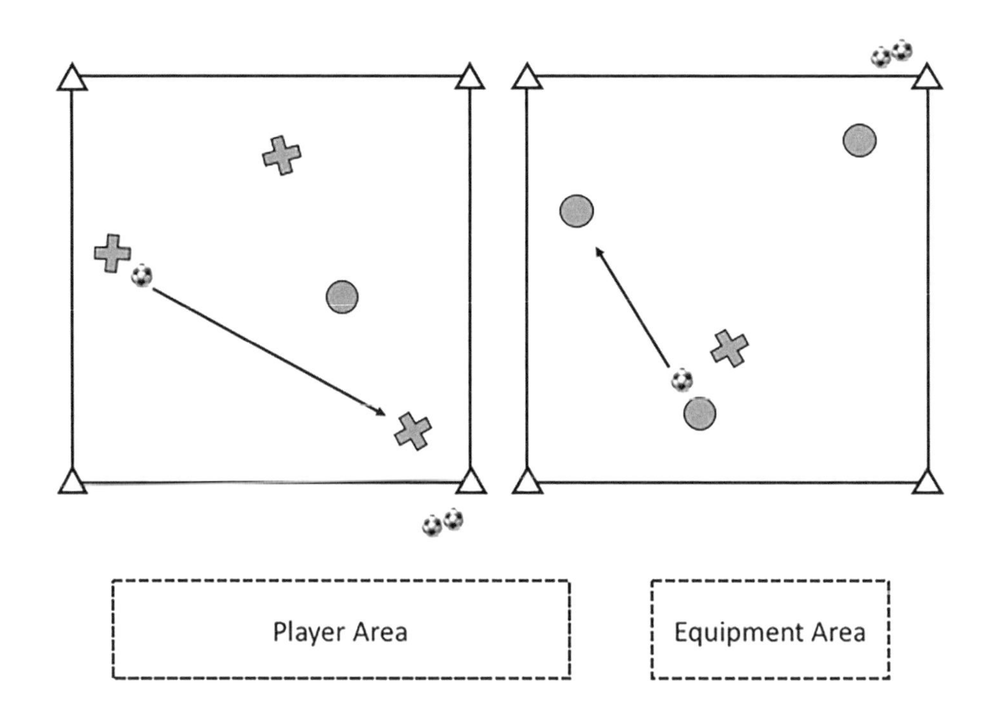

Practice Three

Three-versus-one practice, where the three attacking players look to retain possession of the ball. The player looking to intercept the ball remains as a defender for a set period of time or until they gain possession of the ball. During the practice, consider rotating the participants between the different grids so that they play with and against a range of players. Or you may want to organise the players so that they are playing with and against players that will challenge them.

Possible Variations

- Consider the width and length of the pitches to meet the needs of your players. Each pitch does not have to be identical in size or shape.
- Limit the number of touches that the attacking players can have.
- Use a smaller ball to make it more difficult to pass and control.
- The balls can be transferred between areas, but the players remain locked in.
- Players stay as defenders for a set period of time. If they win the ball, they look to keep it from the attacking players for as long as possible.

Practice Four:

First Practice / **Main Practice** / Game Practice

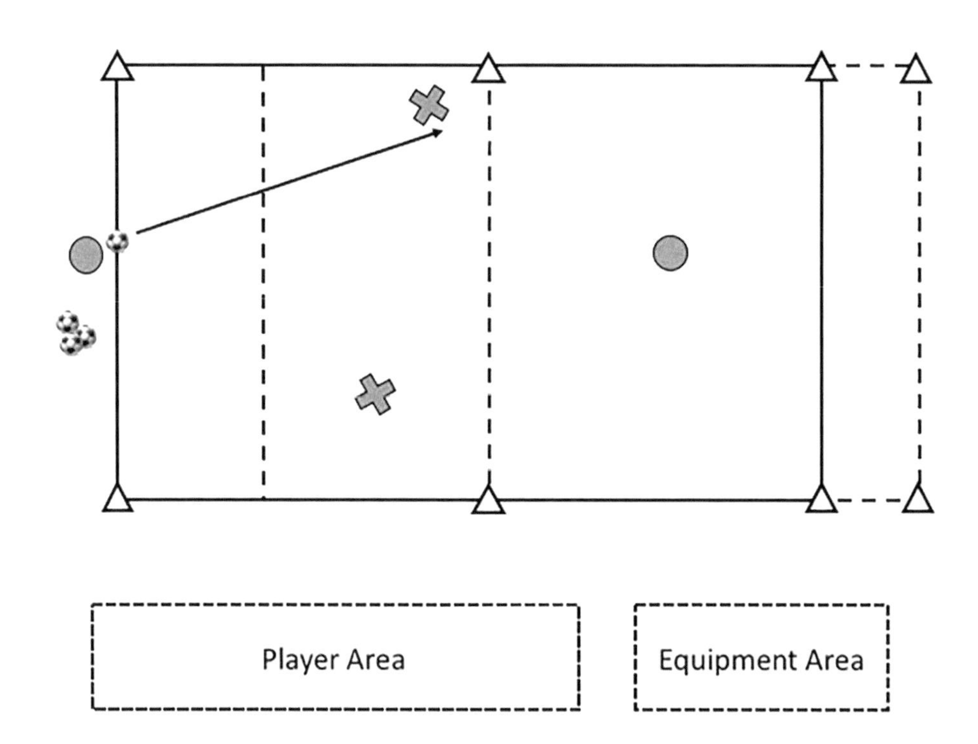

Practice Four

Two-versus-two practice, with the area split into thirds (the thirds are not equal in terms of size and need to be set up to meet the needs of your players). The server plays the ball into the attacking players who enter the final third and look to score a point when one of them receives a pass in the 'target zone'. Once the attacking players have entered the final third, the server then becomes a second defender and makes a recovery run to support their team-mate who has been attempting to delay and prevent the attacking players from scoring a point. Should the defending players win the ball, they look to get the ball back to the first third by having either one of the players dribbling the ball into it or receiving a pass within it.

Possible Variations

- Consider the width and length of the pitches and each individual area to meet the needs of your players. Each pitch does not have to be identical in size.
- Replace the 'target zone' with a small goal that the attacking players have to pass into.
- Allow the defender to start where they want.
- Allow the server to enter the area as soon as they have made the initial pass.
- One attacking player starts in final zone with the defender, and the initial pass is played to them.
- Add a goal and goalkeeper for once the attacking players enter the 'target zone'.

Practice Five:

First Practice / Main Practice / Game Practice

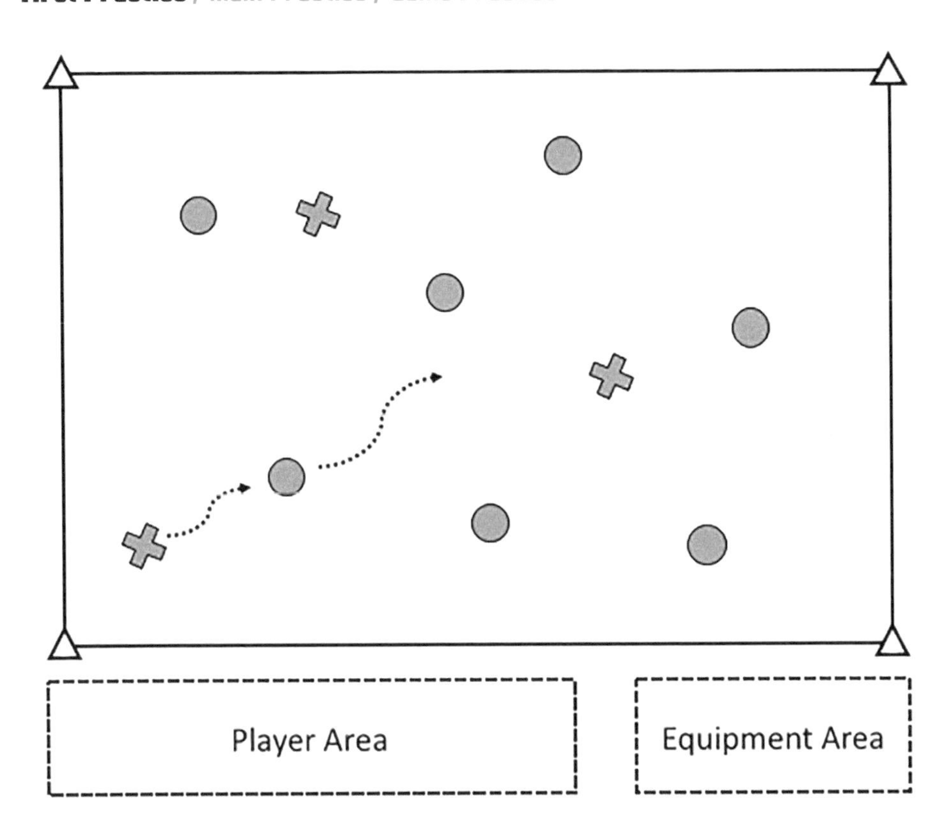

Practice Five

A small number of taggers attempt to tag the rest of the players. If a player is tagged, they are 'frozen' and must remain still until they are released by one of their team-mates. (This could be with a 'high five' or by running under the frozen players outstretched arms.) Taggers aim is to try and tag all of the players so that they are all frozen.

Possible Variations

- The players are given a challenge to complete whilst they are frozen to increase the physical returns; for instance, you might challenge them to balance on one foot.
- Consider the width and length of the area to meet the need of your players and the outcomes you want from the practice. For instance, a small area will mean more agility, and a larger area will require more speed.
- Different shaped areas will lead to different outcomes. A circle means no corners to get caught in, whereas a triangle makes it easier to get cornered, and so on.
- Add an additional area and use as needed. For example, it could be a 'No Go Zone' for all players, just the taggers or just the players who are trying to avoid being tagged.
- Add balls and use as needed. All players have a ball and dribble whilst either tagging or avoid being tagged; only a small number of balls are introduced, and the players in possession cannot be tagged.

Practice Six:

First Practice / Main Practice / Game Practice

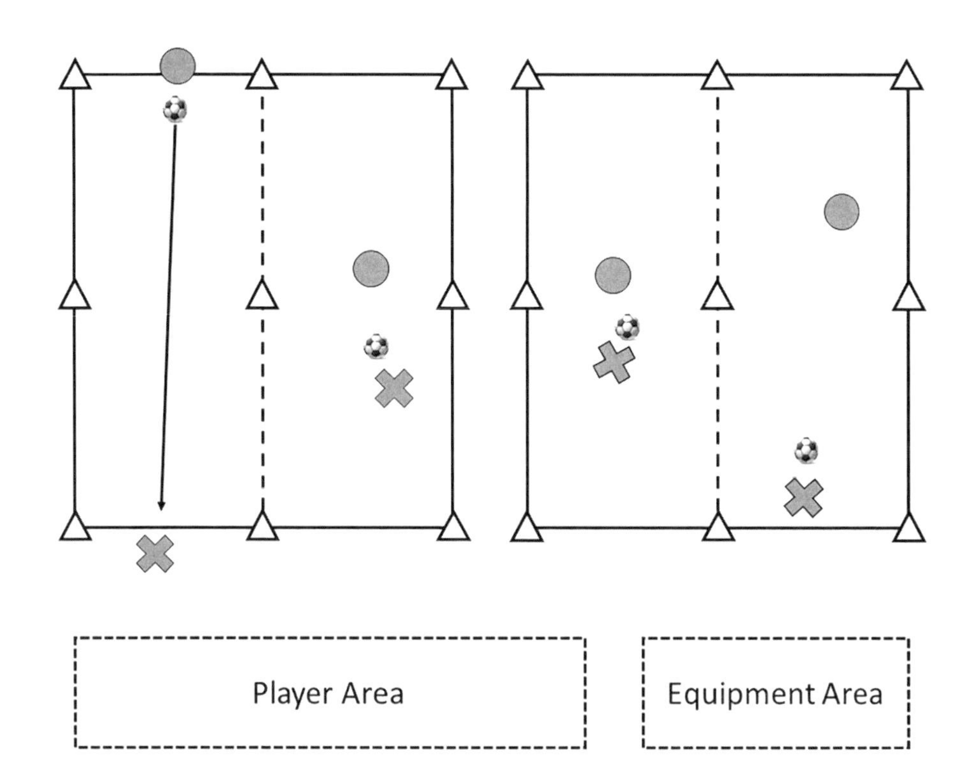

Practice Six

Defender plays the ball to the attacker who looks to dribble the ball over the defender's line. If the defender wins the ball, they look to dribble over the attacker's line. After each go, rotate the roles of the players.

Possible Variations

- Consider the width and length of the pitches to meet the needs of your players. Each pitch does not have to be identical in size or shape.
- Have different start positions for the defenders to replicate different scenarios within the game and also to differentiate the different level of players within the practice.
- Allow players to go into the adjoining the pitch with a different points system for dribbling over the defender's line on the two different sides of the pitch.
- Have an extra task for the attacking players to complete once they have dribbled over the line: a shot at goal, a pass through a set of cones, and so on.
- Split the pitch in half and have a defender in each half.
- Progress the practice into a two-versus-two.

Practice Seven:

First Practice / **Main Practice** / Game Practice

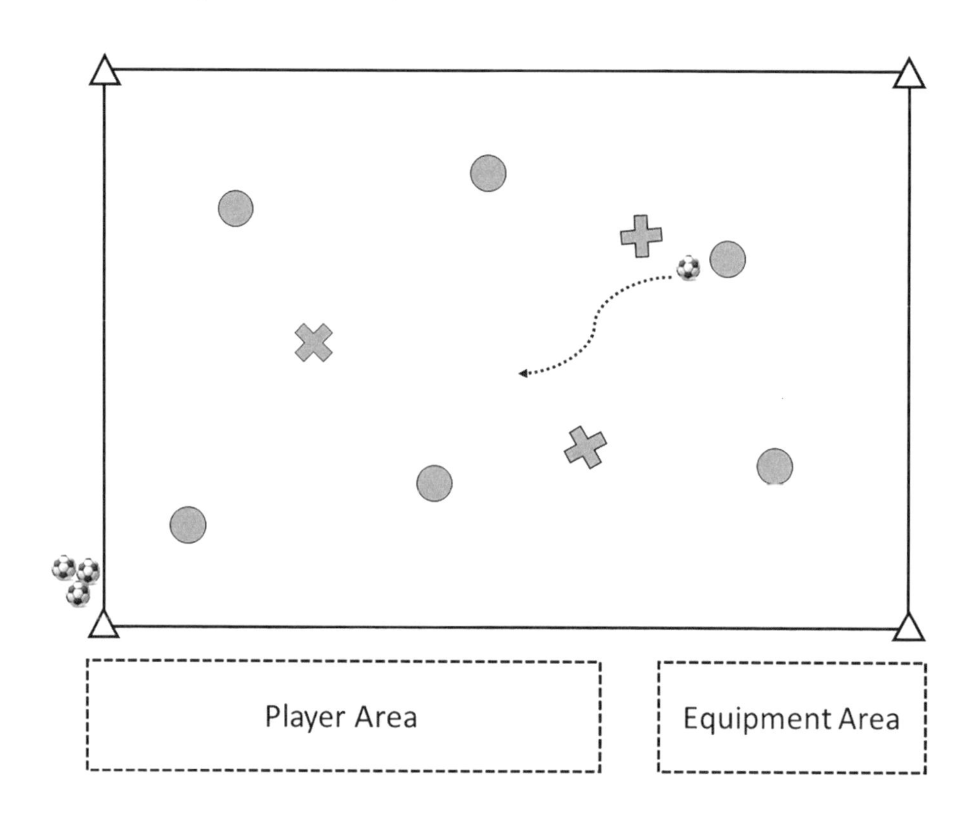

Practice Seven

The attacking team looks to complete a set number of passes to achieve a point. In doing so, they will gain a point and the practice will continue. Should the opposition win the ball or if the ball goes out of play, the pass counter is reset, and the practice continues. If the defenders win the ball, they win a point if they successfully break out of the area. Rotate the role of the defenders regularly throughout the practice.

Possible Variations

- Consider the width and length of the pitch to meet the need of your players.
- Different shaped area will lead to different outcomes: length of passes, intensity of play and so on.
- Change the ratio of attacking players and defenders.
- Add an additional area and use as needed. For example, it could be the ball either cannot be or must be passed through this area, or a player has to receive a pass in this area.
- Add small goals or gates outside of the area (one to each side) upon completing the set number of passes, or when the defenders win possession, the ball has to be passed into one of the goals.

Practice Eight:

First Practice / Main Practice / Game Practice

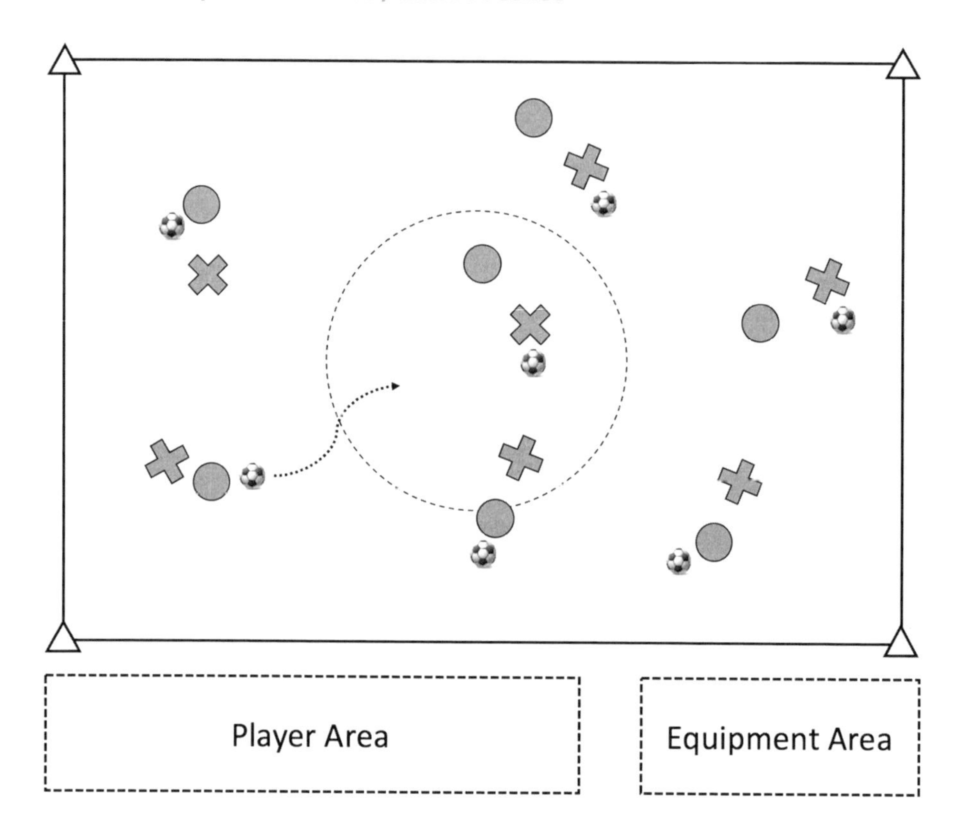

Practice Eight

Players are split into pairs, with a ball between each pair. The players look to keep the ball away from their partner for as long as possible. If the partner wins the ball, they then look to retain the ball. An additional area can be introduced to the practice and can be used in a number of different ways. For instance, players are challenged to dribble through the area to achieve a point.

Possible Variations

- Consider the width and length of the pitch to meet the needs of your players.
- Different shaped areas will lead to different outcomes: a circle means no corners to get caught in, a triangle makes it easier to get cornered and so on.
- Split the area in half. When players are in possession of the ball, they must travel to the side of the pitch that their team has been allocated to.
- Add a number of small areas within the main area that the players cannot travel through.
- Reduce the amount of balls slightly, so that when a player is in possession of the ball they can be supported by a team-mate who does not have a ball.
- Use smaller balls to make it more difficult to dribble.

Practice Nine:

First Practice / **Main Practice** / Game Practice

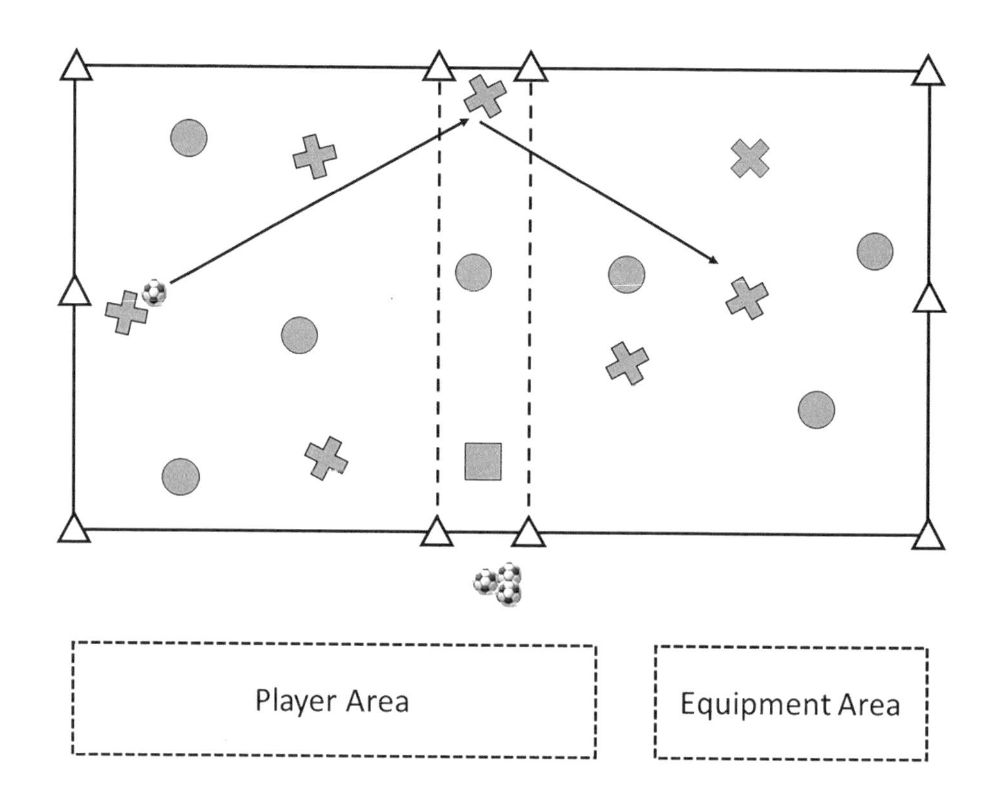

Practice Nine

Players are split into two teams with three versus three in each of the two zones. In between the two zones there is a central zone where there is a player from each team, with an additional neutral player. The neutral player always stays in their wide position, whilst the other two players rotate their position depending on which team has possession of the ball. If your team has possession of the ball, you go into the wide position; when your team loses the ball, you move into the central position. Teams have to complete a set number of passes before they look to transfer the ball from one zone to the other via the central zone using either their own player or the neutral player.

Possible Variations

- Extra neutral players are added to each area to make completing the set number of passes easier.
- The players in the central area are removed, and the ball can just be transferred between the two areas.
- The players in the central area are removed, and a player can drop in to receive a pass when it is being transferred from one area to another.
- A goal is added to each end of the area, so when the ball is transferred from one area to the other, the team then has to try and score a goal rather than transfer it back again.

Practice Ten:

First Practice / **Main Practice** / Game Practice

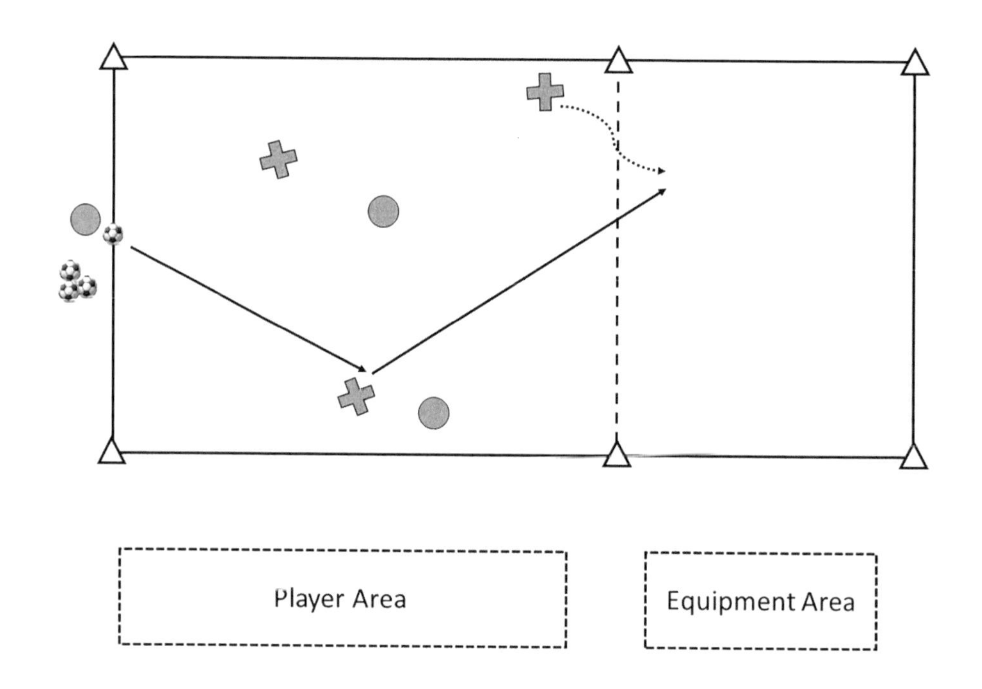

Practice Ten

Server plays the ball to one of the three attacking players who look to release a player into the second area by playing a pass over the line that divides the two areas. (Players cannot dribble the ball over the line.) Once this has been achieved, one defender can enter the area, and the attacking player looks to dribble over the end line. If needed, the attacking players can pass back to the server, and if the defenders win the ball, they look to pass the ball back to the server to achieve a point.

Possible Variations

- Consider the width and length of the pitches and each individual area to meet the needs of your players. Each pitch does not have to be identical in size.
- The attacking players are not allowed to pass back to the server.
- The server can move into the area and join in with the practice once they have made the initial pass.
- A small goal is added to the end of the area for the players to pass into once they have received a pass in the second area.
- The line between the two areas acts as an offside line, so players cannot cross it before the pass is made. (Only use this when players are playing the offside rule.)

Practice Eleven (b):

First Practice / Main Practice / Game Practice

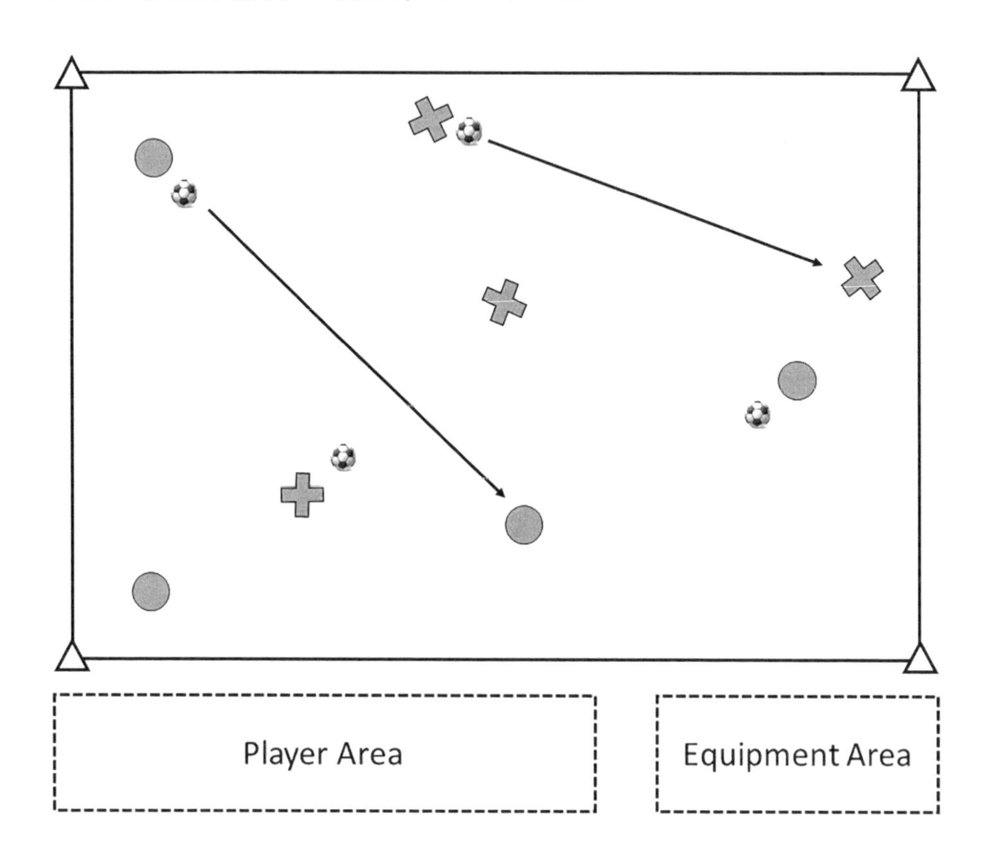

Practice Eleven (b)

Players work in pairs, passing the ball around within the area. Players are encouraged to use as much as the area as they can and are allowed to have as many touches of the ball as they want, passing the ball to their partner when they think it is the right time to do so.

Possible Variations

- Consider the size of the area and adapt it to meet the needs of your players. A larger area will provide more space, but it will also increase the distance the passes have to travel. It will also increase the number of different type of passes that are made.
- One pair (the defenders) starts without a ball, and they have to go and win the ball off any of the other pairs. Whichever pair loses the ball then becomes the defenders.
- One pair just acts as 'taggers' and look to tag any player that is in possession of the ball.
- Add gates that the players have to pass the ball through.
- Split the main area into smaller areas, such as quarters. Players not allowed in the same area as their partners.

Practice Twelve (b):

First Practice / **Main Practice** / **Game Practice**

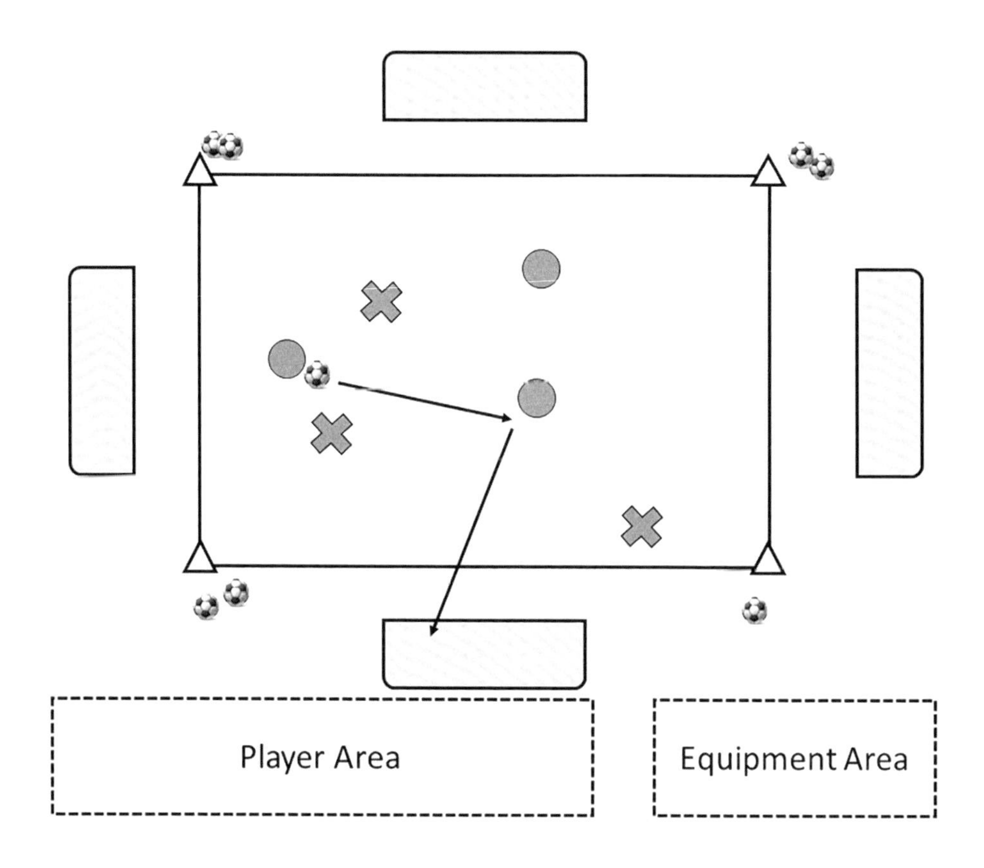

Practice Twelve (b)

Players are split into two teams and look to complete a set number of passes before they attempt to score in one of the four goals. (Players remain inside the area at all times.) Rules are put in place to ensure the players actually have a shot at goal and not just pass the ball towards the goal; this could be that the ball cannot touch the ground until it crosses the goal line.

Possible Variations

- Add players positioned outside of the area who are used to help the teams retain possession until the set number of passes has been completed. Once the set number of passes are completed, the players situated outside of the area then become goalkeepers.
- A support player is added in the area to help teams complete the set number of passes more easily. This ensures more shots are being taken.
- Use different scoring systems depending on the type of finish; for instance, a one-touch finish could be worth two points.
- Teams lose a point if a shot is off target.

When a goal is scored, whichever goal it is scored in is 'locked' and remains 'locked' until another goal is scored in a different goal, which then becomes the 'locked' goal.

Practice Thirteen:

First Practice / Main Practice / **Game Practice**

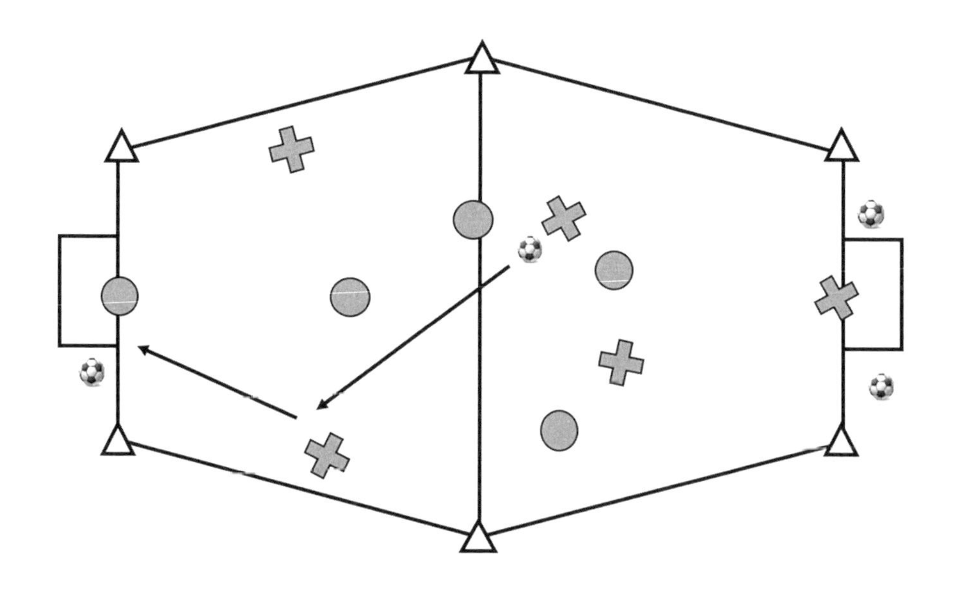

Player Area

Equipment Area

Practice Thirteen

A small-sided game with an emphasis on finishing. Pitch is in the shape of a hexagon to encourage players to shoot from most areas of the pitch.

Possible Variations

- A support player is added in the area to help teams complete the set number of passes more easily, ensuring more shots are being taken.
- Use different scoring systems depending on the type of finish; for instance, a one-touch finish could be worth two points.
- Teams lose a point if a shot is off target.
- Pitch is split into thirds instead of halves with teams unable to score in the final third (to encourage longer range finishing).
- Instead of throw-ins, players kick the ball in and are allowed to shoot directly.

Practice Fourteen:

First Practice / Main Practice / Game Practice

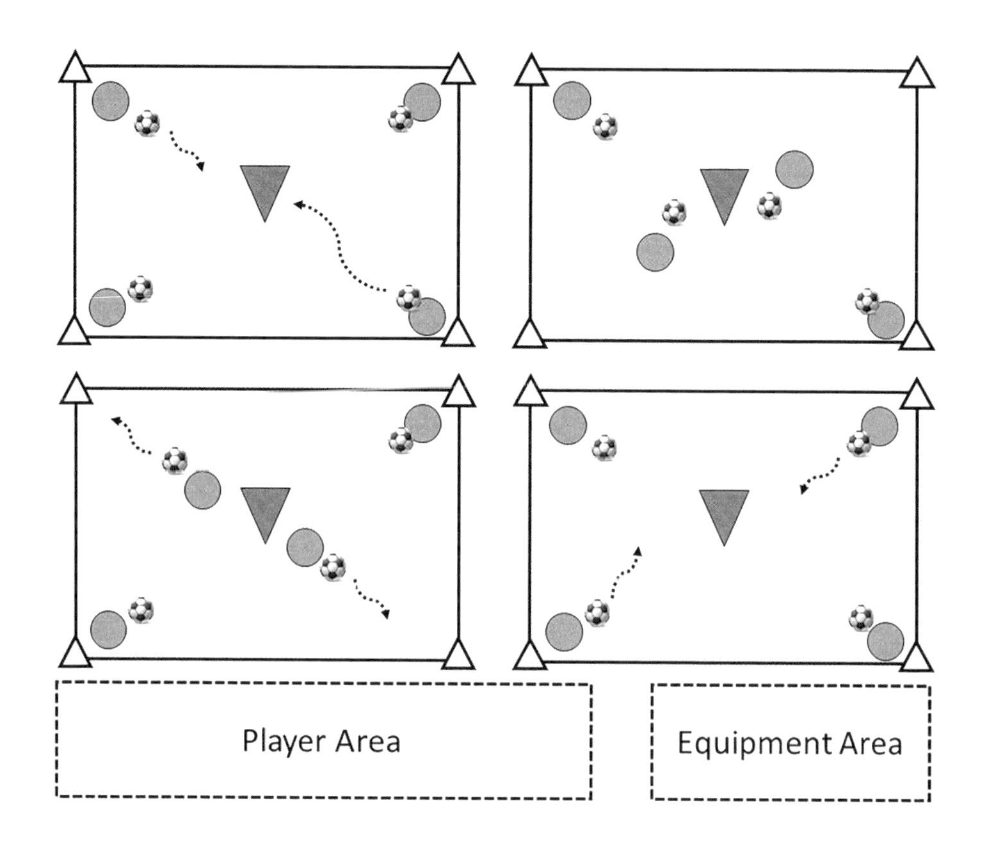

Practice Fourteen

Players work in pairs, with two pairs in each area. One pair at a time dribble towards each other and the large cone in the middle of the area. Once the pair gets to the cone, they complete a skill and go to an agreed side of the cone (i.e. right or left). After they have gone past the cone, they go to the corner of the area where their partner had started, and then the next pair starts and the practice continues.

Possible Variations

- On reaching the large cone, the players travel to a different corner instead of the one facing them, producing a 'turn' rather than dribbling.
- The large cone is removed so that the players dribble towards each other and have to complete the skill as they get close to each other (emphasis on the timing of the skill).
- The large cone is removed, and the players must get from their corner to the opposite corner as quickly as possible, so they are now running with the ball rather than dribbling.
- Only one player has a ball, and the other player becomes a defender.
- Use only two balls between the four players, and once they have reached the large cone, the player passes to a waiting player who is without a ball.

Practice Fifteen:

First Practice / **Main Practice** / Game Practice

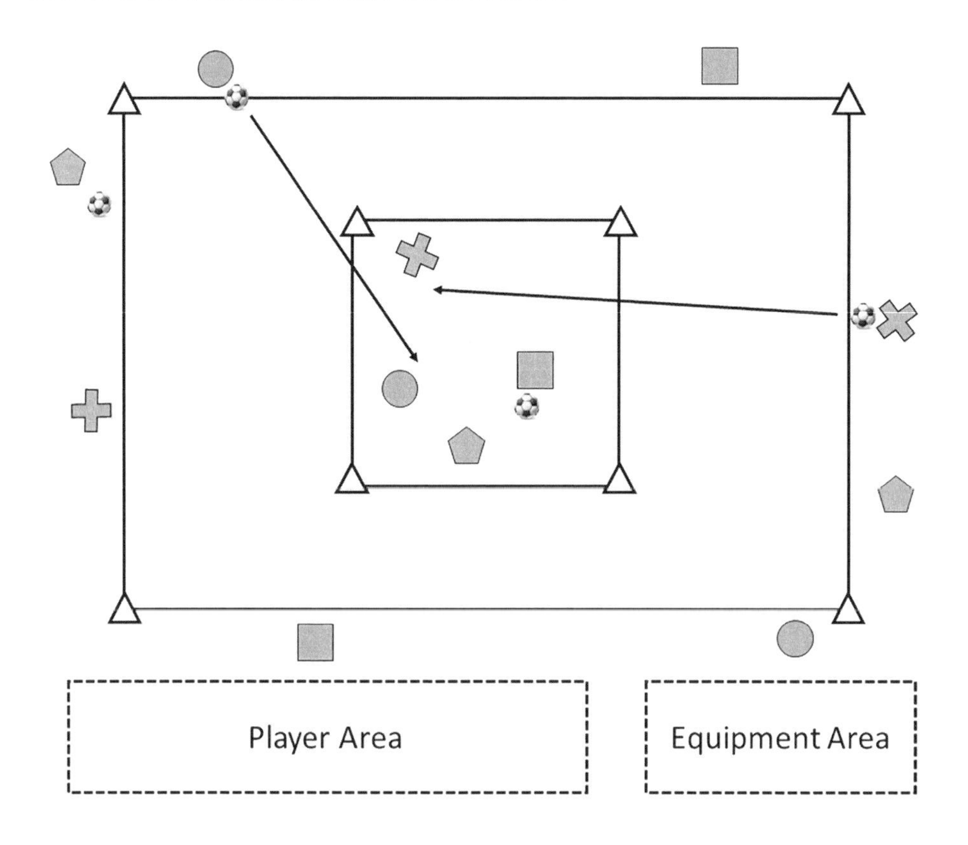

Practice Fifteen

Players work in threes with one player in the central area and the other two players outside of the larger area. The ball is played to the player within the central area who controls the ball before passing it on to the other player on the outside of the area. After the player on the outside of the area has passed the ball, they move to change their position to make it more difficult for the player in the central area to find them. The role of the central player is rotated regularly.

Possible Variations

- Alter the size and shape of the central area to increase or decrease the level of difficulty to receive the ball.
- Change to groups of four instead of three, with two players working in the central area. They must combine before the ball is passed to a player on the outside.
- Add a defender to the central area. If they win the ball, they have to get out of the central area and then pass the ball to a relevant player on the outside.
- After playing the pass into the central area, the player follows their pass; the player in the central area then moves out after playing their pass (rotation of positions).

Practice Sixteen:

First Practice / Main Practice / **Game Practice**

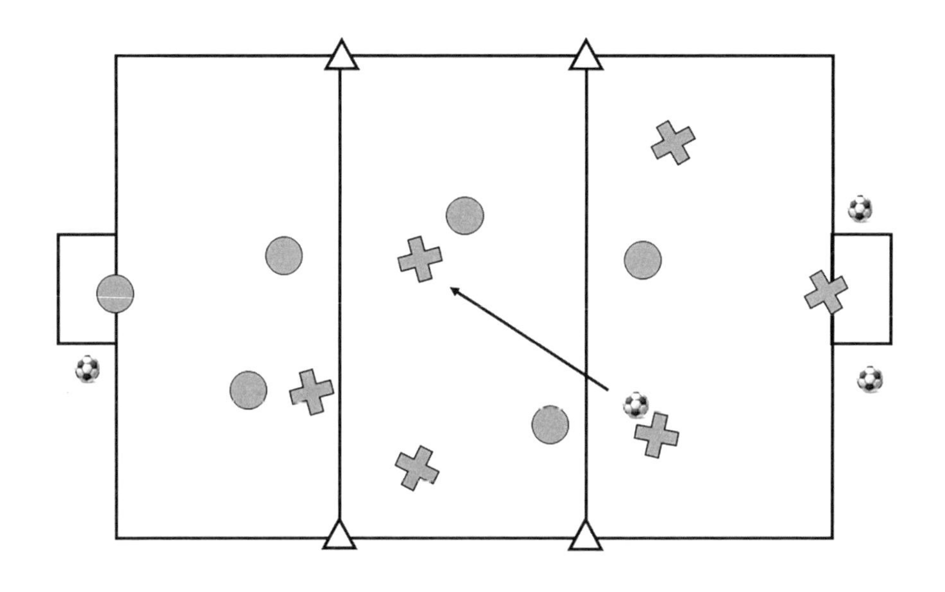

Practice Sixteen

Pitch is split into thirds; these do not have to be equal. Game is played as normal but with relevant rules, restrictions or conditions that support the topic of the session.

Possible Variations

- The thirds do not have to be split using rectangles.
- Players are locked into their zones, and the ball has to be transferred between zones by passing only.
- The ball can only be transferred by a player dribbling over the line. This is also the only way in which a player can move between each area.
- The game always restarts with a goalkeeper (i.e. no throw-ins, corners etc). Also, the ball can only travel forwards until a team reaches the final third.
- A set number of passes has to be completed in specific areas or all of the areas.
- Teams are restricted to the number of passes that they have, either in specific areas or in total.
- Players are restricted to a specific number of touches within the central area.
- The thirds are split vertically instead of horizontally.

Practice Seventeen:

First Practice / **Main Practice** / Game Practice

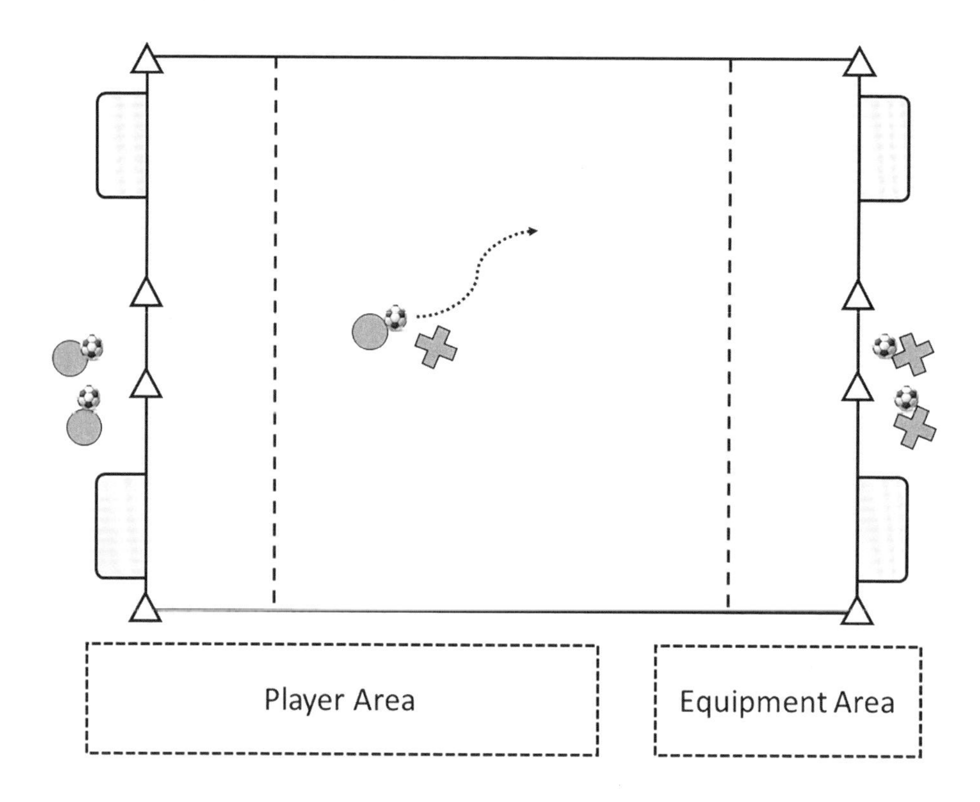

Practice Seventeen

One player enters the pitch through the central gate and attempts to pass into one of the two small goals. They can only attempt to pass into one of the goals once they have entered the 'end zone'. As soon as the player attempts to pass into a goal, a player from the other team enters the pitch and attempts to pass into one of the opposite two goals; the player who was just an attacker becomes a defender and looks to stop the new attacker from passing into the small goals. This rotation of roles continues. Players enter the pitch as the attacking player, then transfer to becoming the defender, then exit the pitch, before entering the pitch as an attacker again.

Possible Variations

- The length and width can be altered to meet the needs of your players and also the planned outcome of the practice.
- The four small goals are replaced by two normal goals with goalkeepers.
- The small goals are replaced by gates which the attackers have to drive through (they can then leave the ball and go and defend).
- Practice is two versus two instead of one versus one.
- In a two-versus-two practice, after attacking, one of the two attackers has to touch the goal or a cone near the goal before they can defend.

Practice Eighteen:

First Practice / **Main Practice** / Game Practice

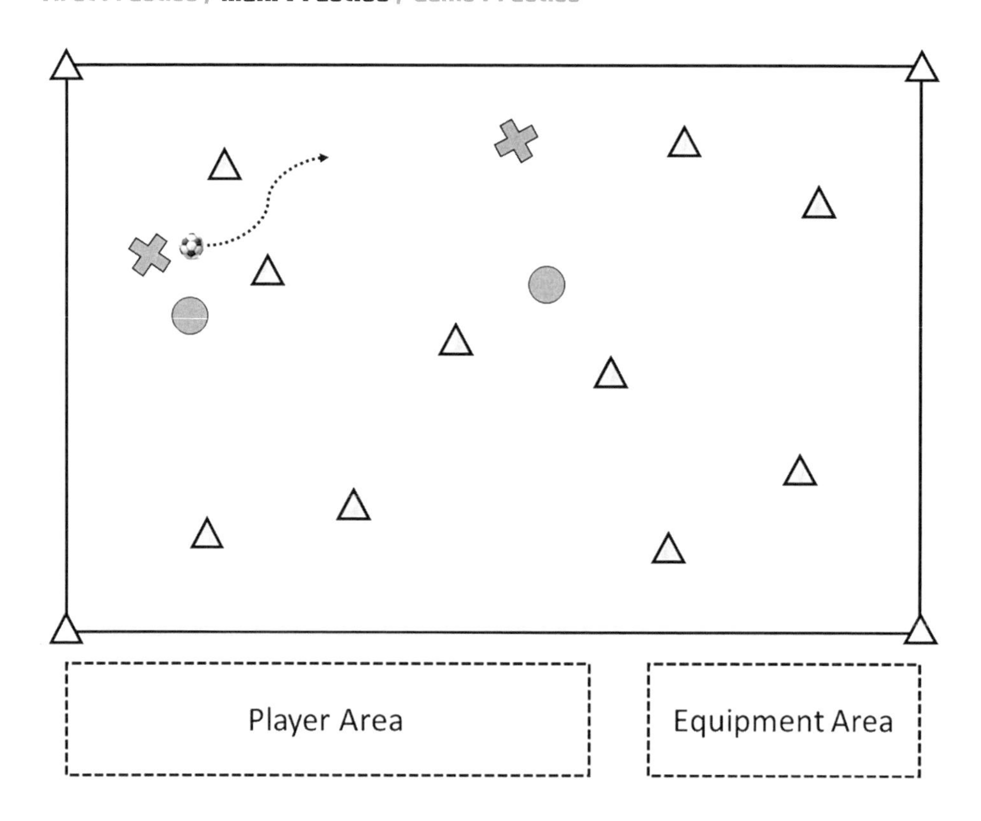

Practice Eighteen

Divide into two teams of equal players (two versus two or three versus three). Teams can score a point when a player dribbles successfully through any of the gates. On achieving a point, the team retains possession and can continue to try and win another point.

Possible Variations

- Consider the width, length and shape of the area to meet the needs of your players.
- A neutral player is used within the area to help the team in possession of the ball.
- Players have to pass the ball through the gates instead of dribbling.
- Players can pass or dribble through the gates.
- Different coloured gates are used. Different colours are allocated to each team, or different colours are worth different points.
- After going through a gate, a further task must be completed, like driving out the area or attempting to score a goal.

Practice Nineteen:

First Practice / **Main Practice** / Game Practice

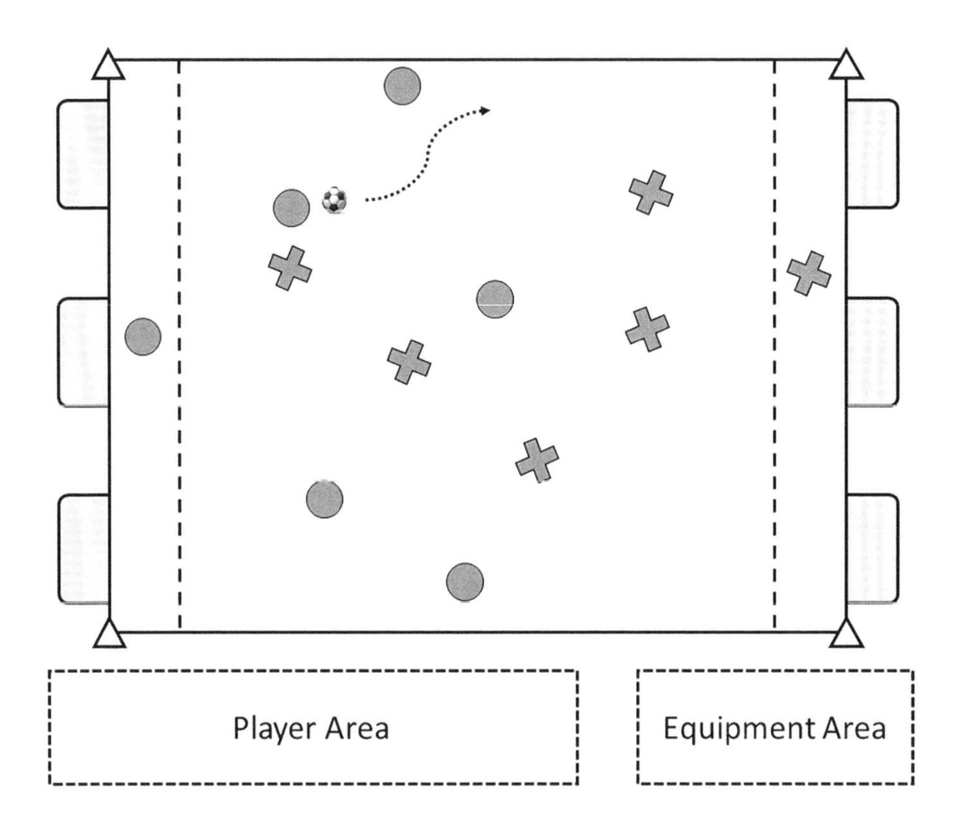

Practice Nineteen

Small-sided game with six small goals. Each team has a 'blocker' that is restricted to the small end zone; the blocker is free to move up and down the end zone. Teams cannot score in the goal that the blocker is standing in front of.

Possible Variations

- Consider the width and length of the area to meet the needs of your players.
- A neutral player supports the team in possession of the ball.
- Teams need to complete a set number of passes before they can attempt to score.
- The centre small goal is replaced by a normal goal which teams can score in at any time, but the blocker can act as a goalkeeper in this goal.
- An attacking player is added to the area with the blocker and they can either pass into a small goal or bounce a pass back to a team-mate.

Practice Twenty:

First Practice / Main Practice / Game Practice

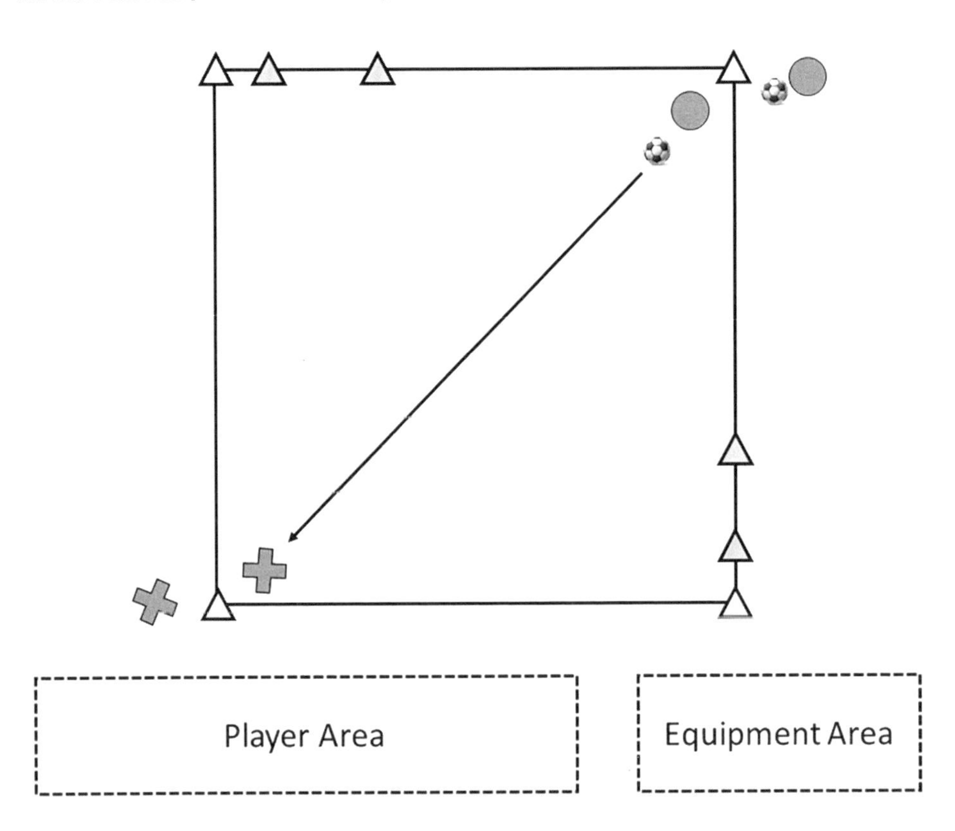

Practice Twenty

Set up a small square with two gates, positioned as shown in the diagram. A defender plays to the attacker who then looks to dribble through one of the two gates; the attacker must have the ball under control as they travel through the gate. If the defender wins the ball, they become the attacker, and they must then attempt to dribble through one of the gates.

Possible Variations

- Consider the size of the area to meet the needs of your players.
- Add a third gate.
- The gates are made wider or narrower.
- Attacking players get to decide how many defenders they want, one or two. They earn more points if they dribble through a gate against two defenders.
- After dribbling through a gate, the attacker has to turn back through the gate into the area again to win the point.

Practice Twenty-One:

First Practice / Main Practice / Game Practice

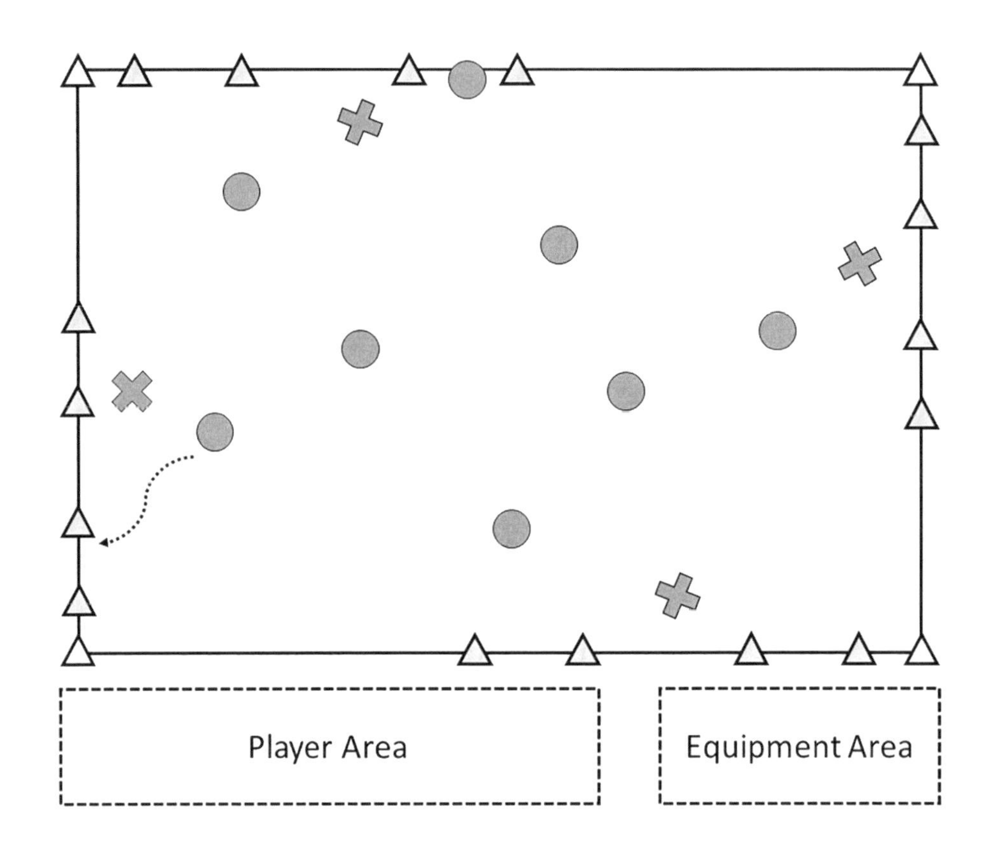

Practice Twenty-One

Players are given the roles of blockers. They are given two gates to protect, which are near each other. Blockers are only allowed to move sideways. The other players look to get through any gate without being tagged by a blocker; if they do, they earn a point. If they get tagged, then the blocker earns a point. Once through a gate, a player can re-enter the area and look to win more points.

Possible Variations

- Consider the width and length of the area as well as the width of the gates and the distance between the two gates to meet the needs of your players.
- Provide the players with a task that they have to complete as they go through a gate: hop, jump, spin, travel backwards and so on.
- Each player has a ball and must dribble it at all times.
- Players are put into three teams: one team guards the gate, and the other two teams compete against each other to win the most points.
- Add an extra defender who can move around the area. If a player gets tagged by this defender, they have to complete a small task, such as a small number of keepy-ups.

Practice Twenty-Two:

First Practice / Main Practice / Game Practice

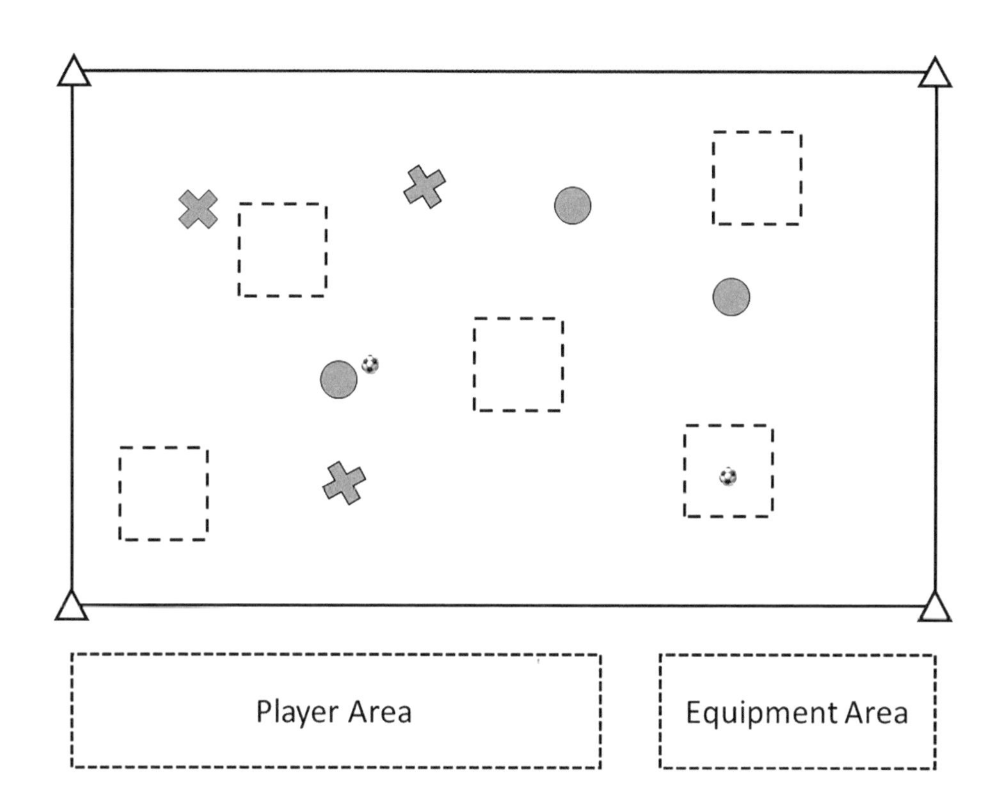

Practice Twenty-Two

Players are split into small teams, ideally three versus three. Using two tennis balls, teams pass one ball between themselves using their hands. If they get tagged whilst in possession of the ball, then possession changes hands. The other ball is left inside one of the five scoring areas. Teams win a point if they are able to place the ball down in one of the five scoring areas (cannot be placed down where the other ball is situated). Once this happens, a player then picks up the other ball, and the practice continues.

Possible Variations

- Consider the width and length of the area as well as the number and positioning of the scoring areas to meet the needs of your players.
- Change the object that they are scoring with. You could use a bean bag or frisbee, for example.
- Play with a soccer ball, and players use their feet instead of their hands.
- Players have to complete a task when in possession of the ball, such as hopping.
- If the ball touches the ground, then the other team gains possession.
- A neutral player is added to support the team in possession of the ball.

Practice Twenty-Three:

First Practice / Main Practice / Game Practice

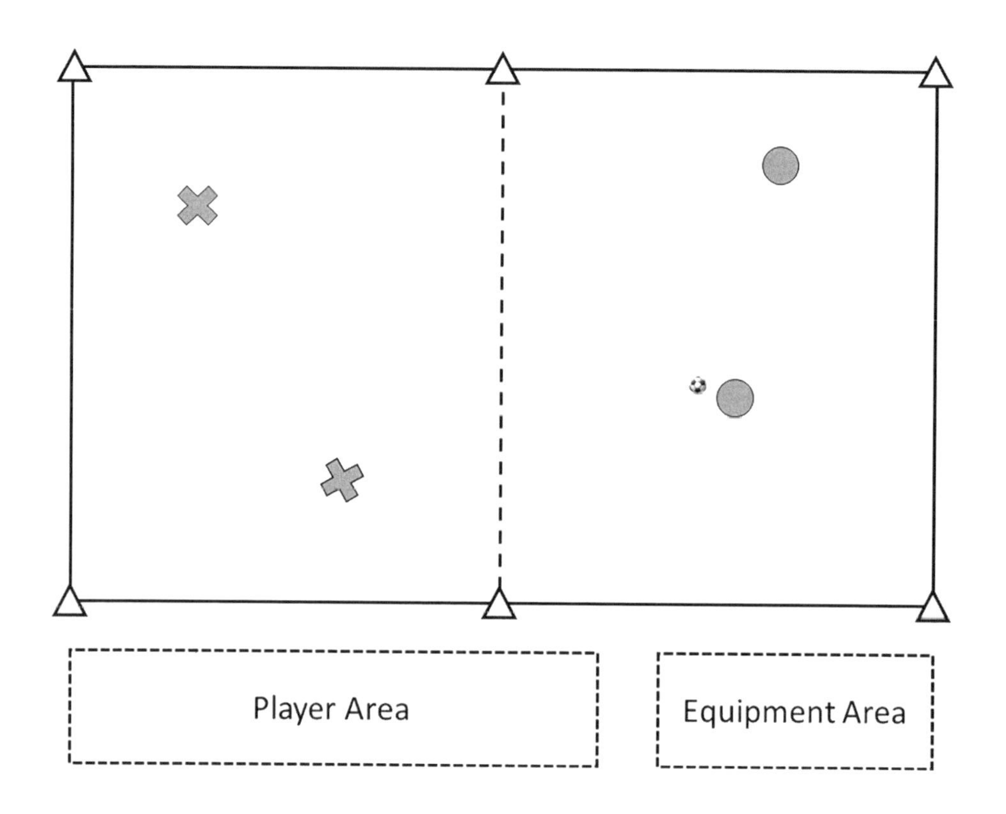

Practice Twenty-Three

Teams of two players work in a small area split in half, with the players locked into their halves of the area. Using a tennis ball, players attempt to throw the ball (underarm) into their opponent's half with their opponents looking to prevent the ball from bouncing by catching it. If the ball does bounce, it is a point to the team throwing the ball; if, however, the ball lands outside of the area, the point goes to the other team. If the ball is caught, then the game just continues.

Possible Variations

- Consider the width and length of the area as well as the number and positioning of the scoring areas to meet the needs of your players.
- Change the object that they are using. You could instead use a bean bag or frisbee, for example.
- Play with a soccer ball, and players use their feet instead of hands (i.e. foot tennis).
- Add small 'bonus zones' to each side of the area; if the ball lands in these areas, then the team wins extra points.
- Players can only catch using one hand.
- Players can only move by hopping.
- Decrease the area size, and the players can no longer move.

Practice Twenty-Four:

First Practice / Main Practice / Game Practice

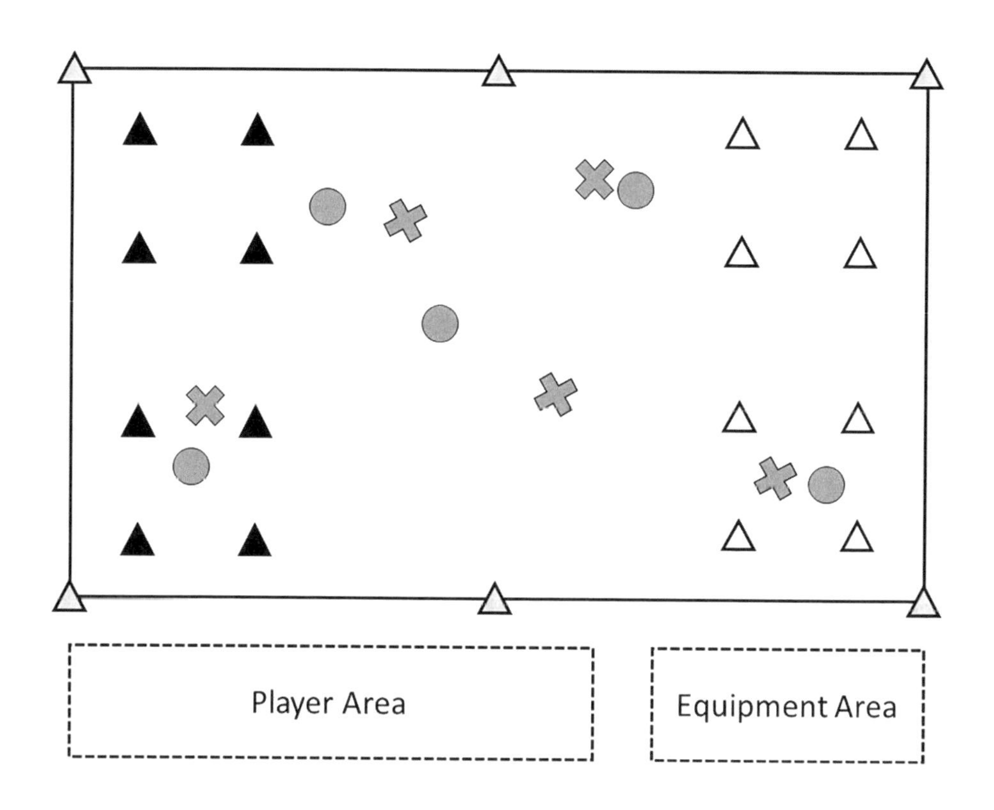

Practice Twenty-Four

Working in pairs, players attempt to travel from one area to another without being tagged by their partner. Players can only be tagged when they are outside of the small areas (i.e. travelling between areas), and the player attempting to score the point decides when to leave the area, with the tagger having to react and chase their partner. Players can get additional points if they travel to an area of a different colour (greater distance).

Possible Variations

- Consider the width and length of the area (this will change the distance the players have to run), as well as the size of the small areas (this will change the distance between the two players) to meet the needs of your players.
- Have a 'safety' area in the middle of the main area which players can use of they think they are going to be caught.
- Players also have balls, so they are now 'running with a ball'.
- Add an extra 'tagger' who can tag any player.
- Have extra cones spread throughout the area. If a player is able to touch one of these as they are running between the areas, they gain extra points.
- Players win bonus points if they travel to a second area after reaching the first area without stopping.

Practice Twenty-Five:

First Practice / Main Practice / Game Practice

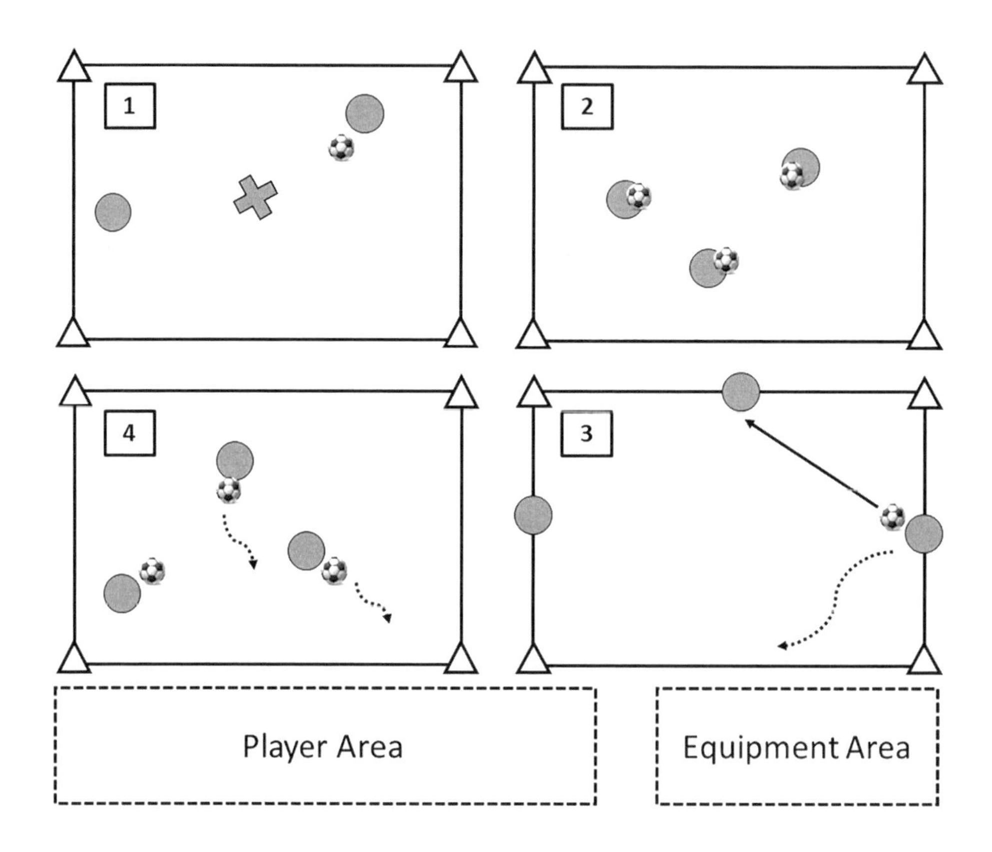

Practice Twenty-Five

Within the first practice, two players look to retain possession against a defender. If the defender wins the ball, they swap roles with the player who lost it. In the second practice, the players look to complete keepy-ups, and in the third practice, the three players each stand on one side of the area and pass the ball between themselves. Once they have passed the ball, they move to the side of the area that is free. Finally, in the fourth practice, the players each have a ball and dribble around the area, completing any skill of their choice.

Possible Variations

- Change the activities to meet the needs of your players or link to the focus of the session.
- Turn each of the activities into a competition, with each group trying to gain as many points as they can in total across all the activities.
- Teams can also choose a 'bonus' activity where their score is doubled.
- Just set up four areas, and the players get to produce their own activities.
- Have the four groups complete each of the activities at the same time and turn it into a competition, such as, first group to complete a set amount of passes or keepy-ups.

Practice Twenty-Six:

First Practice / **Main Practice** / Game Practice

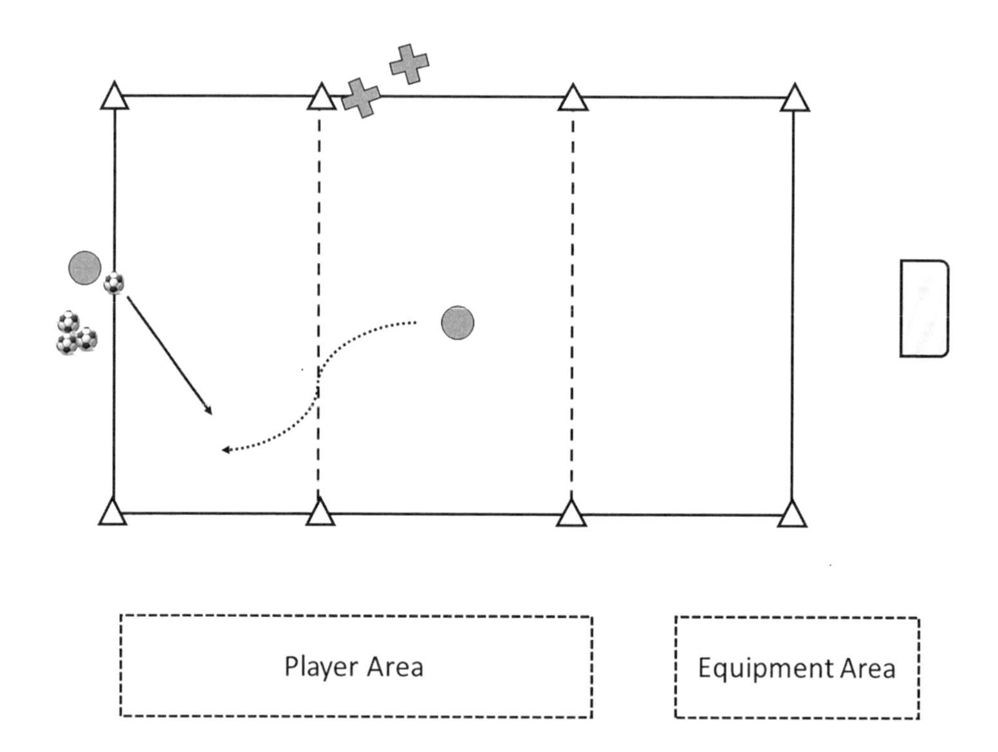

Practice Twenty-Six

Attacking player drops in to receive the ball from the server and then looks to drive towards the third zone where they can pass into the small goal. The defender can go and defend once the player has received the ball.

Possible Variations

- Consider the width and length of the area to meet the needs of your players.
- Allow two defenders to enter the pitch; one is locked into the first zone once they have entered.
- Remove the small goal, and the attacking player must drive over the line instead.
- Remove the goal and have two gates, with the player having to drive through one of them.
- Remove the small goal and add a normal sized goal and goalkeeper. The player now has to score past the goalkeeper.
- Change the starting position of the defender. For instance, they could start just behind the server or in the area next to the attacker's starting position.

Practice Twenty-Seven:

First Practice / **Main Practice** / Game Practice

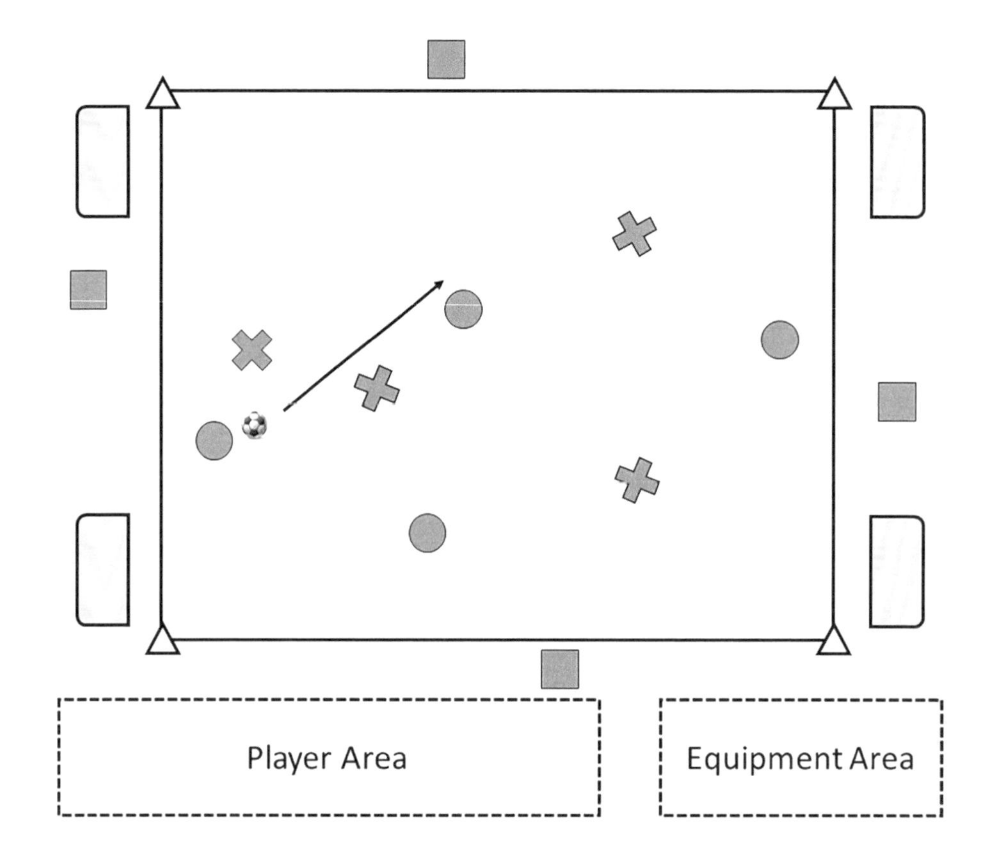

Practice Twenty-Seven

Teams are split into three teams, with two teams within the area and the other team acting as support players around the outside of the area. One of the teams in the area looks to complete a set number of passes before they can attempt to score in one of the small goals. The other team looks to win the ball and in doing so they can look to score immediately, without the need to complete any number of passes. The team that needs to complete the set number of passes can use the support players to help them retain possession, but if they do, then the number of passes they have completed resets to zero. The role of the three teams can be rotated each time a point is scored.

Possible Variations

- Consider the width and length of the area to meet the needs of your players.
- Replace the four small goals with two normal goals with goalkeepers.
- Instead of having goals, players just have to break out of the area.
- Add a support player inside the area.
- On completing the set number of passes, the team just continues and looks to achieve those passes again. The other two teams swap roles immediately without stopping the practice.

Practice Twenty-Eight:

First Practice / **Main Practice** / Game Practice

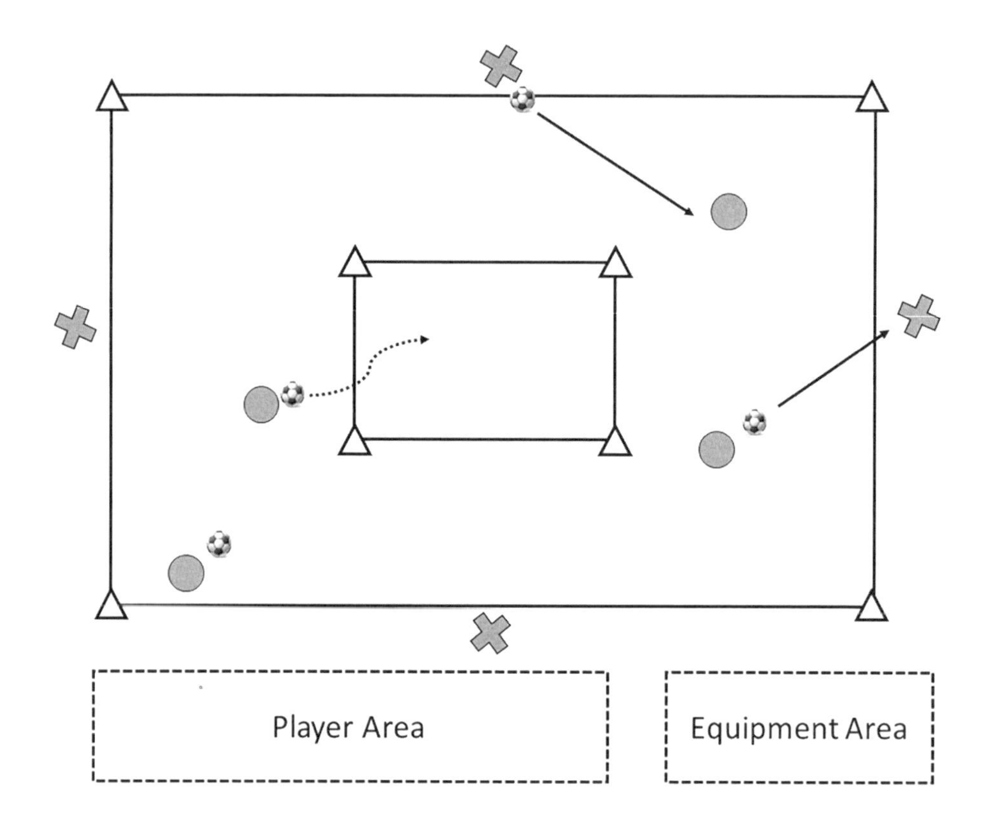

Practice Twenty-Eight

The players are split into two groups, with one group working within the area and the other group spread around the outside of the area, acting as servers. Players within the area receive a pass from a server and then must travel through the centre square before passing the ball to another server who does not have a ball. The player then receives another ball and repeats the process. The roles of the two groups are rotated regularly.

Possible Variations

- Players have to perform a skill when travelling through the central square.
- Players can only travel through the centre square one at a time.
- Add a defender to the centre square.
- Add a defender to the main area.
- Players have to pass from the centre area without stopping.
- Instead of travelling through the centre square, they have to pass through it.

Practice Twenty-Nine:

First Practice / **Main Practice** / Game Practice

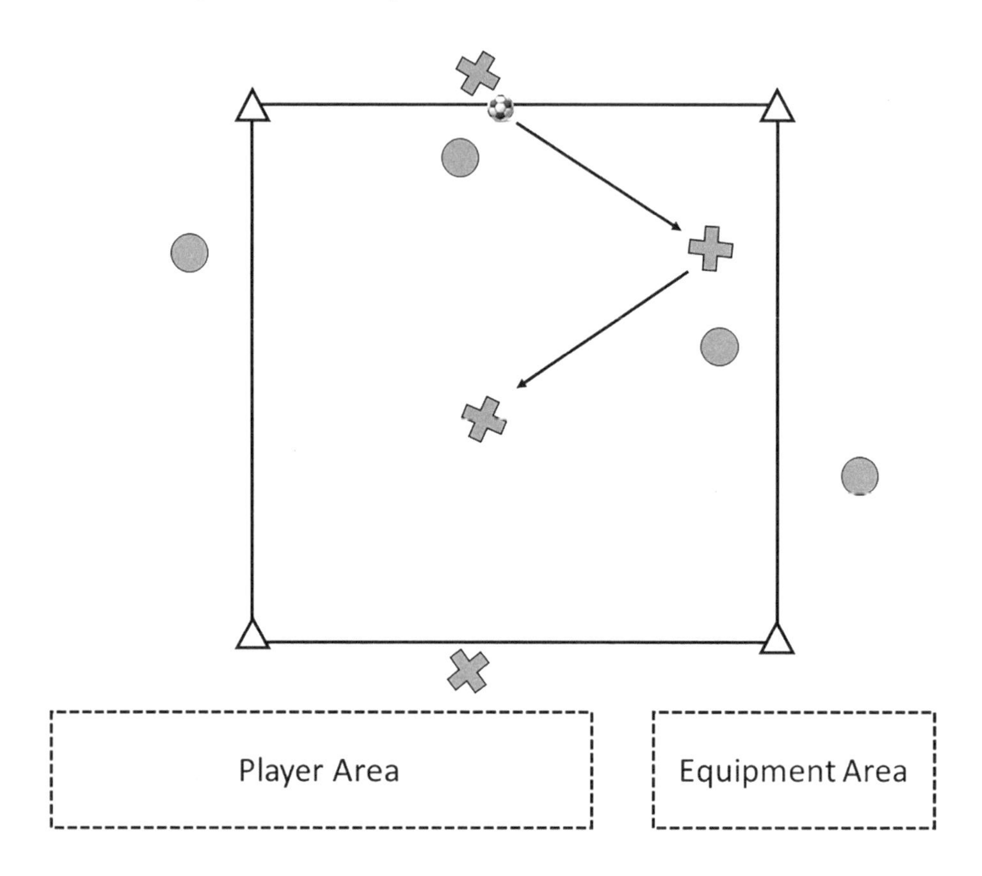

Practice Twenty-Nine

The area is set out as a square, and the players are split into two teams. Each team has two target players facing each other across the square, with the two teams playing in different directions. A point is awarded if a team gets the ball across the area from one target player to the other without the opposition touching the ball. To achieve the point, at least one player in the area must touch the ball (i.e. it cannot go directly from one target player to the other). If a team wins a point, they retain possession of the ball and look to transfer the ball across the area to the other target player. The target player role should be rotated regularly.

Possible Variations

- Consider the width and length of the area to meet the needs of your players.
- Limit the touches that the players in the area have.
- Both players in the area have to touch the ball.
- Players in the area and outside the area can rotate positions.
- A small area is added to the main area; teams get bonus points if, when transferring the ball between target players, the ball travels through this small area.

Practice Thirty:

First Practice / **Main Practice** / Game Practice

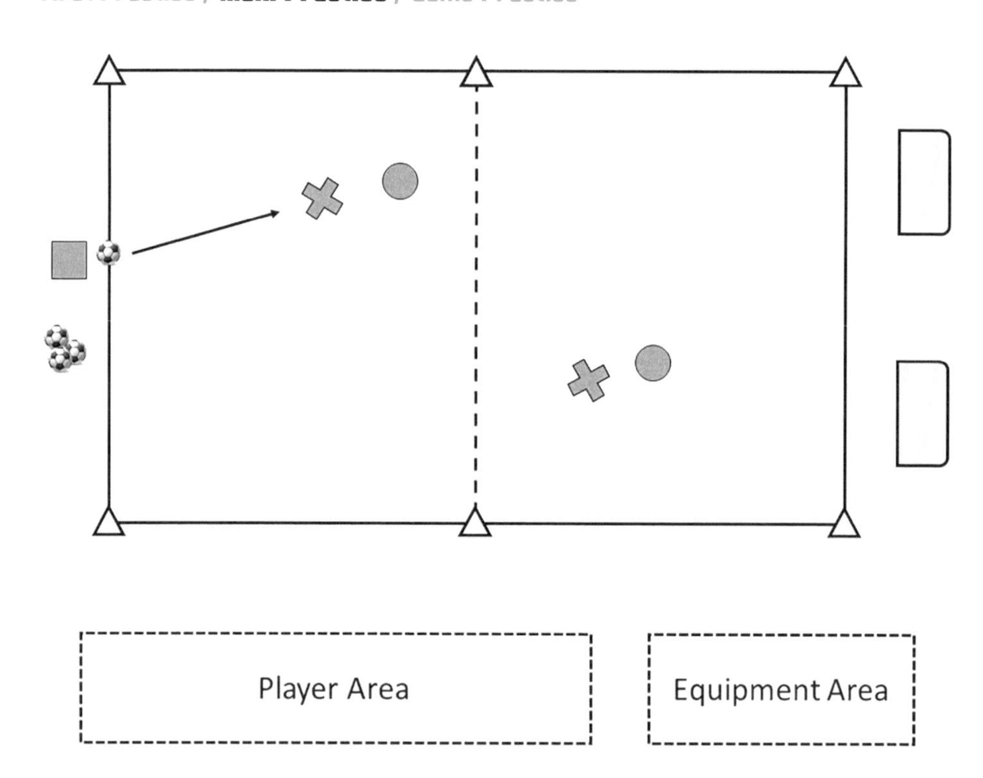

Practice Thirty

The area is split into two, with an attacker and defender in each half. Server plays the ball to an attacker who then looks to transfer the ball by passing or dribbling into the next half. Once in the next half, the attackers look to pass the ball into one of the small goals. At any time, the attackers can leave one half and move into the other half, whereas the defenders are locked into their designated areas. If the defenders win the ball, they look to play it back to the server to win a point.

Possible Variations

- Consider the width and length of the area as well as the size of the different areas (they do not have to be equal) to meet the needs of your players.
- Allow the server to join in and make it three versus two.
- Allow the server to join as an extra defender.
- First defender can move into the end zone once an attacking player has touched the ball inside it.
- Replace the small goals with a normal goal and goalkeeper.
- Consider changing the starting positions of both or one of the defenders.
- The ball can only be transferred into the second area either with a pass or only by dribbling.

Practice Thirty-One:

First Practice / Main Practice / **Game Practice**

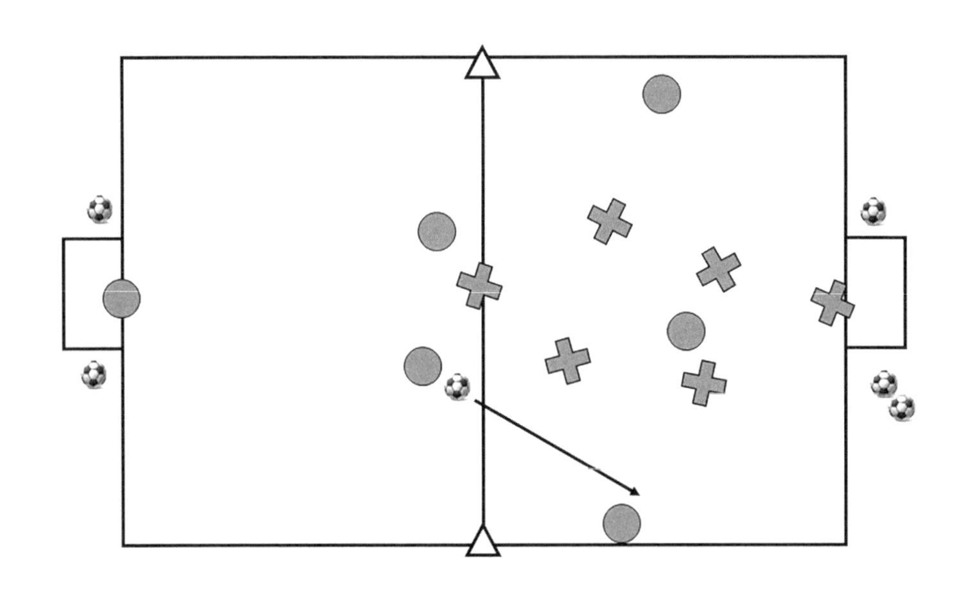

Player Area

Equipment Area

Practice Thirty-One

A small-sided game that always restarts with the goalkeeper whose team has possession of the ball, with the opposition having to retreat to their own half. The team in possession of the ball must then complete a set number of passes in the opposition's half before they can attempt to score a goal. If the opposing team wins the ball, they can just attack without the need to complete a set number of passes.

Possible Variations

- Consider the width and length of the area to meet the needs of your players. The size of the two halves does not need to be identical.
- Add support players around the outside of the pitch for the team in possession of the ball.
- Limit the number of touches the players have in the opposition's half (only for the team that starts with possession).
- The team starting without the ball is restricted to a small amount of passes if they win the ball.
- Each team gets five balls each. When the ball goes out of play, the game always restarts with the same team until they run out of balls. Then the other team has their turn.

Practice Thirty-Two:

First Practice / Main Practice / Game Practice

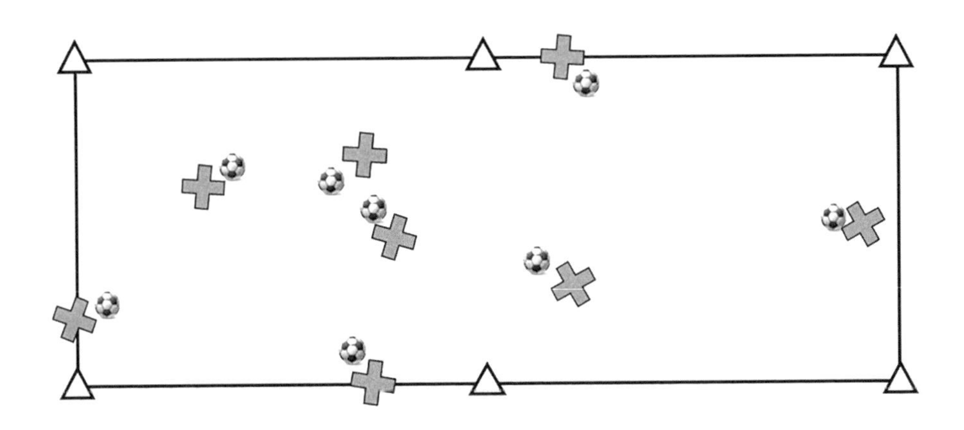

Practice Thirty-Two

Players dribble up and down a long narrow area. When travelling from one end to the other, players must visit each of the two long sides of the area at least once. Once they have reached the end of the area, they turn and travel back down, again visiting each long side at least once. The practice continues in this fashion, with an emphasis on the players scanning and manipulating the ball to avoid the other players.

Possible Variations

- Have players start the practice at different ends of the area to increase the amount of confusion and traffic.
- Add a defender to the area who has to try and tag the players.
- The defender has to dribble a ball as well.
- The area is split into smaller areas, with a defender locked into each area. They all can be given a ball, or a ball can be given to just a few of them.
- Two players work as a pair, passing the ball across the area and trying to avoid the players dribbling. For every set amount of passes they complete, they earn one point. The players dribbling have to avoid the ball being passed between the players.
- Add a small goal for the players to pass into once they have travelled up and down the area a set number of times.

Practice Thirty-Three:

First Practice / Main Practice / Game Practice

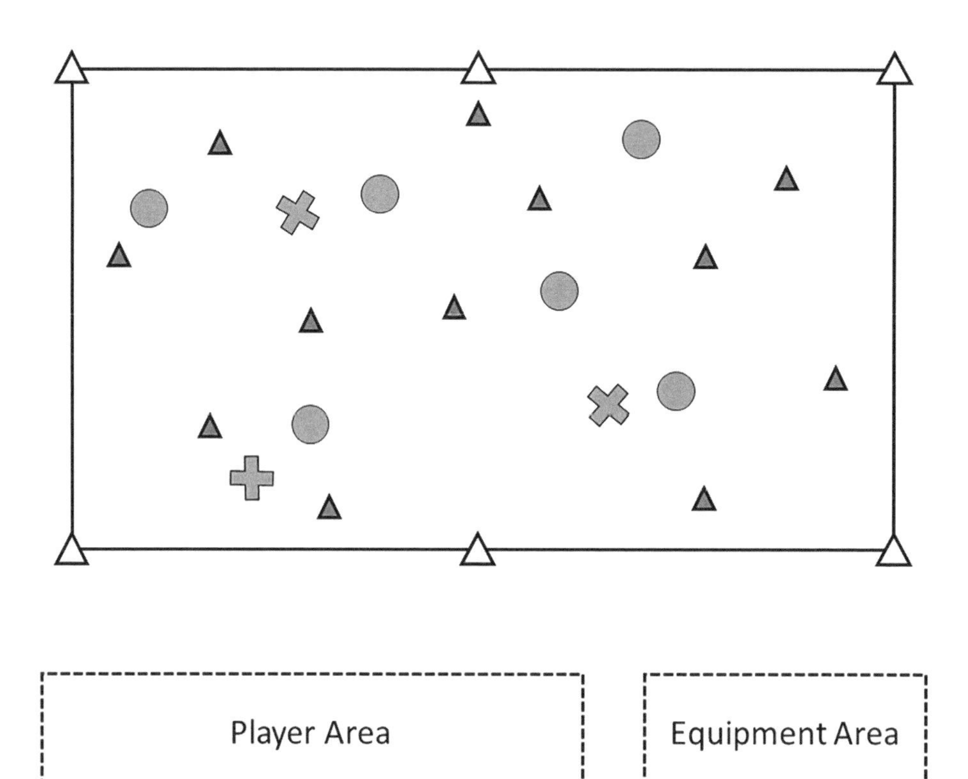

Practice Thirty-Three

This is a game of tag where the taggers gain a point every time they tag one of the other players. The players who are trying to avoid being tagged can win points if they are able to run between two cones, but they lose five points every time that they are tagged. The role of the taggers is changed regularly, and players only take on the role of a tagger for a short period of time.

Possible Variations

- Change the ratio of players tagging and those avoiding being tagged.
- Add or remove gates; also consider where the gates are positioned.
- Use different coloured gates, with a different points system for each colour.
- Split the players into two teams, with each team having a different coloured gate they must run through. Teams have to run through gates and also tag opposition players; points for each task to be decided by the coach.
- Players are given balls to dribble with as well.
- Players have to complete a task as they pass through a gate. For instance, they have to touch the ground with one of their hands, or they need to complete a spin.

Practice Thirty-Four:

First Practice / Main Practice / Game Practice

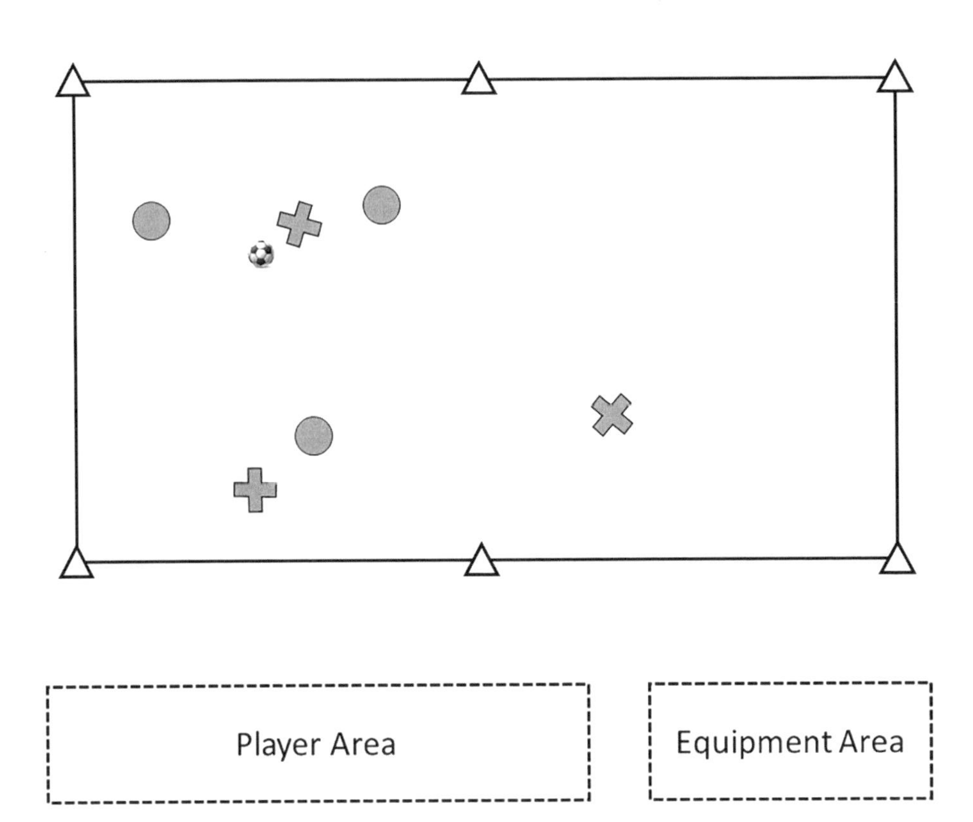

Practice Thirty-Four

A small-sided game consisting of whatever players are available to play. Teams win a point if one of their players dribbles the ball (under control) over the opposing team's line.

Possible Variations

- Consider the width and length of the area to meet the needs of your players.
- Add two gates on each of the end lines. Players either have to dribble through these gates, or they get a bonus point if they do.
- Add a number of gates to the pitch; players have to dribble through one of these gates before they can dribble over the end line.
- Add small goals a distance away from the end lines. Once players have dribbled over an end line, they can get an extra point if they pass the ball into the small goal. This must be attempted with their first touch after they have crossed the end line.
- Split the pitch into areas, with a one-versus-one in each area. Players can only transfer the ball to an area next to them, and it must be transferred with a pass.

Practice Thirty-Five:

First Practice / **Main Practice** / Game Practice

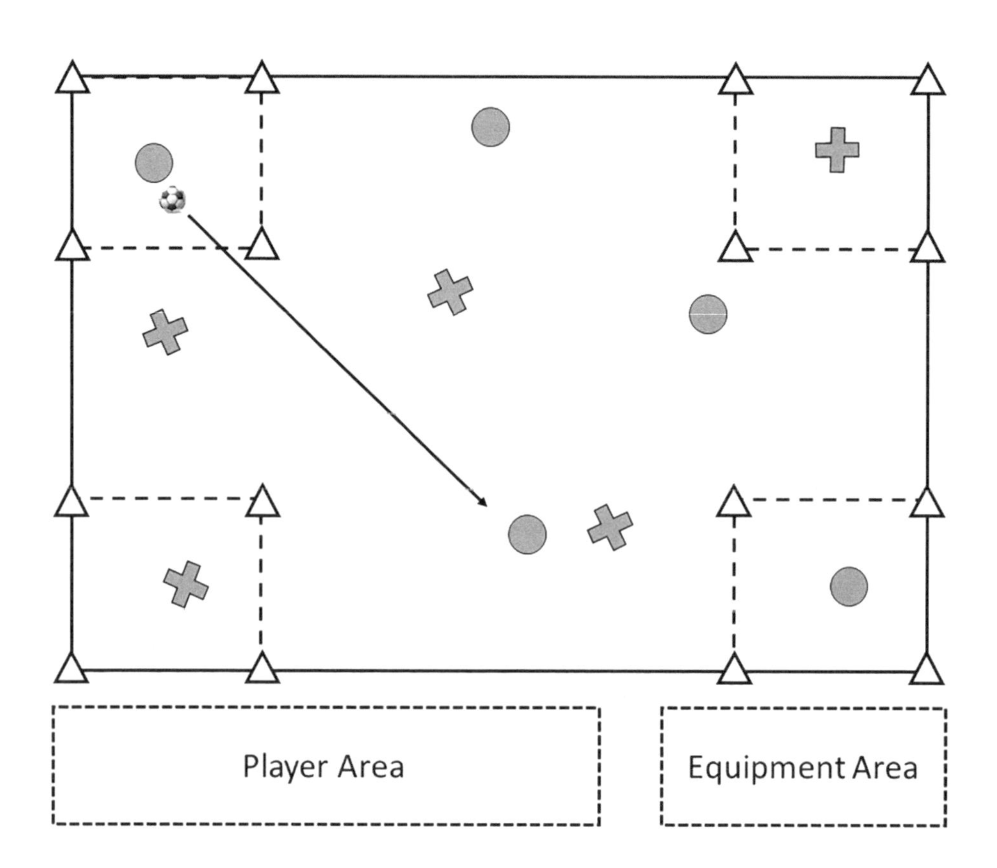

Practice Thirty-Five

Players are split into two teams, with each team having two target players in opposite corners of the area. These target players are locked into their corners, and no other players can enter their areas. Teams achieve points if they pass a ball to one of their target players, and the target player then successfully returns the ball to the same player or one of their team-mates.

Possible Variations

- Consider the width and length of the area as well as the size of the areas that the target players are locked in to meet the needs of your players.
- The four target players are neutral players, so both teams can pass into any four of the target players.
- Limit the target players to one touch.
- Whichever side of the area that the ball is played to the target player, the pass by the target player must come out the other side.
- Whichever player plays the pass to the target player cannot receive the pass back.
- Add small goals to the outside of the area. Once the teams have completed a set number of passes with their target players, they then need to pass into a small goal.

Practice Thirty-Six:

First Practice / **Main Practice** / Game Practice

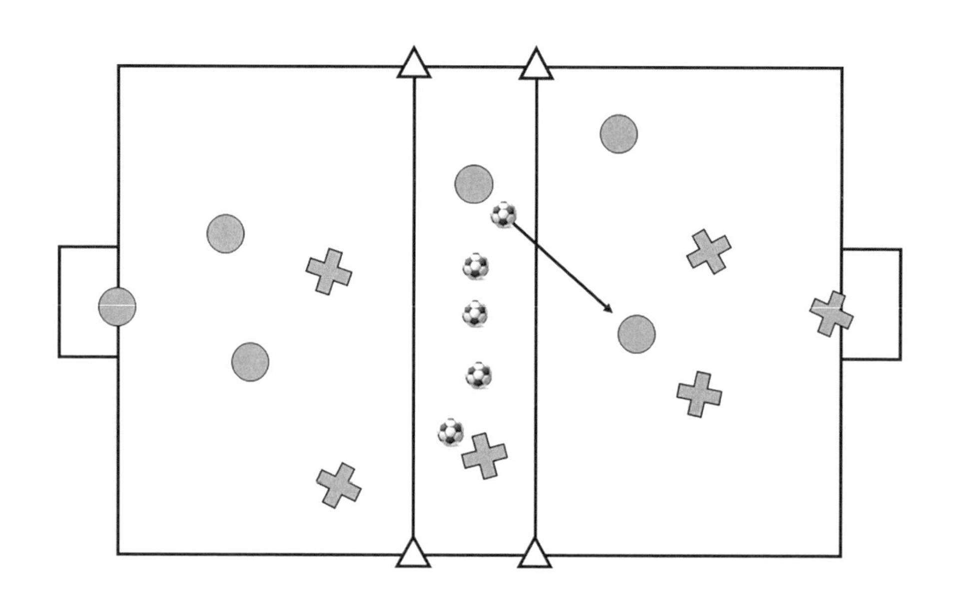

Player Area

Equipment Area

Practice Thirty-Six

Two games of three versus two, plus a goalkeeper. One of the attackers passes a ball from the central area to a team-mate and then joins in with the practice. After they score or the ball goes out of play, one of the attackers passes another ball in from the central area. This continues until all the balls have been used. The exact same thing happens on the other pitch, with the pitches competing against each other to score the most goals. If a defender wins the ball, they attempt to dribble it back to the central area for a bonus point.

Possible Variations

- Consider the width and length of the area to meet the needs of your players. Both halves do not have to be the same size.
- Change the ratio of attacking players and defenders.
- Limit the attacking players to a maximum number of passes.
- Teams earn extra points if they score without passing the ball or only using one pass.
- The attacker serving the ball to their team-mates is locked in the central area but can receive a pass back from the other players.
- If a defender wins possession, they can then go join the other pitch with the ball and attempt to score with the help of the attacking players on that pitch.

Practice Thirty-Seven:

First Practice / Main Practice / Game Practice

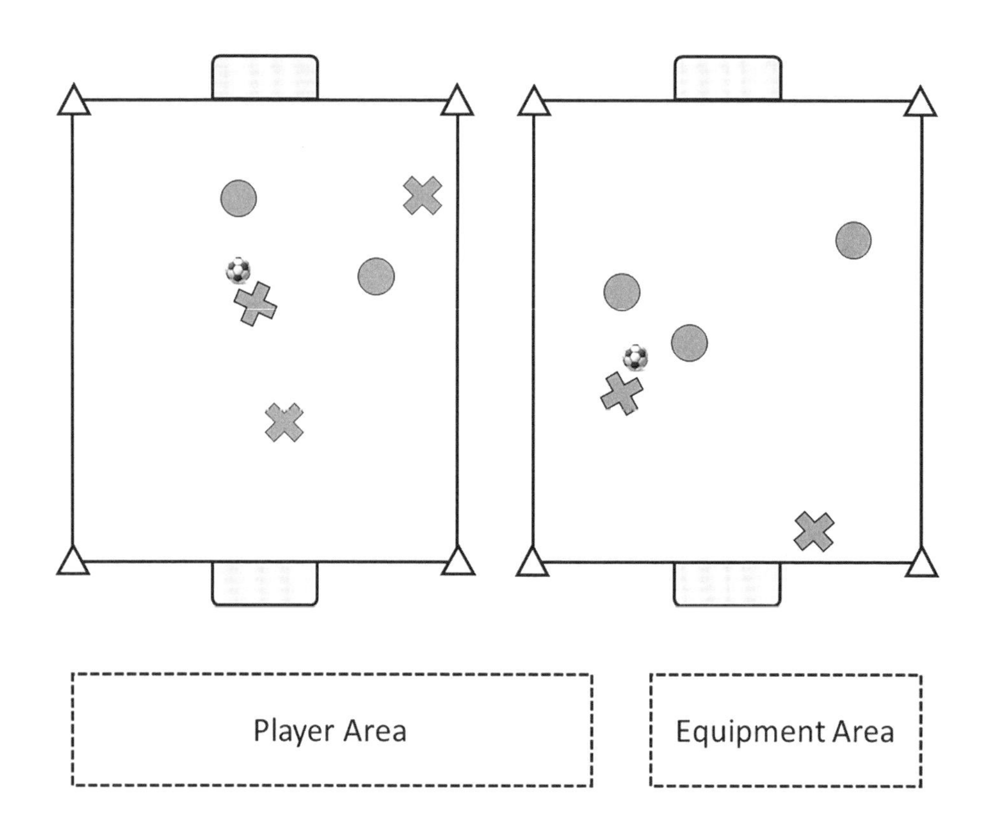

Practice Thirty-Seven

Two small-sided games are played next to each other. Players from both teams are allowed to leave one pitch and join in with the other pitch at anytime and as many times as they want.

Possible Variations

- Only allow the players from one team to change pitches for a set amount of time before then allowing the other team to do it for the same amount of time.
- Set the pitches up differently. For instance, one pitch could be a normal game, whereas on the other pitch there are no goals, and players score points by dribbling over the opposition's end line.
- Have different rules between pitches. For example one pitch has a maximum number of touches for each player.
- Only one chosen player from each team can move between pitches.
- Restrict players to only being allowed to change pitches once.

Practice Thirty-Eight:

First Practice / **Main Practice** / **Game Practice**

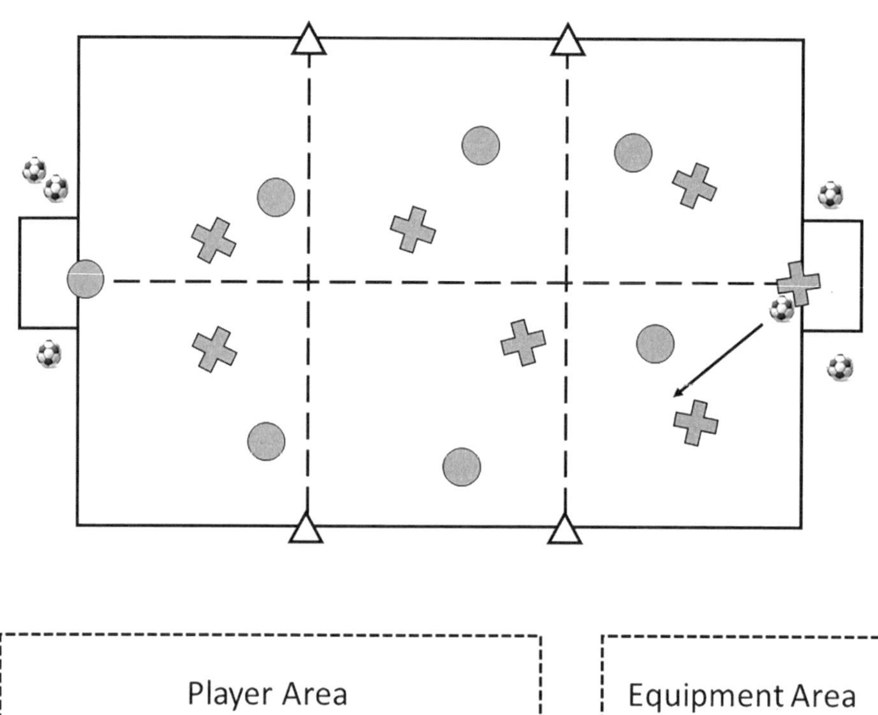

Practice Thirty-Eight

A small-sided game where areas are created, matching the number of outfield players each team has. Each individual player is then locked into a specific area against an opposition player, creating a number of one-versus-one games within the main game. The ball can only be transferred from area to area by passing the ball.

Possible Variations

- Consider the width and length of the area to meet the needs of your players. The areas using the main pitch do not have to be the same size.
- Allow players from the team in possession to move into an adjoining box when the ball is in that box to create a two-versus-one.
- Have a neutral player who can go anywhere on the pitch, supporting the player in possession of the ball.
- Only lock the players from one team into their designated areas for a set amount of time before swapping it over to the other team, and then the players from the other team are locked in for the same amount of time.
- If a team is able to complete a set number of passes, then all their players become unlocked until they lose possession of the ball or it goes out of play. Players must then return to their areas immediately.

Practice Thirty-Nine:

First Practice / **Main Practice** / Game Practice

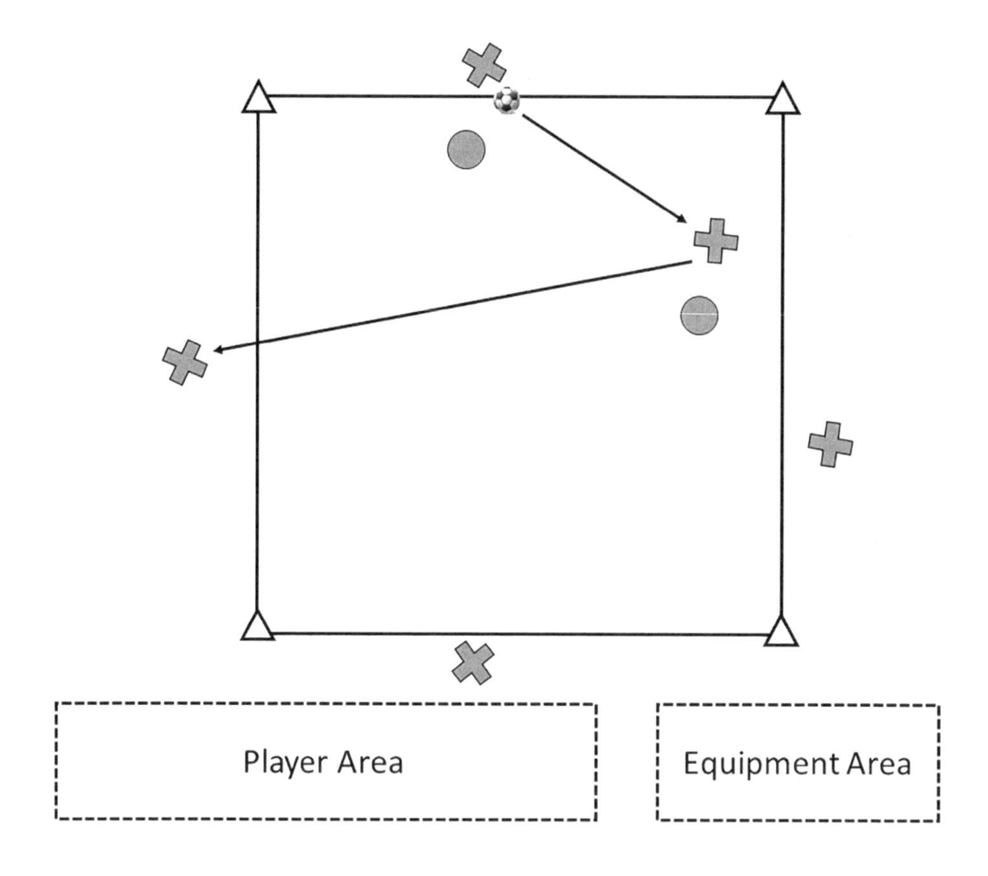

Practice Thirty-Nine

Four attacking players are located outside of the area, one on each side of the square, with an additional attacking player on the inside with two defenders. Attacking players can pass the ball between themselves but only win a point if they can pass the ball into the player within the area. This player can then pass it back out again, but they cannot pass to the player who played the ball in. If the defenders win the ball, they look to retain it for as long as possible. All attacking players can enter the area until they win the ball back.

Possible Variations

- Consider the size of the area to meet the needs of your players.
- The attacking players win a bonus point if the pass from the player within the area goes through the space between the two defenders (split pass).
- Only have three players on the outside. These players are then allowed to move to the side of the area that is free (this will be constantly changing).
- The attacking players win a bonus point if the pass from the player within the area is a one-touch pass.
- Have another area within main the area that can be used in a number of ways. For example, it can be a safety area where the attacking player can go but not the defenders.

Practice Forty:

First Practice / Main Practice / **Game Practice**

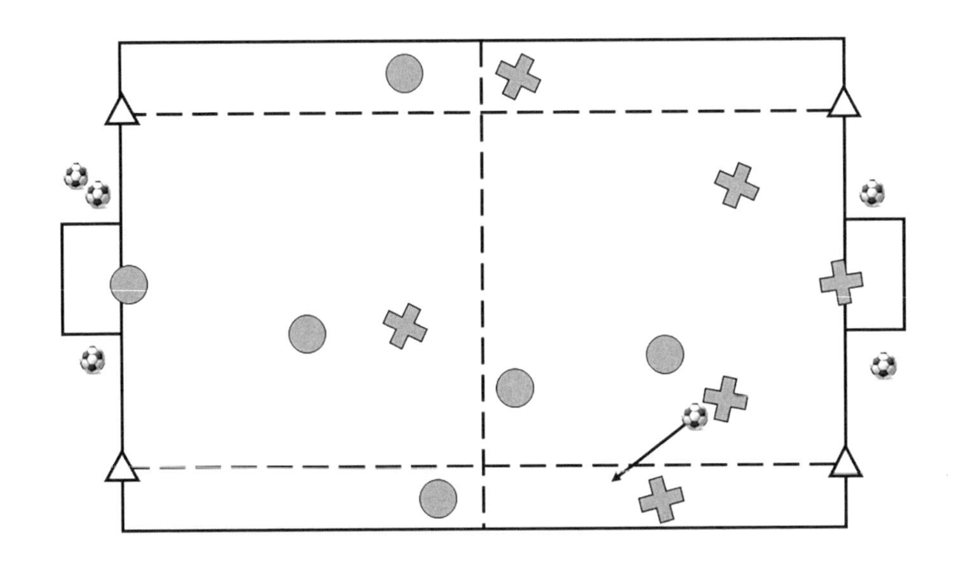

Player Area

Equipment Area

Practice Forty

Small-sided game with two wide channels. Each team must have one player in each of the wide channels, and these players are locked into these areas. When their team is out of possession, the players in the wide channels must retreat to their own half, allowing the attacking players in the wide areas to receive the ball in their own half unopposed if they want to.

Possible Variations

- Consider the width and length of the area as well as the width of the channels to meet the needs of your players. The channels do not need to be the same width.
- The defending players in the channels can enter the opposing half once the attacking player has had their first touch.
- The defending player is now allowed to go anywhere they want within the channel.
- When the ball is in a channel, a player from the team in possession can enter the channel and support the player on the ball, making it a two-versus-one.
- Players in the pitch and the channel can rotate positions, but they must keep the balance of one player in each channel.
- When a player in the channel is in possession of the ball, their team-mate in the other channel can come out of their channel and onto the pitch.

FINAL THOUGHTS

At the very start of this book we spoke about the need to give the players that we work with lasting memories that they can look back on with both fondness and happiness. It was also noted that we have an obligation to provide the players with an environment and an experience that allows them to play soccer without any fear or worries, where they can learn and develop whilst not taking away any of the fun and enjoyment that they get from just playing the game. And most importantly of all, it was stressed that we have an obligation not to let the players down, to make sure that we do what is best for them, both as people and young soccer players.

This may have seemed a little overwhelming at first, that we have such an important responsibility and that we can have such a big influence on these young children. But by taking away the key messages from across all of the chapters, it will hopefully be a lot less daunting and instead it is now actually quite exciting what we can achieve as a coach and what they can achieve as players and also young people. The most important of these messages has to be to remember that they are children, as this leads to a number of key reminders that are essential when working with young players. Because they are children they just want to play, they want to have the freedom to run around and make their own decisions and the overwhelming reason that they come to training is because they just like to play soccer. So let them do this, put them in practices where they can express themselves and have fun, rather than using 'drills' where they are restricted and told where they have to go or where they have to pass the ball. Children also play a different version of the game to adults; therefore we need to link everything that we do to this form of soccer and not the one that they will play when they are older. Similarly, they are at a different stage of their development compared to adults and they will therefore need to learn and practice different things that will allow them to be the best possible version of themselves for when they do start to play the full version of the game. And because they are children we will need to be patient with them, we need to accept that they will behave like children, we need to use language that they will understand and most importantly of all, they want to have fun. Allow them to come to training and enjoy themselves, give them the opportunity to play soccer with their friends and just enjoy the experience of doing so.

The second key message is that we are soccer coaches and therefore we need to support and help our players develop to become soccer players. If the players wanted to be cross-country or long-distance runners they would go to athletics training; they do not come to training to run around a field or to do circuits – they come to play soccer. Nor do they want to be standing around listening to someone telling them what they should be doing or waiting for their turn to have a go; they want to busy and active, they want to be playing soccer. So when planning our practices, we need to look to maximise the ball rolling time for each individual player; they need to be as close to the full version of the game as possible, so that the players can practice what they will be doing when they play the actual game. Quite often the best possible way to achieve this is by using 'game' practices, which are defined by having rules and parameters, competition and scoring systems, some form of target or goals, and situations where the players will come across problems that they need to solve and will therefore need to make decisions – and, of course, they are fun to play. The practices that we plan and design need to look like and represent an element of the actual game, as the players need to be able to use these practices when they are playing in a match. When they face a challenge in a match, there needs to be a familiarity about it, they need to have come across something similar during training so that it is not a surprise to them and they can use what they have learnt to help solve the problem they are facing. They want to be soccer players, so let them practice playing soccer.

The other part of being a soccer coach is the coaching aspect of the role. As coaches we are there to help the players to improve and become better, so we should look to provide the guidance and support that they need to develop and progress. This does not mean that we are there to tell them what to do. Rather, we need to give them the opportunity to work things out themselves and only look to help when they really need it. This help should not come in the format of information and instructions, but instead through using the question and answer technique or with challenges or restrictions. We should provide a 'narrow focus' to our sessions, so that the players have a specific subject to learn and concentrate on. This will prevent the learning process being lost in the players trying to take on and work out too much information. We also need to remember that the team or the squad is made up of a number of individual players, and therefore what is suitable and relevant for one particular player will not necessary be needed for every other player or in fact any player. Remember we are there to develop each individual player, not the team.

The final message that you should take away from the book is to just remember who you are and why you are doing this. We have just discussed that the players are children and, just as importantly, we need to remember that we are the adults. Therefore, no matter what happens, we need to continue to not only do what we believe in, but also what we know is the right thing to do. This might include remembering that there needs to be a long-term approach to our coaching instead of resorting to short-term fixes just because something happened in a game. Or ensuring that every player gets the same amount of time on the pitch during match day and not changing this just because it is a close game, and by giving the perceived 'better' players more time might help us win the game. Or committing to the approach that match day is just an extension of training and therefore should be about the players learning and developing and not about the result, even when there are external pressures to change this. We need to commit to and stick with our values and beliefs and know what we are doing is in the very best interest of every single player. And finally, remember that we stepped forward to take on this role of the coach because we wanted to help allow a group of children to play soccer and that what we are doing is a wonderful, unselfish act. But we will only continue to do this if we are enjoying the experience, so it is just as important for us to have fun as it for the players. Because not only will our enthusiasm transfer to the players, but it will make everything else so much easier – all of the planning that is needed, the set-up of the practices, the delivery of the session and everything else that is needed and usually unseen by everyone else. We are in a unique and privileged position and we owe it to ourselves and the players to do our best and just enjoy it.